PROGRESSIVE Skills in English

in English

Level 4 Teacher's Book

Terry Phillips and Anna Phillips

Garnet
EDUCATION

Published by
Garnet Publishing Ltd.
8 Southern Court
South Street
Reading RG1 4QS, UK

First edition 2013

ISBN: 978-1-85964-687-8

British Library Cataloguing-in-Publication Data
A catalogue record for this book is available from
the British Library.

Production

Project managers:	Richard Peacock, Nicky Platt
Editorial team:	Emily Clarke, Sarah Mellowes, Richard Peacock, Nicky Platt, Rod Webb
Research:	Lucy Phillips
Design:	Ed Du Bois, Mike Hinks
Typesetting:	Mike Hinks
Photography:	Clipart, Corbis, Digital Vision, Getty Images, Image Source, Photodisc, Istockphoto, Shutterstock
Audio and DVD:	EFS Television Production Ltd., Silver Street Studios

Every effort has been made to trace the copyright holders
and we apologize in advance for any unintentional
omissions. We will be happy to insert the appropriate
acknowledgements in any subsequent editions.

Printed and bound
in Lebanon by International Press: interpress@int-press.com

PROGRESSIVE Skills in English

Contents

Listening	Speaking	Reading	Writing	Knowledge area
1 Geography and development	Geography and water problems	Geography and tourism	Geography and the economy	Geography and the modern world
2 Communicating far and wide	Communication aids	Communication inventors	Communication inventions	Communication
3 The case against television	The hidden persuaders	Conventions in narrative fiction	Reality TV – real or fiction?	Media and advertising
4 Life systems	A sporting life	Learning for leisure	Living longer, living better	Living life to the full
5 Agriculture through history	Interfering with nature?	Should man be a herbivore?	GM: The future or the end?	The past, present and future of food

Listening	Speaking	Reading	Writing
1 *lecture with headings and subheadings* • note-taking: scientific numbering	*discussion group* • clarifying • raising / dealing with an objection	*magazine article* • reading for a purpose: highlighting key words • making inferences	*Discussion essay* • linking sentences • restating (first steps to preventing plagiarism)
2 *lecture with sequence of events* • timelines • using handouts of slides	*presentation and discussion* • saying you are lost • helping a speaker	*article with biography* • reacting to a text: opinions and lessons for life	*Description essay* • adding extra information to existing sentences
3 *talk with argument* • understanding the argument • understanding the speaker's concessions	*tutorial* • linking to previous speaker / topic • expressing uncertainty	*textbook; academic website* • recording sources	*Outline essay* • supporting statements with evidence: statistics; quotations; reported speech
4 *talk with fractured text* • adding information (to notes) which comes out of order	*presentation and discussion* • summarizing • reacting to summaries	*student essay with sources and reference list* • highlighting key points • highlighting sources	*Outline essay; Evaluation essay* • writing about graphs: trends, reasons and results
5 *lecture with timeline / sections / problems and solutions* • recognizing digressions and end of digressions	*presentation and discussion* • referring to research • making V agree with S	*research extracts* • sentence relationships: reason, result, example, explanation	*Argument essay* • using lexical cohesions • using *despite / because of*

Book maps

Grammar

Listening	Speaking	Reading	Writing
1 • comparing with *both / neither, and / but, whereas / while*	• correcting statements with *think* + past • showing surprise with *realize* + past • saying weak forms	• understanding linkage between information: *and / but / or, because / so, while / whereas, although*	• writing about the past: *for / since / ago* • linking past and present
2 • verb patterns (1): ditransitive verbs	• *was doing when did* • *did when did*	• complex sentences: understanding participle clauses with active sentences	• complex sentences: joining sentences with active participles
3 • verb patterns (2): verb + *~ing*; verb + *that*	• noun phrases with relative clauses: subject noun phrases: object / complement noun phrases	• complex sentences: understanding participle clauses with passive sentences	• complex sentences: joining sentences with passive participles
4 • cleft sentences • pseudo-cleft sentences	• review of modals: *must* for rules / laws; *may / might / could* for possibility; *should* for advice	• statements with hedging	• tense choice • hedging with verbs / adjectives / nouns / modals
5 • complex sentences with *when / if, although, because*	• complex sentences with *when / if, although, because*	• interrogative clauses	• *because / although* + clause vs *because of / despite* + noun phrases

Phonology, Everyday English and Portfolio work

Listening	Speaking	Everyday English	Portfolio
1 • stress in two-word phrases	• saying weak forms	• expressing opinions politely; persuading	Island tourism
2 • hearing two consonants together	• linking and suppressing	• talking on the phone	Communication aids for the vision-impaired
3 • hearing two vowel sounds together	• intrusive sounds	• complaining	Media debate
4 • predicting pronunciation of new words	• sense groups • rising to pauses	• talking about health problems	The positive and negative aspects of ageing populations
5 • understanding phonemic symbols	• saying vowel letters *e, i, o* • stress in two-word phrases	• at the supermarket	Influences on the environment

Introduction Contents

Introduction

The series

This course is part of the multi-level *Progressive Skills in English* series. The series as a whole prepares students to study wholly or partly in English medium at tertiary level, or to join the world of academic English, on the Internet and in print.

Routes through the course

Progressive Skills in English is an extremely flexible course. There are logical routes through the Course Book, from 25 hours to 120 hours. By adding the Workbook to the package, the course can provide all the input required on a complete academic year of 180 hours.

Some of the possible routes through the book are given at the end of this Introduction. For others, particularly with regard to the use of the extra pages – **Everyday English, Knowledge quiz** and **Portfolio** – see below.

The themes

In each level of *Progressive Skills in English* there are five themes, covering a wide range of areas of human knowledge.

Level 4
Theme 1:   Geography and the modern world
Theme 2:   Communication
Theme 3:   Media and advertising
Theme 4:   Living life to the full
Theme 5:   The past, present and future of food

The sections

Within each theme there are four main sections, each dealing with a discrete skill: listening, speaking, reading or writing. A number of related topics are explored within each theme. For example, in Theme 3 the following areas are explored:
Listening: the case against television
Speaking: the hidden persuaders
Reading: conventions in narrative fiction
Writing: reality TV – real or fiction?

The focus in each section is on **one** specific skill. The Methodology notes in the lessons stress the discrete skills focus and caution against spending too much time on, for example, speaking in a listening section. This is not because the writers dislike integrated skills. Indeed, each theme ends with a section called Portfolio, which provides detailed guidance on integrated skills activities following the completion of a particular theme. The insistence on the target skill is because the writers believe that both the teacher and the students should focus on improvement in a specific skill in a particular lesson, rather than moving constantly between different skills. However, the key word here is *focus*. More than one skill will, of course, be involved in any particular lesson. For example, in listening lessons there is almost always a speaking output, and in writing lessons there is almost always a reading input.

The commonality of theme across the four skill sections means that, by the end of a theme, students have a much deeper knowledge of both the information and vocabulary that it comprises, than is normally achieved in ELT course books.

The lessons

Each skill section contains five lessons, and each lesson has a clear focus and purpose, as shown in the following table. (See top of page opposite.)

Additional pages

Every theme contains three additional pages:

Everyday English
This page is in the speaking section and builds skills in survival language and social English. In Theme 2, for example, this page covers *Talking on the phone* and in Theme 4, *Talking about health problems*. See the **Methodology** section for more guidance.

Knowledge quiz
This page is in the reading section and tests students on their acquisition of common core knowledge and thematic vocabulary from the theme. In Theme 3, for example, this page ask students to remember information about *Advertising, television and narrative fiction*. See the **Methodology** section for more guidance.

Lesson	Focus	Purpose and methodology points
X.1 X.6 X.11 X.16	Vocabulary for the skill	To ensure that students understand and can recognize some basic vocabulary needed for the theme. This lesson also contains all the target words from the section, printed down the outer margin. The positioning is deliberate. You and the students should be able to flick back and find a thematic set easily. Note that only about half of the words in this list will be pre-taught in the first lesson. The remainder will be met in context during the rest of the section. Teachers might like to test students on the list before starting the lesson, and then again at the end of the section or the theme.
X.2 X.7 X.12 X.17	Real-time practice	To practise a skill with the students' available linguistic resources. This lesson can be seen as an informal test of current knowledge and ability in a particular area. The text type encountered in this lesson is met again in the *Applying skills* lesson, so students get a second chance to understand or produce the text type after they have seen and practised relevant sub-skills and grammar.
X.3 X.8 X.13 X.18	Learning skills	To highlight specific sub-skills which are required to complete the task(s) in the second and fifth lessons of the section. Note that the skills taught here are all transferable rather than simple exhortations to 'Listen carefully' or 'Read quickly'.
X.4 X.9 X.14 X.19	Grammar for the skill	To highlight specific grammar points which are related to the text type in the Real-time practice lesson. In many cases, these are syntactic points – see **Syntactic grammar for EAP** below. The content of these lessons is directly related to the skill for that section, as the writers have discovered that there are significant differences between the grammar you need for each skill.
X.5 X.10 X.15 X.20	Applying skills	To apply the skills learnt in the third and fourth lessons of the section to a new text. The text for reception or the target output for production contains the same linguistic features as that in the second lesson of the section.

Portfolio

This section – usually three pages – comes at the very end of each theme and provides an opportunity to integrate skills learnt during the course. Students are provided with tasks and research information in additional listening and reading texts, and asked to produce talks and/or written texts. In Theme 4, for example, students are asked to research and talk about *The positive and negative aspects of ageing populations.* See the **Methodology** section for more guidance.

Approach

Aims

In *Progressive Skills in English,* students learn to understand the main types of academic spoken language, lectures and tutorials, and the main types of academic written language, journal articles and encyclopedia entries. They also learn to produce the main kinds of student academic language, oral presentations, contributions to a tutorial and written assignments.

Moving from teaching general to academic English

Many of the teaching techniques and approaches used in general English teaching can be transferred to the teaching of academic English. The differences are more to do with the syllabus and course content. Some of the key differences we have noted include:

Grammar

Most general English courses are driven by tense grammar. Since 80 per cent of academic English is in a present tense, the focus needs to move from tenses to syntactic grammar. For more details on this point, see **Syntactic grammar for EAP** below.

Skills

A general English course will focus mainly on oral communication. Listening will be extremely varied, from conversations and anecdotes to radio programmes. Reading is often relegated to third place and writing to a very distant fourth. For the academic learner, reading and writing are at least as important as the other skills. For more details, see **Discrete skills or integrated?** below.

Content

In EAP, listening to lectures will be more relevant than listening to anecdotes and stories. Academic students need to learn to 'grab' relevant information from a lecture after one listening only. Similarly with reading, required content will mostly be fact or theory or a mixture, rather than fiction and anecdote. Students need to be able to decide quickly which texts, or parts of texts, are relevant to the task and extract the information. Listening and reading texts in general will be much longer in EAP than in a general English course.

Vocabulary

Students need a wide range of formal language. Academic texts about a single subject tend to use a lot of synonyms for key nouns and verbs, so students need to deepen and broaden their lexical range all the time.

Topics and themes

Sometimes you find very familiar 'EFL' topics in *Progressive Skills in English*, but then you will see that the approach to that topic is different. For example, in a section on friends and family, students are not asked to describe these people but to explore relationship theories and analyze social data.

Critical thinking

Students are encouraged to ask *why* and *how* throughout the course, and to relate information from a particular text to their own selves or their own country/area. They are shown the importance of evaluating information and looking for stance or bias on the part of the speaker or writer.

Discrete skills or integrated?

In terms of presentation, *Progressive Skills in English* is very definitely a discrete skills course. Research has shown that students need to have a clear focus with measurable objectives in order to make real progress, and this is only really possible if the skills are initially separated out. However, integration is the norm in the real world and, since the course aims to mimic real-world skills usage, integration is automatic once one moves from presentation. For example, in the receptive skills lessons, as in the real world, students have to make notes from reading and listening and then discuss their findings, thus bringing in writing and speaking to listening and reading lessons. In the productive skills lessons, as in the real world, students have to research before producing, thus bringing in reading and listening skills.

Receptive skills – listening and reading

Research strongly suggests that listening and reading are based on a continuous interaction between top-down and bottom-up processes. Top-down processes prepare the listener or reader to understand the information in the text. Bottom-up processes ensure that the listener or reader can decode information in real-time, i.e., as it is actually being heard or read.

Top-down processes

Before we can understand information, we need to recognize the context. We expect to hear different things in a restaurant, for example, from a lecture room, or to read different things in a novel and a religious text. We use context and co-text clues (pictures, newspaper headlines, diagrams) to **activate schemata** – pictures, we could say, of familiar situations. In the process, the brain makes available to us vocabulary, discourse structures and **background knowledge** of the real world, which help with bottom-up decoding. We start to develop **hypotheses** about the contents of the text, and we continually **predict** the next word, the next phrase, the next discourse point or the next communicative value as we are listening or reading. In *Progressive Skills in English*, students are taught to bring top-down processing to bear on new listening and reading texts. The course works to build schemata and background knowledge which will help students to predict content, in general and in particular. In the academic world, listening and reading normally have a productive by-product – detailed notes. Throughout *Progressive Skills in English*, students are taught to take notes and to use these notes in later activities to prove comprehension of the text.

Bottom-up processes

Top-down processes enable listeners and readers to get a good general idea of what will be heard or read in a text. However, to get a detailed and accurate understanding, the text must be broken down into meaningful units. In the case of spoken English, this means being able to turn the stream of speech into actual words, which in turn means knowing the phonological code of English. With written English, it is slightly easier, if your first language has a similar orthography to English but will continue to pose problems for students whose L1 is Chinese or Arabic, for example. Research has shown that we use syntax to achieve this breaking into meaningful units (see below on **syntactic grammar**). In *Progressive Skills in English*, students are taught to recognize all the phonemes of English in context and to identify multi-syllable words from the stressed syllable in the stream of speech. They also learn to identify written words from the first two or three letters, a key skill which enables native speakers to understand written text at high speed. Students are also exposed to common syntactic patterns and practise breaking up incoming language into **subject**, **verb**, **object / complement** and **adverbial**.

Productive skills – speaking and writing

Production in speech and writing in the normal EFL classroom is often more or less spontaneous and personal. Students are asked to speak or write about themselves, their lives, families, opinions, etc., with very little preparation. This mimics real-life conversation and, to some extent, real-life informal letter and e-mail writing. This type of production is rare in *Progressive Skills in English* because it is not the model for production in the academic world.

Production in academia begins with an **assignment** which requires **research**. The research almost always leads to **note-taking**. From these notes, an oral presentation, tutorial contribution or written assignment is produced. There are normally three stages to this production: **drafting**, **editing** and **rewriting**. In *Progressive Skills in English,* we teach the idea of the TOWER of writing – **t**hinking, **o**rganizing, **w**riting (for the writer), **e**diting, **r**ewriting (for the reader / listener).

Syntactic grammar for EAP

Grammar in ELT has traditionally been seen as largely a question of verb tense, and that certain tenses are 'easy' and others are 'hard'. Progression through levels conventionally equates to the ability to manipulate different tenses, from present simple of the verb *be* at Beginners to present perfect continuous passive modal at Advanced. Most best-selling courses follow a structural syllabus which is, largely, a verb tense syllabus. However, English is a *syntactic* language where meaning is carried by word order rather than paradigmatic form. We cannot recover the meaning of a word or its role without a sentence or text context, because English words are not marked in most instances for part of speech or case. Many words can be nouns or verbs depending on context; *like,* to take an extreme example, can be a noun, a verb, a preposition or an adjective. Any noun can be the subject or object of a verb; only pronouns are marked for case, e.g., *He told him.*

Research has shown that native speakers use their knowledge of English syntax, together with their vocabulary, to decode sentences, in speech and in writing. They do this in real time. In other words, native speakers are constantly constructing tree diagrams of incoming data which help them to predict the next item and its role in the ongoing sentence.

It is somewhat strange that this key fact seems to have gone unnoticed for so long by ELT practitioners. The reason is probably that most ELT classwork, for many decades, has been based on spoken interaction, often of informal conversation, rather than the individual interacting with and decoding in real time a formal spoken or written text. Corpus research now shows us that conversation in English has an average phrase length of just over one word, and very short sentences, such as *I went there, She likes him, He's working in a bank.* In short sentences like this, the most salient area of difficulty is the verb form which must be dropped between the subject and the object, complement or adverbial. However, in academic or formal discourse, the average phrase length jumps to eight words. Analysis of this genre shows that noun phrases are particularly long, with pre- and post-modification of the head noun, and subject noun phrases are often preceded themselves by long adverbial phrases, so that a sentence may have a large number of words before the subject and more words before the main verb. For example:

> According to research at the University of Reading into the problems experienced by children growing up with a single parent, children from one-parent families in deprived areas have a much greater chance of developing personality disorders.

The native speaker has little problem with this sentence, either in speech or writing, because he/she knows that the phrase *According to* is not the subject and the subject will come along in a while, and that *children* can be post-modified so he/she must wait for this noun phrase to end before encountering the verb, etc. The non-native speaker, trained in decoding simple short utterances, will have considerable difficulty.

Complex tenses are in fact not at all common in academic/formal English. Research shows that the majority of sentences in this genre are in the present simple, including its passive forms, for the obvious reason that most formal English presents facts, theories or states of being, which are rendered in English by this tense. The next most common tense is the past simple, because the genre often contains historical background to current facts, theories or states of being, which in turn is normally rendered in past simple. In one particular corpus study, only one example of the present perfect continuous was found in the whole academic/formal corpus. A student equipped with facility in these two tenses will understand the tense information in around 90 per cent of academic/formal sentences. However, they may not understand the noun phrases and adverbial phrases which surround these 'simple' tenses.

There is a final key issue which applies in general to long texts in the EFL classroom. In the main, when students are exposed to longer texts with a formal structure, they are allowed, even encouraged, to engage in multiple listenings or multiple readings before being asked to complete an after-doing comprehension task such as multiple choice or true/false. This type of activity has no correlate in the real world, where listening has to be real-time – there is no opportunity for a second or subsequent hearing – and reading should be real-time if it is to be efficient. Comprehension occurs as the sentence is being received. However, real-time comprehension is only possible if the receiver understands the syntactic structures possible in the language and identifies, in real time, the structure being used at a particular time. The listener or reader is then ready for the required components of that structure and predicts their appearance and even the actual words. For example, once a native speaker hears the verb *give,* they will anticipate that a person and a thing will complete the utterance. Even if the 'person' noun phrase contains many words, the receiver will be waiting. For example: *The state gives unemployed people with a large number of children under the age of 18 still in full-time education ...* The native-speaker listener or reader is thinking, 'What? What does it give?' Conversely, the construction of extended formal text in speech and writing also requires a deep understanding of syntax, otherwise it is not possible to construct sentences of the complexity required by the genre.

While writing the syllabus for *Skills in English,* first published by Garnet Education in 2003, we were struck by the points above and began work on the implications for classroom practice. In *Progressive Skills in English,* we feel we have gone some way to presenting a coherent syllabus of relevant practice to build the skills required for real-time comprehension.

Syntactic grammar in this course
If students have completed the A1/A2 course in this series, *New Starting Skills in English,* they will be fully familiar with parts of speech and with the most common syntactic patterns (see tables 1 and 2 below) by the time they start *Progressive Skills in English* Level 1. Since we cannot assume this familiarity, however, these points are quickly revised in the first few sections of the course. Thereafter, students are exposed mainly to basic S V O/C/A patterns, with co-ordination. Gradually, the length of the object noun phrase or complement is extended and co-ordination is introduced but with no ellipsis of subject or verb. This should ensure that students begin to get a natural feel for these patterns, can recognize them in real time in listening and reading, and produce them in speech and writing.

Table 1: Sentence roles and parts of speech

Roles in sentences	Possible parts of speech	Notes
Subject	noun, pronoun	extended noun phrase can contain other parts of speech, e.g., *a very large piece of research*
Object	noun, pronoun	
Complement	noun, adjective, adverb	an object becomes a complement when it has the same reference as the subject, such as in sentences with *be* and related verbs, e.g., *She is a doctor. He was late. They seem tired.*
Verb	verb	extended verb phrase can contain adverbs, e.g., *They are still waiting.*
Adverbial	adverb, prepositional phrase	note that this role in a sentence can be filled by a prepositional phrase as well as by an adverb, e.g., *He works hard. She works in a bank.*

Table 2: Main sentence patterns in English

We left.	S V
She is a doctor.	S V C
I am cold.	S V C
They were late.	S V A
We have been to the back.	S V A
I gave her the book.	S V O O
They made him president.	S V O C
I told her to leave.	S V O V
We saw them later.	S V O A
Accept responsibility.	V O

Exercise naming
Many ELT course books give general names to groups of exercises, such as *Presentation* or *Pronunciation. Progressive Skills in English* goes much further and names the target activity for each exercise in its heading, e.g., *Activating ideas* or *Predicting the next word.* By this simple means, both teacher and students are informed of the purpose of an exercise. Make sure that your students understand the heading of each exercise so they can see clearly the point which is being presented or practised.

Exercise types
As is probably clear already, *Progressive Skills in English* contains many original features, but teachers

and course leaders need not be concerned that a wholly new methodology is required to teach the course. On the one hand, exercise naming means that the purpose of new types of exercise is immediately clear. On the other, many traditional types of ELT exercises are used in the course, with only slight changes. The most significant of these changes are shown in table 3 below.

Table 3: Adaptations to traditional exercise types

Traditional exercise	*Progressive Skills* version
grammar tables	- Parts of sentence are clearly shown with subject, verb, object/complement/adverbial columns. - Parts of speech are clearly shown with colour-coding. purple = noun red = verb blue = pronoun orange = adjective green = preposition brown = adverb
gap fill	In some cases, one part of speech is removed so students can see the various contexts in which, e.g., a pronoun can appear. In other cases, one role in the sentence is removed, e.g., the subject, so students can see the different words which can make up this role.
sentence anagrams	Words are jumbled in a number of sentences in the traditional way, but when students have unscrambled them, all the sentences have the same syntactic structure, e.g., S V O A. Words in a particular phrase are kept together during the jumbling, e.g., *in the UK*, rather than all being split; this helps students to think in terms of syntactic blocks rather than individual words.
transformation	Traditional transformation, e.g., positive to negative, appears regularly, but in addition, active to passive is introduced early on in the course, because of the relatively high frequency of passives in academic English.
joining sentences	Sentences are joined by co-ordinators from the beginning of *Progressive Skills in English*, but the second half of the sentence retains all its features, e.g., subject, verb, negation, for most of Level 1. This is because co-ordinated sentences with ellipses hide the kernel syntactic structure with which we want students to become familiar, e.g., *Some people do not know about the problem **or care.*** The second half of this sentence is originally: *Some people do not care about the problem* but with the ellipsis, the subject, the negation and the object disappear.

Vocabulary lists

Vocabulary is a key part of language learning of any kind but it is even more important for the student of academic English. Students need a huge vocabulary in order to understand or produce the lexical cohesion common to this genre. Each skill section in every theme begins with a vocabulary list of about 40 items in the right-hand column of the first lesson. This list contains items from the skill section which are linked to the theme. The part of speech is given in every case for single items. In addition, there is sometimes information on the precise meaning in the context of the theme, e.g., *area (n) [= location]* (as opposed to field of study, for example). There is space at the bottom of each list for students to add three or four more words which they wish to learn.

Most of the items in each list are probably new to the majority of the students in any class. A few of the items are likely to be known, but are so central to the theme that they are included for revision.

Normally, about 40 per cent of the words in the list are presented in the Vocabulary lesson, with some reference made to perhaps another 10 per cent. The remaining words will be encountered in other lessons and either specifically taught or understood in context.

You can use the lists in a number of ways:
- ask students to look at the list before the start of the skill section and tick the words they 'know'; do not test the students this time but encourage them to be honest
- ask students to repeat this activity at the end of the skill section, and again one week and one month later; on these occasions, test the students' knowledge, particularly in the relevant skill, e.g., to check that students can spell the words from a writing section, or pronounce the words correctly from a speaking section
- get students to mark the stress on each word as they encounter it
- get students to underline or highlight in some way unusual spelling and pronunciation points
- put students into pairs or groups to test each other
- allow students to write a translation beside some or all of the words

Please note: flashcards and detailed notes on using them can be found on the *Progressive Skills in English* website, www.skillsinenglish.com.

Skills Checks

In every theme, there is at least one Skills Check. The naming of this feature is significant. It is assumed that many if not all students will have heard about the skills points in these boxes, i.e., they are skills *checks* not skills *presentations*. It is the writers' experience that many students who have gone through a modern ELT course have *heard of* the majority of skills points but cannot make practical use of them. If you feel, in a particular case, that the students have no idea about the point in question, spend considerably longer on a full presentation.

In most cases, the students are given an activity to do before looking at the Skills Check, thus a test-teach-test approach is used. This is quite deliberate. With this approach, there is a good chance that the students will be sensitised to the particular point before being asked to understand it intellectually. This is likely to be more effective than talking about the point and then asking the student to try to apply it. The positioning of the Skills Checks means that the information relevant to an activity or set of activities is available for consultation by the student at any time. Because some students have an inductive learning style (working from example to rule) and some have a deductive style (working from rule to example), the Skills Checks have rules *and* examples.

You can use the Skills Checks in a number of ways:
- ask students to read out the rules and the examples
- get students to give you more examples of each point
- ask students to read the Skills Check and then cover it; read it out with mistakes or with wrong examples of the point being presented
- at the end of the lesson, ask students to tell you the new skill(s) they have encountered, without looking at their Course Books

Pronunciation Checks
In the speaking section, and occasionally in the listening section, there are Pronunciation Checks. In Level 1, these focus on phoneme discrimination. For example, in Theme 2 Listening, one Pronunciation Check deals with hearing the two phonemes /æ/ and /ɑː/, while in Theme 2 Speaking, another deals with the actual production of the two phonemes. The examples in these checks are recorded, so you can give students good models of the target point and then drill the items (see **Further speaking practice / drilling** below). Sometimes there is additional practice material to be completed after working through the check.

As mentioned above, all exercises are named. Many of these names appear regularly throughout the course, sometimes with slight changes. This is because these activities are particularly valuable in language learning.

Activating (background) knowledge / ideas
In line with basic communication theory, the lessons always try to move from the known to the unknown. This activity at the start of a lesson allows students to show that they have knowledge or ideas about the real world before learning new information. It also enables the teacher to gauge what is already known, and build on it if necessary, before moving further into the lesson.

While students are talking about a particular area, they are in effect activating schemata, which means they are more ready for further information in the same area.

Understanding words in context
Research shows that it is possible to work out the meaning of a small proportion (perhaps ten per cent) of words in a text, if the remaining words and structures are well known. This activity guides students, perhaps through multiple matching, to show understanding of new items.

Transferring information (to the real world) / Using new skills in a real-world task
It is essential that information is transferable outside of the classroom. This activity tries to make the bridge between information learnt in class and applications in the real world.

Reviewing key words
Students are often given the opportunity to recall words from the previous lesson(s) of a skill section. This helps students to move information into long-term memory.

Identifying a new skill
The methodology of *Progressive Skills in English*, as detailed above, is that students are presented with a text in the Real-time lesson which contains some recycled skills points and one or more new skills points. The students are not directed formally to the new point(s) but may notice while they are doing the real-time activity. Then in the next lesson, they are formally directed to the point(s). This is in line with the principle of noticing before learning.

Predicting content
Listening and reading are real-time skills. The listener must be ahead of the speaker; the reader must be ahead of the text. Activities in this type of exercise help students to get ahead.

Previewing vocabulary

This is a pre-teaching activity. Sometimes key vocabulary is required in order to complete a task later in a lesson. This key vocabulary is presented and needs to be practised thoroughly so it is fully available to students during the coming lesson.

Hearing / Understanding / Studying a model / discourse structure

Progressive Skills in English follows the principle that students must see or hear what they are later asked to produce in speech or writing. In this exercise, they work with a model in order to recognize key features, such as discourse structure.

Practising a model

Clearly, once students have seen key points about a model, they should be given the opportunity to produce the text.

Producing a model

This is the third stage, after 'understanding' and 'practising'. Students are given a task which requires the production of a parallel text.

Producing key patterns

This is related to producing a model, but is at the sentence level.

Showing comprehension

Comprehension in the real world is a real-time activity and is something which happens in the brain: it is not directly observable. However, it is essential that both teachers and students see that comprehension has taken place. But remember, this sort of activity is a test of comprehension not a sub-skill in comprehension.

Researching information

Progressive Skills in English is not convergent. Students are only sent back to their pre-existing ideas of knowledge at the beginning of lessons, in *Activating knowledge / ideas*. *Progressive Skills* is divergent. Students are sent off to research and bring back information, in order to give a talk, take part in a tutorial or produce a written text.

Developing vocabulary

Students of academic English need constantly to develop their vocabulary knowledge. This exercise extends their existing vocabulary.

Developing independent learning

Clearly, the ultimate aim of teaching a language is that students become independent learners who do not need a teacher to acquire new linguistic knowledge. This activity gives students a particular sub-skill to aid this process.

Developing critical thinking

We must take students beyond the 'what' and the 'when' of information. We must get them to react to information, and to ask why something happened or why it is important.

Remembering real-world knowledge

Progressive Skills in English is based on the theory that people need a framework of knowledge in order to understand new information as they read or hear it. Therefore, they need to remember real-world knowledge from lessons, not just vocabulary, skills and grammar.

Using / Applying a key skill

Skills are learnt, then they need to be applied. This activity always connects directly to *Identifying a new skill* in an earlier lesson in the skill section.

Making and checking hypotheses

Real-time listening and reading is about making and checking hypotheses. This is what makes it a real-time activity. Students need to learn a wide range of points about discourse, vocabulary and syntax which helps with making hypotheses. They then need to be given the opportunity to check these hypotheses.

Methodology

Everyday English

These additional lessons are designed to give university students some survival English for university life. The language and topics are freestanding so the lessons can be done at any time during the skill section or theme, or can be missed out completely should you so wish. The page could last a whole lesson or you could spend a shorter time and only work on two or three of the conversations. The format of all the Everyday English lessons is similar, with between four and six mini-dialogues on a similar topic or with a similar function.

Here are some ways of exploiting each stage of the lesson:

You may wish to highlight the grammar of some of the forms used in the conversations, but in general they can be learnt as phrases without going into too much explanation. Indeed, many of the forms that we often spend a lot of time on in class could probably be better learnt as fixed phrases, since their usage in everyday life is so limited, e.g., *How long have you been learning English?*

Ask students if they think the conversations take place in a formal or informal context. If conversations are formal, it is always important to remind students to use polite intonation.

Once any tasks set in the Course Book have been completed, and you have checked students understand the conversations, you can use the conversations for intensive pronunciation practice. Use one or more of the following activities:

- Play the CD, pausing after each line for students to listen and repeat, chorally and individually.
- Drill some of the phrases from the conversations, chorally then individually.
- Students practise the conversations in pairs, from the full transcript or from prompts.
- Students practise the conversations again, but substituting their own information, words or phrases where appropriate.
- Students extend the conversation by adding further lines of dialogue.
- Students invent a completely new conversation for the situation, function or photograph.
- Add some drama to the conversations by asking students to act out the conversations with different contexts, relationships or emotions (e.g., one student should act angry and the other student bored).

Monitor and give feedback after paired practice. You may want to focus on:

- intonation of closed and open questions
- stressed words in short answers, e.g., *Yes, it is. Yes, it does.*
- accurate use of auxiliary *do* in present simple questions

Knowledge quiz

Although this is an optional part of each theme, the idea behind it is central to the approach of *Progressive Skills in English*. We have found from our work with universities around the world that students often fail to understand a text *not* because the English grammar is above their level, but because they do not have the framework of real-world knowledge or the breadth of topic-specific vocabulary in order to comprehend. This page makes these items central, but revises and tests them in a variety of enjoyable ways. There are several ways in which this page can be used. The Methodology notes for each theme suggest a particular way or ways on each occasion, but broadly the page can be done as:

- a quiz for individuals, pairs or groups where it appears, i.e., at the end of the reading section
- a quiz, but *later* in the course, when students have had a chance to forget some of the knowledge and/or vocabulary
- a quiz, but *before* the students do the theme; keep the answers and see how much they have learnt after doing the theme
- a self-study test; students write their answers and hand them in, or self-mark in a later lesson in class
- a phase of a lesson – the teacher sets the task(s) in the normal way and feeds back orally

Portfolio

The main features of the Portfolio lessons are:

- **versatility**
  It is possible to spend anything from part of a single lesson to four lessons on the activities; in addition, some, all or none of the work can be done in class.
- **integrated skills**
  All four skills are included in this lesson, though the focus will shift depending on the activity.
- **academic skills**
  The focus is on researching, digesting and exchanging information, and presenting information orally or in writing.
- **learner independence**
  At all stages from research through to oral or written presentations, the teacher should be in the roles of monitor, guide and, if necessary, manager, and should try to avoid being the 'knower' and 'controller'!

Here are some ways of exploiting each stage of the lesson:

Activating ideas

Use the photographs in the book or show your own. Make sure students have the key vocabulary for all the activities.

Gathering information

The course provides listening and reading texts. You can suggest extra Internet research if you wish. The information is often presented as an information gap, with groups listening to different texts then regrouping in order to exchange information. At first, you may need to suggest the best way to take notes, e.g., in a table with relevant headings. Later, however, you should encourage students to design their own note-taking tables and headings. At all stages, encourage students to help each other with comprehension or any problems, only calling on you as a last resort. The research stages can be done in class or for homework. However, check the research has been done effectively and reasonably thoroughly before moving on to the presentation stages.

Oral presentations

To start with, these should be no more than a few sentences long. The organization of the presentations is crucial and will depend on how much time you have and the number of students in your class.

- **Formal and teacher-centred**
  Set another activity for the class, or ask another teacher to do something with your class. Remove one student at a time (or one group, if the presentation is a collaboration) to another room so that you can listen to the presentation.
- **Student-centred to some extent**
  Students give presentations to other groups of students in the class. You may have between two and four presentations going on at the same time. Monitor as many as you possibly can. Make a note of students you have listened to and make sure you listen to different students next time round.
- **Student-centred and informal approach, requiring a mature class**
  Students give presentations to their groups as above. However, the 'listening' students give feedback after the talk, rather than you.

It is important that if you have students listening to talks, they are not simply 'passive' listeners. They will switch off and get bored. Wherever possible, therefore, assign tasks. This is relatively easy if students are listening to new information: they can complete notes or write answers to questions. However, if they are listening to talks similar to their own, give the 'listening' students feedback or comment sheets to complete (see below).

Table 4: Example feedback form for group tasks

Did the speaker ...	always	sometimes	never
look up from notes?			
make eye contact?			
speak loudly enough?			
talk at correct speed?			
use good intonation patterns?			
use good visuals / PowerPoint slides?			
give all the important points?			
introduce the talk?			
conclude the talk?			

Please note: many of the above suggestions for oral presentations in the Portfolio lesson, including the feedback form, are also relevant for lessons in the speaking sections.

Feedback on oral presentations

You can choose between giving formal, written feedback to individual students, and more informal oral feedback to each group or the whole class. Formal written feedback could be based on a checklist of speaking sub-skills such as those provided by IELTS or Cambridge ESOL for the FCE. Alternatively, you may prefer to devise your own checklist with broader headings, e.g.,

- accuracy
- fluency
- pronunciation
- grammar
- vocabulary, etc.

Informal feedback should include some positive and encouraging statements, as well as showing students what they need to work on. With the scaffolding in *Progressive Skills in English*, students should not make a large number of mistakes in producing spoken or written work, so it should be easier than otherwise to focus on a small number of areas for improvement. Make a note of grammar or vocabulary mistakes you hear while monitoring the class. Write the incorrect language on the board. Elicit from the class what the mistake is and how to correct it. Drill the correct sentence. Practise any words, phrases, sentences or questions that you noted were poorly pronounced.

Whichever method of feedback you choose, give the class one or two targets to work on for the next oral presentation, e.g., 'Look up from notes more often.' Even better, ask students to each set themselves a target for next time. Suggest ideas, which can be discrete (such as about the pronunciation of a particular sound) or much broader (such as about making clearer notes). Students should make a note of their target for next time and you can check it if you wish.

Dealing with writing

In the Portfolio, you can adapt the final activity as you wish. You may like to give further practice of writing a full assignment-type essay, but there are other writing activities that are worth doing:

- notes only, possibly in a table
- PowerPoint slides
- a poster or wall presentation, particularly if you can display these publicly
- a one-paragraph summary
- a complete project on the topic, containing several different articles with accompanying visuals; this can be worked on individually or produced together in a group

Giving feedback on writing

For work set for completion in class:
Monitor and give some help to individuals. Make a note of common errors, i.e., mistakes that two or more students make. Then give feedback to the whole class. You can use the technique described above for feedback on oral errors; write the incorrect sentences the students have produced on the board and elicit the correct version.

For work that you collect in:
It is important not to get bogged down in detailed corrections and/or piles of written work waiting to be marked. For this reason, do not set too much written work as home assignments! You could, of course, ask students to comment on each other's writing in a phase in a later lesson, but this only works with relatively mature classes. Always set the length of the task, using these teaching notes as a guide.

Establish a marking key with the class early on in the course. For example, *sp* = spelling, *p* = punctuation, *gr* = grammar, and, if you feel it is necessary, provide this as a handout. A marking key means you are able to highlight the problem areas but leave students to make the corrections.

Focus on only two or three key areas each time you mark. Initially, these may simply be presentation and layout, e.g., using paragraphs, but later could include using more complex noun phrases or more formal language. Later you can focus on sub-skills such as organization and discourse, cohesion, longer sentences, etc.

We have tried to provide model answers wherever possible, even for open-ended activities like the writing and speaking assignments. Always show these to the class and discuss possible variations, in order to avoid the models being too prescriptive. If you have students with good writing skills, ask their permission to show their written work to the class as example answers.

Listening

'How many times should I play the DVD or CD of lectures?' This is a question we are often asked by teachers. On the one hand, we need to train our students to deal with the real-life lecture situation, in which students will only have the opportunity to hear the information once. On the other hand, students may simply not understand the lecture on the DVD after only one playing. So what is the solution?

- Firstly, it is important to make sure all the pre-listening activities are carried out effectively so that students can begin to predict the lecture content.

- Next, play the first section of the lecture once only for completion of the exercise or activity; this is a kind of 'test' to find out how well students would perform in the 'real-life' situation. It also trains students to listen for as much information as they can on the first hearing. Check how well students have completed the task and elicit the correct answers.
- Once you have confirmed the correct answers, move on to the next section of the lecture and corresponding exercise. Repeat the above procedure.
- When students have heard all the sections of the lecture, replay the complete lecture, with or without the transcript. This is where learning takes place, because students have the opportunity to see why they missed information or did not fully understand during the first playing.
- Finally, as a follow-up, students should be encouraged to listen to the complete lecture several times on their own at home, both with and without the transcript.

What other strategies can the teacher use?
- Remember that the key to comprehension in a foreign language is prediction, so students must have time to assimilate what they have just heard and predict what is coming next. You can pause the lecture any number of times during the first listening if you think your class needs this extra time. But, of course, pause at logical points – certainly the end of sentences and preferably the end of topic points.

What other strategies can the students use?
- Nowadays, most lecturers in the real world provide pre-lecture reading lists and notes, PowerPoint slides and visuals, and handouts. Summaries are also often available on the university's portal. There are PowerPoints available for all the lectures on the *Progressive Skills in English* website. Students should be made aware of all of these resources and encouraged to use them.

Further speaking practice / drilling

In the notes for individual speaking lessons, we often say 'practise the sentences with the class'. You can use one or more of the example drilling techniques below. There are many other techniques, but we have just given a sample below. (The examples are all based on Level 1, Theme 1 Speaking.)

- **Simple repetition, chorally and individually**
Highlight the pronunciation area you want to focus on when you model the sentence or question, e.g., showing the intonation pattern with your hand, or using an intonation arrow on the board.

- **Question and answer**
  When do you take national exams in your country?
  We take them at 16 and 18.
  (Do not simply accept *16 and 18* in a controlled
  practice phase – encourage a full sentence.)
  Alternatively, you can practise short answers. Tell
  students if you require *yes* answers or *no* answers:
  Is a nursery school for young children?
  Yes, it is.
  Does primary *mean 'first'?*
  Yes, it does.
  Do most children leave school at 18?
  Yes, they do.

- **Transformation**
  These examples focus on forms of the present
  simple tense.
  Many children begin school at seven.
  Sorry, but they don't begin school at seven. OR
  Actually, they begin school at five.

- **Substitution**
  Say a phrase or sentence and ask the class to
  repeat it. Then give prompts that can be
  substituted as follows:
  History is a very important subject at school.
  useful
  History is a very useful subject at school.
  isn't
  History isn't a very useful subject at school.
  university
  History isn't a very useful subject at university.
  Drama
  Drama isn't a very useful subject at university.

- **Prompts**
  These can be given orally or they can be written on
  the board. They are particularly good for practising
  question forms:
  Nursery / young children?
  Is a nursery school for young children?
  When / take / A levels?
  When do you take A levels?

Setting up tasks

The teaching notes for many activities begin with the
word *Set* ... This single word covers a number of vital
functions for the teacher, as follows:
- Refer students to the rubric, or instructions.
- Check that they understand **what** to do: get one or
  two students to explain the task in their own words.
- Tell the students **how** they are to do the task, if this
  is not clear in the rubric (as individual work,
  pairwork, or group work).
- Go through the example, if there is one. If not,
  make it clear what the **target output** is: full

sentences, short answers, notes, etc. Many activities
fail in the classroom because students do not know
what they are expected to produce.
- Go through one or two of the actual prompts,
  working with an able student to elicit the required
  output.

Use of visuals

There is a large amount of visual material in the book.
This should be exploited in a number of ways:
- **before** an activity, to orientate the students; to get
  them thinking about the situation or the activity
  and to provide an opportunity for a small amount
  of pre-teaching of vocabulary
- **during** the activity, to remind students of
  important language
- **after** the activity, to help with related work or to
  revise the target language

Pronunciation

Only the speaking section of each theme directly
focuses on oral production. In this section, you must
ensure that all the students in your group have
reasonable pronunciation of all target items.
Elsewhere, in the other skill sections, it is important
that you do not spend too long on oral production.
However, do not let students get away with poor
production of basic words, even if the focus of the
lesson is not speaking.

Comparing answers in pairs

This activity is suggested on almost every occasion
when the students have completed an activity
individually. This provides all students with a chance to
give and to explain their answers, which is not possible
if the teacher immediately goes through the answers
with the whole class.

Monitoring

Pairwork and group work activities are, of course, an
opportunity for the students to produce spoken
language. This is clearly important in the speaking section
but elsewhere, these interactional patterns provide an
opportunity for the teacher to check three points:
- that the students are performing the correct task,
  in the correct way
- that the students understand the language of the
  task they are performing
- the elements which need to be covered again for
  the benefit of the whole class, and which points
  need to be dealt with on an individual basis with
  particular students

Feedback

At the end of every activity there should be a feedback
stage, during which the correct answers (or a model

answer, in the case of freer activities) is given, alternative correct answers (if any) are accepted, and wrong answers are discussed.

Feedback can be:
- high-speed, whole class, oral – this method is suitable for cases where short answers with no possible variations are required
- individual, oral – this method is suitable where answers are longer and/or where variations are possible
- individual, onto the board – this method is suitable when the teacher will want to look closely at the correct answers to highlight points of interest or confusion.

Remember, learning does not take place, generally speaking, when a student gets something right. Learning usually takes place after a student has got something wrong, and begins to understand why it is wrong.

Confirmation and correction

Many activities benefit from a learning tension, i.e., a period of time when students are not sure whether something is right or wrong. The advantages of this tension are:
- a chance for all students to become involved in an activity before the correct answers are given
- a higher level of concentration from students – tension is quite enjoyable!
- a greater focus on the item as students wait for the correct answer
- a greater involvement in the process – students become committed to their answers and want to know if they are right and if not, why not

In cases where learning tension of this type is desirable, the detailed teaching notes say *Do not confirm or correct (at this point)*.

Highlighting grammar

This course has specific grammar lessons but, in addition, in other lessons the expression *Highlight the grammar* is used in the teaching notes. This expression means:
- Focus the students' attention on the grammar point, e.g., *Look at the verb in the first sentence.*
- Write an example of the target grammar on the board.
- Ask a student to read out the sentence/phrase.
- Demonstrate the grammar point in an appropriate way (see below).
- Refer to the board throughout the activity if students are making mistakes.

Ways of dealing with different grammar points:
- for **word order**, show the order of items in the sentence by numbering them, e.g.,

1	2	3	4
They	*often*	*have*	*a special party.*

- for **paradigms**, show the changes with different persons of the verb, e.g.,

  I   *go*
  He   *go**es***

Self-checking

On a few occasions during the course, the teaching notes encourage you to ask the students to check their own work. This can be done by referring students to the full transcript at the end of the course. This is an excellent way to develop the students' recognition and correction of error. Listening, in particular, obviously happens inside someone's head, and in the end each student has to understand his/her own error or misunderstanding.

Gap fill

Filling in missing words or phrases in a sentence or text, or labelling a map or diagram, indicates comprehension of both the missing items and the context in which they correctly fit. It is generally better to provide the missing items to ensure that all the required items are available to all the students. In addition, the teacher can vary the approach to gap fills by sometimes going through the activity with the whole class, orally, pens down, then setting the same task individually. Gap fills or labelling activities can be photocopied and set as revision at the end of the section or later, with or without the missing items box.

In *Progressive Skills in English*, gaps often contain the same kind of word (e.g., nouns) or the same role in a sentence (e.g., the subject) in order to reinforce word class and syntax.

Two-column activities

This type of activity is generally better than a list of open-ended questions or gap fill with no box of missing items, as it ensures that all the target language is available to the students. However, the activity is only fully effective if the two columns are dealt with in the following way. Ask students to:
- **guess** the way to complete the phrase, sentence or pair
- **match** the two parts from each column
- cover column 2 and **remember** these parts from the items in column 1
- cover column 1 and **remember** these parts from the items in column 2

Additional activities are:
- students test each other in pairs
- you read out column 1 – students complete with items from column 2, books closed
- students write as many of the items as they can remember – Course Books closed

Ordering

Several different kinds of linguistic elements can be given out of order for students to arrange correctly. The ability to put things in the correct order strongly indicates comprehension of the items. In addition, it reinforces syntactic structure, particularly if:
- you present a number of jumbled sentences together with the same underlying syntax
- you keep elements of each phrase together, e.g., *in the UK* rather than breaking everything down to word level

This type of activity is sometimes given before students listen or read; the first listening or reading task is then to check the order. To make the exercise more enjoyable, and slightly easier, it is a good idea to photocopy the items and cut them into strips or single words. Students can then physically move the items and try different ordering. The teacher can even make a whiteboard set of sentences and encourage students to arrange or direct the arrangement of the items on the board.

Tables and charts

Students are often asked to transfer information into a table. This activity is a good way of testing comprehension, as it does not require much linguistic output from the students at a time when they should be concentrating on comprehension. Once the table has been completed, it can form the basis of:
- a checking activity – students compare their tables, note and discuss differences
- a reconstruction activity – students give the information in the table in full, in speech or writing

The second method should be used with caution, bearing in mind the focus on the receptive skill in the course rather than on written or spoken production.

Error correction

It was once thought that showing students error reinforced the error, that students would be even more likely to make that error in the future. We now know that recognizing errors is a vital part of language learning. Rather than reinforcing the error, showing it can serve to highlight the problem much better than any number of explanatory words. Students must be able to recognize errors, principally in their own work, and correct them. For this reason, error recognition and correction activities are occasionally used.

The 25-hour course

Firstly, each skill section contains 25 lessons which stand alone from the other skill sections. In other words, students do not need to have studied the listening section of a theme, for example, in order to use the speaking section effectively. However, there is a thematic link between all the skill sections in one theme, so if students *do* study more than one skill, they will broaden and deepen their ability to understand and/or produce text about the theme. Course leaders can, of course, choose more than one skill – for example, listening and speaking, or listening and reading, to match the exact needs of their students.

The 40-hour course

Each skill section has two core lessons, the second and third lessons in the section. The first core lesson is called *Real-time*, e.g., *Real-time listening*, and includes a particular kind of text which contains new sub-skills and new grammar points. The second core lesson is called *Learning new skills*, e.g., *Learning new listening skills*. In this lesson, the new sub-skills are highlighted and practised. Ideally, the first core lesson should be prefaced by the vocabulary lesson, and the second core lesson should be followed by the grammar skills lesson, but it is possible to set the first for homework preparation *before* and the second for homework consolidation *after* the core lessons. In this case, all the themes can be covered in 40 hours.

The 60-hour course

Each skill section contains a lesson which focuses on a grammar point related to the skill. Although there is quite a large amount of common core grammar in the genre of EAP, there are many points which are directly related to specific skills. For example, it is easy to *see* negation in English because the word *not* is clearly evident in negative sentences. However, it is very hard (often impossible) to *hear* negation, so understanding that spoken sentences are negative requires different skills. The 60-hour course is the 40-hour course plus the grammar lesson in each skill.

The 80-hour course

Each skill section begins with a vocabulary lesson. Research has shown how important vocabulary is in the acquisition of language, and this is particularly true of academic English, which uses a very large number of synonyms in order to achieve lexical cohesion in a text. The 80-hour course is the 40-hour course plus the vocabulary lesson and grammar lesson in each skill.

The 100-hour course

A key feature of the *Progressive Skills* approach is the use of parallel texts. In all listening and reading sections and in nearly all speaking and writing sections, the fifth lesson contains the same text type as that in the second lesson, requiring understanding and use of the same sub-skills and grammar points. The fifth lesson, *Applying new skills*, therefore gives students the immediate opportunity to prove that they have understood and can apply the new points presented. The fifth lesson in each section adds another 20 hours to the course.

The 120-hour course

This involves using all the material in the Course Book, including the three extra pages in each theme.

Table 5: Possible routes through the course

Listening	Vocabulary	D	can be set for self-study preparation
	Real-time	A	core material
	Learning new skills	A	core material
	Grammar	B	can be set for self-study
	Applying new skills	C	can be omitted
Speaking	Vocabulary	D	can be set for self-study preparation
	Real-time	A	core material
	Learning new skills	A	core material
	Grammar	B	can be set for self-study
	Applying new skills	C	can be omitted
Reading	Vocabulary	D	can be set for self-study preparation
	Real-time	A	core material
	Learning new skills	A	core material
	Grammar	B	can be set for self-study
	Applying new skills	C	can be omitted
Writing	Vocabulary	D	can be set for self-study preparation
	Real-time	A	core material
	Learning new skills	A	core material
	Grammar	B	can be set for self-study
	Applying new skills	C	can be omitted
Extra pages	Everyday English	E	can be omitted
	Knowledge quiz	E	can be omitted
	Portfolio	E	can be omitted
Key	Route 1 = A	40 hours	
	Route 2 = A + B	60 hours	
	Route 3 = A + B + D	80 hours	
	Route 4 = A + B + C + D	100 hours	
	Route 5 = A + B + C + D + E	120 hours	

Theme 1

Geography and the modern world

- Geography and development

- Geography and water problems

- Geography and tourism

- Geography and the economy

Listening: Geography and development

1.1 Vocabulary for listening: The HDI

Objectives

By the end of this lesson, students should be able to:

- demonstrate understanding of key target vocabulary for the section in isolation and in context;
- relate spoken vocabulary to its written form;
- demonstrate understanding of information about the UN HDI (Human Development Index).

Introduction

Avoid exploiting the heading *The HDI* as this would pre-empt Exercise A. Instead, use Exercise A as the introduction to the lesson.

A Activating ideas

Check understanding of the items in the list. Ask students to give one more example in each case. Here are some possible points for each area:

population	total size; density; life expectancy
climate types	tropical; desert; polar; temperate; Mediterranean
natural resources	fossil fuels (oil, coal); gold; water; wood; copper
minerals	coal; gold; salt; iron (ore); copper
cultivation	wheat; oats; rice; corn; vegetables; fruit
development	economic; social; political

Then set the task for pairwork. After a few minutes, elicit ideas, but do not confirm or correct.

Answers

See Exercise B.

B Understanding vocabulary in context

1. Set the task and warn students this is quite a short extract. Play 🎧 **1.1**. Students discuss the answer in pairs. Elicit answer. Write on

the board *HDI = Human Development Index*. Reassure students they will learn more about what this means in the next extract. For the moment it is enough they understand it means how rich a country is.

2. Give students time to read the beginnings of the four questions. Tell students this extract is quite long. Play 🎧 **1.2**. Students then compare answers in pairs. Elicit answers.

   Summarize the four key points for human development and write them on the board:

   - *life expectancy*
   - *literacy*
   - *education*
   - *standard of living*

   Tell students they should learn these four key points.

3. Check students can find the three countries on the map. Set the task. Play 🎧 **1.3**. Students discuss answers in pairs. Elicit answers. Elicit further ideas for the similarities between the less developed countries (and the reasons for their poverty). Do the same for the developed countries.

   Finally, play the whole lecture (all three extracts), with students following the transcript.

Answers

1. The map shows development (HDI) for all the countries in the world.

2. a. How long can people expect to live in that country? (life expectancy)

   b. What percentage of people can read and write? (literacy)

   c. How many years of education do children receive? (enrolment at each level)

   d. What is the average income per person? (standard of living)

3. The three countries are mentioned as examples of highly developed countries (Canada and Norway) and a country with a low development (Sierra Leone number 177). Norway is also mentioned because it is number 1 on the HDI. The other items are mentioned as possible reasons for high or low scores on the HDI.

Transcripts

🌐 1.1

Presenter:	**1.1. Theme 1: Geography and the modern world Lesson 1.1. Vocabulary for listening: The HDI**
	Exercise B1. Listen to Extract 1. Check your ideas from Exercise A.
Lecturer:	Now, I'd like you to look at this map. And I want you to notice the colours in particular. What do they represent? Well, the map shows human development for every country in the world. We'll look at exactly what we mean by human development later in the lecture. Now every year, the United Nations Development Programme looks at human development in every country in the world. So this UN programme produces an index of human development – the HDI, or Human Development Index.

🌐 1.2

Presenter:	**1.2. Exercise B2. Listen to Extract 2. What questions does the UN ask about each country?**
Lecturer:	According to the UNDP, we can measure human development in a particular country by finding answers to four questions. The first one is this, and it's very simple: *How long, in that country, can people expect to live?* This is called life expectancy. In some countries, life expectancy can be as high as 80 years of age. In the poorest countries of the world, it is only about 40 years old.
	Now, the second question. *What percentage of people can read and write?* In other words, what is the level of literacy in the country? Here, in the UK, the literacy rate is 99 per cent. In Afghanistan, however, it is only 28 per cent of the population.
	Our third question is linked to the second question about literacy. *How many years of education do children receive?* The important thing here is the enrolment rate at each level. What percentage of children complete primary, secondary and tertiary education?
	And finally, the fourth question. Any ideas what it is? No? Well, it's this. *What is the average income per person?* We call this the standard of living. It is measured by dividing the total income of the country by the total population. The total income is sometimes called Gross Domestic Product or GDP. When we divide by the population, we get GDP per person, or per capita, as we say.
	So our four questions are about life expectancy, literacy, education and income, or standard of living.

🌐 1.3

Presenter:	**1.3. Exercise B3. Listen to Extract 3. Why does the lecturer mention the following: a) Canada, b) Norway, c) Sierra Leone, d) natural resources, e) location, f) freshwater?**
Lecturer:	Now, at the beginning of this lecture, I asked you to notice the colours on the map. Let's think about what they represent. Countries with the

highest human development achieve scores of around .9, or 90 per cent. Examples include the USA and Canada and several countries in Northern Europe. In fact, Norway is number 1 in the world on the HDI. So these are the dark green countries on the map. Countries with very low development score only .3 or .4 – 30 to 40 per cent. Several countries in Africa are in this category, including Sierra Leone, which in 2010 was ranked 177 in the world. As you can see, these countries are coloured red, orange or brown.

So what are the similarities between the dark green countries, the ones with the high HDI? Is it their location in the world and their climate? Is it their natural resources? Is it their style of government? And what about the poorest countries in the world? What factors do they have in common? It could be population, poor agricultural land or a lack of fresh water. I want you to consider these ideas and ...

C Researching information

In class, students can discuss possible answers for each question. They may be able to make an educated guess for the HDI number for their country/ies and some of the other answers.

Elicit students' ideas or guesses and if possible, make a note of them. Then when the exact answers have been researched, it will be interesting to compare them with the students' earlier ideas.

Set the task, and if necessary elicit phrases that could be typed into a search engine in order to find the relevant information, for example *HDI list*.

Answers

Answers depend on students.

Closure

Choose one of the following ideas:

- Work on identifying the stressed syllables for some of the multi-syllable words from the lesson:

  a'ccording

  de'velopment

  edu'cation

  ex'pectancy

  'literacy

  par'ticular

  per'centage

  popu'lation

  u'nited

- Discuss further some of the topics from the lesson. For example, you could write the following countries on the board and ask students which ones they think are in the top 10 on the HDI:

UK	Hong Kong
USA	France
Italy	Germany
Canada	UAE
Japan	Australia

In 2011, the following countries were in the top 10: Australia (2), USA (4), Canada (6), Germany (9).

1.2 Real-time listening: Qatar and Lebanon

Objectives

By the end of this lesson, students should be able to:

- use existing skills in order to complete notes on a geography lecture comparing two countries;
- demonstrate understanding of knowledge about the geography of Qatar and Lebanon;
- recognize target vocabulary in context.

Introduction

Revise the four UN Human Development Index questions from Lesson 1.1:

a. How long can people expect to live in that country? (life expectancy)

b. What percentage of people can read and write? (literacy)

c. How many years of education do children receive? (enrolment at each level)

d. What is the average income per person? (standard of living)

If you set the research task (Exercise C) at the end of the previous lesson, discuss students' answers to the four questions about their own country/ies now.

A Activating ideas

1. Make sure the right-hand page is covered, or do the activity with books closed. Write the title of the lesson on the board, *Qatar and Lebanon*, and introduce the activity. Students discuss the question in pairs. Elicit some of their ideas.

2. Students uncover the photographs and other visuals on the right-hand page, then discuss the question in pairs. Elicit ideas.

Methodology note

A few years ago, Qatar was not a well-known country outside of the Middle East. However, many students may now have heard of it, if only because it will be hosting the 2022 football World Cup.

Answers

Answers depend on students but here are some ideas from the maps and the photographs.

Qatar is a peninsula and Lebanon is a coastal country.

Qatar is in the Gulf and Lebanon is on the Mediterranean.

Both countries have skyscrapers – urban development.

Qatar is a desert country, or has a desert.

Lebanon has fields and crops.

Qatar is very hot, has solar power.

Lebanon has a lot of rain.

Qatar has oil.

Lebanon has mining of some sort.

B Understanding an introduction

1. When students have finished reading the handout for the lecture, elicit ideas for the *geography of a country*. Check students understand the question on the handout. It is asking *Is climate, location, etc., important for the HDI of a country?* Remind students about the lecture extracts they listened to in the previous lesson, 1.1. In that, the lecturer asked what the rich countries had in common, and also the poor countries. You can spend a couple of minutes discussing students' ideas about this if you wish.

2. Set the task. With a less able class you can tell them there are four sections to listen for. Play DVD 1.A. Students discuss the sections in pairs. Elicit answers.

3. Point students to the handout under Exercise C. Set the task and go over the examples. Tell students not to worry too much about spelling at this point. Play DVD 1.B. Students complete individually then compare answers in pairs.

After a few minutes, use an electronic projection to show the correct answers. You can draw students' attention to the scientific numbering, but this will be dealt with in more detail in the next lesson, 1.3.

Remind students that the word *area* can have at least three meanings: size, region and topic / subject. In this context it means size, or square kilometres.

Give students time to correct spelling mistakes. Before moving on to the next activity, check understanding of some of the sub-headings by asking students to remember some of the definitions / explanations given by the lecturer, e.g.,

density = the average number of people per square kilometre

urban = living in a town

Answers

1. location, population, land / area, climate, natural resources

2. The lecture sections will be:
   - subheadings
   - a comparison of Qatar and Lebanon
   - Human Development Index ratings
   - Does geography affect HDI?

3. See completed handout for Exercise C.

Transcripts
🌐 1.4 DVD 1.A

Presenter: **Lesson 1.2. Real-time listening: Qatar and Lebanon**

Lecturer: Right, so, today we are looking at the effect of geography on human development. I'm going to focus on two small countries in the Middle East. Next time, by the way, we'll look at two large countries. This week, the two countries are Qatar and Lebanon. First, I'll explain how we can divide the main information about a country, like location, etc., into subheadings. Then I'll compare the two countries in terms of each subheading. Finally, I'm going to tell you the rating of each country on the United Nations Human Development Index, and I'm going to ask you to consider this question: Does the geography of each country affect the human development of its population? There are many similarities between the countries but there are also some differences. Perhaps these differences affect human development.

🌐 1.5 DVD 1.B

Lecturer: Now, I've given you a handout to fill in today. Can you get that out? Right. As you can see, I'm going to look at five key headings for each country. Together, these points give us a picture of the country. The key points are location, population, land, climate and natural resources. We can divide each of these headings into subheadings. I'd like you to fill in the subheadings.

So under *location*, we have *region* and *borders*. We could have *latitude* and *longitude* as well, but *region* and *borders* is fine for us today.

Secondly, *population*. Under this heading, we look at three points: the *total population*, the *density* and the *urban:rural split*. I just want to make sure that you understand the special terms in this section. *Density* means the average number of people per square kilometre. Some countries have a very high density: small countries with a large population, for example. Some countries have a very low population density. *Urban* means 'living in a town', and *rural* means 'living in the country'. The urban:rural split, therefore, is the percentage of people who live in towns compared with the percentage who live in the country.

Thirdly, *land*. Obviously we need to know the area, but more important really is the amount of agricultural land. That's a percentage, of course. Some countries have a lot of agricultural land, but some have deserts or mountains so the amount is very small. Finally in this section, fresh water – that is, lakes and rivers. This last one is particularly important, because of the global shortage of water nowadays.

Next … ah, yes, climate. Well, we start with *type*. As you know, there are a number of main types, like temperate or desert. Then there's average rainfall – that's an annual figure, usually. And temperature range. You know, from 1 degree Celsius to 24 degrees Celsius, for example.

Finally, natural resources. Some people include things like forests in natural resources – in other words, things *above* the ground. But in this analysis, I am only going to consider resources *under* the ground. There are two main types of underground natural resources. They are fossil fuels and minerals. Fossil fuels are things we can burn, like oil and gas and coal. Minerals are things like iron, gold, copper. Oh, sorry. There is one more section, isn't there? Human Development Index. We'll come to that at the very end.

C Understanding a lecture

1. Make sure students understand the task; each student should listen for the information for ONE country only and make notes on that. Play DVD 1.C. Do not elicit answers.

2. Monitor while students exchange information in pairs. Play DVD 1.C again so that students can check their answers for both countries. Show the completed table using an electronic projection so that students can do a final check.

3. Elicit ideas for the answer to the question about human development but do not confirm or correct.

   Play the final part of the lecture, DVD 1.D. Elicit the correct answer for the country with the highest HDI.

Optional activity

Use the numerical information about the two countries to revise pronunciation of numbers, especially percentages, square numbers and decimals, and also the abbreviations for measurements: *mm* = millimetres, *km* = kilometres.

Answers

See table below.

Transcripts
🌐 1.6 DVD 1.C

Lecturer: OK. So, I hope you've got the subheadings now. Now we are going to compare two countries, using these headings and subheadings.

Both countries are located in the Middle East, but Qatar is in the Gulf whereas Lebanon is at the eastern end of the Mediterranean Sea. Qatar is a peninsula, only bordered to the south by Saudi Arabia, while Lebanon is almost completely surrounded by Syria. Has anybody here been to Qatar? No? Well, it is an extremely interesting place. It's a Muslim country, of course, with a very open outlook on the world. Lots of modern buildings and wide roads. Lebanon is also an extremely interesting place. The capital, Beirut, was once called 'the Paris of the East' because it is beautiful and very cosmopolitan – I mean, there are many different nationalities there and many religions. Does the location of these countries affect their human development?

Right, so, population. We're going to look at the total, then the density and finally the urban:rural split. Firstly, the total size. Neither country has a large population but Lebanon's is three times the size of Qatar's. Qatar has 1.5 million people while the Lebanon has around 4.3 million. This difference in population is reflected in density. Qatar has 120 people per square kilometre while Lebanon's is 413 per square kilometre. The people of both countries live mainly in the towns. Ninety-six per cent of Qataris are urban – they live mainly in the capital Doha, whereas the figure for the Lebanese is 87 per cent. Do any of these points about population affect the human development of this country?

Thirdly, land. We've got area in total, and the amount of that land which is agricultural. We also need to consider fresh water – lakes and rivers in each country. So, neither country is large in area. In fact, they are almost the same size. Qatar comprises 11,400 square kilometres while the Lebanon is slightly smaller, at 10,400 square kilometres. Qatar does not have much agricultural land, because most of the country is desert, but Lebanon has a great deal of land for cultivation. Finally, in this category, Qatar has no fresh water. Literally, none. The country relies on

heading	subheading	Qatar	Lebanon
location	region:	Middle East, Gulf region	Middle East, eastern end Med. Sea
	borders:	peninsula, only border – Saudi Arabia	main border – Syria
population	total:	1.5 million	4.3 million
	density:	120 people per sq km	413 people per sq km
	urban:rural:	96% urban	87% urban
land	area:	11,400 sq km	10,400 sq km
	agricultural:	low percentage	high percentage
	fresh water:	none, relies on desalination	surplus
climate	type:	desert	Mediterranean
	ave. rainfall:	<75 mm per annum	825 mm per annum
	temperature range:	15–40 degrees C	5–38 degrees C
natural resources	fossil fuels:	oil and natural gas	poss. oil offshore
	minerals:	no	yes, esp. limestone, iron ore
HDI		0.831	0.739

desalination – I mean, getting fresh water from salt water. Lebanon, on the other hand, has a water surplus. Do any of these points about land area and usage affect the human development of the country?

Fourthly, climate. Here we are interested in the basic type, in the average rainfall, and in the temperature range. So first, type. One country, Qatar, has a desert climate. This means hot, dry summers and warm, dry winters. By contrast, Lebanon has a Mediterranean climate. This means hot, dry summers and cool, rainy winters. So both countries have hot, dry summers ... but Qatar is also warm and dry in winter whereas Lebanon has cool, rainy winters. Rainfall in Qatar averages less than 75 millimetres per annum, while Lebanon has around 825 millimetres a year. Both countries have a similar temperature range, but Qatar goes from 15 to 40 degrees Celsius while Lebanon's range is 5 to 38, so Qatar is much hotter all year round. Does the climate of either country affect human development?

Finally, natural resources. With regard to fossil fuels, Qatar has fuels but Lebanon has none, although it is said that there is oil offshore. In terms of minerals, the situation is the reverse. Lebanon has minerals, especially limestone and iron ore, which is used to make steel. Qatar, on the other hand, has no minerals. Does the presence or absence of natural resources affect human development?

🌐 1.7 DVD 1.D

Lecturer: So we've heard about some of the geographical features of the two countries.
Now, the key question is: What is the Human Development Index of each of these two countries? As you know, this index is a measure of life expectancy, literacy, education in general and standards of living. The figure for Qatar is very high, at 0.831. For Lebanon, the figure is slightly lower, at 0.739.

OK. So, I want you to think about the key question for our next tutorial: Does geography affect human development? Both Qatar and Lebanon have quite a high figure – they are both in the top half of the table of world countries. But Qatar's figure is higher than Lebanon's. Why?

D Developing critical thinking

Set the task and go over the examples. Elicit other possible phrases for comparing the two countries:

They are both ... (in the Middle East)

They are / have (approximately) the same ... (area)

Lebanon / Qatar has more ... (water, rainfall, oil)

The population is higher / lower in ...

Qatar doesn't have any ... but Lebanon does. etc.

Students make more comparisons in pairs. Monitor and give feedback, telling students they will have more practice on ways of comparing in Lesson 5.4.

Students work in pairs, at the same time discussing if each subheading affects the human development. For example, a small population in Qatar means there is more money per capita. After a few minutes, elicit ideas.

Answers

Answers depend on students, but here are some ideas:

- Location can mean that a country is close to large markets for its goods or far away.
- A coastline is good for exporting and importing goods.
- A large population can be good for development, but it can also hold a country back.
- A high urban population usually means more development.
- Agricultural land is good for growing food crops and raising animals for food, but many agricultural countries are very poor.
- All countries need a supply of fresh water.
- It is hard to develop very hot countries, which can't afford air conditioning.
- Fossil fuels are a good source of income and are needed for a country's own development. Minerals can also be very valuable.

Closure

Use the discussion of the points raised in Exercise D to close the lesson if students have suggested some good ideas.

If not, you could play the DVD again with students following the transcript. If there's time, play the whole lecture, if not, choose a short section.

1.3 Learning new listening skills: Using lecture structure

Objectives

By the end of this lesson, students should be able to:

- recognize the stressed word in noun + noun and noun + adjective phrases;
- use scientific numbering for taking notes;
- use appropriate strategies to deal with 'getting lost' when following a lecture.

Introduction

Give students two minutes to look back at Lessons 1.1 and 1.2 and study the vocabulary.

A   Reviewing vocabulary

1. Students work in pairs to predict the possible collocation for each word in the list. Do not elicit or confirm or correct. Do not allow students to refer back to Lessons 1.1 and 1.2 again.

2. Check students understand they will hear the phrase in complete sentences, not in isolation. Play ⊙ 1.8. Elicit answers.

3. Students read the Pronunciation Check. Discuss with the class why it is necessary to know this information about stressed words in these phrases – see Language note below. Set the task by asking students to decide in pairs which are noun + noun phrases and which are adjective + noun phrases. Replay the sentences from A2 so that students can check their answers. Elicit answers.

   Tell students they should learn these collocations.

Optional activity

With students' books closed, say the first word in each phrase; students should give you the second:

T: Natural ...?

Ss: resources.

Language note

In noun + noun phrases, the first noun is normally stressed, unless the sentence is contrasting. The assumption by speakers is that listeners will be able to 'fill in' the unstressed second noun in context. We must therefore teach students to recognize the common collocations of noun + noun phrases. Incidentally, it is not quite so important with adjective + noun collocations, because the noun will normally be stressed therefore at least students will know the broad area which is being talked about.

Note that it is very hard for native speakers to say which word they normally stress in these two-word phrases because we can stress either word if we wish to contrast, so both possibilities sound acceptable.

Transcript
⊙ 1.8

Presenter:	1.8. Lesson 1.3. Learning new listening skills: Using lecture structure Exercise A2. Listen to some sentences from the lecture and check your ideas.
Lecturer:	1. Some people include things like forests in natural resources. 2. And temperature range from the coldest to the hottest. 3. So we've heard about some of the geographical features of the two countries. 4. Some countries have a very low population density. 5. Density means the average number of people per square kilometre. 6. But more important really is the amount of agricultural land. 7. They are fossil fuels and minerals.

Answers

a. natural resources	adj + noun
b. temperature range	noun + noun
c. geographical* feature	adj + noun
d. population density	noun + noun
e. square kilometre	adj + noun
f. agricultural land	adj + noun
g. fossil fuels	noun + noun

- *geographic* and *geographical* can both be used; there is no change in meaning

B   Identifying a new skill (1)

Focus students' attention on Skills Check 1 and tell them they will learn another useful skill for note-taking – *scientific numbering*. Reassure them this is not as complicated as it sounds!

Once students have finished reading, build up a framework for scientific numbering on the board.

Note that each level of heading is normally indented.

1. (main heading)
    1.1. (subheading)
    1.2.
    1.3.

(It is possible to go up to 1.11 or even 1.20, etc., if points are still relevant to the main heading.)

2.
    2.1.
    2.2.
    2.3.
    2.4.
3.
    3.1.
    3.2.

Note also that we can continue to subdivide (although we don't go to this degree of complexity here):

4.
    4.1.
        4.1.1.

Set the task for Exercise B. Students complete individually. Show correct answers on an electronic projection so that students can correct their own work.

Answers

4. Climate
    4.1. Type
        Mediterranean
    4.2. Ave. rainfall
        900 mm
5. Natural resources
    5.1. Fossil fuels
        none
    5.2. Minerals
        limestone, iron ore

C Practising the new skill (1)

The three topics are from previous themes (and levels) of *Progressive Skills in English*. Spend a minute or two finding out how much students can remember about each topic. If they haven't studied these themes before, then simply elicit one or two ideas about each.

Check students understand the task. Play 🎧 **1.9**. Students complete individually then compare answers in pairs. Once again, show answers on an electronic projection so that students can correct their own work. Go over any problem areas. Play 🎧 **1.9** again, with students following the transcript if you wish.

Answers

1.

Time management

1. People
    1.1. colleagues
    1.2. employees
    1.3. the boss
2. Things
    2.1. work
    2.2. energy
    2.3. distractions

2.

Memory

1. Process
    1.1. sensory
    1.2. short term
    1.3. long term
2. Types
    2.1. autobiographical memory
    2.2. procedural memory
    2.3. stories
    2.4. shocking events / flashbulb

3.

Desertification

1. Causes
    1.1. climate change
    1.2. farming methods
    1.3. deforestation
2. Greening

Transcript
🎧 1.9

Presenter: **1.9. Exercise C1. Listen to the introductions to three lectures.**

Lecture 1: Time management.

Lecturer 1:	OK. So this week I'm going to talk about time management. There are two main topics, or areas, within time management. Firstly, managing people; and secondly, managing things. So that's people and, er, things.
	But under each heading we have several subheadings. So under the heading *people* we have three subheadings: *colleagues*, *employees* and, most important of all, *the boss*! While under the heading *things* we have three more subheadings. They are *work*, *energy*, and, unfortunately, *distractions*.
Presenter:	**Lecture 2: Memory.**
Lecturer 2:	So, where have we got to? Right, yes. Memory. This week, I want to summarize everything about this subject so far. So, first, I'm going to look at the *process* of remembering, which involves three stages, according to the Multi-stage memory model. We will look at each stage again – that's sensory, short-term and long-term. Then I'm going to go quickly through the *types* of memory. If you remember, there are four main *types* of memory. Firstly, of course, there is autobiographical memory, like name, date of birth, personal holidays. Then, secondly, there is procedural memory, which is how to do things like drive a car. Thirdly, we have stories, like fairy tales. Finally, shocking events – sometimes called flashbulb memory, because it is like a picture of a moment in our heads.
Presenter:	**Lecture 3: Desertification.**
Lecturer 3:	In today's session, I want to give you an overview of desertification. In the first part of the lecture, I'm going to describe the causes of desertification. We will look at three main causes: climate change, then farming methods, and finally deforestation – that means cutting down trees. Then in the second part of the lecture, I will describe some ways of greening the desert – that is, reversing the process.

D Identifying a new skill (2)

1. Ask students if they ever 'get lost' in lectures (either in their own language or in English). Discuss why this happens. Answers could include:
   poor concentration
   problems with English
   information is difficult to understand
   lecturer speaks too quickly, quietly, etc.
   Tell students that Skills Check 2 will give them some strategies for dealing with the problem. Students read the Skills Check and complete the task.

2. Do not elicit answers but play 🌐 **1.10** so students can check.

Ask students if there are any other strategies for completing missing notes. Examples could include:

- Ask other students if you can borrow and

copy their notes – but remember you must be able to provide better notes than other students sometimes, so the help is mutual.

- Ask the lecturer for PowerPoint slides.
- The lecturer may have a synopsis or lecture notes available online.
- Make sure you have all the handouts, etc.
- If there is a follow-up tutorial, you may be able to complete notes then.

Transcript and Answers
🌐 1.10

Presenter:	**1.10. Exercise D2. Listen and check your answers.**
	During the lecture.
Voice:	OK. So that's climate. Now, let's look at natural resources. Right. We've heard about fossil fuels. What about minerals? Next, natural resources. Let's move on to minerals.
Presenter:	**After the lecture.**
Voice:	I missed the bit about fossil fuels. What did she say about climate type? Did you get the information for average rainfall?

E Practising the new skill (2)

1. Set the task. Check students realize the extract is about *communication*. Play 🌐 **1.11**. Pause at a suitable point and quickly go round the classroom to check that students are completing the task correctly. Re-set the task with an example, if necessary, then continue. Elicit answers.

2. Repeat the procedure for Exercise E1, playing 🌐 **1.12**. Reassure students that the lecturer speaks quickly and they may not hear all the information.

3. Remind students how to ask for missing information. Students practise the questions in pairs to find out any missing information. If students think they got all the information, they can ask questions to check the information is correct. Finally, use an electronic projection to show the correct completed notes. Give feedback on the pairwork activity.

Optional activity

Replay 🌐 **1.11** and 🌐 **1.12** with students

following the transcripts.

Answers

1.

Communication

1. Barriers to communication
    1.1. physical
    1.2. mental
    1.3. linguistic
    1.4. emotional
    1.5. cultural
2. Breaking down barriers
    2.1. giver
    2.2. receiver

2.

Communication

3. Barriers to communication
    3.1. <u>physical</u>
        must be able to hear and see
    3.2. <u>mental</u>
        speaker must form ideas correctly;
        listener must have knowledge and
        ability to understand them
    3.3. <u>linguistic</u>
        not going to talk about this
    3.4. <u>emotional</u>
        can be worst; can't understand if angry,
        depressed, worried
    3.5. <u>cultural</u>

Transcripts

🌐 1.11

Presenter:	1.11. Exercise E1. Listen to an introduction to a lecture about communication. Prepare a page for your notes with scientific numbering.
Lecturer:	I want to talk to you today about communication. We communicate … or, perhaps I should say, we *try* to communicate all the time. But communication – real communication – is not easy. So, I'm going to talk about the process of communication.
	Firstly, I am going to talk about barriers to communication. There are several main barriers to communication. I'm going to look at five. We have physical barriers: for example, you can't hear me well. Then there are mental barriers: you can't understand my ideas. There are linguistic barriers, of course – if we don't have a common language. Fourthly, emotional barriers. Perhaps you are angry with me. Finally, there are cultural barriers. Perhaps we have a different

view of the communication. So, five main barriers, I will look at each one in more detail. Then, in the second half, I will talk about breaking down the barriers. In this section, I'm going to mention two ideas. Firstly, the role of the information giver, and secondly, the role of the information receiver. So that's giver and receiver.

OK. Let's start with barriers …

🌐 1.12

Presenter:	1.12. Exercise E2. Listen to the first part. Make notes.
Lecturer:	OK. Let's start with barriers to communication. Firstly, physical barriers. This is really quite obvious but sometimes people try to communicate, even quite important messages, in completely the wrong place. For example, a lecturer tries to announce an assignment at the end of a lecture, when the students have already started to get up, walk around, talk. It is better to announce information like this in a quiet room and to make sure that everyone can hear you and everyone is listening. You must remember that people need to be able to hear you and, preferably, to see you as well. Seeing a speaker helps you to understand the words. Secondly, we have mental barriers. There are two possible reasons for mental barriers – me and you. Perhaps you don't understand me because I have not formed my ideas clearly or because I don't express them clearly. Perhaps you don't understand me because you are not paying attention, or you are not knowledgeable enough or clever enough to understand them. We shall see in the second part how to deal with this barrier, whether it starts with the speaker or the listener. Thirdly, there can be linguistic barriers. I'm sure you are very familiar with those so I'm not going to dwell on it. Fourthly, emotional barriers, which can be the worst kind of all. You cannot understand perfectly what someone is saying to you if you are in an emotional state, angry, depressed, worried. Of course, you can't express yourself perfectly in those circumstances, either. Finally, cultural barriers …

Methodology note

With a more able class, you can set all three stages of Exercise E together and then feed back on everything at the end. With a less able class, set each task one at a time, feed back, then move on to the next stage. Make sure you keep reminding students about what to do if they 'get lost' in all future listening lessons.

Closure

Practise pronunciation of the stressed words in the following sentences and questions:

*I **missed** the bit about **minerals**.*

***What** did he say about **natural resources**?*

*Did you get the **information** for **fossil fuels**?*

***What** was the **point** about **climate change**?*

*I didn't understand the **last point** about **time management**.*

1.4 Grammar for listening: *both / neither; and / but; whereas / while*

Objectives

By the end of this lesson, students should be able to:
- identify similarities about two locations in spoken sentences with *both, neither*;
- identify differences in two locations in spoken sentences with *but, whereas, while, against, other*;
- recognize agreement of subject and verb with *both* and *neither*.

Introduction

Do the following revision activity to prepare students for the sentences in the tables.

Divide the class into pairs. Each student has one minute to give as much information as they can remember about the two countries from the lecture in Lesson 1.2. Student A talks about Qatar and Student B talks about Lebanon.

Grammar box 1

Tell students they will learn the grammar for describing two things or places that are the same. Focus students' attention on the first table. When students have read it, elicit answers to the question below the table. This focuses on the fact we use a plural noun and a plural verb with present tenses (*are, have*, etc.) with *both*, but singular nouns and verbs with *neither* (*is, has*, etc.) – see Methodology note below.

Use the board to show (or elicit) the kernel ideas for the sentences with *both*:

Qatar is located in the Middle East.

Lebanon is located in the Middle East.

= Both countries are located in the Middle East.

Qatar has some natural resources.

Lebanon has some natural resources.

= Both countries have some natural resources.

Repeat the procedure with the *neither* sentences:

Qatar does not have a large population.

Lebanon does not have a large population.

= Neither country has a large population.

Tell students to study the sentences for describing two **different** things or places.

The key point here for the listener is hearing the discourse marker – *but, whereas, while, against* or *the other* – which tells you that the speaker has moved on to talking about the second item. Point out that information after the discourse marker is often incomplete, e.g., *Lebanon has a great deal* (of what?). So the listener must hold the first part of the sentence in mind and then complete mentally the full idea for the second half of the sentence.

Methodology note

In reading, it is easy to see that two items are either positively the same (*both*) or negatively the same (*neither*). These words may also be salient in speech, but if students miss the first word in one of the sentences, there is a second indicator of whether the similarity is positive or negative. Positive (*both*) is followed by a plural verb, whereas negative (*neither*) is followed by a singular verb.

Point this out clearly to students. There is often a third indicator. We use *some / a lot of* with positive similarities, but *any / much / many* with negatives. Sometimes listeners will need all three indicators to be sure whether the similarity is positive or negative.

A Identifying similarities

Exploit the visuals of Singapore and Tonga. Find out how much students already know about Singapore. (They have probably never heard of Tonga!) Discuss possible reasons why they have been selected for comparison (they are both island nations). Tell students, as they will hear in the lecture extract, the two countries have many similarities. However, one is very successful economically, and the other is not. They will find out some of the reasons for this.

Give students time to read through the list of features and set the task. Play 🎧 **1.14**. Students complete individually then compare answers in pairs. Elicit answers by asking students to make sentences with *both* and *neither*:

Both places are surrounded by water.

Neither place has high rainfall in summer.

Optional activity

- Replay 🎧 **1.14**. Students write the figures for each heading.
- Replay 🎧 **1.14** with students following the transcript.

Answers

small land area	✓
surrounded by water	✓
small populations	✓
tropical climate	✓
desert areas	✗
high rainfall in summer	✗
high rainfall in winter	?
high summer temperatures	✓
high winter temperatures	✓
mountains	✗
river and lakes	?

Transcript
🎧 1.14

Presenter: **1.14. Exercise A. Listen to an extract from a lecture about Singapore and Tonga.**

Lecturer: OK, now we're going to look at two island nations, Singapore and Tonga. Singapore is in southeast Asia and Tonga is in Western Polynesia in the South Pacific. They have some similarities but many differences. One is very successful in economic terms, and very rich. The other is not very successful, economically, and is quite poor. What role has geography played in these differences?

Anyway, let's consider the similarities first.

Obviously, both countries are surrounded by water but Tonga has over 150 beautiful, tropical islands and Singapore has about 60. However, many of Tonga's islands are uninhabited, and, in the case of Singapore, only the large main island is important. Surprisingly, perhaps, tourism is not a major part of the economy in Tonga although the government has plans to develop this industry. Now, my next point: both countries

are small in land area and both have small populations. We'll look at the actual figures later. Let's look at climate. As you've probably guessed already, the two countries have a tropical climate and neither has any actual deserts. On the other hand, neither has much rainfall in summer. Unlike desert climates, both countries have high temperatures in summer *and* in winter whereas of course deserts can be cold in winter. And lastly, both countries are very flat and neither has any mountains.

B Identifying differences

Tell students that this time they will hear the differences between Singapore and Tonga. Give students time to read through the headings. Explain they do not have to write detailed figures. They only have to decide which country is bigger in terms of the particular item. Go through the example.

Play 🎧 **1.15**. Students complete the task individually. Elicit answers and encourage students to give sentences such as:

Tonga is much bigger than Singapore.

Singapore is much more densely populated than Tonga.

Optional activity

- Replay 🎧 **1.15** and ask students to write the exact figures for each heading.
- Replay 🎧 **1.15** with students following the transcript.

Answers

	Singapore	Tonga
area		✓
population	✓	
density	✓	
highest point		✓
agricultural land		✓
highest rainfall	✓	
urban %	✓	
GDP per capita	✓	
HDI	✓	

If students complete the table after a second hearing:

	Singapore	Tonga
area	660 sq km	748 sq km
population	over 5 million [2010]	122,000 [2010]
density	7,000 per km²	165 per km²
highest point	Bukit Timah 166 m	unnamed point [on Kao] 1,033 m
agricultural land	1%	48%
highest rainfall	288 mm	210 mm
urban %	100: 0	25: 75
GDP per capita	$57,000 per capita	$2,900 per capita
HDI	0.846 (27th)	0.677 (85th)

Transcript
🌐 1.15

Presenter: 1.15. Exercise B. Listen to another extract about Singapore and Tonga.

Lecturer: So we have seen some of the similarities between Tonga and Singapore. Now let's consider the differences between these island nations. I said that both are small, but there are big differences between them.

Singapore has an area of 660 square kilometres, and Tonga has 748. However, Singapore is much bigger in terms of population. Singapore has over 5 million people and the population density is very high, at over 7,000 per square kilometre. In fact, it is one of the most densely populated, or crowded, countries in the world. Tonga, on the other hand, has a much smaller population, at 122,000, and a much lower density of 165. Many of its islands, in fact, are uninhabited.

Both countries are flat, as we have heard. The highest point in Singapore, Bukit Timah, is at 166 metres against 1,033 metres in Tonga. The area in Tonga has no name, by the way.

What about agricultural land? Well, Singapore only has one per cent agricultural land – yes, that's right, one per cent, whereas nearly half of Tongan land is under cultivation. Forty-eight per cent, to be precise. The wettest month in Singapore is December, which has an average of 288 millimetres, while Tonga's is March, at 210. So there is not a significant difference there.

Now, we heard about the agricultural land in Singapore – well, the lack of agricultural land, I should say. There is no agricultural land because the whole main island is one large city. So most people in Singapore live in the city and the urban:rural split is 100 to 0. But Tonga is very different. Only 25 per cent of people live in towns. Finally, Singapore is a very rich country with a GDP per capita of $57,000, which is third

place in the world, while Tonga only has a GDP per capita of $2,900.

OK. What does all this mean for the HDI? Which is higher, do you think? Let's see. The HDI for Singapore is 0.846, which means it is 27th in the world. By contrast, the figure for Tonga is 0.677, which puts it in 85th place.

Why is Singapore higher? Does the remote location of Tonga give it a major disadvantage …?

Closure

Discuss with the class why Singapore has a much higher HDI than Tonga because of its geography. You might want to explain that there are also other reasons (e.g., Tonga has a great deal of corruption, and Singapore was developed by the British when Malaya was part of the British Empire), but the focus here is on geography and development. Here are some points that may be raised:

- Singapore is very close to other Asian countries, including Indonesia, which has a very high population for Singapore's goods. In fact, there is a causeway to Malaysia, which also has a high population. Tonga is very remote in the middle of the South Pacific.

- Singapore is really one big island whereas Tonga is many islands, which means communication is quite difficult.

- Tonga is hotter than Singapore and has less rainfall so there may be a problem with fresh water.

1.5 Applying new listening skills: Pakistan and Chile

Objectives

By the end of this lesson, students should be able to:

- produce notes for comparing two countries using correct headings and scientific numbering;

- demonstrate understanding of a lecture comparing two countries through accurate note-taking;

- apply critical thinking in order to analyze reasons for the HDI position of the two countries.

Introduction

Choose one of the following:

- Use Exercise A.

- Revise information about one or more of the countries studied in this section: Qatar, Lebanon, Singapore or Tonga. Which country has the highest / lowest HDI?

A Reviewing vocabulary

1. Students should recognize all the words in the box but if you like you can give them a minute to look back at the headings and subheadings in Lesson 1.2.

   Set the task, pointing out that the words are all subheadings. Students must group them and write the word for the heading. Students complete individually then compare answers in pairs. Do not elicit answers.

2. Play ⏺ **1.16** once for students to check their answers to A1. Then play it again for students to mark the stressed syllable. Use an electronic projection to show the correct answers and elicit the stressed syllable for each word.

Answers

heading	subheading
Lo'cation	'Region
	'Borders
Popu'lation	'Density
	'Urban:rural split
Land	'Area
	Agri'cultural
	'Lakes and rivers
'Climate	'Rainfall
	'Temperature range
Natural re'sources	'Fossil fuels
	'Minerals

Transcript
⏺ 1.16

Presenter: 1.16. Lesson 1.5. Applying new listening skills: Pakistan and Chile

Exercise A2. Listen and check your answers. Mark the main stressed syllable in each word or phrase.

Voice: *Region* and *borders* come under *Location*. *Density* and *urban:rural split* are concerned with

Population.
Area, agricultural and *lakes and rivers* describe *Land*.
Rainfall and *temperature range* are part of *Climate*.
Fossil fuels and *minerals* come under *Natural resources*.

B Activating ideas

Check students can find Pakistan and Chile on a world map. If you can show any photographs of the two countries on an electronic projection it would help with the prediction activity.

Set the task. Students should work in pairs and make a note of their ideas, even if they are not sure. Do not confirm or correct answers. However, find out which country they think has the higher HDI; you could take a class vote on it. Also find out the reasons for their opinion.

Answers

Answers depend on students. They should keep notes of their ideas to check at the end.

C Understanding the lecture

1. Set the task. You will need to remind students about:

   - using scientific numbering for note-taking (see Lesson 1.3);

   - what to do if they get 'lost' (see Lesson 1.3);

   - the headings and subheadings from Exercise A (above).

   Emphasize that students should simply leave a space if they miss any information.

   If necessary, give the class an example of the notes: play the first few lines of [DVD] 1.E and use an electronic projection to show how the corresponding notes should look so far.

   Play the rest of [DVD] 1.E, monitoring to check students are taking notes in the correct way. If not, pause, use an electronic projection again for another example and then continue.

2. In pairs or groups, students ask for any missing information. If students still have gaps in their notes, try this role play. Take on the role of the lecturer from the DVD. Students have to ask you about missing information as they would perhaps after the lecture has finished or in a later tutorial. For example:

S1: *I missed the information about Pakistan's density of population. What was it exactly?*

T: *That's 177 people per square kilometre.*

S2: *What did you say about the climate in Chile?*

T: *I said Chile has every type of climate.*

Finally, use an electronic projection to show the completed notes for the answers.

Answers

Model answers: see table below.

Transcript

1.17 DVD 1.E

Lecturer: I'm going to talk today about two large countries. There are many similarities between the countries but there are also some differences. As you know, when we analyze the geography of a country, we look at five areas: location, population, land, climate and natural resources. Then, as before, at the end of the lecture I'm going to give you the Human Development Index number – or HDI – for each country. Like last time, I'm going to ask you to consider this question: *Does geography affect human development in these countries?*

First, then, location. We need to consider region and borders. One country, Pakistan, is in western Asia whereas the other, Chile, is in South America. Pakistan is bordered in the east by India, in the west by Iran and Afghanistan and in the north by China. Chile has borders with Peru in the north, Bolivia in the northeast and Argentina in the east. Chile also has a very long coastline on the South Pacific Ocean.

OK. Let's look at population now. As before, I'm going to look at three sub-areas under this heading: the total population, the density and the urban:rural split. Pakistan has a large population, but Chile's is quite small. The population of Pakistan is 185 million whereas Chile's population is around 10 per cent of that size, at 17.3 million. Pakistan therefore has a much higher density of population than Chile: 177 people per square kilometre against 20 per square kilometre. What about the urban:rural split? Well, the population of Pakistan is more rural than the population of Chile. The split in Pakistan is 34 to 66, whereas in Chile it is 87 to 13.

Thirdly, land. As you know, we consider area, percentage of agricultural land and availability of natural water, that is, lakes and rivers. Both countries are large. In fact, they are almost the

	Pakistan	Chile
1. Location		
1.1. Region	western Asia	South America
1.2. Borders	India to the east; Iran and Afghanistan to the west; China to the north	Peru to the north; Bolivia to the northeast; Argentina to the east; long coastline on S. Pacific
2. Population		
2.1. Total	185 million	17.3 million
2.2. Density	177 per km²	20 per km²
2.3. Urban:rural split	34:66	87:13
3. Land		
3:1. Area	803,000 km²	756,000 km²
3.2. Agricultural %	30%	21%
3.3. Lakes and rivers	the Indus	the Loa
4. Climate		
4.1. Type	desert in the north	every type, from desert in the north through to Mediterranean to Arctic in the extreme south
4.2. Ave. rainfall	125 mm – 1,500 mm	0.2 mm – 2,900 mm
4.3. Ave. temperature	13 – 34°C	-18 – 38°C
5. Natural resources		
5.1. Fossil fuels	coal	coal, small amount of oil and natural gas
5.2. Minerals	iron ore, copper	iron ore, copper
6. HDI	0.504	0.805

same size. Pakistan has an area of 803,000 square kilometres, while Chile is slightly smaller at 756,000 square kilometres. Both countries have quite a high percentage of agricultural land. Pakistan has 30 per cent agricultural land and Chile has 21 per cent. Both countries have permanent lakes and rivers. The most important river of Pakistan is the Indus, while the most important river of Chile is the Loa.

Fourthly, climate. If you remember, in this area we consider the broad type of climate, then we look at average annual rainfall and temperature range. Both countries are very large so they have different climates in different areas. In fact, Chile has every main type of climate, from *desert* through *Mediterranean* to *Arctic* in the extreme south. Both countries have desert regions in the north of the country. The rainfall range in Pakistan is much lower than in Chile. In Pakistan, rainfall ranges from 125 mm, which is very low, to 1,500 mm, which is very high. Meanwhile, in Chile, average rainfall is between 0.2 mm in the north and 2,900 in the south. The temperature range is also wider in Chile. Whereas in Pakistan there is a temperature range throughout the year between 13 degrees Celsius and 34 degrees Celsius, in Chile the range is much bigger, between minus 18 … that's minus 18 degrees Celsius … and plus 38 degrees Celsius.

Finally, natural resources. As you know, we can divide natural resources into fossil fuels and minerals. Both countries have coal, but Chile also has a small amount of oil and natural gas. With regard to minerals, both countries have iron ore and copper.

OK. So we have heard about some of the geographical features of the two countries. What are their HDI ratings? They are very different. On the one hand, the HDI for Pakistan is 0.504, which puts it in the bottom half of the world's countries. On the other hand, the HDI for Chile is 0.805, which means Chile is in the top half. Why is there that difference? Is it connected to geography?

D Developing critical thinking

Students discuss the two questions in pairs or small groups. Suggest phrases students can use (or refer them back to Lesson 1.4) for talking about similarities and differences:

Both countries are / have …

Neither country is / has …

Chile has … but Pakistan has …

After a few minutes, elicit their ideas.

Answers

Answers depend on students.

Closure

Either use Exercise D or, if there is time, show the lecture again with students following the transcript.

Speaking: Geography and water problems

1.6 Vocabulary for speaking: Water resources

Objectives

By the end of this lesson, students should be able to:

- demonstrate understanding of meanings of target vocabulary;
- pronounce target vocabulary in isolation and in context;
- use knowledge about water resources in order to complete tasks.

Introduction

Write the following sentences on the board:

1. *Canada is a country which has many natural* **resources**. *(minerals, oil, coal, gas, etc.)*

2. *The company has survived because it has good financial* **resources**. *(money, property, etc.)*

3. *The language centre has really good* **resources**. *(educational resources, e.g., books, computers, DVDs, CDs, etc.)*

4. *My boss is a really* **resourceful** *person. (skilled, good at dealing with problems)*

5. *In many African countries, water* **resources** *are very limited. (not enough rain, rivers, etc., and not enough ways of storing water)*

Ask students to discuss the meaning of the word *resource* in each sentence. After a few minutes, elicit ideas. Tell students that in today's lesson they are going to look at water resources.

A Understanding a diagram

1. This is a problem-solving activity. Briefly exploit the diagram but do not teach any of the words in the box. Elicit the fact that the diagram shows a water system. Spend a minute or two revising words such as *mountain, cloud, rain, river, town, fields*.

   Now set the task. Say the words in the box for the students. Tell them not to worry if they are not sure about the answers. Students work individually then compare answers in pairs.

2. Play ⓓ **1.18**. Students check their answers. Use an electronic projection of the completed diagram so that students can check their answers again. Play ⓓ **1.18** once

more with students following the transcript. Ask students to listen carefully to the pronunciation of the new words. Target words are each repeated two or three times in the extract so this will help students to learn the correct pronunciation.

Check understanding of other words and phrases: *streams; foot of the mountains; soak; (under)ground; flow*.

3. Practise pronunciation of the words in the box and any other words you think students may have difficulty with for this activity.

   In pairs, students describe the diagram to each other. (Make sure the transcript is covered.) You will probably need to provide some prompts on the board, or you can write the first few words of each sentence for students to complete. Remind students to use the present simple to describe a system or process.

   Monitor while students are working and give help with pronunciation of new words.

   Give feedback; in particular you may need to focus on the correct use of prepositions.

Answers

See opposite page.

Transcript
ⓓ 1.18

Presenter:	**1.18. Lesson 1.6. Vocabulary for speaking: Water resources**
	Exercise A2. Listen to an extract from a lecture about water resources, and check your ideas.
Lecturer:	Now, I want you to study this diagram. It shows a water system in a mountainous area. OK. All the water comes from rainfall in the mountains. You can see small streams ... here. They all join together into one big river ... here. Now, look at the foot of the mountains. There is quite a large dam. It probably holds several billion cubic metres of water. So the dam holds the water for some time and allows it to soak into the ground. What happens next? Well, if you look here, you can see some of the water from the dam goes to an underground aquifer. An aquifer is a kind of underground store of water. People take water from the aquifer through wells. You can see the wells in the diagram just here. OK, let's return to the river. The river then flows past a reservoir. A reservoir is another method of storing water; it's a kind of artificial lake. Some of the water from the river is diverted into the reservoir and, from there, into irrigation channels for the fields. In other words,

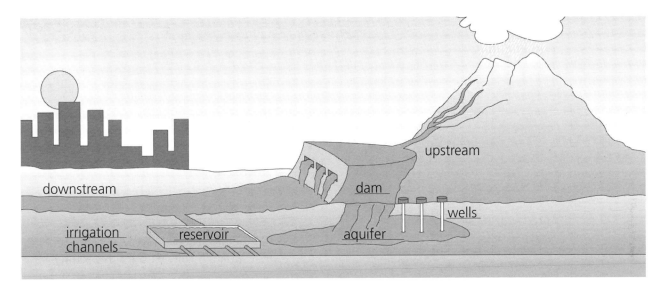

downstream

irrigation channels

reservoir

dam

upstream

wells

aquifer

farmers use water from the reservoir to irrigate their crops. So there you have the complete system, from rain falling in the mountains, to stored water in the dam, aquifer and reservoir.

Methodology note

Students may be surprised to discover this meaning of the word *well*. The word can be different parts of speech. It can be an adverb, as in *I didn't sleep very well last night* and an adjective, as in *I am very well, thank you*. In this context it is, of course, a noun.

B Using new vocabulary in context

1. In this activity, students will hear the pronunciation of the target words in context in each question. Words from Exercise A are also recycled.

   Before you set the task, you could play the questions on ⊘ **1.19** and ask students to listen out for new words. When they hear a new word, they can tick it off on the list.

   For example:

   Question a: *What is the **source** of the water in the system?*

   Students tick off the word *source* in the wordlist.

   Do not elicit answers during this phase.

   Now set the task and give students time to read through the answers.

Play ⊘ **1.19**. Pause after each question. Increase speaking practice by allowing students to discuss the answer in pairs each time, but do not elicit yet. Replay the question if necessary. Repeat the procedure until the last item, then elicit correct answers. Go over any items students had difficulty with and replay the relevant questions if necessary.

2. Set this as a pairwork or small group activity in order to increase speaking practice. Students should try to recall each of the questions from the previous activity. If necessary, provide prompts or the first two or three words of each question. When students have discussed what the question should be, they should write it down.

   For feedback you can either:

   - replay ⊘ **1.19**, pausing after every question so that students can compare with their own, then drill each question;

   - elicit each question, then drill using ⊘ **1.19** as a model.

   Finally, in pairs, students can practise asking and answering all the questions. Monitor and give feedback.

Answers

a. What is the *source* of the water in this system?	e	Yes, into the reservoir.
b. What is *upstream* of the town?	j	No, because a lot of the rainfall is stored in the dam, the aquifer and the reservoir.
c. Which parts of this water system could *leak*?	i	No, because there is a lot of fresh water.
d. How do people *extract* water from this system?	a	It comes from rainfall on the mountains.
e. Do the people *divert* any of the water?	c	Several parts – the dam, the reservoir, the irrigation channels, the wells.
f. What *feeds* the irrigation channels?	f	The reservoir.
g. What could lead to *flooding* in the town?	b	There's a dam.
h. What could lead to *shrinkage* of the aquifer?	d	They draw water from the wells and take it from the reservoir into irrigation channels.
i. Does this area need a *desalination* plant?	h	It could happen if there was a reduction in rainfall.
j. Do the people of this area ever *run out of* water or suffer from *drought*?	g	It could result from the dam breaking.

Transcript

🔊 1.19

Presenter: 1.19. Exercise B1. Listen and find an answer to each question about the water system in the diagram above.

Tutor:
a. What is the *source* of the water in this system?
b. What is *upstream* of the town?
c. Which parts of this water system could *leak*?
d. How do people *extract* water from this system?
e. Do the people *divert* any of the water?
f. What *feeds* the irrigation channels?
g. What could lead to *flooding* in the town?
h. What could lead to *shrinkage* of the aquifer?
i. Does this area need a *desalination* plant?
j. Do the people of this area ever *run out of* water or suffer from *drought*?

C   Building vocabulary

Students discuss answers in pairs. Elicit answers. Focus on:

1. Pronunciation of the vowel sound in one-syllable words:

   dam /æ/

   flood /ʌ/

   leak /iː/

   flow /əʊ/

   shrink /ɪ/

2. Stressed syllable of multi-syllable words. Point out that *extract* changes its stress depending on the part of speech; second syllable when a verb, first syllable when a noun.

   Drill the words if you wish.

Answers

1. dam – dam
2. divert – diversion
3. extract – extract
4. flood – flood
5. flow – flow
6. irrigate – irrigation
7. leak – leak/leakage
8. shrink – shrinkage
9. supply – supply

Closure

1. Students' books closed. Say some of the nouns from this lesson, students say the verb. For example:

   T: *flood*

   Ss: *flood*

   T: *diversion*

   Ss: *divert*

   Other nouns with verb forms are: *irrigation; dam; flood; flow; shrinkage; supply; extract; feed.*

2. Set a home assignment. Students research one of the world's largest dams, e.g., the Hoover or Aswan dams. They can find out:
   - location;
   - source of the water;
   - uses for the water, e.g., *irrigating crops, hydroelectricity,* etc.;
   - cubic capacity;
   - date of construction;
   - cost of construction.

1.7 Real-time speaking: Water problems in a developed country

Objectives

By the end of this lesson, students should be able to:
- use existing skills to talk about water problems and solutions;
- pronounce target vocabulary in context.

Introduction

Either use Exercise A or ask students to explain again the water system in the diagram in Lesson 1.6; you could even ask them to draw it from memory and describe the diagram as they recreate it.

A Reviewing vocabulary

1. Check students can remember the meanings of the words in the box. If necessary, refer them back to the previous vocabulary lesson, 1.6. Set the task and go over the example. Students complete individually then compare answers in pairs.

2. Play 🔊 **1.20** once so that students can check their answers. Replay any items students are not sure about. Play 🔊 **1.20** again, pausing after each word so that students can repeat it.

Answers

1. 'a/qui/fer
2. di/'vert
3. ex/'tract – note that this is the verb so the stress is on the second syllable
4. i/rri/'ga/tion
5. 'rain/wa/ter
6. 're/ser/voir
7. 'shrink/age
8. 'un/der/ground

Transcript
🔊 1.20

Presenter:	1.20. Lesson 1.7. Real-time speaking: Water problems in a developed country Exercise A2. Listen, check your answers and repeat each word.
Voice:	aquifer divert extract irrigation rainwater reservoir

B Gathering information

1. Check the meaning of the word *aquifer* (from Lesson 1.6) if you have not already done so. Give students time to read the map and notes. Students discuss the two questions from the assignment in pairs. Avoid too much explanation of the abbreviations used for the notes; encourage students to try to work them out independently while discussing the problem and solution. Elicit ideas.

2. Set the task. Revise the meaning of the multi-word verb *run out of*. Students should make a note of each 'mistaken' point while they listen. Play 🔊 **1.21**. After listening, students compare notes in pairs. Elicit answers to questions a and b. If you like, play 🔊 **1.21** again before you elicit the answer to question c.

Transcript and Answers
🔊 1.21

Presenter:	1.21. Exercise B2. Listen to the student giving information to a discussion group.
Student 4:	OK. So we are talking about water problems and proposed solutions, right? Who wants to start?
Student 1:	OK then, *I* will. I looked at the problems in the United States. Apparently ...
Student 2:	I didn't realize they had problems with water there!
Student 1:	Well, they do. Big problems, apparently. It seems that the central part of the US is running out of underground water. There's an underground reservoir, called the Ogallala Aquifer and ...
Student 3:	The *what* Aquifer?
Student 1:	Ogallala. So, basically, the Ogallala Aquifer provides half of all the water for the United States.
Student 4:	Um ... just a second! Half of all the water?
Student 1:	Sorry. Did I say half? I meant a third.
Student 4:	And do you mean for drinking *and* irrigation?
Student 1:	No, sorry. I mean just for irrigation. Um, yes, irrigation.
Student 2:	No problem. And, er, why is the water running out?
Student 1:	Because the water was formed in the reservoir thousands of years ago, but the reservoir is no longer ... er ... refilled by rainwater.
Student 3:	What? Thousands of years ago? I thought these underground reservoirs were millions of years old.
Student 1:	Oops! Did I say thousands? I meant to say millions.
Student 3:	Oh, right, OK. So how serious is the problem?
Student 1:	It's really serious. Research shows that the reservoir is shrinking fast. The level of the water in the reservoir is falling by one metre every year.
Student 3:	Wow!

Student 1:	Er, yes ... so it will dry up within 200 years. Yes, um, 200.
Student 4:	So, what's the proposed solution?
Student 1:	Well, farmers in the area are suffering shortages, er, so they, er, stopped ... um are going to stop, er, growing crops which require irrigation.
Student 2:	But that's not really a solution, is it? Surely we have to continue to irrigate crops? And what about ...
Student 3:	Well, not necessarily. Farmers could grow crops which are local ... er ... to the area. They ... um, the crops ... probably grow without irrigation.

C Studying the model

1. Set the task. Reassure students it does not matter if they cannot fill in many of the spaces at this point. Do not elicit answers.

2. Play ⏺ **1.22**. If necessary, pause after each answer to give students time to check or write the missing words. Focus on some of the questions in the extracts and discuss:

   - the speaker's purpose or function of each utterance;
   - the stress and intention patterns used.

   For example:

   Half of all the water? / _Thousands_ of years ago?

   - function = surprise, checking
   - stress – the word _half_ is stressed in the first case because that is the key point being checked; the word _thousands_ is stressed in the second for the same reason
   - rising intonation is used at the end of both questions, again to show surprise

   That's not _really_ a solution, is it?

   - function = polite disagreement – the word _really_ makes the objection weaker and less confrontational
   - stress = the word _really_
   - intonation = rising (tentative) intonation to express politeness

Transcript and Answers
⏺ 1.22

Presenter:	**1.22. Exercise C2. Listen and check your answers.**
Student A:	Basically, the Ogallala Aquifer provides half of all the water for the United States.
Student B:	Just a second. _Half_ of all the water?
Student A:	Sorry. Did I say half? I meant a third.
Student B:	And do you mean for drinking _and_ irrigation?
Student A:	No, sorry. I mean just for irrigation.
Student A:	The water was formed in the reservoir thousands of years ago.

Student B:	_Thousands_ of years ago? I thought these underground aquifers were _millions_ of years old.
Student B:	So, what's the proposed solution?
Student A:	Well, the farmers are going to stop growing crops which require irrigation.
Student B:	I'm not sure that's a very _good_ solution.
Student A:	Perhaps not, but it solves the problem in the short term.

Pronunciation Check

You can work through the Pronunciation Check at this point or before Exercise C if you prefer.

If you worked through Exercise C as suggested above, students should easily be able to answer the first question, _How does the speaker show surprise?_

Play the example questions on ⏺ **1.23** and ask students to repeat for correct stress and intonation. Use an electronic projection to elicit the stress and intonation patterns for the two questions:

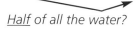

Half of all the water?

Thousands of years ago?

Transcript
⏺ 1.23

| Presenter: | **1.23. Pronunciation Check. Listen to these sentences.** |
| Voice: | _Half_ of all the water?
Thousands of years ago? |

Play ⏺ **1.24** for the remaining sentences. Pause after each question for students to repeat.

Transcript
⏺ 1.24

| Presenter: | **1.24. Pronunciation Check. Listen and repeat some more sentences. Copy the stress and intonation.** |
| Voice: | _Ten_ metres a year?
A _tropical_ climate?
Four _thousand_ per square kilometre?
Thirty degrees centigrade?
Visual learners or _aural_ learners?
Last _month_ or last _year_? |

D Practising the model

Play ⏺ **1.22** again. Pause, for repetition, after each checking question showing surprise. Check students are using good stress and intonation. If you wish, you can ask students to mark up the extracts by underlining stressed words and using arrows for intonation.

Now divide the class into pairs to practise the extracts. Monitor and make a note of common errors. Give feedback.

E Developing critical thinking

Put students into two groups to discuss the two questions. If they are struggling to think of other solutions, give them prompts as follows:

divert / other areas / refill / aquifer	They should divert streams / rainwater from other areas to refill the aquifer.
irrigate / crops / waste water	They could irrigate the crops with waste water.
tran'sport / other areas	They could transport water from other areas.
GM crops / need less water	They should develop GM (genetically modified) crops, which need less water.
build dams / rivers / store	They could build dams on the rivers to store water for irrigation.

Closure

1. In pairs or groups, students take turns to give a talk about the Ogallala Aquifer using the notes under the map. If you wish, the 'listening' students can ask simple checking questions for some of the information.

2. Give some sentences about the information in the lesson with mistakes in each, as follows (error in *italics* and correct information in brackets):

   a. The Ogallala Aquifer provides *half* (a third) of all the water for *drinking* (irrigation) in the United States.

   b. The water was formed in the reservoir *thousands* (millions) of years ago.

   c. The level in the reservoir is falling by one *millimetre* (metre) a year.

   d. The reservoir will dry out in *20* (200) years.

   e. Farmers in the area *have stopped* (are going to stop) growing *crops* (which require irrigation).

Everyday English: Expressing opinions politely; persuading

Objectives

By the end of this lesson, students should be able to:

- express opinions politely with appropriate intonation;
- persuade others of their point of view in a discussion.

Note: This Everyday English is a little different from many of the others in that it is not situational. Instead, it helps students to have discussions and express opinions politely. Students learn phrases for persuasion, important not only for academic argument but also in everyday life. There is also a focus on tentativeness and hedging, which are cultural traits of British people (though not all other English-speaking cultures). These 'British' characteristics may form the basis of a discussion with the class.

The important thing, however, is that students are aware that it is easy to fall into the trap of sounding rude, unless they learn to use appropriate intonation and more tentative language, especially when expressing opinions, or even facts of which they are absolutely sure. If a British person knows, for example, that the population of their town is 204,000, and they are asked for this information, they will probably say *It's just over 200,000, I think* rather than *It's 204,000*.

Introduction

Use Exercise A.

A Activating ideas

Check students understand the captions and the headlines, in particular the words *poverty*, *pollution*, *preventable* and *sanitation*.

Ask students how they feel about the headlines and elicit phrases such as:

That's / It's terrible / shocking / appalling.

We should do something about this situation / problem.

I feel angry / frustrated / shocked.

Students discuss the question *What are the reasons for some of the problems?* in pairs or small groups. Elicit a few ideas if necessary to start the discussion off.

Answers

Answers depend on students but here are some reasons for the problems in the headlines:

- lack of rain in hot countries = poor harvest, etc.
- lack of vaccines for malaria and other diseases
- water is not stored
- water / food is expensive
- poverty
- pollution
- too many people
- government corruption, disorganization, poor infrastructure, etc.
- lack of education – people do not know that they should avoid using the same water for sanitation, washing and drinking, for example, or wash clothes downstream of a sanitation outlet.

B Studying a model

1. This conversation is an example of how **not** to speak English! In the next exercise, students will hear the more polite version.

   Set the task and explain the conversation is based on the first headline. Check understanding of the words *charities* and *aid*. Play ⊕ **1.25**. Elicit answers to the question.

   Ask follow-up questions:

   What is Student A's solution to the problem? (We should give money to charities so that they can help poor people.)

   What is Student B's solution? (The UN should do more; they should help people to help themselves.)

   Discuss with the class which person they agree with.

2. Play ⊕ **1.26**. Elicit answers. Focus on the phrases used to agree or disagree politely. Discuss how the extra phrases in the conversation make it more polite. Build up the table opposite on the board.

   Most phrases come at the beginning of the sentence but we often use tag questions at the end. You can also point out that using a conditional sentence is also a polite way of expressing an opinion, as in *If the UN doesn't do the job, charities have to do it.*

polite phrases	basic sentences
I think …	Everyone should give money to charities.
I agree, but don't you think …?	The UN should do more.
That's true, but …	Ordinary people can't just ignore the problems.
Perhaps, but … can we?	We can't leave it to charities.
Anyway, surely …	We shouldn't just give aid.
Shouldn't we …?	We should help people …
Well, OK …	In the long term.
But, in the meantime …	People are dying …
Mustn't we?	We must do something about that …

Drill the phrases and sentences with the class, making sure students use polite intonation.

3. Students practise the conversation in pairs. Encourage them to use the sentences in version 1 of the conversation as prompts. Students should try to remember some of the 'polite' phrases and add them at appropriate points in the conversation. Students can swap the 'polite phrases' around if they wish. Monitor and give feedback.

Answers

1. The speakers do not use polite intonation or phrases to express opinions or disagree. Many British speakers would find the speakers rude or think they were angry.

2. The intonation is more polite. Both speakers use phrases for agreeing and disagreeing and giving an opinion. They sound a little hesitant (tentative).

Transcripts
⊕ 1.25

Presenter:	**1.25. Everyday English: Expressing opinions politely; persuading**
	Exercise B1. Listen to the conversation below about the first headline. What do you notice about it?
Voice A:	Did you know that over 20,000 children die every day unnecessarily?
Voice B:	You mean from poverty and hunger and so on?

Voice A:	Yes. Everyone should give money to charities.
Voice B:	The UN should do more.
Voice A:	Ordinary people can't just ignore the problems.
Voice B:	We can't leave it to charities. And we shouldn't just give aid. We should help the people in developing countries to help themselves.
Voice A:	In the long term. But people are dying, including thousands of children. It's terrible. We must do something about that.

🌐 1.26

Presenter:	**1.26. Exercise B2. Listen to a second version of the conversation. What differences do you notice?**
Voice A:	Did you know that over 20,000 children die every day unnecessarily?
Voice B:	You mean from poverty and hunger and so on?
Voice A:	Yes. I think everyone should give money to charities.
Voice B:	I agree, but don't you think the UN should do more?
Voice A:	That's true, but ordinary people can't just ignore the problems. If the UN doesn't do the job, charities have to.
Voice B:	Perhaps, but we can't leave it to charities, can we? And anyway, surely, we shouldn't just give aid. Shouldn't we help the people in developing countries to help themselves?
Voice A:	Well, OK, in the long term. But in the meantime people are dying, including thousands of children. It's terrible. We must do something about that, mustn't we?

C Practising the model

1. Remind students about the second headline, *2.5 billion people do not have access to clean water and good sanitation*. Set the task. Students work in pairs to discuss possible ways to complete each sentence. Elicit answers. Discuss ways of making some of the sentences more polite, for example:

   I think governments should dig more wells.

   Surely governments should dig more wells, shouldn't they?

   Drill some of the sentences.

2. Set the task and remind students of the 'polite' phrases they can use. Divide the class into groups of between three and five to discuss the solutions. Students can add their own solutions too, if they wish. Students can also discuss the disadvantages of solutions, e.g., some solutions may be too expensive. Monitor and give feedback.

Optional activity

Write the following further headlines on the board. Ask students to discuss each one and

suggest solutions:

148 million under-5s in developing countries are underweight for their age

100 million children do not attend primary school

22 million infants are not protected from disease by routine immunization

500,000 women die each year from causes related to pregnancy and childbirth

Closure

Give feedback on the speaking activities if you have not already done so.

Spend a few minutes summarizing the discussion points made during the lesson.

1.8 Learning new speaking skills: Contributing to discussion groups

Objectives

By the end of this lesson, students should be able to:

• identify when to use the schwa sound in words and sentences;

• use phrases for clarification at appropriate points in a tutorial discussion;

• use phrases with polite intonation for objecting and dealing with objections in a tutorial discussion.

Introduction

Write the key words (in *italics*) from Exercise A on the board and get students to say them until they are using reasonable pronunciation.

A Reviewing vocabulary

Set for pairwork, then feed back orally. Give the answers and ask students to try to remember the questions.

Answers

Possible answers:

1. You can use a pump, or dig a channel from the river.

2. Because the rainfall in the areas goes down.

3. You can pipe water from a river.

4. Because the population in the area is rising, or because people are using more water, in car washes, swimming pools, etc.

5. Because crops need water to grow and there isn't enough natural rainfall in the area.

B Saying vowels

1. Students can discuss in pairs or you can elicit ideas from the class, but do not confirm or correct.

2. Students check their ideas in the Pronunciation Check. Play 🎧 **1.27** for the Pronunciation Check and then go through the list of underlined words.

3. Students practise saying the phrases in pairs or you can drill them. However, the pronunciation of the schwa sound is something you need to follow up at every opportunity during speaking phases as it is such an important part of English pronunciation.

Answers

1. The connection is that all these words are pronounced with the schwa sound.

2. Pronunciation Check sentences:

   - *It provides a third of all the water for irrigation in the US.*
   - *The water was formed millions of years ago.*
   - *The farmers are going to stop growing crops.*
   - *They could grow crops which are local to the area.*

Note that some other words contain schwa as well, as follows:

provides, water, irrigation, ago, farmers, local, area

Note also that *the* is not pronounced with schwa in the final sentence because it is followed by a vowel sound in *area*.

Transcript
🎧 1.27

Presenter:	**1.27. Lesson 1.8. Learning new speaking skills: Contributing to discussion groups**
	Pronunciation Check. Listen and check your answers.
Voice:	It provides a third of all the water for irrigation in the US.
	The water was formed millions of years ago.
	The farmers are going to stop growing crops.
	They could grow crops which are local to the area.

C Identifying a new skill

1. Students focus on the Skills Check. Elicit answers to the three questions.

2. Work through the example, showing that this is the main stressed word in this sentence. Play 🎧 **1.28**, and work through the stressed words. Get students to repeat, then set for pairwork. Play 🎧 **1.29** and remind students to use the schwa sound. Monitor and assist. Feed back on general problems.

Answers

1. clarify = when you don't understand

2. object = when you don't agree

3. deal with = agree with the objection or make another point

Transcripts
🎧 1.28

Presenter:	**1.28. Skills Check. Listen to some more contributions. Mark the main stressed word in each sentence.**
Voice A:	Do you mean for drinking *and* irrigation?
Voice B:	No, sorry. I mean just for *irrigation*.
Voice A:	Did you say *thousands* of years ago?
Voice B:	Sorry. I meant to say *millions* of years ago.
Voice A:	They are going to *stop* growing crops.
Voice B:	I'm not sure that's a very *good* solution.
Voice A:	No, but it solves the problem in the *short* term.
Voice B:	They could bring water from *another* area.
Voice A:	But that would be very *expensive*.
Voice B:	Yeah.

🎧 1.29

Presenter:	**1.29. Skills Check. Listen again. Copy the polite intonation.**
	[REPEAT OF SCRIPT FROM 🎧 1.28]

D Practising the new skill: clarifying

Check students understand the task. Do the first one or two mini-dialogues with the class as examples, perhaps by asking a pair of your most able students to demonstrate.

Students continue in pairs. Monitor and then give feedback.

Answers

Example dialogues:

1. Visual learners like sounds.

   Do you mean sounds?

   No, sorry. I mean colours.

2. Aural learners learn by reading.

Did you say reading?

Sorry. I meant to say listening.

E Practising the new skill: objecting

Refer students to the ideas and opinions in the Resources section, or photocopy the ideas and hand one out to every student in each group. Set for group work. Note that the exponents in the Skills Check, particularly for *Objecting and dealing with objections*, are only a tiny subset of what they can say. With a more able group, point this out and suggest that they try out other ways of objecting and reacting, but remind them that they must be polite: *That's rubbish!* is not acceptable.

Statements in the Resources section:

I think governments should make water very expensive.

Water companies should restrict the amount of water each family can use.

We should not allow people to water garden flowers.

The government should stop people digging wells.

We should make people recycle water in their own homes.

It should be illegal to have baths. Showers are much better.

People should be put in prison for wasting water.

We should close all car washes.

Closure

Keep students in the same small groups. Ask students to think of very strong opinions or ideas (they don't have to agree with them!). Ask the other students to object and then for the speaker to deal with the objection.

You might also want to give some of the following shocking facts about water:

- Three and a half million people die each year from water-related disease.
- 98 per cent of water-related deaths occur in the developing world.
- 884 million people do not have access to safe water supplies, which is approximately one in eight people.
- Dirty water claims more lives through disease than any war claims through guns.
- At any given time, half of the world's hospital beds are occupied by patients suffering from a water-related disease.
- An American taking a five-minute shower uses more water than the typical person living in a slum in a developing country uses in a whole day.
- Poor people living in the slums often pay 5–10 times more per litre of water than wealthy people living in the same city.
- Over 50 per cent of all water projects fail; less than 5 per cent of projects are visited, and far less than 1 per cent have any longer-term monitoring.

1.9 Grammar for speaking: Showing surprise with *think* and *realize*

Objectives

By the end of this lesson, students should be able to:

- show surprise in statements with *I thought ...* and *I didn't realize ...* with appropriate intonation and stress;
- use the patterns *I thought* + past tense and *I didn't realize* + past tense in spoken sentences.

Introduction

Replay the conversation from Lesson 1.7 with students following the transcript. Discuss with the class how the speakers in the conversation expressed surprise (stressed words and intonation).

Grammar box 2

Give students time to study the tables. Elicit the answer to the question (it changes to the past simple tense). Point out, though, that the verb does not change if it is past already, e.g.,

The aquifers were formed thousands of years ago.

I thought they were formed millions of years ago.

Ask students why the word *that* is in brackets (because it can be left out). Point out that if you say it, you must use schwa. Point out also the use of the pronoun, *they*, in place of the noun the *aquifers*.

Play 🔊 **1.30** so that students can listen to the stress and intonation in the sentences with *I thought ...* The intonation rises to the stressed (or 'checking') word and then falls at the end of the sentence.

Ask students to listen to 🔊 **1.30** again and repeat. Students practise the two mini-conversations in pairs.

Transcript
🔊 1.30

Presenter:	1.30. Lesson 1.9. Grammar for speaking: Showing surprise with *think* and *realize*
	Grammar box 2. Listen to each statement and comment.
Voice A:	The aquifers are thousands of years old.
Voice B:	I thought they were *millions* of years old.
Voice A:	The reservoir provides half of all the water for irrigation.
Voice B:	I thought that it provided a *third* of all the water.

Language and culture note

In English, we often put *I think* at the front of information we are absolutely sure is true. This is polite tentativeness. It sounds rude to native speakers to make bald statements that contradict another speaker, e.g.,

The Moon goes round the Sun.

No, it doesn't. It goes round the Earth. = rude!

Point this out to your students if you think they will be able to understand it.

A Showing surprise with *think*

Set the task and go over the example. Practise the example sentence with the class. Point out the use of pronouns in response, e.g., *the Moon – it.*

You can deal with the remainder of the activity in either of two ways:

• Do the activity as a drill, with the Course Books closed. Say the sentence from the book, students respond with the correct sentence. Do this chorally and individually. Once you have worked through all the items, students open their books and practise in pairs.

• Set the activity for pairwork first. Monitor and make a note of items students find difficult. Elicit from the class which word was stressed in each sentence. Then drill the items students had problems with. The answers can be written in class or for homework for consolidation.

Answers

1. I thought (that) it went round the Earth.
2. I thought (that) they lived in the Antarctic.

3. I thought (that) they started talking at one year.
4. I thought (that) they used the euro.
5. I thought (that) most of the water was stored in the oceans.
6. I thought (that) they released it into the atmosphere at night.

Optional activity

Make some more statements that are clearly wrong. Students have to show surprise with *think*.

Grammar box 3

Repeat the procedure for Grammar box 2 above (🔊 1.31).

Focus on:

• the change in verb tenses
  provides – provided
  is falling – was falling
• the stressed information
  A *third* of all US irrigation water
  By *one metre* every year

Transcript
🔊 1.31

Presenter:	1.31. Grammar box 3. Listen to each statement and comment.
Voice A:	The aquifer provides a third of all US irrigation water.
Voice B:	I didn't realize it provided a *third*.
Voice A:	The level is falling by one metre every year.
Voice B:	I didn't realize that it was falling by *one metre*.

B Showing surprise with *realize*

Repeat the procedure for Exercise A. However, there is more than one possible way to complete the information in each response so accept anything reasonable.

Answers

1. I didn't realize (that) they were greening the desert there.
2. I didn't realize (that) there was a lot of water once.
3. I didn't realize (that) ice could change straight to vapour.
4. I didn't realize (that) sugar was composed of carbon, hydrogen and oxygen.

5. I didn't realize (that) they released carbon dioxide when they respire.

6. I didn't realize (that) whales were mammals.

Closure

Say these 'false' sentences or put them on an electronic projection so that students can practise in pairs. Students should give a response beginning *I thought (that)* ...

- Water is cheap all over the world.
- Most people in the world can get clean drinking water easily.
- Global warming is a more serious problem than access to clean water.
- You don't die from drinking dirty water.
- People in the West are careful about the way they use water.
- Access to clean water is only a problem in Africa.

Students make sentences beginning *I didn't realize (that)* ... with the following facts about water, some of them from Everyday English.

- Three and a half million people die each year from water-related disease.
- 98% of water-related deaths occur in the developing world.
- 884 million people don't have access to clean water.
- Poor people living in the slums often pay 5–10 times more per litre for water than wealthy people living in the same city.

1.10 Applying new speaking skills: Water problems around the world

Objectives

By the end of this lesson, students should be able to:

- research and present information about water supply problems in a particular part of the world;
- clarify information when necessary during a presentation;
- express surprise when listening to facts during a presentation.

Note: The following websites may be useful for further research on the topics for this lesson.

National Geographic (http://www.nationalgeographic.com)

Environmental Protection Agency (http://www.epa.gov)

American Museum of Natural History (http://www.amnh.org)

Discovery Education (http://www.discoveryeducation.com)

water.org

blueplanetnetwork.org

Introduction

Focus students' attention on the photograph of the woman collecting water from a well and write the following quotation from http://water.org on the board:

In just one day, more than 200 million hours of women's time around the world is consumed for the most basic of human needs – collecting water for domestic use.

Discuss the quotation with the class, perhaps by asking a few questions:

- Why is it 'women's time'? What are the men doing?
- Why does it take so long to collect water? (wells are often far from the villages, water extremely heavy to carry)
- How can we improve the lives of these women? (pump clean, safe water to the villages = less disease, women free to do other work – break cycle of poverty)

A Reviewing vocabulary

Before you set the task, use the photos to revise / teach some nouns, for example: *well, dam, pipe, river bed*, etc. Set the task. Elicit one or two ideas, then students make more sentences orally in pairs. Elicit ideas and check for correct use of tenses, especially the present perfect simple (see Answers below).

Answers

Answers depend on students but here are some suggestions:

1. The river has dried up. / The area has run out of water.
2. The field has flooded. / The area is flooded.
3. The pump is irrigating the farm.
4. The woman is drawing / collecting / taking water from the well.
5. The lake is shrinking / has shrunk a lot.

6. A huge amount of water is stored by the dam. / They have dammed the river to store the river water.

7. The desalination plant extracts salt from sea water. / This plant desalinates sea water.

B Researching information

Ideally, for this activity, photocopy the information using pages 53–54. Hand out the relevant texts as students choose.

After students have read the assignment, check understanding.

Refer students to the *Table of contents* for the Reading pack in the Course Book. Ask them to choose **one** topic each for research. You may need to give students a little background information for each to help them with their decision. Students should **not** choose their country or an area close to their home country.

Set the task. Students read about their topic on the relevant page. However, students could also do further Internet research, focusing on:

• the exact cause of the water problem;

• the solution(s);

• any disadvantages the solutions may have.

Tell students how long the presentation should be and if necessary set a strict time limit, e.g., three minutes. On the other hand, if your students are reticent, you might need to set a minimum time!

Students research and make notes on their topic individually. If this is done in class, go round and give help where necessary. Any students working on the same topic can exchange notes and ideas at a suitable point in the lesson if you wish. There are several new words in each extract so students may need to check meaning with each other or with you.

Methodology note

Students can choose their own topics but make sure you have a reasonable distribution so that at least two or three students are working on each topic. If you have an uneven spread, you may need to ask a few students to choose another topic. The research can be done in class or in the library if you have one. If not, then the research can be set as a home assignment.

An alternative methodology is as follows. Students choose, or you allocate a different topic, to each group of three or four students. The groups research and practise their presentation on one topic together. When they are ready, re-divide the groups so that each has a selection of different topics. Students then present their topic to the rest of the group.

C Taking part in a discussion

Divide the class into groups of four or five, making sure that every student in each group has researched a different topic (as far as possible).

Revise phrases for checking information and for showing surprise (1.7–1.9). Remind students to do the following for their presentations:

• Give an introduction and a conclusion.

• Speak at the right speed, and loudly enough.

• Use eye contact.

• Speak from notes only, not full sentences.

• Refer to PowerPoints or visuals if relevant.

Give the 'listening' students a task. This can be a questionnaire or table to complete. Alternatively, they can complete a feedback form (see Introduction, page 17).

Monitor while students are giving their presentations and make a note of common errors. Give feedback.

D Developing critical thinking

The question can be briefly discussed in class and researched properly as a home assignment. Students can then discuss the questions more fully, or present their findings in another lesson.

Closure

Choose one of the following:

- Give feedback on the presentations if you have not already done so.
- Use the discussion in Exercise D.
- Ask students which facts from the section they have found most shocking / surprising about water.
- Recap on any vocabulary items students are still struggling to pronounce, particularly if they are still getting the stressed syllable wrong.

Mexico City

Mexico City is sinking. The city is one of the most populous in the world. In the distant past, it was an area of lakes. Mexico City takes 80 per cent of its water from an underground reservoir. As a result, the ground has dried out and the city has sunk nine metres in the last 20 years. The city is going to buy its water from other areas of Mexico. The water will be delivered to the city by lorries.

India

There is a problem with fresh water supply in many parts of India. For example, in the capital, New Delhi, 36 million cubic metres of water is needed each day to meet demand. However, only 30 million cubic metres is supplied and only about 17 million cubic metres reaches consumers because a great deal of the water leaks out. The World Bank is supporting a proposal to privatize water supply in India. They say that private companies will be able to supply the whole of India with clean water, although they admit that the price will be higher than at present.

Southern China

The south of China floods most years while the north of the country suffers from drought. In the north, water for irrigation is reducing underground supplies by more than 30 cubic kilometres per year. If this continues, China will have to reduce the production of grain and will rely on imported crops. The government has begun the largest-ever construction project in China. They plan to divert billions of cubic metres of water from the Yangtze River to refill the Yellow River.

Southern Australia

Australia has the lowest rainfall of all the continents, with the exception of Antarctica. One of the largest rivers, the Murray, is drying out. As a result, salt has risen to the surface and destroyed agricultural land. The government is going to limit the extraction of water from the Murray.

Southeastern Spain

The southeastern coast of Spain receives a reasonable amount of rainfall every year, but needs to meet a huge demand, mainly from the tourism industry. The government announced a 4.2 billion euro plan to divert water from the River Ebro in the north of the country, but it was stopped when a large number of people objected. The government is going to build several desalination plants to provide fresh water for the southeastern coast.

Egypt

The Nile River rises in Uganda but flows north through Sudan and Egypt to the Mediterranean. The river is the only real source of fresh water for the majority of the population of Egypt. Several countries south of Egypt, including Tanzania and Ethiopia, have plans to extract water from the Nile. The government of Egypt has threatened to use force against any country that takes Nile water without Egypt's permission.

Turkey

Turkey is reasonably well supplied by natural fresh water. In fact, it sells water from the Manavgat River to other countries in the region. However, it still suffers from water shortages from time to time. The government plans to build 22 dams on the Tigris and Euphrates rivers, but this will have a very bad effect on water supplies downstream, in Syria and Iraq.

Chad

Lake Chad was once one of the largest lakes in the world. In fact, the word *Chad* means 'large lake' in the local language. The area of the lake has shrunk in the last 50 years from nearly 30,000 km^2 to less than 1,500 km^2. This shrinkage is due to less rain and more usage for irrigation. Nine million people now suffer severe water shortages. The government is talking to its neighbours about diverting waters from the Congo River to refill the lake.

Reading: Geography and tourism

1.11 Vocabulary for reading: The impact of tourism

Objectives

By the end of this lesson, students should be able to:

- demonstrate understanding of the vocabulary for the section;
- recognize the spelling of new vocabulary;
- use new vocabulary to critically evaluate the benefits and drawbacks of tourism in different countries.

Introduction

If possible, bring in a world map to the lesson or show one on an electronic projection.

Exploit the photographs by writing the following questions on the board and asking students to discuss them in pairs:

Where was each photograph taken? (possibly the Middle East, Africa, Caribbean, etc.)

What type of holiday / tourism does each show? (golf, safari, diving, culture / archaeological, etc.)

What are the advantages for the local economy? (employment and money to local people; often helps people in rural areas – they don't have to move to big towns to find work, etc.)

What are the problems for local people and the environment? (damage to countryside, coral reefs, etc.; money goes to big businesses rather than local people; uses up too many water resources; pollution; culture may be damaged, etc.)

A   Activating ideas

Students discuss in pairs or small groups. After a few minutes, elicit ideas. This is a chance to see how much real-world knowledge your students have. They may be able to tell you specific sights in some of the locations, like the hotels in Dubai or the ruins of the Coliseum in Rome.

Answers

Answers depend on students, but here are some ideas:

1. Dubai: luxurious accommodation, sun, beaches, safari / desert trips, shopping, restaurants, golf

2. Rome: language learning, food, history, culture

3. Malaga: sun, beaches, nightlife, possibly food and language, golf

4. Egypt: sun, beaches, archaeology, history, culture

5. the Alps: skiing, climbing, walking, nature

6. Disneyland: rides and activities

7. another part of their own country: same language, same currency, cheaper, more convenient, to find out more about own country

8. a foreign country: to learn another language, culture, for better weather, etc.

B   Understanding new vocabulary in context

Exploit the visual of a cruise ship and ask students if they would like to go on a holiday like this.

If you like, you can give students one minute to look at the words in the list before they cover them. Then set the task and ask students to cover the word list. Encourage students to read through the whole text first and think about the part of speech for each missing word before they start writing in the answers. After a few minutes, students can uncover the word list and check their answers. Go over any words students had difficulty with.

Answers

Join us on the *cruise* of a lifetime!

Go diving on beautiful coral *reefs*.

Take a *safari* into the rainforest to shoot wild animals – but only with your camera!

Visit the *ruins* of ancient civilizations.

Enjoy the exciting *nightlife* on board every evening – we have clubs, a theatre and a cinema.

Go shopping in our *upmarket* stores.

Fly from London Heathrow (*seasonal* flights from other airports).

Book early! *Demand* for our cruises is high.

C Developing critical thinking

Give students time to read through the questions then check understanding of some of the vocabulary: *impact, damage, offend, environment*.

Set the task and tell students they can use the words in the box and their own ideas as well. Teach or elicit the meaning of *carbon emissions*, but avoid explaining every word as they should become clear as students work through the activity.

Students discuss the questions in pairs or small groups. Encourage students to talk about a range of countries or locations. Be prepared while monitoring to step in and suggest places. When the discussion has finished, elicit some ideas.

Optional activity

Students write a paragraph about the impact of tourism around the world based on answers to the questions.

Closure

Recap on the meanings of some of the vocabulary from the lesson or use your feedback for Exercise C.

Refer students to the photographs at the top of the lesson and ask:

What impact can each kind of tourism have on the local environment?

Possible answers:

All of these types of tourism can bring in tourist dollars but:

- golf courses may take scarce water resources from people and agriculture
- desert safaris may damage the local eco-system and offend tribes in remote areas
- diving on coral reefs can damage them – people break off pieces as souvenirs; in addition, cruise ships taking people to locations can damage the reefs
- too many visitors to a ruin can damage the stone; treasures underground can be damaged by photography

Objectives

By the end of this lesson, students should be able to:

- use headings and maps to predict information in a text;
- identify relevant and accurate information for a research task;
- use existing skills to deal with web resource texts.

Introduction

If possible, show some visuals of Tunisia and the Roman sites near Zarzis. Use visuals to pre-teach or revise the meanings of *ruins* and *marble statues*.

Students will probably, of course, know a little about Tunisia due to the recent political upheaval there. Find out what else they know about the country, but make sure you do not pre-empt the reading activities.

A Preparing to read

Students read the assignment handout. Check understanding of the verb *attract* in this context. Set the task. Students discuss the questions on the assignment handout in pairs and try to predict answers. Reassure them they will not be able to give all the information now, of course, but should make 'educated guesses'. Make sure students do not start looking at the texts on the opposite page, or the notes in Exercise B.

After a few minutes, elicit a few of their ideas.

Answers

Answers depend on students, but here are some suggestions:

1. Zarzis has a good climate, long coastline so good for beach resorts, not far from Europe, etc. Some students may be aware of Carthage and other Roman sites.

2. 'sun, sea and sand' type holidays, water sports, archaeological tourism

3. Extend tourist season, attract tourists from other parts of the world (not just Europe).

4. More tourism might use too many water resources, more flights to the country increases carbon emissions, higher prices in tourist towns may drive out locals. Local Muslims may be offended by the behaviour / dress of westerners.

B Understanding the text

Focus on the notes and elicit the phrase for the way the notes are organized: *scientific numbering*. (This was taught in the listening section of this theme.)

Give students time to read through the notes. Check the meanings of some of the words, for example: *ruins, marble statues, offend*. Revise the meaning of the word *impact*; a good synonym for this context is *effect*.

Focus on the texts on the opposite page. Ask students to scan them quickly and elicit answers to the following:

• *How many texts are there?* (five)

• *What kind of information is in each one?* (Tunisia = general / background information; Zarzis = facts and figures; Zarzis, Tunisia = description of the town; Djerba Airport = flights, Roman sites = archaeological information)

Set the task. Tell students it is not necessary to understand every word, especially in the section about Roman sites. Give a reasonable length of time for students to complete individually, then compare answers in pairs. Use an electronic projection to give feedback.

Methodology note

The information for the notes in section 4 (Impact) is not given explicitly in the texts. It has to be inferred. Inferring information is covered fully in the following lesson (1.8) in this section. (Both lessons 1.8 and 1.9 will help with deeper understanding of the texts in this lesson so it is not necessary to go into too much detail here.)

Answers

Zarzis, Tunisia

1. Features
    1.1. long, hot summers
    1.2. *v. little* nightlife
    1.3. *Roman* ruins
    1.4. marble statues *moved to Paris*
2. Types of tourism
    2.1. sun, sea and sand
    2.2. *no* cruise holidays (*no marina*)
    2.3. *no* shopping
    2.4. diving
    2.5. archaeological
    2.6. *desert* safari
3. Development?
    3.1. more flights, e.g., from Tunis (*already daily from Tunis – perhaps Switzerland?*)
    3.2. high-speed transport from airport
    3.3. restore *Roman* ruins
    3.4. *build* 5-star hotels
4. Impact?
    4.1. water shortages
    4.2. damage *ruins or even the desert*
    4.3. offend local people
    4.4. damage to agriculture = no water

C Understanding new words in context

Set the task and go over the example. Warn students that several of the words in this activity have more than one meaning. So they need to find the synonym for this context.

There are a few options for carrying out this activity in a student-centred way, rather than simply eliciting from the whole class:

• Students can work in pairs or individually.

• Students can work on all of the words.

• Or, if you are short of time, and in order to really encourage student independence, allocate a few different words for each pair or individual to work on. After a few minutes, students work with different individuals or pairs in order to exchange their answers. In this way, students should build up a list of all the synonyms by the end of the activity.

Monitor and give help where necessary. Students can use dictionaries if they wish. At the end of the activity, only elicit answers for words students had difficulty with. Alternatively, show the synonyms using an electronic projection so that students can compare their list of answers. Elicit the part of speech of each word in the text.

Methodology note

The word *supplement* can be a noun and indeed with the suffix ~*ment*, students might find it hard to believe that it can also be a verb.

Answers

direct (*adj*)	= without any stops
republic (*n*)	= state, nation – specifically, without a monarch
get by (*multi-word v*)	= survive, manage
proximity (*n*)	= nearness
followers (*n*)	= believers, supporters
comprises (*v*)	= is made up of
dates (*n*)	= a kind of fruit
reasonable (*adj*)	= quite good
supplement (*v*)	= add to
served (*v*)	= helped, provided for
vast (*adj*)	= very large
available (*adj*)	= existing, easily found
treatment (*n*)	= dealing with, management
suffer (*v*)	= experience

D **Transferring information to the real world**

Set the two questions for students to discuss in pairs or small groups. If you think students will not have many ideas for question 2, you can write the names of some locations on the board for students to discuss (see Possible answers below). After a few minutes, elicit their ideas.

Optional activities

- Students could discuss possible locations for tourist development in their own country. What kind(s) of tourism would the location be suitable for?
- Students could research a location for an assignment or oral presentation.

Methodology note

There are so many different types of tourism these days that the only places where tourism is restricted tend to be trouble spots and war zones. When selecting locations for discussion in this activity, students may wish to talk about these less obvious forms of tourism:

- Hobby (painting, cookery holidays)
- Educational (language learning, historical)
- Religious (pilgrimage, retreats)
- Activity (walking, skiing, climbing, potholing)
- Children's holiday camps
- Outdoor (camping, caravans)
- Natural world (safaris, wildlife, spring flowers, rainforest)

The following even exist:

- Disaster (going to see the results of an earthquake, tsunami)
- Eco (going to visit remote areas like rainforests and glaciers)
- Industrial (looking at particular kinds of landscape caused by industry, e.g., mining)

Answers

1. Answers depend on students.
2. Some possible locations for further tourist development in Europe and Africa could include: Croatia, Montenegro, the Atlantic coast of Portugal including Coimbra, the Black Sea area, Libya (also has important Roman ruins), Morocco, Jordan.

Closure

Choose one of the following:

- Recap on some of the vocabulary from the lesson.
- Use the discussion in Exercise D.

1.13 Learning new reading skills: Reading for a purpose; inferencing

Objectives

By the end of this lesson, students should be able to:
- do reading research for a purpose;
- use real-world knowledge to infer meaning in a text.

Introduction

1. Briefly exploit the visual of Carthage, Tunisia. Point out that the Romans fought the Carthaginians over 2,000 years ago in this area (the Punic Wars).

2. Write some words on the board and ask students what they expect to come next, as follows:

transport	*links*
road	*system*
democratic	*government*
high	*mountains / peaks*

Elicit answers, then add the word in italics in each case.

A Reviewing vocabulary

This activity is a little different from ones students have done before. Set the task. Students work individually, then compare answers in pairs. If students find it difficult, give them one or two more letters for each word on the board.

Elicit answers and ask students to suggest a possible noun to follow each adjective (students should be able to remember some collocations from previous lessons).

Answers

Possible nouns for collocation given in brackets, but accept any reasonable suggestions.

1. rea*sonable* (access)
2. avai*lable* (resources)
3. incre*asing* (demand)
4. sea*sonal* (flights)
5. his*toric* (building)
6. commer*cial* (building, port)
7. archae*ological* (interest, site)
8. upm*arket* (restaurants, shops)

> **Methodology note**
>
> Research shows that native speakers sample most words in a text, but they do not look at every letter. They appear to identify some words from the first letters. This activity tests this skill in your students and could be used many times with flashcards, by only exposing the first part of each word as you flash it.

B Identifying and practising a new skill (1)

1. Set the task. Point out the word *study* has a different meaning here. Usually it means *learn*. Here it means *look carefully* or *analyze*. After a minute, elicit answers from the class. Discuss the example marked-up assignment below Skills Check 1.

2. Set the task. Students complete individually

then compare answers in pairs. Elicit answers using an electronic projection. Students can underline and circle rather than using highlighters if necessary but highlighters are much better.

Answers

2. Research one country in Europe or Africa Make a list of the key geographic features.

Read either the paper by Sengupta (2003) or Laukenmann (2003) Be prepared to talk about the main conclusions.

Research Eric Berne and Thomas Harris. What is the main similarity between their ideas of Transactional Analysis?

We can use the DIGEST approach for decision-making.

1. How can this approach reveal management style?

2. Describe a personal example of autocratic participatory or democratic decision-making

Read Robbins, pages 38–45.

a. What are the main differences between an environment and an ecosystem?

b. List three ways that animals adapt to changes in their environment.

C Identifying and practising a new skill (2)

1. When students have studied Skills Check 2, elicit answers. Teach the verb *infer* and write it on the board with the noun *inference*. You can also teach the phrase *draw inferences (from something)*.

2. Set the task for pairwork. Students find and discuss evidence for or against each statement. After a few minutes elicit ideas.

3. Set the task. Students work individually to start with and can then discuss their ideas in pairs. Elicit ideas. If students are struggling, give them some of the inferences in the Answers below and ask them to tell you where they can find the relevant information.

> **Methodology note**
>
> There is often confusion even amongst native speakers about the difference between the two verbs *infer* and *imply*. Strictly speaking, a listener or reader *infers* something, but a speaker or writer *implies* it.

Answers

1. By looking at one or more pieces of information in the text and, sometimes, using your own world knowledge.

2.

a. Tunisia is a good destination for tourists from India.	F = India in Asia – no direct flights from Asia
b. Tourists from Sicily might be interested in Tunisia.	T = very close, visitors to the archaeological sites in Sicily would probably like to see those in Tunisia
c. Egyptian tourists have no trouble in communicating with Tunisians.	T = Egyptians speak Arabic – as do Tunisians
d. Tunisia has a low population density.	T = density = area / pop – area high, pop low
e. It does not rain very much in southeastern Tunisia.	T = rain = rivers – one permanent in northwest / most of southern part of country is desert
f. Agriculture is more important than tourism at the moment.	T = vast majority of water resources for agriculture, but tourism demand growing

3. Possible inferences:

Zarzis, Quick facts text

Tourism is possible in the winter, but not very desirable.	mild, wet winters
It takes quite a long time to get from the airport to Zarzis.	45 km

Zarzis, Tunisia text

Arabs have lived in the area for some time.	historic buildings with Arabic influences
Town has existed for 2,000 years.	port has been centre of the town's economy since Roman times
Fishing is a main part of the economy.	many kinds of fish are landed
There is water in underground streams or aquifers.	most (trees) are fed by well water
Berbers live(d) near Zarzis.	it is possible to visit the Berber settlement
It is a good area for swimming and diving.	wide beaches of fine sand and sponge reefs off the coast

Djerba Airport text

Most tourists come from France and Germany.	flights from all major cities in these two countries
The area does not get many tourists from Africa, Asia or the Americas.	no direct flights, even seasonal ones

Roman sites near Zarzis text

The marble statues from Zitha were very important.	since been moved to the Louvre in Paris
The local authorities did not think the Roman ruins are a priority for expenditure, but they have changed their minds.	the tower is in danger of collapsing, but there are plans to restore and renovate the tower as a museum

Closure

Recap the two sub-skills students have learnt in this lesson.

1.14 Grammar for reading: Understanding *as* and *since*

Objectives

By the end of this lesson, students should be able to:
- identify different meanings of *as* and *since* in context;
- use *as* and *since* to predict the next piece or type of information in a sentence.

Introduction

Elicit information students learnt about tourism in Tunisia in Lesson 1.7.

Tell students that today's lesson is about two 'small' words in English, *as* and *since*.

Methodology note

One option here is to ask students to find all the examples of *as* and *since* in the text in Lesson 1.7 at this point, rather than in Exercise A. Ask students to discuss the meanings of the two words in the examples in the text in pairs. Then ask students to check their ideas in Grammar box 4 and the explanation underneath.

Grammar box 4

Give students time to study the table and the explanation underneath. Check understanding. Give the start of each sentence in random order up to *as* or *since* and ask students to tell you the meaning of the word in this situation and what will come next.

A Understanding *as / since* in context

This could be done before students study the table (see the Methodology note above).

Set the task. Working in pairs, students find the examples of each word and discuss the meaning. Elicit answers.

Answers

However, there are no people in large parts of Tunisia *since* most of the south of the country comprises the northern edge of the Sahara desert.	*because*
However, some reports suggest that the country may suffer water shortages *as* demand increases.	*at the same time that*
0.683 = 81st (up from 0.436 *since* 1980)	*from a time in the past until now*
The town has a busy commercial port, which has been the centre of the town's economy *since* Roman times.	*from a time in the past until now*
paving slabs and many marble statues which have *since* been moved to the Louvre, Paris.	*from a time in the past until now*

B Predicting information after *as / since*

1. Set the task and go over the example. If the students have done *Progressive Skills* Level 3, tell them that all the sentences have been taken from the reading texts in those themes.

   Students should cover Exercise B2. Tell students to discuss each sentence in pairs and predict what kind of information should come next.

Make a note of common errors. Make sure there is enough time left at the end of the lesson for you to give feedback on common errors. With very able classes, you can ask students to predict the **exact** information, but do not confirm or correct in this case. Elicit ideas.

2. Set the task. Students should match the exact information to each sentence in Exercise B1. Elicit answers and ask students if they predicted correctly in Exercise B1.

Answers

There has been a great deal of research into memory since	the 1960s.
It is better to spend a short time on memory retrieval every few weeks since	retrieval and storage makes memory connections stronger.
Revise difficult ideas early in a revision period as	you remember more from the start than from the end.
Eric Berne believed that people behave as	Parents, Adults or Children in interactions.
Thomas Harris worked in the Navy for several years as	a psychiatrist.
The cost of weddings in the US has risen by 30 per cent since	the start of the 21st century.
Wedding dresses should be hired since	they are only worn once.
You cannot use the creative side and the logical side of your brain at the same time, so you must not evaluate ideas as	you generate them.
Tell other people about any decision since	it might be difficult to stick to it later.
Many scientists say the Earth has been getting warmer since	1000 CE.
Fish in deep water see better in blue light since	there is only blue light in the ocean.

Methodology note

The word *as* can be an adverb, preposition or a conjunction. We have not distinguished between the parts of speech in this lesson as we felt it would not be useful.

Closure

Use the feedback from Exercise B1.

Objectives

By the end of this lesson, students should be able to:

• use new reading sub-skills, vocabulary and grammar from the theme in order to research and make notes on a text;

• demonstrate understanding of, and select relevant information from web texts about the tourist industry in Cyprus.

Introduction

Use Exercise A.

A Activating ideas

Students discuss in pairs or elicit ideas from the class. In order not to pre-empt too much of the later activities, do not spend too long on this activity.

Answers

Possible answers:

Size: small island

Location: Mediterranean

Climate: hot (but cold in mountain region)

Culture: ancient ruins

Tourism: beach, skiing

Political: island divided into two halves

B Preparing to read

Remind students about the sub-skills learnt in Lesson 1.8, Skills Check 1. Students mark up the assignment accordingly. Check understanding of the words *assist* and *restrict*. Elicit answers using an electronic projection.

Answers

Case Study 4: Island tourism

Tourism is already big business for Cyprus, but the government wishes to develop it further.

Research the island and make notes for an oral presentation on the following:

1. What geographical features may:

    1.1. assist

    1.2. restrict

    ... the development of tourism?

2. What non-geographic factors may:

    2.1. assist

    2.2. restrict

    ... tourism to the island?

C Understanding a text

1. Remind students to use scientific numbering for their notes. Set the task. Students complete individually.

2. After a reasonable amount of time, students can compare answers in pairs. Elicit ideas.

    Show the model notes on an electronic projection. Go over any vocabulary problems.

Optional activities

• Ask students to find all the examples of *as* and *since* in the text. Students decide the meaning of each use as described in Lesson 1.9.

• Some words in the text have more than one meaning. Write the following words on the board and ask students to use dictionaries to check the meanings for this context:

distinction

remains

cut

demand

spread

Answers

Model notes:

1. Geographical features which may:

    1.1. assist

        1.1.1. location – Eastern Med, near Europe and the Middle East

        1.1.2. sandy beaches

        1.1.3. World Heritage site

        1.1.4. archaeological remains

        1.1.5. climate – Mediterranean

        1.1.6. snow for skiing in winter

        1.1.7. transport links

    1.2. restrict

        1.2.1. good beaches some distance from airports

        1.2.2. rocky coastline in places

        1.2.3. no permanent rivers, little or no rain = water shortage

1.2.4. snow in winter only, so short skiing season

1.2.5. too hot in summer?

2. Non-geographic factors which may:

2.1. assist

2.1.1. high HDI = no problems of begging, etc.

2.1.2. in the Eurozone – same currency as 17 Euro countries

2.2. restrict

2.2.1. conflict with Turkey = may deter some tourists + difficult to get tourists from nearest country, Turkey

2.2.2. energy shortage – no oil

D Inferring information

Remind students about the inferencing skills they learnt in Lesson 1.8, Skills Check 2. Set the task and go over the example. Students complete individually, then compare answers in pairs. Elicit answers.

Answers

1. Population density is very low in Cyprus.	*density = population / area = 9,000,000 / 9,000 = 1,000*
2. Nicosia is not divided now.	*... the last divided capital in the world until quite recently*
3. Turkey took over the north because many people in the north are ethnic Turks.	*... Turkish-speaking in the north*
4. There is tourism in the northern part of the island.	*tourist areas of both parts of the island*
5. There is no fighting on the island.	*The UN has kept the peace*
6. Only certain parts of the Cyprus coast are suitable for bathing.	*... rocky coastline*
7. There were permanent rivers and lakes in the past.	*Nowadays, there are no permanent lakes or rivers ...*
8. You can't go skiing in Cyprus in summer.	*thick snow ... in the winter months*

9. Tourist hotels in Cyprus are a higher priority for water than local residents.	*supplies to hotels and restaurants are rarely cut*
10. Tourists from Germany do not need to change money when they visit Cyprus.	*Cyprus is part of the Eurozone = same currency = Euro; Germany is in the Eurozone too*

E Reacting to information in a text

Students discuss in pairs or groups. Elicit ideas.

Closure

Choose one of the following:

* Use the discussion from Exercise E.
* Ask students to find some sentences in the Cyprus resources with *as* and *since* and tell you the meaning of the word in each case:

... English is widely spoken in the tourist areas of both parts of the island, *as* the country was under British administration until 1960.	*because*
It has been divided roughly in half *since* the occupation of the northern part by Turkish troops in 1974.	*from a time in the past until now*
The island has been inhabited *since* at least 10 000 BCE.	*from a time in the past until now*
Nowadays, there are no permanent lakes or rivers *as* there is almost no rainfall on the island, ...	*because*
Nicosia International Airport has been closed *since* 1974.	*from a time in the past until now*
Cyprus is part of the Eurozone, which means it has the same currency *as* 17 countries in Europe.	*part of a fixed phrase: same ... as*
At one time, Cyprus was rich in water (with many rivers and lakes), but annual rainfall has gone down steadily *since* the 1970s, as the population and the number of tourists has gone steadily up.	*since = from a time in the past until now; as = at the same time that*
As a result, reserves are at an all-time low and, from time to time, it is necessary to divert water from agriculture to domestic, industrial or tourist use.	*part of a fixed phrase*
However, these plants use oil so this is not a long-term solution, *since* Cyprus has no oil reserves.	*because*

- Recap on some of the vocabulary from the complete section.
- Focus on some of the vocabulary in the text in this lesson.
- Ask some comprehension questions (or write them on the board) to further check understanding.

Answers
See opposite page.

Closure
Tell students to learn the information or vocabulary for any of the answers they got wrong in class.

Knowledge quiz: What? When? Where? How?

Objectives

By the end of this lesson, students will have:
- reviewed core knowledge from Theme 1;
- recycled the vocabulary from Theme 1.

Introduction
Tell students they are going to do a knowledge and vocabulary quiz on this theme of the book. If you like, while you are waiting for everyone in the class to arrive, students can spend a few minutes looking back over the theme.

Methodology note

See notes in the Introduction (page 16) for further ideas on how to do the quiz. As usual, the focus should be more on content than using correct grammar.

Question 1
Divide the class into groups of three or four. Make sure the final column is covered (if you prefer, photocopy the quiz with the final column left blank for students to make notes). Students discuss the questions and make notes of their ideas. Do not elicit answers.

Question 2
Students match the questions and answers in their groups, or you could reorganize the students into pairs. Finally, elicit answers, preferably using an electronic projection.

Question 3
Tell students to cover the final column, or hand out another version of the quiz with only the answers. Elicit questions round the class, or put students into groups to complete the activity.

1. What are *fossil fuels*?	17	a boat
2. What are *minerals*?	16	a large ship for passengers on holiday
3. What are *natural resources*?	11	an area for storing water
4. What can you *cultivate*?	13	being able to read and write
5. What can you *raise* on farms?	6	change planes somewhere
6. What do you have to do if there are no *direct* flights to a country?	5	crops or cattle
7. What does a *dam* do?	8	eat it – it is food like vegetables
8. What do you do with a *crop*?	23	from lack of maintenance or damage in war
9. What happens if a water pipe *leaks*?	21	into deserts or jungles
10. What happens in a *drought*?	4	land to grow crops
11. What is a *reservoir*?	1	oil, natural gas, coal
12. What is *desalination*?	9	some of the water gets out of the pipe
13. What is *literacy*?	7	stop water from flowing down a river
14. What is population *density*?	12	taking salt out of sea water to make drinking water
15. What is the *urban:rural* split?	14	the average number of people in, e.g., a square kilometre
16. What do you *cruise* in?	15	the ratio between people living in towns and people living in the country
17. What can you leave in a *marina*?	10	there is no rainfall, or very little
18. When do you *get by* in a language?	2	things like copper, iron, gold
19. When do you *irrigate* crops?	3	things like wood, oil, fish
20. When does water need *treatment*?	20	when it is dirty
21. Where do *safaris* go?	19	when there is not enough rainfall in a particular area
22. How can you make an *inference*?	18	when you don't speak it very well but can make and understand simple points
23. How does a building become a *ruin*?	24	with a well
24. How do people *extract* water from an underground aquifer?	25	you do work regularly to make sure there is no problem with the roof, the walls, etc.
25. How do you *maintain* a building?	22	you put pieces of information in a text together and use real-world knowledge

Writing: Geography and the economy

Objectives

By the end of this lesson, students should be able to:

• demonstrate understanding of and be able to spell target vocabulary for the section;

• demonstrate understanding of geographical factors which determine economic success according to Sachs and Gallup.

Introduction

Write the title of the lesson on the board.

Elicit the parts of speech of the two words *economic* and *success* and build up a table on the board as follows:

verbs	nouns	adjectives
economize	economy	economic – *having to do with the economy*
	economist	(un)economical – *careful or money-saving*
succeed	success	(un)successful

If there's time, students can write a sentence for each word (leave enough time for Exercise B, which will take up most of the lesson).

A Activating ideas

Students discuss the questions in pairs. Monitor and help with pronunciation of new words if necessary. Students should be able to work out the meanings of new words from the context. In particular, students can guess the meaning of Gross Domestic Product from the lessons about HDI earlier in the theme, and from the fact that the 'Western' countries on the map are all the same colour. Therefore, the map must show economic success or wealth.

After a few minutes, elicit ideas.

Answers

1. GDP = the value of all the goods and services produced by a country; per capita = per person – the term is used when something, in this case GDP, is divided by population.

2. Infectious diseases = diseases that can be passed to people from the environment, e.g., malaria, tetanus, small pox, measles, rabies, cholera, etc.

3. The link is this, generally speaking: dark on Figure 1 map = light on Figure 2 map.

4. Figure 1: the darker the colour, the higher the GDP. Figure 2: the darker the colour, the more tropical disease.

B Understanding new vocabulary in context

Ask students to read the left-hand column only and check understanding of the basic sentences and vocabulary. Now set the task and go over the example. Point out that, on this occasion, all the extra information is in the correct order, so students only have to decide where it goes.

Students should write the sentences individually. They should try to work out the meaning of new words from context first, but can then check with a dictionary. Give students time to compare answers in pairs before playing the recording, one sentence at a time. Give students time to mark their own sentences and correct them. Go over any sentences students had difficulty with.

Answers

The words in *italics* relate to the Closure.

1. According to a major *survey* for the World Bank, geography *contributes* to economic success.

2. In 1998, two American *economists*, Sachs and Gallup, looked at data for 150 countries.

3. They *reached* a conclusion about the economic *performance* of countries.

4. They reported that three geographic factors affect the economic success of a country.

5. They defined success *in terms of* gross domestic product (GDP) per capita.

6. Firstly, they found that countries in the northern *hemisphere* were more successful, *in general*, than countries in the southern hemisphere.

7. Secondly, they discovered that, generally speaking, countries with temperate climates had a higher GDP than hotter countries …

8. … perhaps partly because these countries do not *suffer from* tropical diseases.

9. Finally, they reported that successful countries usually have *access* to a seaport and large, *navigable* rivers into the interior so trade is easy.

10. Twenty-four countries in the survey met all three *criteria*.

Closure

Recap on the meaning of italicized words from Exercise B with one or more of the following:

- reverse dictionary / synonyms – students give the word from this exercise, e.g., *came to = reached; half a sphere = hemisphere*

- in context – say key sentences up to a target word; students say the next word, e.g., *According to a major ... survey ... geography ... contributes*

1.17 Real-time writing: Economic performance – the UK

Objectives

By the end of this lesson, students should:

- **know more about the effect of geographical location on the UK economy;**
- **demonstrate understanding of the organization of a discussion-type essay;**
- **have produced sentences to complete an essay.**

Introduction

Dictate some words and phrases from Lesson 1.16 to check spelling, e.g.,

contributory

hemisphere

performance

criteria

gross domestic product

generally speaking

A Previewing vocabulary

Check students understand the task and go over the example.

Students complete individually, then compare answers in pairs. Elicit answers and accept any reasonable suggestions.

Answers

Possible answers:

1. *reach*	a conclusion
2. analyze	data
3. list	contributory factors
4. meet	criteria
5. suffer from	a disease
6. be	a member of a group
7. have	natural resources
8. contribute to	success

B Understanding the assignment

1. Give students time to study the assignment handout. Spend a few minutes revising the findings of the Sachs and Gallup research from the previous lesson.

   Remind students to underline key information (see Lesson 1.13). Remind them also that with this kind of essay – Discussion – they must work out the thesis first. Ask students to complete the following sentence in order to show they understand the thesis:

   Countries often become rich because of ... (their geographical location / geography)

2. Ask students to guess the answer to the question. For example, is the UK in the top 10 countries, top 20 or 50? Then ask students to check the notes to see who was closest.

3. This activity focuses on the discourse of the essay (the organization). You can do it at this point in the lesson, or later.

Answers

1. Discussion essay

2. The UK is number 20 in terms of economic success in the world.

3. Possible answer:

   Para 1: introduction

   Para 2: defining terms

   Para 3: points in favour of the thesis

   Para 4: points against or additional

   Para 5: conclusion

C Gathering information

Set the task and go over the example. Students write more sentences individually. Elicit answers and write the sentences on the board. Alternatively, show the suggested answers (below) and discuss with students any differences with their own.

Answers

Possible answers:

location:	The UK is located in Europe, which is in the northern hemisphere.
climate:	The UK has a temperate climate and therefore has no tropical diseases.
access to seaport:	It is a number of islands so it has many ports and easy access to trade.
stable government:	The UK has a stable government with the last invasion in 1066 and the last civil war in the 17th century.
natural resources:	The UK has fossil fuels and minerals.
member of EU:	The UK is a member of the EU, which has 27 members. This gives the UK an easy market of 500 million people.

D Writing the essay

1. Set the task, making sure students understand they may have to change their sentences in order for them to fit grammatically. Do at least one sentence with the class as an example. Monitor while the class is writing and give help where necessary. Make a note of common errors.

   Use an electronic projection to show possible answers. Discuss possible variations on each sentence. As usual, the majority of the essay is in the present, but point out the use of tenses in the following sentences:

   - *I am defining* = present continuous because this is a one-time definition
   - *The UK was placed* = past simple because the data was produced in 2008
   - *The country has not been … invaded* = present perfect because past up to now

2. Discuss the question with the class. Set the task, giving students the first sentence of the model answer to start them off, if necessary.

   Less able classes: Build up the final paragraph from the model answer on the board. Make sure students' pens are down during this phase. Then erase the paragraph, perhaps leaving a few words as prompts. Students then write the paragraph themselves.

   Monitor during the writing phase and give help where necessary. Give feedback.

Answers

Model answer:

According to the Sachs and Gallup survey (1998), economic performance is largely the result of three factors. The three factors are *location in the northern hemisphere, a temperate climate and access to a seaport*. In this essay, I will analyze *the data on the economic performance of the United Kingdom*, consider to what extent *the Sachs and Gallup analysis explains it* and then list *other possible contributory factors*. Finally, I *will reach a conclusion*.

In this essay, I am defining economic success in terms of *gross domestic product (GDP) per capita*. The United Kingdom is *an extremely successful country in these terms*. The UK was placed *20th out of 180 countries in data produced in 2008 by the International Monetary Fund*. The GDP *per capita was $43,734 in that year*.

The United Kingdom meets all of the criteria for economic success in the Sachs and Gallup analysis. Firstly, *it is located in Europe, which is in the northern hemisphere*. Secondly, it has a temperate climate with an average temperature *between 5 and 15°C* and average rainfall *between 500 and 2,500 mm per annum*. As a result, the country does not *suffer from any tropical diseases*. Finally, the UK is a *number of islands, there are many seaports and nearly every part of the United Kingdom has easy access to the sea*. It is possible, therefore, that these three factors have contributed to the economic success of the United Kingdom.

However, there are other possible contributory factors. Firstly, the UK has a very long history of stable government. *The country has not been successfully invaded since 1066 and the last civil war in the country was in the 17th century.* Secondly, the UK has many valuable natural resources, including fossil fuels and minerals.

Finally, the UK is a member of the European Union, which comprises 27 countries at present. This means it has an easy market of nearly 500 million people for its goods and services.

In my opinion, the Sachs and Gallup analysis partly accounts for the economic performance of the UK because it meets all three criteria. However, there are other factors, including stable government, natural resources and membership of the EU, which have made a significant contribution.

Closure

Give feedback on the writing activities if you haven't already done so.

1.18 Learning new writing skills: Paraphrasing

Objectives

By the end of this lesson, students should be able to:
- **use a variety of methods to paraphrase information in order to avoid plagiarism.**

Introduction

Discuss the meaning of the word *plagiarism* and explain the importance of avoiding this in students' work.

A Reviewing vocabulary and grammar

Set the task. Students complete individually, then compare answers in pairs. Tell students to learn the correct preposition for each phrase and write and highlight on the board as follows:

according to + person

the result of

the data on + subject

success of + country, person, company, etc.

in economic terms

in 2008 (in + year)

first, second, etc., *out of* + plural noun

with a per capita

criteria for

success in + subject, field

Point out that *success* can be followed by *of* or *in*, depending on the type of word that follows.

Answers

1. According to Sachs and Gallup, economic success is largely the result *of* three factors.
2. In this essay, I will analyze the data *on* the economic success of the UK.
3. The UK is a successful country *in* economic terms.
4. *In* 2008, the UK was placed 20th out of 180 countries, *with* a per capita GDP of $43,734.
5. The UK meets all three criteria *for* economic success *in* the Sachs and Gallup analysis.

B Identifying a key skill

1. Students discuss in pairs. Elicit ideas.
2. Give students plenty of time to study all the information in the Skills Check. Ask: *Why must you paraphrase another writer's words?* (Because you can only use another writer's words in a direct quote with attribution. We will see how to do this in Theme 3.)
3. Check students understand the task. Students can rewrite the paraphrases individually or you can elicit and write them on the board.

Optional activities

These can be done at this point in the lesson, or left until the Closure phase.

With students' books closed:

1. Students rewrite the original sentences using the paraphrases from Exercise B3 as prompts.

   On the board: *The UK has a temperate climate.*

   Students write: *The UK climate is temperate.*

2. Give the first sentence from each pair of example sentences in the Skills Check. Students write the paraphrase.

   On the board: *Geography is responsible for economic performance.*

   Students write: *Geography accounts for economic performance.*

Answers

1. The second sentence is a paraphrase or restatement of the first sentence.
2. a. a different order of information
   b. replacement subject – *there*
   c. active to passive
   d. synonym – *belongs to*

C Practising the new skill (1)

Set the task. Students discuss each answer in pairs and help with spelling, etc. With less able classes, you can write all the answers on the board in the wrong order. Students then match the pairs of words. Elicit answers. Then ask students to cover the first column of words. Ask students to recall the original synonym in the first column using the words in the second column as prompts:

T: *report, analysis*

Ss: *survey*

Tell students they should learn all these synonyms.

Answers

1. survey	report, analysis
2. largely	mainly
3. partly	to some extent
4. located in	situated in
5. therefore	so
6. goods and services	products
7. comprise	consist of
8. the result of	caused by
9. as a result	because of this
10. significant	important

D Practising the new skill (2)

Here are two possible approaches, depending on the level of your class.

More able classes: Set the task. Students complete individually. Show the correct sentences on an electronic projection. Discuss any differences students have with the model answers.

Less able classes: With students' pens down, elicit answers and build up the target sentences on the board. Then erase the correct sentences (or leave a few words as prompts). Students then write the sentences individually. Show the correct sentences on an electronic projection so that students can correct their own work.

Optional activity

Students' books closed. Use the paraphrases (answers below) for students to recall the original sentences in their course books, preferably in writing:

On the board: *Three factors largely lead to economic success.*

Students write: *Economic success is largely the result of three factors.*

Answers

1. Three factors largely lead to economic success.
2. Economically, the UK can be considered a successful country.
3. There is an average temperature range of between 5 and 15 degrees Celsius.
4. All three of the criteria of the survey are met by the UK.
5. The UK consists of a number of islands.

Closure

Use one or more of the optional activities above if you haven't already done so.

1.19 Grammar for writing: *in, ago, since, for*

Objectives

By the end of this lesson, students should be able to:

- produce paraphrases for sentences with *for, since* and *ago*;
- produce sentences with correct tense with *for, since* and *ago*.

Introduction

Say the irregular verbs from this section – ask the students to write the past tense and the past participle.

infinitive	past	past participle
be	was / were	been
have	had	had
meet	met	met
place	placed	placed
contribute	contributed	contributed

Grammar box 5

Ask students to study the tables. Elicit the name of the tense in each section and summarize the grammar on the board as follows:

past simple + *in / ago*

present perfect + *since / for*

It is + *since* + past simple

Remind students how the present perfect is formed, if necessary.

A Using *since* and *for*

Set the task. Students complete individually, then compare answers in pairs. Elicit answers.

> **Optional activity**

Set this for now, later in the lesson or for homework. Ask students to select six of the answers and write a full sentence for each.

Answers

1.	*for*	ten years
2.	*since*	1963
3.	*since*	9.00 a.m.
4.	*for*	a long time
5.	*for*	ever
6.	*for*	half an hour
7.	*since*	he graduated
8.	*since*	I saw you
9.	*since*	midday
10.	*since*	the 15th century
11.	*for*	the whole of her life
12.	*for*	three months

B Paraphrasing

Set the task and go over the example. Remind students of the importance of being able to paraphrase sentences in English. This is not only to avoid plagiarism; finding different ways to express the same thing makes your writing more interesting.

Point out that the sentences for numbers 2 and 3 contain passive verbs, and the answers should also be in the passive where appropriate. Spend a couple of minutes revising how passive verbs are formed, if necessary.

Students complete individually, then compare answers in pairs. Elicit answers, preferably using an electronic projection, making sure students have used the correct tense each time.

Answers

1. The UK joined the EU in 1973.

a. *ago*	*The UK joined the EU over 30 years ago.*
b. *since*	The UK has been a member of the EU since 1973.
c. *for*	The UK has been a member of the EU for over 30 years.
d. *it*	It is over 30 years since the UK joined / became a member of the EU.

2. The UK was last successfully invaded in 1066.

a. *ago*	The UK was last successfully invaded nearly a thousand years ago.
b. *since*	The UK has not been successfully invaded since 1066.
c. *for*	The UK has not been successfully invaded for nearly a thousand years.
d. *it*	It is nearly a thousand years since the UK was successfully invaded.

3. Oil was discovered off the coast of the UK in 1970.

a. *ago*	Oil was discovered off the coast of the UK 40 years ago.
b. *have / since*	The UK has had oil since 1970.
c. *have / for*	The UK has had oil for 40 years.
d. *it*	It is more than 40 years since oil was discovered off the coast of the UK.

C Using *in / ago / since / for / it is* + time period

Elicit some ideas for writing about the students' country/ies. They could write about the dates for a president or government, civil war, a natural disaster, etc.

Remind students to use the correct tense for each sentence. Students complete individually. Monitor and give help where necessary. Give feedback.

Ask a few students to read out one or two of their sentences.

Closure

Use your feedback for Exercise C.

Objectives

By the end of this lesson, students should be able to:
- organize research notes and ideas about the economic performance of their country in preparation for the written task;
- use target vocabulary, language and discourse structure from the section in order to produce a discussion-type essay about economic performance.

Introduction

Exploit the first two visuals. They indicate non-geographic factors that might affect economic performance.

The first one shows an extremely famous piece of tapestry (work in cloth) which illustrates the Battle of Hastings, when the Normans conquered the Ancient Britons and successfully invaded Britain for the last time in 1066. The second one shows an offshore oil rig – which represents the discovery of oil off the coast of the UK in 1970.

A Reviewing vocabulary and grammar

Briefly revise some of the paraphrasing work students have done in the previous lesson in this section, particularly Lesson 1.18.

Set the task and go over the example. Students complete individually, then compare answers in pairs. Show the answers on an electronic projection. Students correct their own work. Discuss any differences students may have had from the target sentences.

Answers

See table in the next column.

B Thinking and organizing

Give students time to read through all the task instructions and information. Check understanding and revise the Sachs and Gallup survey from Lesson 1.16 if necessary.

You can ask students to work individually to do the research and notes, or you can organize the class into pairs or groups. This will partly depend on whether you have students from a monocultural or multicultural background.

1. The UK is in the northern hemisphere. (location)	The location of the UK is the northern hemisphere.
2. The UK has a temperate climate. (is)	The climate in the UK is temperate.
3. The UK does not suffer from tropical diseases. (exist)	Tropical diseases do not exist in the UK.
4. Three factors contribute to the success of the UK. (contributory)	There are three contributory factors to the success of the UK.
5. The UK has had a stable government for a very long time. (history)	The UK has a very long history of stable government.
6. The UK has an easy market for its goods and services. (sell)	The UK can sell its goods and services easily.

Encourage students to look back at the model notes and essay in Lesson 1.17 while they are working.

If the research is done in class, monitor while students make notes and give help where necessary.

C Writing

Go through each point, referring back to the relevant pages and lessons in this section.

Set the task for completion in class or as a home assignment.

D Editing and research

Remind students to edit their work after the first draft, and then write a second draft. They should show their work to other students to make sure their organization and explanations are clear.

Closure

Give feedback on any written work done in class.

Objectives

By the end of this lesson, students will have:

- worked independently to produce presentations in speech and/or in writing about the effect of geographical factors on the HDI and GDP of an island country;
- used vocabulary, grammar, sub-skills and knowledge from the theme in integrated skills activities.

Introduction

Recap on other islands mentioned in this theme: Singapore, Tongan islands, Cyprus.

Methodology note

Research, note-taking and other preparation may have to be set as assignments. The presentations can then be given at a later date in class.

As usual, the Portfolio draws on many of the topics and sub-topics throughout the theme. Before you start this lesson, you may want to recap on the following:

- geographic location and HDI and/or economic success
- water resources
- tourism and its impact on resources

A Activating ideas

Exploit the visuals and establish the name of each island and their geographical locations.

Answers

Malta – island in the Mediterranean

Mauritius – island off the coast of Africa

Sri Lanka – island off the coast of India

B Gathering and recording information

When students have finished reading the assignment handout, check understanding and clarify some of the points.

Students choose which country they wish to research. They should highlight it and mark up the important points in the assignment. Divide the class into groups according to the country they have chosen. Students can then:

- divide the research tasks up between them and then come back and exchange notes later;
- or, each student does research for every question, then students come back and compare.

Students make suggestions to improve each other's notes and make comments about interesting or unusual facts.

Remind students about the work they did in Lesson 1.8 on sharing research and point out this is a good opportunity to practise those phrases.

C Preparing a presentation

Decide if you want students to give presentations individually or to give a pair or group presentation for their country.

At this point, students should practise saying sentences for the talk and prepare slides and/or visuals, if possible. Monitor and give help where necessary. If they are working in pairs or groups, students should decide who is going to say what, and the order of each speaker.

D Giving and hearing a presentation

Check students understand the task and the questions. Monitor while students are giving their presentations and check the 'listening' students are making notes to answer the questions.

When the presentations are finished you can:

- give feedback on the presentations;
- discuss answers to the questions – this can be done as a whole-class activity or students can discuss in small groups.

E Writing

Remind students to follow the usual procedure for writing activities. They have already researched most of the information, so now they should: organize notes, write a first draft, edit and then rewrite.

During the editing stage, students can show their work to other students for feedback.

Once again, this is a very flexible exercise. Choose one of the following procedures:

- You can allow individual students to choose one of the writing activities.

- You could select one activity yourself for the whole class to work on.

- Elicit ideas for how to approach each activity, then take a vote on which activity the class should work on.

- You could allocate different activities to individuals or groups according to their levels of ability (for example, the poster activity may be easier for students whose writing ability is less fluent).

- As usual, the activity can be set in class or for homework.

Closure

Give feedback on oral or written presentations if you haven't already done so.

Discuss further some of the points raised in the lesson, or you could ask students to discuss the following with regard to the countries researched:

Will the development of tourism damage the things that tourists come to the country to enjoy?

Theme 2

Communication

- Communicating far and wide

- Communication aids

- Communication inventors

- Communication inventions

Listening: Communicating far and wide

2.1 Vocabulary for listening: Communication mediums: benefits and drawbacks

Objectives

By the end of this lesson, students should be able to:

- recognize new vocabulary on the topic of communication in isolation and in context;
- develop understanding of new vocabulary in preparation for the section.

Introduction

Write the title of the lesson on the board and elicit the meaning of the key vocabulary: *medium* (in this context = method, way); *benefits and drawbacks* (= advantages and disadvantages). If you want to, you can briefly elicit other common meanings of the word *medium* (average, middle). Tell students that this lesson will be about the benefits and drawbacks of different methods of communication.

A Activating ideas

1. Set the task. Go through the headings in the table; check students understand that *sender* and *receiver* are people in this context.

   Play ● **2.1**. Students complete the first row of the table individually then compare

answers in pairs. Elicit and check the meaning of the following new words:

convenience – convenient

security

delivery

Briefly discuss with students the cost of posting a letter in their countries and how long it takes for a letter to arrive.

2. Divide the class into small groups. Elicit possible questions students could use to discuss the information, such as:

   How much does this method / medium cost?

   How fast is this medium?

   It's very convenient for the receiver, isn't it?

   Do you think this is a very secure method?

   Monitor during the activity. Although the focus in this lesson should be listening, you can make a note of common errors, e.g., in forming questions, and give feedback at a suitable point. However, do not spend too long on this activity – five minutes should be enough to complete most of the information.

   Use an electronic projection to show the completed table. Ask students to tell you if they agree or disagree with the answers.

Answers

Possible answers:

medium	speed	cost	convenience for sender	convenience for receiver	security
posted letter	*slow*	*cheap*	*not very convenient – have to go to post box or post office*	*very convenient if postal delivery*	*very secure in most countries*
letter through courier	*quite fast*	*expensive*	*quite high if courier comes to you*	*very convenient if courier delivers to house*	*very high*
e-mail	*fast – speed of light*	*very – almost free*	*very – on your PC or even smart phone*	*very – on your PC or even smart phone*	*very, very high*
fixed-line telephone call	*fast – speed of light*	*can be expensive*	*quite high if near fixed line*	*quite high if near fixed line*	*very high*
mobile telephone call	*fast – speed of light*	*can be very expensive*	*very – on your PC or even smart phone*	*very – on your PC or even smart phone*	*very, very high*

Transcript
🔊 2.1

Presenter: 2.1. Theme 2: Communication

Lesson 2.1. Vocabulary for listening: Communication mediums: benefits and drawbacks

Exercise A1. Listen to some students working with Table 1. Fill in the information for *posted letter*.

Student A: OK. So we've got the example here for a posted letter. It is slow but cheap. What does the next bit mean?

Student B: Well, we have to consider convenience for the sender and for the receiver. It's not the same thing. Posting a letter is not very convenient for the sender …

Student C: Because you have to go find a post box or go to a post office.

Student B: Exactly.

Student A: Ah, right. I see. But it's very convenient for the receiver.

Student B: Well, only if there is postal delivery. In my country, you have to go to a post office to collect your letters.

Student A: Right. So what about letter through a courier. What's a courier? …

B Word-building

1. Set the task. Students complete individually then compare answers in pairs. Do not elicit answers – the next activity will confirm all the words for the table.
2. Set the task. Students discuss each word in pairs.
3. Play 🔊 2.2. Students check their answers. Go over any words students were not sure about.

Answers

noun	adjective	opposite adjective
con'venience	con'venient	incon'venient
se'curity	se'cure	inse'cure
ex'pense	ex'pensive	inex'pensive
'benefit	bene'ficial	'useless
'scarcity	'scarce	'common
com'plexity	'complex	'simple

Transcript
🔊 2.2

Presenter: 2.2. Exercise B3. Listen and check your answers.

Voice: convenience, convenient, inconvenient
security, secure, insecure
expense, expensive, inexpensive
benefit, beneficial, useless
scarcity, scarce, common
complexity, complex, simple

C Recognizing words in context

Check students understand the task and go over the example. Play 🔊 2.3. Students complete individually then compare answers in pairs. Replay 🔊 2.3, pausing after each sentence. Elicit the correct answer.

Optional activities

Choose one of the following:

- Students try to remember the full sentence from the transcript for each answer (word).
- Students' books closed. Play some of the sentences from 🔊 2.3 again. Students write the full sentence.

Answers

	noun		adjective		opposite adjective
5	convenience		convenient	3	inconvenient
	security	2	secure		insecure
	expense	1	expensive	6	inexpensive
4	benefit		beneficial		useless
	scarcity	8	scarce		common
	complexity	7	complex		simple

Transcript
🔊 2.3

Presenter: 2.3. Exercise C. Listen to some sentences. Number the words in the table above.

1. Mobile phone calls can be very *expensive*.
2. E-mail is very *secure*, even if you don't put your e-mails into code.
3. The postal system is *inconvenient* if there is no home delivery.
4. The speed of e-mail is one of its main *benefits*.
5. The mobile has largely replaced the fixed-line phone because of its *convenience*.
6. Letters are *inexpensive* but very slow, compared with e-mail.
7. Some people don't use e-mail because they think it is too *complex*.
8. You don't see many public phone boxes in some countries now. They are quite *scarce*.

Closure

Do one of the optional activities in Exercise C. Alternatively, ask students, in pairs, to take turns to summarize the benefits and drawbacks of different methods of communication in one or two sentences. For example:

A posted letter is slow but it's cheap and very secure. It's not always convenient for the sender but postal deliveries are convenient for the receiver.

2.2 Real-time listening: Long-distance communication and business principles

Objectives

By the end of this lesson, students should be able to:

- use existing skills to understand a business studies lecture about a case study of the history of communication;
- demonstrate understanding of the lecture through using PowerPoint slide headings;
- recognize new vocabulary in context.

Introduction

Refer the class to the illustrations. Put students into pairs or small groups and ask them to find the following:

a building	2	a phone box	6
a satellite	5	wires	7
a postage stamp	8	a hand	10
a fire	3	a country lane	8
horses	8	a tower	9
the Earth	5	a telegram	11

A Activating ideas

Set the three questions together. Students discuss in pairs or small groups. Elicit the answer for question 1. Elicit ideas for questions 2 and 3 but do not confirm or correct at this stage.

Answers

1. They are all long-distance communications.
2. Possible answers in table opposite, including chronology in brackets (but do not confirm at this stage):
3. Answers depend on students, but see above.

1. telephone	(7)
2. semaphore	(4)
3. smoke signals	(1)
4. writing (the earliest form)	(2)
5. satellite, e.g., for some radio / television messages	(8)
6. telephone	(6)
7. telephone (and, in an earlier age, telegraph)	(5/6)
8. post	(3)
9. mobile telephone	(9)
10. Morse code = telegraph	(5)
11. telegram – which is linked to telegraph and telephone	(5/6)

Methodology note

You can refer to the illustrations on the right-hand page at any point during the lesson. Keep building the students' knowledge about each method of communication. Alternatively, leave until the Closure activity at the end and round off the lesson with it. You may even wish to return to this at later points in the listening section.

B Preparing for a lecture

Ask students to read the title slide on the right. Then ask:

What is a successful business? (It makes money; it grows / expands.)

What are the links between a successful business and the history of communication? There is probably no obvious answer to this question at this point; simply ask the question so that students are prepared to listen for the answer during the activity.

Tell students they may wish to change or add to their answers to *What is a successful business?* once they have listened to the lecture.

Set the numbering task. It does not matter if students cannot number all of the slides, although there is a 'Western' logic to the actual structure of the lecture – chronology, then principles, then example. Students discuss the slides in pairs. Elicit ideas but do not confirm or correct. Check that students remember the meaning of the word *benefit* – something that has a good effect, is an advantage or a 'good thing'.

Answers

Answers depend on students at this stage.

Methodology note

The title of the lecture is deliberately a little quirky as this tends to be the style of many business presentations. The link between business and the history of communication will become clear by the end of the lecture.

C Understanding a lecture

1. Set the task and play DVD 2.A. Students complete individually then compare answers in pairs. Elicit answers for the correct order using an electronic projection. Elicit the slides the lecturer did not have time to deal with. Replay any sections of DVD 2.A students had difficulty with.

2. Set the task. Students complete individually then compare answers in pairs. Elicit answers, once more using an electronic projection if possible.

3. This activity focuses on the discourse function for each main part of the lecture. Elicit the meaning of, or give brief explanations for each word in the box, e.g.

   biographical = facts about a person's life

   chronological = dates or timeline for facts

   classification = organization of a basic idea into subheadings

   exemplification = relating a theoretical idea to a particular example

   description = how something works, or what it looks like

   pros and cons = points for and against an argument

   Set the task, explaining that not all the words in the box are used. Students discuss in pairs. Elicit answers.

Optional activity

Do these at this point, or after Exercise D (possibly as a closure activity).

- Select a section of DVD 2.A for intensive listening. For example, you may wish to focus on a particular grammar point, new vocabulary, or pronunciation. You could give students the relevant section of the transcript, perhaps with gaps in order to provide an activity.

- Ask students to read the transcript either in class or at home. This can be done at the same time as listening to the lecture again.

Methodology notes

1. Ideally, in order to reflect 'real life', students should watch the whole lecture without pausing. However, if you are short of time, or with less able classes, you can divide the lecture into two or three sections. Play a section of DVD 2.A. Go over the correct answers, then play the remainder (in another lesson if necessary).

2. In the next lesson, 2.3, students will hear some extracts which will complete the information about the telegraph and telephone.

Answers

4	Three key business principles • benefits • personnel • infrastructure	classification
2	Early systems: Sumeria, China, Egypt Sumeria: invention of writing China: first postal service Egypt: horse riders + relay stations	chronological
1	Early systems: before writing • smoke signals and drums	chronological
6	The telegraph: how did principles apply? • faster, more secure	exemplification
	The telephone: how did principles apply?	(not dealt with)
3	Early systems: France • semaphore stations	chronological
	Early systems: A new approach	(not dealt with)
5	The telegraph: how did it work? • Morse code	description

Transcript and Answers

2.4 DVD 2.A

Presenter:	2.4. Lesson 2.2. Real-time listening: Long-distance communication and business principles
Lecturer:	Everybody here? Yes? OK. I'm going to talk to you today about communication over long

distances. It's quite an interesting subject in its own right, but we are not here to learn about smoke signals or telephones specifically. We are going to look at the history of long-distance communication to see what the modern businessperson can learn from it. History is a very good case study. Who said that? That's right. Me.

OK. So, first, a quick outline of the history of long-distance communication *before* the telephone, then we'll see how basic business principles applied, even in those early days. Finally, we'll look at the development of the telephone in the light of these principles.

So, where do we begin with the history of communication over long distances? Obviously, human beings have been able to communicate over *short* distances since ancient tribes in Africa and wherever first learnt to speak. But unless you can shout very, very loudly, you cannot communicate with someone in the next town or city by using your *voice*. You need another medium of communication. First, we had things like smoke signals, I guess. They must be thousands of years old. People used to bang drums as well, in some areas, I suppose. But this kind of signal only works over a few kilometres. People wanted a way of communicating over much longer distances. They couldn't use *spoken* language – that's the telephone and, of course, that came much later. They had to use *written* language.

As you probably know, the Sumerians invented writing in about 3000 BCE – that's over 5,000 years ago. Once people had a script, they could send a letter. In other words, they could write something down and give it to a messenger, who could take it to someone in another town or even another country. There is some evidence that the Sumerians sent written messages to each other but we need to move on a couple of thousand years to …

… the earliest recorded postal system. That appeared in about 900 BCE. The Chinese invented it. Couriers carried messages around the country, from the national leaders to their local rulers. They were diplomatic messages, in other words, not things like *Having a lovely time. Wish you were here.* The messages didn't travel very fast. The couriers walked, so speed of transmission was about eight kilometres an hour. They weren't very secure either. Thieves could stop a messenger and take the message from him.

In about 150 BCE, the Egyptians started using horses to carry messages more quickly. Horses can go faster than people but they cannot travel for very long carrying a person – and the messages, of course. So the Egyptians set up a system of relay stations for messengers on horseback. Urgent messages now travelled at about 15 kilometres an hour for the next few thousand years. They still weren't secure, of course. *Why is all of this important to the modern businessperson?* I hear you ask. *Why do I need to know all this rubbish?!* Let's go on a bit and then we'll see.

We have to wait a long time for the next big idea. In 1793, a man called Claude Chappe invented the long-distance semaphore in France. The

French government built a network of 556 relay stations all over the country. These were houses with arms on the roof. The arms could move to make different symbols. Urgent messages could travel at about 20 miles an hour now – faster and much more secure. It was very difficult to intercept and stop the message from reaching its destination. It was in code, too, so even if you did intercept it, you couldn't understand it. But the system was very expensive, both to build and to maintain. It was very expensive for the customers who wanted to use it, too. But Napoleon used it all the time to send urgent messages about troop movements – you know, how his armies were moving around the country.

Why have we looked at these ancient systems? Well, they demonstrate in a simple way three basic business principles. Firstly, at the centre of any successful business is a benefit. What does that mean? A successful business satisfies a want. Let me explain. A potential customer *wants* to do something. In the case of long-distance communication, people simply wanted to send messages to a distant location. This want did not change, through thousands of years. But it was met in different ways through the generations. The different ways were faster, or more secure, or cheaper, or more convenient. But they always satisfied the basic want.

We can go further. Customers do not buy *products*. They buy *satisfaction of wants*. In other words, they buy *benefits*. Companies sometimes forget this. They try to sell customers products. They give them details of the product. 'It works at three million mega somethings per kilo something.' 'It's got a widget in the thingamabob.' But most customers aren't interested in products. You can't sell customers products. Customers want to enjoy the *benefit* of the product. The Sumerians didn't want *writing*, the Chinese did not want *messengers*, the Egyptians did not want *horse riders* and the French people certainly did not want *semaphore stations* waving their arms all over the place. They simply wanted to send a message over a long distance. So that's the first point. Always think about the customer's wants, about the needs that your product or service satisfies.

Secondly, successful businesses have trained or skilled *personnel*. The Chinese system had men who knew the way to another town or area. The Egyptian system was more complex. It had horse riders and personnel who looked after the horses at each stop. The French system was even more complex. It had skilled operators who worked the semaphore machinery. The Chinese probably didn't teach their couriers the routes – they knew them already. The Egyptians probably didn't train their horse riders. They employed skilled riders. But the French certainly trained their semaphore operators. So here's the second point. A successful business needs skilled personnel. It either employs them *or* teaches them the special skills which the business needs.

So, to recap. A successful business supplies customers with benefits, and employs or trains skilled people. But successful businesses need something else, and this is sometimes out of their control. What is it?

Well, the Chinese system needed a road between A and B. So did the Egyptian system. The French system didn't need roads, but it needed buildings every few kilometres to relay the signal. This is the third key element. Most businesses need an *infrastructure* – a system of roads, railway lines, air routes, sea lanes, plus buildings – shops, offices, warehouses. The Chinese and the Egyptian message businesses didn't build the roads. They were there already. But the French message system needed a new infrastructure system, and the French government agreed to build it. Businesses must work with existing infrastructure or they must be prepared to allocate scarce resources to new infrastructure.

Oh, I nearly forgot. Final very important point. The semaphore system was very expensive to build and to maintain. Of course, you can spread the cost over all messages, but still each message was expensive. But the system was very fast and very secure, so the government was prepared to pay the high cost. In this case, the government was also the customer, but the principle is the same. If you provide higher benefits, some people will be prepared to pay more for the same basic product or service.

Right. So, think about the key principles – benefits, personnel and infrastructure – as we consider the next invention. It's the telegraph. First I'll tell you how it worked and then we'll look at how it met the principles. The name *telegraph* comes from two Greek words: *tele*, which means 'distant', and *graph*, which, in Greek, means 'writing'. How did the telegraph work? One person keyed in letters on a machine. They travelled as electrical signals to another machine, in another town. The second machine printed the letters on strips of paper. Mostly, the system was used by the railways, so there were telegraph wires between all the stations to carry the messages. But there were problems with the telegraph. Firstly, the letters were in code. It was called Morse code, after the inventor, Samuel Morse. Someone had to turn the letters into Morse at one end, and decode the Morse into letters at the other end. Secondly, only one message could travel along the telegraph line at one time. That is like a road between two towns which can only carry one car at a time. Thirdly, you needed wires connecting each telegraph office. However, in terms of speed, the telegraph was a big improvement on semaphore – and, of course, couriers on foot or horseback. The message travelled at the speed of electricity along a wire, which is, of course, the speed of light. In some ways, it was secure, because only a Morse operator could decode the message. But, on the other hand, the operator read the message before delivering it, so in that way it was insecure. So, bearing all that in mind, what benefits did the new system deliver for customers? What problems did it pose for the business, in terms of personnel and infrastructure?

So that's how the telegraph worked. Now, how did it meet the principles? Well, first, benefits. It was faster and more secure than the postal system ... Oh, dear. I see we are running out of time. So let me leave those questions with you. Benefits, personnel and infrastructure for the

telegraph. We'll look at the answers next time. Then we'll move on to the telephone and the mobile. Dear me, I didn't get through very much, did I? Well, anyway, you've got the basic principles. Thank you. See you next week.

D Developing critical thinking

Set the task. Students discuss in pairs and produce the written summary between them.

Elicit the two sentences and write them on the board. Check understanding.

Answers

The history of long-distance communication shows that successful businesses must provide benefits to customers. People use new technology when it offers greater benefits.

Closure

Choose one of the following:

- Do one of the optional activities suggested in Exercise C (above).
- Ask students which words from the vocabulary lesson (2.1) they heard in the lecture, e.g., *communication, principles, medium, signal, script,* etc.
- Follow up on Exercise A3 and elicit the correct chronological order for the communication methods, and any other further information students have learnt about each method.

2.3 Learning new listening skills: Taking notes onto handouts

Objectives

By the end of this lesson, students should be able to:

- identify 'swallowed' consonants in connected speech;
- use PowerPoint slides to make notes.

Introduction

Tell students they are going to hear some words from the lecture in Lesson 2.2. They must identify them. Say the stressed syllable of the following words, and underspeak the rest of each word.

'me di um	'sig nal
're lay	trans 'mi ssion
'cou rier	'sem aphore

inter 'cept   'net work
'sym bol   per so 'nnel
'in fra struc ture

A Reviewing vocabulary

1. Set the task. Students complete individually then compare answers in pairs. Do not elicit answers yet.

2. Play ⦿ **2.5**. Check understanding of the phrases *electrical device* and *Morse code*.

3. Ask students if they noticed a particular pronunciation problem with each pair of words. Encourage them to try saying each pair to themselves. Elicit ideas, without confirming, then ask students to read the Pronunciation Check. Play ⦿ **2.7**. There are four additional pairs of words from those listed in the Pronunciation Check. Elicit what they are.

4. Students discuss the questions in pairs. Elicit ideas and ask students what the parts of speech are for the words in each pair. Students should begin to realize that the pairs of words are either noun + noun or adjective + noun. Replay ⦿ **2.5**. Elicit answers / rules for stressed words in these phrases.

Answers

1.

a. electrical	*f*	beings
b. Morse	*e*	business
c. postal	*b*	code
d. skilled	*a*	device
e. successful	*g*	message
f. human	*d*	personnel
g. urgent	*c*	system

4. The rule is that adjective + noun phrases are normally stressed on the noun, while noun + noun are normally stressed on the first noun. This stress changes when we wish to contrast, e.g., *su'ccessful businesses* as opposed to *'unsuccessful businesses*.

   a. electrical de'vice (*adj + n*)

   b. 'Morse code (*n + n*)

   c. postal 'system (*adj + n*)

   d. skilled perso'nnel (*adj + n*)

   e. successful 'business (*adj + n*)

   f. 'human being (*n + n*)

   g. urgent 'message (*adj + n*)

Transcripts

⦿ 2.5

Presenter:	2.5. Lesson 2.3. Learning new listening skills: Taking notes onto handouts
	Exercise A2. Listen and check your answers.
Voice:	a. electrical device b. Morse code c. postal system d. skilled personnel e. successful business f. human beings g. urgent message

⦿ 2.7

Presenter:	**2.7. Pronunciation Check. Listen to the pronunciation of some pairs of words. Can you hear the first consonant?**
Voice:	1. send messages 2. write letters 3. make progress 4. ask questions 5. eat dinner 6. take back 7. lend money 8. find friends

B Identifying a new skill

1./2. Set questions 1 and 2. Students discuss in pairs; do not elicit ideas.

3. Ask students to read the Skills Check. Check understanding of all the information, especially how the slide headings can be used for note-taking. You could use an electronic projection of the diagram in the Skills Check to highlight the key points.

Answers

See Skills Check.

C Practising a new skill

1. Remind students about the lecture they listened to in Lesson 2.2. Recap on some of the points or play a short extract of DVD 2.A again. Remind students that the lecturer did not have time to finish all the PowerPoints. Check students understand what to do: look up new words, check meaning and pronunciation, especially stress, etc. Elicit ways to check meaning and pronunciation. For example, students can:

• ask each other;

• use a dictionary or online resource;

• ask you.

When they have checked the pronunciation, they should say the word in their heads many times so they are more likely to recognize it when they hear it in the lecture.

Students work through the slides in pairs. Encourage them only to ask you for help as a last resort. Monitor, giving help only where absolutely necessary.

2. Remind students how to use the points on the slides as headings when note-taking. Set the task. Play ⏺ **2.6**. Students complete individually then compare answers in pairs. Use an electronic projection to build up complete notes.

Answers

On this occasion, there is no model, as the model will appear in C2. But students should only be adding a few additional words / numbers to the information on each slide.

Transcript
🔊 2.6

Slide 1.

Lecturer: OK. Let's consider the telephone as a business model. Remember, we need to look at three elements – the benefits of the product or service, the personnel required and the infrastructure. The fixed-line telephone provided lots of benefits over the telegraph. Firstly, it was very fast – in fact, it worked at the speed of light, because that is the speed of electricity. And it went straight from the sender to the receiver – you did not need a person to take down the message and then deliver it. And, of course, because there was no operator, the system was much more secure. It was years before people learnt how to bug, or listen in, to telephone conversations. But, coming onto personnel and infrastructure, there were drawbacks too. First, personnel. Well, of course, when the telephone was invented, there were no trained personnel. In fact, a new word was coined in about 1912, for people who answered telephone calls and connected people – *telephonist*. These people had to be trained. The company also had to train *linesmen* – people who put up the lines between towns and maintained them. They *were* all men then, but times have moved on a little. Finally, there was no infrastructure. The company needed to build telephone *exchanges* – another new term. They had to put up telephone lines to link the system together, and to lay millions of kilometres of telephone cables, including cables under the Atlantic Ocean and even the Pacific. As a result, the telephone developed really slowly.

Presenter: Slide 2.

Lecturer: Right, so let's compare the development of fixed-line phones and mobiles. In the process, we will learn an important business principle. First, the fixed-line phone. The device was invented in 1876 by an American, Alexander Graham Bell, but by 1890 there were only 5 million in use, most of them in the US, and even 30 years later, in 1922, there were only 20 million subscribers – that is, people with a telephone. In 1965, the total reached 300 million, doubling to 600 million by 1995 and doubling again to 1.2 billion in the next 20 years. So it took over 130 years to reach this number.

What about the mobile? Well, the device was invented in 1973 by a researcher working for Motorola, Martin Cooper. By 1985, there were 340,000 subscribers, which rose to 33 million by 1995. In 2003, just 30 years after its invention, there were 1.5 billion mobiles in the world, more mobiles than fixed-line phones. The figure stood at 4.6 billion in 2010. That's almost one telephone for every man, woman and child on Earth!

Presenter: Slide 3.

Lecturer: How can we explain the differences? Why did the mobile-phone customer base grow so quickly? Was it because of very high benefits to customers? Well, mobile phones certainly have high benefits for customers – for example, you can use them anywhere. You don't call a place anymore, you call a person. But fixed-line telephones probably had higher benefits back in 1876. What about personnel? To what extent did companies need to train personnel? Well, perhaps not as much as the early days of fixed-line telephones because so much of the system is automatic, so there was a saving there. But in terms of infrastructure – the mobile phone towers, for example – the phone companies had to build everything. So, in many ways, mobile phones had a similar business model to fixed-line phones. But there was one big difference. Mobile phone companies learnt an important lesson from the slow development of the fixed-line telephone. Mobile phones cost about $500 to make in the early days, but companies did not try to pass on that cost to customers. They did not charge customers $500 to have a mobile. In many cases, they gave away the handsets in return for a service contract. As a result, the installed customer base grew very quickly. How could the companies afford to give away their products? Well, they got a service contract in return and the customers paid regularly for the calls. If a business has more customers, its unit costs – its cost per customer – usually go down. So the installed customer base grew quickly *and* the mobile phone companies made money.

Closure

Discuss briefly the benefits and drawbacks of PowerPoint slides to accompany lectures, for example:

Benefits

- emphasize key points
- help you remember / understand key information
- make lecture more interesting
- give you the written word as well as the spoken word

Drawbacks

- sometimes lecturer talks to slide rather than audience
- sometimes lecturer simply reads points on slide without expanding further
- sometimes problems with electricity supply or technology
- sometimes slides are badly produced or not clear

2.4 Grammar for listening: Ditransitive verbs; verbs with prepositions

Objectives

By the end of this lesson, students should be able to:

- recognize sentence patterns for ditransitive verbs and verbs with prepositions;
- use verb patterns to predict the end of sentences when listening.

Introduction

Students' books closed. Write the following verbs on the board and ask students what they have in common: *offer, give, buy, teach, send, steal* (note that *steal* needs a preposition, but is still ditransitive).

Elicit they are all *ditransitive verbs*; these verbs can – and in many cases must – have two objects. Students need to be prepared for the second object when they have heard the first, e.g., *I offered him …* = not a complete idea. We must say *what*. Similarly, *They stole money …* = not really a complete idea. We would normally say *from whom*.

Tell students they will learn more about this type of verb in this lesson. If possible, leave the list of verbs on the board until the closure activity at the end of the lesson.

Grammar box 6

Students study Tables 1 and 2. Ask *What do you notice about the two different word orders?* (If the 'person' object comes first, you don't need the word *to*.)

A common error is for students to include *to* in sentences with the first pattern. Emphasize that this is wrong by writing the following sentence on the board and striking out the word *to*:

You can't sell ~~to~~ customers products.

Students then study the information in Table 3. Elicit the answer to the question *What do you notice about the objects in this case?* (They can be a 'person' in either position or can both be 'things'.) The point to emphasize here is that the objects cannot be switched round. Write the following on the board and put a line through it:

Thieves could steal ~~from the courier the messages.~~

A Hearing the two objects

Set the task and go over the example. Make sure students see that they have to label the objects, e.g., *1a* and *1b* **not** *1* and *2*. Play 🎧 **2.9**, pausing just long enough for students to find the answer each time. When you have played all the items, students can compare answers in pairs.

Elicit answers, replaying items students had difficulty with (the later items are more difficult than numbers 1–6).

Optional activity

Students look at the pairs of objects and try to remember the complete sentence.

Answers

object 1

3a	a message
8a	customers
4a	her
2a	me
5a	the book
9a	the government
7a	the Social Sciences lecturer
10a	thousands of francs
6a	us
1a	you

object 2

8b	a lot of money
2b	a message
7b	a present
1b	a question
3b	for me
10b	for the government
9b	his invention
6b	some money
4b	the truth
5b	to school

Transcript and Answers

Presenter: 2.9. Exercise A. Listen to each sentence. Number the two objects you hear in each case.

Voice:
1. I'm going to ask you a question.
2. Can you send me a message?
3. He took a message for me.
4. They told her the truth.
5. I'll bring the book to school tomorrow.
6. Could you lend us some money?
7. We are going to buy the Social Sciences lecturer a present at the end of term.
8. Telephone companies charged customers a lot of money for calls in the early days.
9. Claude Chappe showed the government his invention.
10. The semaphore stations cost thousands of francs for the government to build.

B Consolidation

Set the task and go over the examples. Students complete individually. Monitor and make a note of any common errors. Give feedback. Ask a few students to read out one or two of their completed sentences.

Answers

Answers depend on students but here are some suggestions:

1. He gave me *a message*.
2. The courier took the letter *to the government office*.
3. I offered her *a cup of coffee*.
4. The company sold its main business *to a competitor*.
5. Mobile phone companies often give customers *phones*.
6. Telegraph offices delivered telegrams *to people's homes*.
7. The employment agency found a good job *for me*.

Closure

Choose one of the following:

- Give feedback on Exercise B, if you have not already done so.
- Dictate some sentences from the lecture in Lesson 2.2 or some sentences with two objects.
- Add to the list of ditransitive verbs on the board (see Introduction) by eliciting all the verbs from the lesson:

offer	*give*	*teach*
steal	*supply*	*print*
ask	*send*	*take*

bring	*lend*	*buy*
charge	*show*	*cost*
rent	*deliver*	*give*
offer	*sell*	*find*
earn	*owe*	*tell*

2.5 Applying new listening skills: The Internet and business principles

Objectives

By the end of this lesson, students should be able to:

- produce notes for building a successful business infrastructure, using PowerPoint slide handouts;
- demonstrate understanding of a lecture about building a successful business through accurate note-taking;
- apply critical thinking in order to analyze reasons for a successful etailing company.

Introduction

Say the following sentences from the first lecture extract in Lesson 2.3, 2.6, and ask students to complete each one.

OK. Let's consider the telephone as a business model. Remember, we need to look at three elements – the benefits of the product or service, the personnel required and the	infrastructure. The fixed-line telephone provided lots of benefits over the telegraph.
Firstly, it was very fast – in fact, it worked at the speed of light, because that is the speed of	electricity.
And it went straight from the sender to the receiver – you did not need a person to take down the message and then	deliver it.
And, of course, because there was no operator, the system was much more secure. It was years before people learnt how to bug, or listen in, to telephone	conversations.
But, coming onto personnel and infrastructure, there were drawbacks too. First, personnel. Well, of course, when the telephone was invented, there were no	trained personnel.

In fact, a new word was coined in about 1912, for people who answered telephone calls and connected people –	*telephonist.*
These people had to be	trained.
The company also had to train *linesmen* – people who put up the lines between towns and	maintained them.
They *were* all men then, but times have moved on a little. Finally, there was no infrastructure. The company needed to build	telephone *exchanges* –
They had to put up telephone lines to	link the system together,
and to lay millions of kilometres of	telephone cables,
including cables under the Atlantic Ocean and even the Pacific. As a result, the telephone developed	really slowly.

A Activating ideas

Spend a few minutes revising some of the key points from the lecture in Lesson 2.2 about the link between successful businesses and the history of communication.

Students discuss the three questions in pairs or small groups. Elicit ideas, checking that students have remembered the meanings of the three words:

benefits

personnel

infrastructure

Answers

Answers depend on students but here are some ideas:

1. It's fast, cheap (free, sometimes), secure; huge amount of useful information.

2. web designers, possibly software engineers, helpline personnel

3. Students may know about modems, relays, servers, satellite systems, but most of this is revealed in the lecture to come so do not pre-empt.

B Preparing for a lecture

Set the task. In this activity students should:

- start to predict the content of the lecture;
- make sure they know the meaning and

pronunciation of any new words in PowerPoint slides, so that they recognize the new words when they arise in the lecture (this was covered in Lesson 2.3).

Students can work individually or in pairs. Monitor and give help where necessary.

C Following a lecture

Remind students how to use the PowerPoint slides to make notes (see Lesson 2.3). Play the introduction to the lecture on DVD 2.B, then pause to check everyone is on track.

Play the rest of DVD 2.B.

If you are short of time, or with less able classes, you can divide the lecture into two or three sections. Play a section of DVD 2.B. Go over the correct answers, and then play the remainder (in another lesson if necessary).

Use an electronic projection to show the completed notes. Ask students to compare with their own. Find out where students had gaps or problems making notes. Replay the relevant section of DVD 2.B where possible or use the transcript.

Optional activity

- Select a section of DVD 2.B for intensive listening. For example, you may wish to focus on a particular grammar point, new vocabulary, or pronunciation. You could give students the relevant section of the transcript, perhaps with gaps in order to provide an activity.

- Discuss the kind of information in the lecture; biographical, chronological, classification, exemplification, pros and cons.

- Ask students to read the transcript either in class or at home. This can be done at the same time as listening to the lecture again.

Answers

The Internet – history

date	idea / purpose	invention / inventor
1945	link information in a library	*Vannevar Bush*
1946	first computer	*ENIAC / US army*
1960s	link documents	*hypertext / Nelson*
1974	first PC	*several inc. IBM*
1975	link computers in same place	*TCP /IP / Cerf*
1977	link computers in different places	*modem / Hayes*
1990	find information on the **inter** (national) **net**(work)	*http; browser / Berners–Lee*

The Internet – purpose

not a business opportunity, at first!

❖ **see information**   *Bush and Lee's dream*

❖ **market a company**   *cheaper than ads, etc.*
marketing tool
saw co. on web, went to it

❖ **sell goods**   *shop itself*
why need high street presence?
see online, buy online

4

Retailing *vs* etailing

retailing	etailing
high street presence	*web presence*
customer ...	*customer ...*
walks down high street	*goes online*
enters shop	*finds website*
walks around	*navigates website*
talks to salespeople	*uses online data*
pays at till	*pays online*
takes goods home	*receives goods by post/courier*
takes goods back if necessary	*returns goods if necessary*

6

Transcript and Answers

2.10 DVD 2.B

Lecturer:

In our last lecture, we heard about three key principles of business development – real benefits for customers, skilled personnel and effective infrastructure. We looked at the case of long-distance communication where businesses began with a want. But there is another way to develop a new business. We can start with *infrastructure* and think – *What customer wants can I satisfy by using this infrastructure? What benefits can I deliver with this infrastructure?* Am I making sense? You can start with a benefit or with an infrastructure. I suppose you can even start with personnel, but that's a bit weird!

So this week, I'm going to talk about the most important infrastructure of the 21st century. No, it's not the M25 or any other road, and it's not Eurostar or any other railway line. It's certainly not British Airways or Ryan Air! It's the international network of computers which now covers the globe – the Internet. First, a brief bit of history, and then we're going to look at the principles of *etailing* – online selling – as opposed to *retailing* – selling on the high street.

Right, so, let's get the history out of the way. The Internet really starts at the end of the Second World War. In 1945, a man called Bush – no, not *that* one, or his father! This one is called Vannevar Bush. He had a dream. 'It must be possible,' he thought, 'to link all information in a library together.' His dream went further. 'Then we could look at the information on a screen. We wouldn't need to go to the actual books or the documents in the library at all.' He was only thinking about all the information in *one* library, but still, for Bush's dream to become a reality, a lot of inventions had to come together. Let's look at five of them quickly.

Firstly, in 1946, scientists who were working for the US Army built the first real computer. It was called ENIAC. That's E-N-I-A-C. It was enormous and it only worked for a few minutes before breaking down, but it was the start of the computer age.

Secondly, in the 1960s, a man called Ted Nelson invented a name for the connection between documents. He called it *hypertext* because *hyper* means 'over', or 'extra'. We'll come back to this important word later.

Thirdly, in 1974, the first personal computer appeared. Several companies claim the credit, including IBM, of course. The personal computer, or PC, brought the world of computing into the small business and the private home. But these PCs were 'stand-alone'. In other words, they only worked with the information on their own hard drive.

But one year later, in 1975, a man called Vincent Cerf, that's Cerf with a C, invented a way for one computer to talk to another computer. Not chatting about the weather. Sending digital data along a wire. The method was called TCP/IP. The P stands for *protocol* – rules. At that time, the two computers had to be in the same place, the same room or the same building.

But just two years later, in 1977, Dennis Hayes invented the PC modem. This connected one computer to another computer in a *different* location. And yes, you've guessed it, the connection was through the telephone lines. The name *modem* means *modulator / demodulator* by the way, if you are a computer nerd, but that's just another way of saying 'encoder' and 'decoder'. Modems put digital information into analogue form for the telephone lines and turn the analogue back into digital at the other end. This was a very important invention. But it was just like the telegraph of 100 years earlier. The connection was like a single road between two towns. Only one car could travel on it at one time. Bush's dream was still some way away.

Still, by the late 70s, we had most of the parts for the Internet. But two important pieces were missing. The big breakthrough came in 1990. Tim Berners-Lee was a British scientist working in Switzerland. He had the same dream as Bush. He wanted all the scientists in his laboratory to be able to look at each other's documents. For research, of course, not to plagiarize them! He realized that every document needed an address so you could find the document on another computer. He knew about Ted Nelson's word *hypertext*. Berners-Lee invented a way of addressing documents. He said – 'Dear document …' No, he didn't. He called the address *http – hypertext transfer protocol*. Berners-Lee also invented a simple program, called a browser. This program allowed the user of one computer to look at documents on another computer. And, hey presto – we had the Internet. You see, Al Gore really didn't invent it at all.

Berners-Lee's inventions changed the *road* from one computer to another into a *web*. This web allowed documents to appear on any computer screen on the Internet. Berners-Lee called it *the worldwide web* – or *WWW* for short. Actually, it's longer but you get the point.

Before Berners-Lee's inventions of the document address and the browser, the growth of the Internet was slow. In 1981, 213 computers could talk to each other around the world. In 1985, that number was 1,961. Just before Berners-Lee's inventions in 1990, the number reached 150,000. After Berners-Lee's inventions, the growth was incredible. By 1991, 300,000 computers could talk to each other. Five years after that, the number of computers communicating with each other was nearly 6 million and by 2000 it was 80 million. Today, it is over 4 billion.

At first, the Internet was not seen as a business opportunity. This is an important point! Write it down! In its early years, it did what Bush and Lee had imagined. It enabled academics to see the information on other computers in universities. But gradually, some businesspeople began to realize that you could market your company on the Internet. It didn't cost a lot of money to have a web presence. It was much cheaper, for example, than renting or buying advertising space in newspapers or on billboards. So, in the second phase of the Internet, it became a marketing tool. People saw a company on the Internet and then went to that shop, or restaurant, or hotel. Finally, some companies began to see the Internet as the shop itself. *Why do we need expensive high street premises?* they asked themselves. Nobody else was listening! Customers can see our products online and buy them online. Can you see the problem for a company which takes this route to developing a successful business?

To answer that question, we first have to think about how a normal retailer of books or clothes or whatever works. The company has a high street presence – a shop. Why do they have a shop in the high street? Because that's where customers go. As they say in business, always be where your customers go. Someone goes into the shop, walks around looking at the goods on display, and sees something they want. They talk to a salesperson, who is usually a skilled employee. They buy the item and pay at the till – nowadays, usually with a card. They take it home. If they don't want it, or if there is something wrong with it, they take it back to the shop and, nowadays, in most cases, they can get a full refund.

How is an online retailer – or etailer – different? Well, firstly, of course, there is no shop, no high street presence. Instead, there is a web presence. This can be a good thing. As we have seen, customers go to the web in huge numbers, but, of course, you have to make sure they come to your site – your e-shop – so perhaps you need to spend some money driving customers onto your site. Secondly, there are no salespeople, no skilled personnel. Again, this may not be a problem if customers can navigate around your e-shop easily. Thirdly, there are no tills. Again, no problem, if you have efficient, secure systems for taking payment. Fourthly, you cannot take the goods home with you. The company has to deliver them. So, although the company is an etailer, using the *virtual* infrastructure of the Internet for marketing, sales and payment, it still needs to use the *real* infrastructure of postal delivery to get the goods to you. Finally, you cannot take the goods back, so the company also needs to use the real infrastructure of courier collection to enable you to return the goods – and, of course, it needs an efficient system of crediting back the payment to you.

OK. I see we have overrun again, so I'm going to ask you to do the next bit. Can you research either Boo.com or Amazon.com and be prepared to talk about the reasons for success or failure at the next tutorial? That's Boo – B-double O, and of course Amazon you know anyway. Thank you.

D Developing critical thinking

With a more able group, set this as a classroom task and elicit feedback.

With a less able group, set this as a research task – half the class should research Amazon and the other half research Boo.com – and feed back on it at a later date.

Answers

Answers depend on students but some possible ideas are:

1. Amazon started quite slowly, built its customer base on a small range of products and then expanded. It employs excellent people in customer services and has a website which is very easy to negotiate.

2. Boo.com grew very quickly, did not have a good website or good people in customer service. It did not have a good system for returning goods.

Closure

Use any of the optional activities above if you have not already done so, or go over some of the vocabulary from the lesson.

Speaking: Communication aids

Objectives

By the end of this lesson, students should be able to:

- demonstrate understanding of meanings of target vocabulary;
- pronounce target vocabulary in isolation and in context;
- use knowledge about communication disabilities in order to complete tasks.

Introduction

Exploit the visuals:

What parts of the body do they show? (eye, ear, mouth, throat, etc. – do not go into details of all the small body parts)

What senses do they represent? (sight, hearing and speech)

Which senses are not shown? (touch, smell)

A Activating ideas

Write the following questions on the board for students to discuss in pairs.

- *What do social workers do?* (help people who are struggling with everyday life)
- *What sort of people do they help?* (elderly, disabled, mentally ill, families with young children 'at risk', etc.)
- *Why do we need social workers?* (identify and prevent more problems)
- *Would you like to be a social worker? Why (not)?* (hard work with low pay, sometimes dangerous or very stressful)

After a few minutes, elicit ideas. You should be able to teach or revise the meaning of a few words for the lesson, including *disabilities, (in)dependent*.

Focus on the lecture handout and point out it is from the Department of Education and *Social Work*. Set the task. Allow a minute or two for reading then elicit answers to the two questions in Exercise A.

Language and culture note

As well as the traditional terms *deaf, dumb* and *blind*, three more modern terms are included: *hearing impaired, speech impaired* and *sight impaired*. The terms *deaf, dumb* and *blind* tend to imply a total lack of a faculty, whereas *impaired* can include anything from 100 per cent loss of the faculty to partial loss.

Note that the expression *a dumb person* does exist, but it can mean 'a stupid person', because *dumb* in American English can also mean 'stupid'. Students should therefore use it with care.

The word *mute* can also be offensive. However, students need to be aware of these words for studying the history of these topics when, of course, they were used freely.

Answers

1. Communication disabilities include people who are *blind (visually / sight impaired), deaf (hearing impaired)* or *speech impaired*. (We have deliberately avoided the use of *dumb* or *mute* – see Language and culture note above.)

2. There are a number of possible reasons for this:

   - The disability limits the type of work people are able to do.
   - Disabled people may be able to do the job but the workplace may not be suitable or the person may not be able to get to the workplace.
   - There is discrimination against disabled people.

B Understanding new vocabulary in context

Give students time to read the questions before you play 🔊 **2.11**. Suggest students make notes for each person while they listen. Warn students it is quite a short extract.

Play 🔊 **2.11**. Do not elicit answers. Students ask and answer the questions in pairs. Monitor for correct pronunciation of target words and for good intonation for the questions.

Elicit answers, correcting and drilling pronunciation as you do so.

Drill the four questions if you wish.

Optional activity

- Play ◉ **2.11** again with students following the transcript.
- Photocopy the transcript with gaps for the target vocabulary. Students fill in the missing words, then listen to ◉ **2.11** again to check their ideas.

Answers

	Maria	Alfred	Elena
Disability?	blind	deaf	speech impaired
How?	car accident	illness	deaf from birth
Aids?	guide dog, Braille	lip reading, sign language	none stated
Employment?	call centre	UN signer	none – age 7

Transcript

◉ 2.11

2.11. Lesson 2.6. Vocabulary for speaking: Living with communication disability

Exercise B. Listen to the case studies of Maria, Alfred and Elena from the lecture.

Lecturer: In this lecture, I'm going to talk about communication disability from the point of view of employment. Can people with communication disabilities work? Of course they can. But society needs to help them in many ways to get into the workplace. We need to make sure employers do not discriminate against people because of their disabilities. I mean, employers mustn't reject people for recruitment or promotion simply because of their disability.

OK. We're going to consider three cases during this lecture. We'll come back to them on several occasions. Firstly, we have the case of Maria. Maria is 55 now. She can't see but she was not blind from birth. She lost her sight in a car accident. However, she deals with her blindness extremely well. She has learnt Braille so she can read and write again. She has a guide dog. She now works full time in a call centre. Secondly, there is Alfred. He's 28. Alfred can't hear but he wasn't deaf when he was born. He lost his hearing as a result of an illness when he was 18. He deals with his deafness very well. He has learnt lip-reading and sign language. He now works as a signer at the United Nations. He listens to speeches at meetings and signs the information for people who are deaf or hearing-impaired.

Finally, Elena. Elena is only seven. She can't speak. She has impaired speaking. As you probably know already, it is unacceptable these days to refer to people as *mute* or, even worse, *dumb*. She was born deaf, and deaf people have great difficulty in learning to speak. There is nothing wrong with Elena's speech *organs*, but her deafness means that she does not know how to make speech *sounds*. However, she is working intensively with a speech therapist to help her to produce speech.

OK. So, those are our three cases. As I said, we will return to them several times ...

C Recognizing vowel sounds

Set the task and go over the example. Students complete individually then compare answers in pairs. Elicit answers and practise pronunciation of any words students found difficult.

Answers

Note that the exercise moves from short vowels to long vowels to diphthongs.

1. let — deaf
2. but — tongue / lung / dumb
3. six — lip
4. eat — teeth
5. two — lose / mute
6. four — chords
7. nine — eye / sight / blind
8. way — brain / Braille
9. we're — hear / ear
10. boy — voice
11. how — mouth
12. go — nose

D Consolidating vocabulary

Set the task. Students work in pairs. Show the correct answers on an electronic projection so that students can check their ideas. Focus on the verb phrases and make the following points:

- *go blind / deaf* (we can also use *become*)
- *lose your sight / hearing / the power of speech* (*lose your voice* is for temporary loss, e.g., when you have a cold)

We use many other phrases with *lose*, for example: *your memory, your balance, your temper, interest,* etc.

Answers

sense noun	sight	hearing	speech
parts of the body	eyes, brain	ears, brain	mouth, tongue, lips, lung, nose, teeth, vocal chords, etc.
disability nouns	blindness, visual impairment	deafness, hearing impairment	speech impairment
disability adjectives	blind, visually impaired	deaf, hearing impaired	~~dumb / mute*~~, speech impaired
verb phrases	can't see, go blind, lose your sight	can't hear, go deaf, lose your hearing	can't speak, lose your voice*, lose the power of speech
aids to disability	Braille, guide dogs	hearing aids, hearing dogs	speech synthesizer

* see notes above on these words and phrases

Closure

Write questions on the board for students to discuss in pairs. These will encourage students to use the target vocabulary:

How can we stop discrimination against disabled people in the workplace?

How can we make workplaces easier for disabled people to manage?

What sort of jobs could you do if you are speech, hearing, or sight impaired?

2.7 Real-time speaking: Braille – reading and writing for the blind

Objectives

By the end of this lesson, students should be able to:

* use existing skills to give a biographical talk about Louis Braille;
* pronounce target vocabulary in context.

Introduction

Check whether students know that Louis Braille was the inventor of the Braille system for reading and writing. Tell them that this is the topic of today's lesson.

A Activating ideas

Make sure the notes about Louis Braille (right-hand column) are covered. Exploit the visual of the Braille printer. Elicit one or two ideas for questions students could ask, for example:

* *When was he born?*
* *Was he French?*
* *Did he get married?*

Students continue in pairs. After a few minutes, elicit the questions and find out if any of the students know the answers. Write all the questions on the board and keep them there throughout the lesson so that you can refer to them. Do not confirm or correct answers.

Answers

Answers depend on students but here are some ideas:

Did …	he get married? / have children? / go to university? / become famous?
Was …	he French? / blind? / rich? / successful?
When …	was he born? / did he die? / did he invent the Braille system?
Where …	was he born? / did he live? / did he go to school/university?
What …	happened to his eyesight? / gave him the idea for the Braille system?
How …	did he become blind? / did he invent the Braille system?
Why …	did he invent the Braille system?

B Gathering information

Set the task. Students discuss the vocabulary in pairs. Give help with pronunciation where necessary.

Elicit the connection between *saddle* and *leather*. (Saddles are made of leather.) Check the meaning of *awl*; the meaning is given in the notes but further explanation may be necessary. You can demonstrate the purpose of an awl with belts or shoes students are wearing. The pronunciation is /ɔːl/.

Methodology note

Students do not need to learn the words *awl*, *saddle*, etc. They are for the purposes of this lesson only.

Answers

1. a saddle = a 'seat' for the rider of a horse. It is made of leather.
2. leather = animal skin that has been dried, used for shoes, belts, etc.
3. raise = make something higher
4. symbols = + - x / (plus, minus, multiplication, division, etc.)
5. adopt = start to use a new idea or method
6. standard = model

Methodology note

There is often confusion between the meanings of the words *raise* and *rise*. Something is *raised* when people have done it: *He raised his hand*. We use *rise* when things move upwards on their own: *The balloon rose into the sky.*

C Studying the model

1. Point out that the notes are written in the present tense but when the information is put into sentences, in speech or in writing, the tense will change to the past. Quickly revise the pronunciation of the dates in the first section of the notes; this will help students to recognize them when they are heard in context.

   Check students understand the task. Play 🔊 **2.12**. Students compare lists in pairs. Elicit answers.

2. Find out if students can answer the question about the range of expressions, but do not confirm or correct. Refer students to the Skills Check. Now elicit answers to the question.

Answers

in 1809

when he was three

for three years

from 1815 to 1819

in 1819, at the age of ten

Transcript
🔊 2.12

Presenter:	2.12. Lesson 2.7. Real-time speaking: Braille – reading and writing for the blind
	Exercise C1. Listen to a student giving information about Braille to a study group. How does she talk about dates, ages and time periods?
Student A:	I'm going to tell you about the inventor of Braille. In fact, he gave his name to the system – I mean, he was called Braille – Louis Braille. He was born in 1809 in a small town near Paris. His father was a saddle-maker. Louis wasn't blind from birth. He had an accident in his father's workshop when he was three. He was playing with an awl when he hit his eye with the tool.
Student C:	That's terrible! What an awful thing!
Student B:	Sorry. What's a nawl?
Student A:	It's not a nawl. It's an awl. A-W-L.
Student C:	I don't understand. Was he blinded in both eyes at once?
Student A:	No. He damaged his right eye and then his left eye got infected.
Student B:	That's dreadful.
Student A:	Yes, it is. Anyway, where was I?
Student B:	I can't remember.
Student C:	I've forgotten, too.
Student B:	Oh, yes. You were talking about the accident.
Student A:	That's right. He lost his sight in both eyes. He went to normal school for three years but he didn't learn much. From 1815 to 1819 he didn't go to school. Then in 1819, at the age of ten, he went to the National Institute for the Blind in Paris. While he was studying there, he learnt a system of reading for the blind. It involved large raised letters of the normal alphabet. Braille thought there must be a better way.

D Practising the model

1. Play 🔊 **2.13**. Pause after each line for students to repeat, making sure they pause where appropriate.

2. In pairs, students take turns to tell each other the information from the first set of notes. Remind students to vary the way they give the dates and to use the past

tense. The sentences do not have to be exactly the same as on the audio. Monitor and give feedback.

Transcript
🎧 2.13

Presenter: **2.13. Exercise D1. Listen and repeat some of the sentences from the presentation. Copy the pronunciation, including the pauses.**

Student A: a. When he was three, he had an accident in his father's workshop.
b. From 1815 to 1819, he didn't go to school.
c. At the age of six, he left normal school.
d. Then in 1819, at the age of ten, he went to the National Institute for the Blind in Paris.
e. Sixteen years after his death, Braille became the worldwide standard.

E   Producing the model

1. Go through the information in the second page of the notes about Braille and check understanding. Elicit one or two sentences based on the notes. Remind students to vary the way dates are expressed and to pause if the date is given at the beginning of the sentence.

   Divide the class into small groups. Students take turns to give a complete sentence about Braille. Monitor and give help where necessary. Give feedback.

2. Set the task: ask students to notice any extra information, comments or opinions when they listen. Play 🎧 2.14 and elicit students' ideas about the differences between the presentation on the CD and their own in E1. Replay 🎧 2.14, pausing after a few of the sentences for repetition. At this point you could ask students to represent the information about Braille in their groups (i.e., students perform a second version of the presentation incorporating some of the extra comments, etc.).

3. This activity also makes a good closure activity. Refer back to the questions you wrote on the board at the beginning of the lesson. Students discuss the answers in pairs. Elicit answers and ideas and ask if students have more questions about Braille or if any of their questions are still unanswered.

Answers

2. The listeners comment on the coincidence – the awl blinded him and he used it to invent his system; the speaker comments on the stupidity of him not being allowed to teach his own system and says how well he coped with his blindness.

Transcript
🎧 2.14

Presenter: **2.14. Exercise E2. Listen to a student presenting the information. What extra comments do the students make?**

Student A: For eight years, from 1821, he worked on his own system. He raised dots instead of letters. In his system, he used …
Student B: Sorry. What are dots?
Student A: They're small circles. He used an awl to raise the letters. In fact, he used the same tool which blinded him.
Student B: That's an incredible coincidence!
Student C: I don't know. He was probably thinking about the accident all the time.
Student A: That's true. Now, … I've forgotten what I was going to say.
Student B: You were going to tell us about his system.
Student A: Oh, yes. In his system, he used six dots. He finished it in 1829. A year before then, he became a teacher at the institute. However, he was not allowed to teach his own system. Isn't that stupid?! But while he was teaching the old method, he continued to work on his new one, and in 1837 he added symbols for maths and for music. So he didn't stop with symbols for the alphabet. Braille died in 1852 when he was only 43, but his system went on to be used all around the world. Just six months after his death, the National Institute switched to Braille's method and in 1868, his system was accepted as the world standard. So, a poor blind boy invented a system which is used all over the world today. Isn't it amazing, the way he dealt with his blindness and achieved so much?

Closure
Students write some sentences about Braille (using dates) for consolidation.

Everyday English: Talking on the phone

Objectives

By the end of this lesson, students should be able to:
• use appropriate language when talking on the phone.

Introduction
Exploit the visual. Elicit or teach the term *mobile phone* (*mobile* for short). The general term *phone* is both noun and verb for all types of telephone. **Note:** Students may know the standard American term *cell phone* (or *cell*).

Elicit what students say when they answer the phone. In the UK, this is usually simply *Hello?*

In office environments, people may answer with their

name, e.g., if Mr Jones answers his desk phone:

A: *Peter Jones.*

B: *Hello Peter. Tom here.*

At home, some people answer by giving the number, so that the caller can be sure he/she has phoned the correct person; for example, speaker A answers the phone:

A: *774614.*

B: *Hello. Can I speak to Martin, please?*

A Activating ideas

Elicit one or two ideas. Then briefly put students into small groups to discuss their ideas.

Feed back orally. Encourage students to compare and explain their phone habits.

B Studying models

1. Cover the conversations. Go through the sentences with the class. Clarify any vocabulary problems. Elicit some ideas for the first sentence. Set the task for individual work and pairwork discussion. Feed back using an electronic projection.

Answers

a	Can you speak up?	e	leaving voice messages
b	Sorry, I think you've got the wrong number.	a	a bad line
c	If you are calling about bus times, press 1.	d	sending SMS messages
d	I'll text you later.	b	a mistake in dialling
e	Give me a call when you pick up this message.	c	an automated menu
f	Certainly. It's d.marshall@hadford. ac.uk.	f	phoning the college for information

2. Set the task for individual work and pairwork checking. Play ⊚ **2.15**. Elicit answers.

Transcript and Answers

⊚ 2.15

Presenter:	**2.15. Everyday English: Talking on the phone**
	Exercise B2. Listen and complete the conversations.
	Conversation 1.
Voice A:	Hello. Could you give me David Marshall's e-mail address please?
Voice B:	Certainly. It's d dot marshall, with two l's, at hadford dot a-c dot u-k.
Voice A:	Thank you.
Voice B:	You're welcome. Bye.
Presenter:	**Conversation 2.**
Voice A:	*[recording]* The person you have called is not available. Please leave a message after the tone.
Voice B:	Hi Katia. It's Piera. Give me a call when you pick up this message. OK, talk to you later. Bye.
Presenter:	**Conversation 3.**
Voice A:	Hi Stef. It's Peter. How are you?
Voice B:	Hi. Fine. I can't hear you very well. Can you speak up?
Voice A:	Do you know Alan's mobile number?
Voice B:	You're breaking up. Can you hang up and redial?
Presenter:	**Conversation 4.**
Voice A:	Hi, is that Carlo?
Voice B:	Sorry, I think you've got the wrong number.
Voice A:	Oh, sorry.
Voice B:	No problem. Bye.
Presenter:	**Conversation 5.**
Voice A:	[recording] If you are calling about bus times, press 1. If you require information about family or student passes, or about Day Rover tickets, please press 2. For all other enquiries, please hold. … You are in a queue. One of our operators will be with you as soon as possible.
Presenter:	**Conversation 6.**
Voice A:	Send me a text this afternoon. My phone's always on.
Voice B:	OK. What's your number?
Voice A:	It's oh double-seven four, triple-five nine, one seven three.
Voice B:	Got it. I'll text you later.

C Practising the model

Put on the board and drill all the expressions in the lesson for talking on the phone:

- Could I speak to …
- It's Piera (note that *I am Piera* is not possible in English)
- Is that Carlo? (*Are you Carlo?* is not possible)
- give somebody a call
- pick up a message

- Talk to you later.
- Can you speak up?
- You're breaking up.
- hang up / redial
- get the wrong number
- send a text (n) / text (v) somebody

1. Set the task for pairwork. Monitor and assist with pronunciation. Note any common pronunciation errors. Play 🎧 **2.15** again if you wish.

2. Continue with pairwork. Ask students to do two or three of the explanation tasks. Monitor and assist. Get students to demonstrate some of the best ones to the rest of the class.

Answers

2. Answers depend on students but here are some suggestions for the kind of language that they should use:

   a. *say your phone number* – double and triple numbers; numbers given in groups of three or four, mobile/land line, network, *What network are you on?*

   b. *send a text* – go to Contacts, select the name, press this button, delete/clear a mistake, space

   c. *use an Internet video phone system* – go to a website, www. (*double-u double-u double-u dot*), sign in with your ID and password, click on a link

   d. *phone the tutors in your department* – phone/call/ring the switchboard, put in the tutor's extension number, ask for the person, they put you through

   e. *use some of the applications on your phone* – go to a screen, select an application

   f. *find out times of trains by phone* – listen to a menu, press a number, wait in a queue

   g. *visit your social networking page on the web* – go to www. (*double-u double-u double-u dot*), log in (v), type in your ID, password, log out (v)

   h. *say your college e-mail address* – dot, at (@)

   i. *leave a message on your mobile's voicemail system* – give me a call/ring, This is (Joe)

   j. *use the college intranet* – go to www. (*double-u double-u double-u dot*), log in (v) type your login (n), type in/put in a key word, click on *Search*

Optional activity

Give students some further situations to role-play, as follows. Some of the situations are similar to the Course Book conversations in order to give practice of the phrases in them. Add your own situations if you wish:

- getting information from the Tourist Office
- returning a call after picking up a message
- leaving a voice message
- asking for another friend's number
- getting a wrong number
- talking in a very noisy place
- making an appointment at the Careers Office

Closure

1. Go over errors that you picked up during your monitoring.

2. Ask students to cover the texts in the Course Book. Say the sentences from Exercise B2. Elicit and build up the full conversations.

2.8 Learning new speaking skills: Repairing communication

Objectives

By the end of this lesson, students should be able to:

- pronounce linked and suppressed consonant sounds accurately in target vocabulary and phrases;
- use phrases for sharing research at appropriate points in a tutorial discussion.

Introduction

Exploit the visual. Ask students if they notice any patterns in the Braille system, for example:

- letters a–j use top two rows of dots only;
- letters k–t use the first column of the bottom row;
- only letters u–z have dots in the second column of the bottom row, etc.

A Reviewing vocabulary

1. All these words are from Lesson 2.7 so students should know the meanings. In pairs, students mark the stressed syllable on each word.

2. Play ⊘ **2.16** for students to check their ideas. Pause after each word for repetition. Note that the pronunciation of *cc* in *accept* and *accident* is /ks/.

Transcript and Answers
⊘ 2.16

Presenter:	2.16. Lesson 2.8. Learning new speaking skills: Repairing communication
	Exercise A2. Listen, check and practise.
Voice:	a. accept
	b. accident
	c. adopt
	d. institute
	e. inventor
	f. standard
	g. system
	h. worldwide

B Saying consonants

1. After students have read the Pronunciation Check, play ⊘ **2.19** so that students can practise the sentences.

2. Set the task and tell students the sentences are all about the life of Louis Braille. Do the first sentence with the class as an example. Students work on the sentences in pairs.

3. Play ⊘ **2.17**. Pause after each sentence for students to check and if necessary edit their marked-up sentences. Write the correctly marked-up sentences on the board. Replay ⊘ **2.17**. Pause after each sentence again for students to repeat (preferably with books closed / sentences covered in the Course Book).

Answers

a. He was born in a small town near Paris.
b. He wasn't blind from birth.
c. He left normal school three years later.
d. He invented a system of reading.
e. He became a teacher at his old school.

Language note

Letters sometimes disappear completely when they appear before another letter, e.g., *next month*. In other cases, the rules of assimilation are extremely complicated, for example:

/p/ replaces /t/, e.g., *not me* becomes *nop me*

/b/ replaces /d/, e.g., *good morning* becomes *goob morning*

/m/ replaces /n/, e.g., *gone back* becomes *gom back*

Do not set out to teach these but students may notice some strange sounds in native-speaker speech now they have been alerted to the issue.

Transcripts
⊘ 2.19

Presenter:	2.19. Pronunciation Check. Listen and copy the linking and suppressing.
Voice A:	He was blinded in an accident.
	It's a pointed tool.

⊘ 2.17

Presenter:	2.17. Exercise B3. Listen, check and practise.
Voice:	a. He was born in a small town near Paris.
	b. He wasn't blind from birth.
	c. He left normal school three years later.
	d. He invented a system of reading.
	e. He became a teacher at his old school.
	f. He died in Paris in 1852.

C Identifying a new skill

1. Set the task. Students complete individually then compare answers in pairs. Do not elicit answers.

2. Refer students to the Skills Check. Students discuss the phrases in pairs. Ask students to mark the stressed words.

3. Play ⊘ **2.18** so that students can check their answers. Play ⊘ **2.18** again, pausing after each line, and ask students which words are stressed. Then ask students to repeat each line.

It should become clear that the verbs *was* and *were* are unstressed in all the sentences except for *Where was I?* In this question, it is stressed.

Highlight the grammar and word order of some of the phrases at a suitable point during this activity:

I've forgotten what *I was going to say*. = present perfect + *what* + past continuous + *to do*

(Note that this could also be analyzed as *future in the past*, but this analysis is perfectly adequate.)

*You **were going to tell** us about* ... = past continuous + *to do*

However, encourage students to learn these **as phrases** rather than going into lengthy grammar explanations. The students do not need to be able to do the paradigm – *He's forgotten, she's forgotten, they've forgotten*, etc. Use the context of the tutorial discussion to convey the function of each phrase.

4. Divide the class into groups of three. Students practise the tutorial extract. Monitor and give feedback.

Transcript and Answers

🌐 2.18

Presenter:	2.18. Exercise C3. Listen to the extract. Check your answers.
Voice A:	He was playing with an awl when he hit his eye with the tool.
Voice B:	Sorry. What's a nawl?
Voice A:	It's not a nawl. It's an awl.
Voice C:	I don't understand. Was he blinded in both eyes at once?
Voice A:	No. He damaged his right eye and then his left eye got infected.
Voice B:	That's dreadful!
Voice A:	Yes, it is. Anyway, where was I?
Voice B:	I can't remember.
Voice C:	I've forgotten, too.
Voice B:	Oh, yes. You were talking about the accident.
Voice A:	That's right.

D Practising the new skill

This is an information gap activity. Set the task. Divide the class into groups of three and allocate text A, B or C to each student. Make sure each student understands which piece of information they should be looking at. Go round and give help where necessary while students are reading their texts. If you wish, students working on the same text can move over to each other and help with

comprehension (i.e., A students work together, B students work together, etc.).

When students are ready they should share the information they have learnt with the rest of the group. Monitor, reminding students to use phrases from the Skills Check at appropriate places. Give feedback.

Methodology note

As usual with presentations or information gap activities, students should not simply read out the information they have been allocated. The points should be put into sentences (orally, not in writing) and/or paraphrased. Extra phrases should be included to guide the listener: *firstly, that means, in fact,* etc. You might wish to spend a few minutes reminding students about other relevant sub-skills they have learnt in the speaking sections of this course before you set the activity.

Closure

Check students have understood the key information from Exercise D.

• Ask B and C students about the information presented by A students.

• Ask A and C students about the information presented by B students.

• Ask A and B students about the information presented by C students.

2.9 Grammar for speaking: Using the past continuous

Objectives

By the end of this lesson, students should be able to:

• use the past continuous for interrupted actions;

• discriminate between past simple and past continuous;

• pronounce unstressed *was* and *were* in past continuous sentences.

Introduction

Ask students to remember as many dates and facts about Louis Braille as they can (see Lesson 2.7).

Grammar box 7

Remind students about the life of Louis Braille. Ask *How did he become blind?* Then focus on the first example sentence.

Give students time to study all the information in the tables. Ask questions about each example sentence in the tables to further check understanding:

What was Braille doing when he hit his eye? (Playing with an awl.)

What happened next? (He lost his sight.)

Focus students' attention on the questions under the tables. Elicit answers. Use the paradigm table to remind students of the forms of the past continuous.

Play 🎧 **2.20**. Pause after each sentence for students to repeat, making sure they do not stress *was* and *were*.

Answers

- action or situation 1?   past continuous
- the interrupting action 2?   past simple
- the result or consequence 3?   past simple

If you wish, go quickly through the paradigm for the past tense of *be*, which is of course the same as for *was/were doing*. Check the formation of questions with inversion of the auxiliary, e.g., *What was Braille doing when he hit his eye?*

Language note

The words *result* and *consequence* are, in a sense, synonyms, in that they both describe events after a particular action. But *result* is normally good and *consequence* is normally bad. You can explain this to the students if you wish.

Transcript
🌐 2.20

Presenter:	2.20. Lesson 2.9. Grammar for speaking: Using the past continuous
	Grammar box 7. Listen to the sentences in the tables.
Voice:	Braille was playing with an awl when he hit his eye. When he hit his eye, he damaged it. While the children were studying at the institute, they learnt a system of reading.

Language and culture note

Surprisingly perhaps, the past continuous tense is used more in spoken English than in written. According to the *Longman Grammar of Written and Spoken English*, it is four times more common, although it is rare in both spoken and written English. In academic English, its usage is largely confined to accidents – *The Titanic was crossing the Atlantic when it hit an iceberg* – and accidental discoveries.

A What happened … and what happened next?

Set the task and do the first answer with the class as an example. You can either ask students to write the remaining sentences, or if you want to keep the focus on oral work, students can discuss possible ways to complete each answer in pairs.

After a few minutes, elicit answers. Write some of them on the board for students to compare with their own answers. Some of the answers can be drilled, if you wish.

Answers

Answers depend on students but here are some ideas:

1. I was doing my homework when … (I got a text message / I had a brilliant idea)
2. We were driving home when … (the police car overtook us / we had a puncture)
3. She was beginning to get worried when … (her daughter phoned / she heard her husband come home)
4. While I was studying yesterday evening, … (my computer crashed / I got a phone call)
5. While they were waiting for the bus, … (they saw a taxi / they saw a child run into the road)
6. While he was living in Paris, … (he became ill / he met an important artist)

B Describing action / situation, interruption and result or consequence

There are many different ways this activity can be carried out – see Methodology note below. If you are short of time, you do not have to do all the pieces of information with the class.

Set the task and go over the example. Students make notes in the table individually then compare answers in pairs. Elicit answers.

Divide the class into pairs or small groups. Students use the notes in the table to make sentences about each discovery / invention.

Methodology note

- The written research can be used as a wall dictation with students taking it in turns to read the information on the wall, remember it, and then report to their group. Each group should write down a maximum of four or five pieces of information. Then remix groups so that the students have to exchange information until they can complete all the sections of the table in the Course Book.

- Divide the class into groups of three. Allocate three different pieces of research information for each student to study and make notes on. Students explain the information to each other (without looking at the original research) and make notes in the table in the Course Book.

Closure
Discuss some of the information students learnt in Exercise B.

2.10 Applying new speaking skills: Sign language and speech synthesis – the early days

Objectives

By the end of this lesson, students should be able to:
- research and present information about either sign language or speech synthesis;
- use sub-skills for sharing research during a presentation.

Introduction
Tell students in this lesson they are going to give another presentation. Elicit from the class what they have learnt about giving good presentations so far. (This may include points from earlier levels of *Progressive Skills*.) Make a list on the board:

Answers

date	person	situation / action 1	action 2	discovery / invention	T / F?
1665	*Newton*	*sitting under apple tree*	*apple fell on head*	*gravity*	*?*
1905	Einstein	travelling to work	thought about riding on beam of light	theory of relativity	T
1745	Watt	watching a kettle boil	realized power of steam	steam engine	F
1946	Spencer	working with radar waves	melted chocolate in pocket	microwave	T
1970s	Fry	working for 3M	discovered mild adhesive	Post-Its	T
		singing in a choir	wanted a bookmark		
1895	Roentgen	exploring path of electrical rays	rays passed through his hand, showed bones	X-rays	T
1937	Sveda	working on a new medicine / smoking	put down cigarette, picked it up, tasted sweet	cyclamate	T
1924	Wakefield	making chocolate cookies	ran out of baker's choc, used pieces of choc, didn't melt	chocolate chip cookies	?
1928	Fleming	studying bacteria	left slides overnight, no bacteria on them because of penicillium mould	penicillin	T
1865	Kekule	studying the structure of carbon compounds	had a day-dream of snake with tail in mouth = benzene is ring of carbon atoms	structure of benzene	T?

- Use signpost language.
- Make eye contact.
- Speak from notes (don't read sentences aloud) … etc.

Ask students to decide on one area to focus/improve on in this lesson. Remember to ask students at the end of the lesson if they succeeded in this and if they think they have improved.

A Previewing vocabulary

Refer students to the illustrations. Set the two tasks for students to discuss in pairs. Elicit ideas.

If you want, you can get students to try to make some of the signs to each other for identification, and to try to explain how the artificial mouth works – air is pumped in on the right, etc.

Answers

1. The first illustration shows hands, fingers, thumbs. The second shows the other items.

2. The first is a system of sign language for people who cannot hear and perhaps cannot speak. The second is much harder to understand and students may not have any real idea at this point. However, the title of the lesson should give it away: it is a very early form of speech synthesis – an artificial mouth, complete with nose.

B Researching information

Give students time to read the assignment then check understanding. In pairs, get students to ask their partner *Which topic do you want to work on? Why?*

Once students have chosen their topics, remind them that they should highlight the assignment for exactly what they have to do. Put them into groups so that they work with others with the same topic.

Remind students to read the notes and discuss with their group any new words or anything they do not understand. Also, to practise pronunciation of words and sentences.

Tell students how long the presentation should be and if necessary set a strict time limit, e.g., three minutes. On the other hand, if your students are reticent, you might need to set a minimum time!

Monitor and give help where necessary.

Methodology note

1. If the resources are available, students can make electronic projections to accompany their presentations at this point. They could also research further information to add to their presentations.

2. With more able classes, or if your class is small, individual students can deliver the complete presentation instead of just a section.

C Presenting

If necessary, revise and practise some of the sub-skills listed in the Course Book for this activity. Tell students which presentation sub-skills you want them to work on besides the ones mentioned, such as:

- eye contact;
- speed and loudness of delivery;
- sticking to a time limit;
- introduction / conclusion, etc.

Re-divide the class into groups with students for each topic. Make sure listening students take active part while each presentation is happening by asking questions and/or taking notes. Monitor and give feedback.

D Developing critical thinking

Students discuss in pairs or small groups. Elicit ideas and prompt if students are struggling.

Answers

Answers depend on students but could include information about:

- T-loops in offices for people who are hearing impaired;
- markings on pavements for blind people to use to find crossing places;
- information in Braille, e.g., in documents and on toilets, etc.;
- markings on telephones so blind people can dial correctly;
- markings on dangerous products so blind people don't drink/eat by accident;
- signers to help in court.

Closure

Finish with your feedback for Exercise C, or use Exercise D.

Reading: Communication inventors

Objectives

By the end of this lesson, students should be able to:

- demonstrate understanding of vocabulary for the lesson;
- use new vocabulary to predict and complete written sentences.

Introduction

Exploit the visuals:

- *What period of time did the people live in?* (19ᵗʰ century)
- *What is the machine?* (early 'computer' / calculating machine)
- *What did the two people do?* (Charles Babbage designed the machine; Ada Lovelace wrote the first computer program.)

It does not matter if students do not know some of the answers. You can give the information yourself.

A Understanding paragraph development

1. Set the task, telling students not to worry if they do not have many ideas at this stage. Students discuss in pairs. Avoid explaining the meaning of new words and phrases at this point. Elicit some ideas but do not confirm or correct.

2. Students complete individually then compare answers in pairs. Elicit answers, but again, avoid explaining the meaning of new words and phrases at this point.

Answers

1. Answers depend on students but here are some ideas:
   a. facts about an invention; why it might be ahead of its time
   b. advice for students, dealing with a problem at university or college
   c. modern history, sociology
   d. psychology, sociology
   e. biographical details
2. c, e, a, b, d

B Understanding phrases in context

Set the task and go over the example. Students can use dictionaries if they wish – they must look up using a key word, e.g., *ahead*. Students discuss in pairs. Elicit answers. Highlight the prepositions used in many of the verb phrases. Focus on the word *strong* and discuss some of the different meanings it has.

Optional activity

1. Use the answers below as the basis for a matching activity. (Write the words and phrases in one column and the meanings, mixed up, in the second column.)

2. Divide the class into two halves, A and B. Give A the phrases in the topic sentences to work on. Give B the phrases in the paragraphs. When students have worked on the meanings, re-divide the class into pairs, Student A and Student B. In these pairs, students take turns to explain the meanings of their words and phrases to each other.

Answers

word / phrase	meaning
ahead of its time	*people are not ready for this idea or invention*
feel strongly about	*have a strong opinion*
heading towards	*move in a direction*
have a big influence on	*when you have power over someone or something*
get through to (him)	*communicate by overcoming difficulties of some sort*
go on to become	*later in someone's life*
give an indication of	*give a sign, probably have to look quite closely to understand it*
first love	*most important thing in a person's life*
the basis of	*the starting point or beginning, the main theory*
come up with	*to think of an idea, usually for the first time*
come into its / their own	*to become very good or useful*
no commercial use	*is not profitable, cannot be made into a saleable product*

word / phrase	meaning
put someone's / something's interests ahead of your own	*make A more important than B in your actions*
look like	*be similar in some way (like = preposition)*
get in the way of	*stop, prevent or slow something down*

C Predicting information from phrases

Elicit ideas for completion of two or three sentences, then ask students to write the remainder. (Alternatively, students could discuss in pairs if you are short of time.) Elicit answers, checking that:

- the answers show students have understood the meaning;
- the words and phrases have been used with correct tense, preposition, etc.

Answers

Answers depend on students but here are some possible endings:

1. The invention was ahead of its time so … *people did not understand it.*
2. The Internet came into its own when … *people got access to broadband connections.*
3. The behaviour of pop stars clearly has an influence on … *many young people.*
4. You should not put work ahead of … *family life.*
5. If you feel strongly about green issues, you should … *get involved in recycling projects.*

Closure
Use feedback for Exercise C.

Objectives

By the end of this lesson, students should be able to:

- use research questions, scanning and topic sentences to predict information and cohesion of text;
- react to information in a text about Edison;
- use existing skills to deal with a biographical and chronological encyclopedia article.

Note: The exploitation of the text continues in the next lesson (2.13). It is important therefore, in this lesson, not to over-exploit the Edison quotes or possible inferences as they are dealt with there in more detail.

Introduction
Write the title of the lesson on the board: *Inspiration and perspiration*. Elicit/teach the meanings of the two words. Discuss possible reasons for having this as a lesson title.

In fact the words come from a quote of Edison's, 'Genius is 1 per cent inspiration and 99 per cent perspiration.' You can explain this now or leave it until later in the lesson.

A Activating ideas

Set the task. Students discuss in pairs. Elicit answers for question 1. Question 2 is a 'teasing' question. It is unlikely that students will be able to answer it. You can return to it at the end of the lesson.

Answers

1. designs / inventions / (technical) drawings / signatures / dates
2. They are, in fact, the patent applications for three of Edison's inventions, but you do not need to explain that at this point.

B Preparing to read

Give students a minute or two to read the end-of-term paper question. Elicit how much information students already know about Edison. Can they give rough dates for his life?

Why is he famous? Do not confirm or correct any points.

Remind students what 'research questions' are if necessary. Elicit one or two ideas. In pairs, students think of further research questions and make a note of them. Elicit ideas.

Answers

Suggested answers:

Who was Edison?

What did he invent? / How many things did he invent?

How important were the inventions?

Are they still important today?

C Understanding the text

Remind students to use strategies to help with understanding the text before they read the complete article, e.g., reading headings, studying illustrations, graphs and tables, etc., and topic sentences. Students should not do detailed reading until they reach Exercise C3.

1. Set a time limit for the scanning activity of one minute. Then elicit answers.

2. If possible, show the topic sentences using an electronic projection. Students close their books or cover the text. In pairs students discuss what each paragraph will be about. Elicit ideas.

3. Set the task. Tell students to answer as many questions as they can without worrying too much about any new words or phrases. Students complete individually then compare answers in pairs. Elicit answers. At this point, you can explain a few difficult words or phrases. However, the meanings of some words, such as *hereditary* and *phonograph*, are dealt with in the next activity. If students are not sure about any of their answers, leave them until after Exercise D, then go back to them.

4. Elicit answers to the question, encouraging students to say why they think Edison is or is not the greatest inventor of modern times. Alternatively, you can leave discussing the answer to this question until the end of the lesson (see Closure).

Answers

1. a. on the web

   b. biographical information

   c. chronological

2./3./4.

Answers depend on students.

- As this is a biographical article there is not really an introductory paragraph. This means students will not be able (as they usually are) to predict information, particularly about the discourse structure, from the first paragraph.

- If students did the speaking section, they will have learnt quite a lot about communication disabilities. You might like to use the fact that Edison was deaf as a quick reminder of that section.

D Developing critical thinking

Remind students about the sub-skill of finding evidence in the text. Set the task and do the first answer with the class as an example. Students complete individually then compare answers in pairs. Elicit answers. Ask students how much information they can add to their research questions from Exercise B.

Answers

1. Edison's mother taught him to read.	*once he could read …*
2. *Hereditary* means 'something you get from your parents'.	*his father and later his son had the same hearing loss*
3. Edison knew sign language.	*once telling a group of deaf people*
4. The telegraph was used on the railway system.	A station-master taught him so probably something to do with the railways + Edison did the job in railway stations.
5. Edison knew people wanted the Stock Exchange device before he made it.	*Edison followed his own advice* (only invent things that people want to buy)
6. Edison stopped working as a telegrapher in about 1870.	*Edison was now (1870) able to work full-time as an inventor*
7. A tape recorder is a kind of phonograph.	It means 'sound writing' and a tape recorder writes sounds.
8. Before Edison, people made light bulbs with different materials.	*he discovered the best materials …*
9. A digital movie camera is a kind of kinetograph.	It means 'movement writing' and a digital movie camera writes movement.

Closure

If you have not already done so, discuss with the class the question from the assignment handout.

Alternatively, ask students to find and underline vocabulary from Lesson 2.11. They should check they can remember the meanings.

2.13 Learning new reading skills: Reacting to a text

Objectives

By the end of this lesson, students should be able to:

- react to opinions and facts in a text;
- react to a text by applying to self.

Introduction

Use Exercise A as this will revise the information from the text in the previous lesson about Edison.

A   Reviewing vocabulary

Set the task. Ask students not to look back at the text until they have made at least one attempt for each answer. Students complete individually then compare answers in pairs. Write the list of correct words on the board so that students can correct their own work.

Answers

1. cellar
2. bright
3. nature
4. hereditary
5. patent
6. inventions
7. bulb
8. industry
9. movies
10. fire

B   Identifying a new skill

Set the task and discuss the meaning of *popular sayings*. Students discuss the two questions in pairs. Elicit ideas. Ask students if they have a popular saying with a similar meaning in their language.

Focus on the Skills Check. After students have finished reading, ask one or two questions to check understanding.

Answers

Answers depend on students but here are some ideas:

1. The quote shows that Edison was optimistic, very hardworking and determined to succeed.

2. His early inventions were not successful but he continued to think of new ideas. His laboratory burnt down but he built a new one.

C   Practising a new skill

1. Students complete individually to find quotes. Then discuss the question in pairs or small groups. Elicit ideas.

2. This is a bit of a 'trick question' as there is no evidence for some of the sayings. You might wish to warn students about this or let them work it out for themselves! Students discuss the sayings in pairs or small groups. Monitor and give help with the meanings of any sayings if necessary. Use an electronic projection to display the text and elicit where the evidence is for each saying.

Answers

1. Students should say whether they agree with each point.

Quote	Attitude / opinion
'The present system does not encourage original thought or reasoning.'	education should teach critical thinking
'I prefer the quiet of deafness to the noise of conversation.'	accept your disabilities / make the most of them
'I learnt a good lesson then. Only invent things that people want to buy.'	understood that there is a relationship between invention and the commercial world
'Pay me what it's worth.'	did not want to negotiate – although actually, this is a clever way of negotiating
'I am 67, but I'm not too old to make a fresh start.'	optimistic
'Genius is 1 per cent inspiration and 99 per cent perspiration.'	modest, but perhaps also understood truth about success

2.

Saying	Example(s) from Edison's life
If at first you don't succeed, try, try again.	Edison's whole life is an example of this; in particular he said re. the light bulb; his failure to sell his first invention didn't lead him to give up inventing, but to change the things he invented.
A poor workman blames his tools.	He didn't blame his tools for not finding the answer straight away.
Behind every great man there's a great woman.	no evidence
Concentrate on what you can do, not on what you can't do.	He knew he was good at inventing so he did that; he didn't worry about being deaf.
Count your blessings.	He accepted his deafness and went on with using his inventive genius.
Forgive and forget.	no evidence
God helps those who help themselves.	He made things happen – he didn't sit around waiting – the incident of the fire at his laboratories, perhaps.

Saying	Example(s) from Edison's life
If a job is worth doing, it's worth doing well.	The 10,000 ways with the light bulb show this.
Life is what you make it.	He made his life from quite poor beginnings – no proper schooling.
One good turn deserves another.	He saved the boy and the boy's father taught him to use the telegraph – which was the start of his working life.

Closure

Ask students how many of the sayings are similar in their own language. You could elicit a translation for some of the sayings. In multilingual groups, divide the class into pairs or groups of students with the same mother tongue and ask them to translate a few of the sayings.

2.14 Grammar for reading: Understanding participle clauses

Objectives

By the end of this lesson, students should be able to:
- identify the 'missing' subject of participle clauses;
- identify the 'missing' tense of participles;
- discriminate between a participle in two-clause sentences and a gerund.

Introduction

Revise *Progressive Skills* Level 3, Lesson 3.14, in which students learnt to find the 'missing' subject in sentences with *and* and *but*.

Examples from text:

Edison jumped down and ~~he~~ pulled the boy back ...

The boy's father was the station master, and ~~he~~ thanked him by teaching him how to use the telegraph.

He wanted $4,000 for the device but ~~he~~ did not ask for this amount.

Grammar box 8

Before they look at the tables, ask students:

What was Edison's first job? (a newspaper seller)

How did he get the job of telegraph operator? (He rescued the station master's son from the railway tracks. The station master taught him to use the telegraph.)

Give students time to study Tables 1 and 2, then elicit answers to the question. Explain it is an important reading skill to work out the subject and the tense of the participle clause. Make sure students have grasped the information here before moving on to the next table.

Move on to Table 3. Give students time to study the information. Point out that this time, the participle comes at the beginning of the sentence rather than in the middle. Elicit the answer to the question. Elicit the two sentences that have been joined to make the one longer sentence and write them on the board:

He (Edison) wrapped tin foil around a container. He connected a receiver and a speaker.

Answers

Tables 1 and 2:

The two tables contain the same information but in the second table, clause 2 has no subject and the verb has changed from *got* to *getting* (= participle). The full stop has changed to a comma. The information is given in two clauses, rather than two sentences.

Table 3:

The subject is *he* and the tense is past simple, because the subject and tense of the participle is the same as clause 2.

A   Recognizing participle clauses

Set the task and elicit the first participle clause in the text as an example. Students find the other participle clauses individually then compare with a partner. Use an electronic projection to elicit answers.

Then move on to the two questions. Do the answers for the first participle clause, *telling a group of deaf people*, with the class as an example. Students discuss the remainder in pairs. Elicit answers.

Answers

telling a group of deaf people	*He told …*
doing the job in railway stations all over America	*He did …*
selling it to them in 1870	*He sold …*
experimenting with hundreds of materials	*He experimented …*
starting the motion picture industry	*The kinetograph started …*
holding 1,093 patents for inventions	*He held …*
covering mass communication	*The patents covered …*

B   Participle or gerund?

Do at least two or three sentences with the class as examples. Set the task for individual completion then students compare answers in pairs. However, if students are struggling, work through more examples with the whole class.

The word *forgetting* is therefore a gerund and students do not need to look for a missing subject.

(You could also replace *forgetting* with *forgetfulness* or *poor memory*.)

Closure
Students' books closed. Ask students to reproduce the tables from this lesson from memory. This can be done individually, in pairs, or elicit the information from the class and build up the tables on the board.

2.15 Applying new reading skills: The actress who invented wireless communication

Objectives

By the end of this lesson, students should be able to:
- use new reading sub-skills, grammar and vocabulary from the theme in order to make notes on a biographical text;
- demonstrate understanding of a biographical text about a technology inventor.

Introduction
Write the title of the lesson on the board. Ask for reactions. Students may say that it is surprising, which opens the door to discuss stereotyping. What do we normally think about actresses? And about people who invent things?

A   Activating ideas
Students discuss in pairs. Elicit ideas but do not confirm or correct – they will discover answers after reading the text.

Answers
No answers at this stage.

B   Preparing to read
After students have looked at the end-of-term test, focus on:
- which faculty has set the test;
- the meaning of *did not get the recognition she deserved*.

Set the task. Students make a list of research questions individually then compare ideas in pairs. Elicit answers and write the points on the board.

Answers
Possible questions:

What did Hedwig Kiesler do in the field of telecommunications?

How important were her inventions / achievements?

What recognition did she receive?

C   Understanding the text
1. Exploit the visual of Hedwig Kiesler and elicit a possible date the photo was taken (probably 1940s, judging from the hair style, make up and pose).

    You could focus on the topic sentences before you set the task if you wish. Elicit/highlight the fact that the article appears to be organized in a similar way to the Edison one, with biographical and chronological information. As in the previous text about Edison, there is not really an introductory paragraph in the accepted sense.

    Set the task. Monitor while students are making notes and give help where necessary.

2. Students compare notes in pairs. After a few minutes, elicit ideas.

Answers
Answers depend on students but here are some possibilities, based on the research questions above:

What did Hedwig Kiesler do in the field of telecommunications?	She invented a communication system …
How important were her inventions / achievements?	… which is the basis of modern wireless telecommunication.
What recognition did she receive?	She eventually got the Electronic Frontier Foundation prize + Inventor's Day celebrated on her birthday in Austria, Ger., and Switz.

D Showing comprehension

1. Students discuss in pairs. Elicit answers.

2. Remind students of the work they did on reacting to a text in Lesson 2.12. Ask students to find and underline Hedwig's opinions first. Then discuss with a partner if they agree or disagree with the opinions. Elicit some of their ideas.

3. Remind students about finding evidence in a text from Lesson 2.11. Set the task. Students complete individually then compare answers in pairs. Elicit answers.

Answers

1. How did these people feature in Hedwig's life?	
a. Fritz Mandl	She married him and learnt about weapons from being with him.
b. Hedy Lamarr	She used this name in her acting career.
c. Louis B. Meyer	He gave her her first job in a Hollywood movie.
d. George Antheil	She worked with him on her invention.
2. Which of Hedwig's opinions do you agree with?	Answers depend on students.

3. These statements about Hedwig are true or probably true. Find evidence in the article.	
a. She was very intelligent.	She understood about weapons and invented something which was years ahead of its time.
b. She had many abilities.	She was an inventor, an actress, a song-writer, a writer.
c. She didn't admire Hitler.	She *escaped* from Austria.
d. She lived to see her invention in use.	She died in 2000 and there were certainly devices in use by then.
e. She realized the importance of her invention.	She won the award so presumably recognized the importance.

E Understanding vocabulary and grammar in context

1. Set the task. Students find the words individually then discuss the meanings in pairs. Students should be very familiar with *invent, invention, inventor,* etc., but you could revise the part of speech for each form of the word.

2. Spend a minute or two revising participle verbs and how they are used to join sentences. If necessary, refer back to the grammar lesson, 2.13. Students complete individually then compare answers in pairs. Elicit answers using an electronic projection.

Answers

1. invention(s), inventor, invented, industrialist, intercept, intimacy, independence

2.

making her first full-length movie	Hedwig made ...
going to all his business meetings	Hedwig went ...
also giving her a new name	Meyer gave her a new name ...
working with	she worked with ...
using the title	they used ...
forming the basis	the system formed the basis ...
expiring before	the patent expired before ...

F Developing critical thinking

1. Remind students about the 'lessons for life' they learnt about in the Skills Check in Lesson 2.13.

   Divide the class into small groups to discuss the questions. After a few minutes, elicit ideas.

2. Revise the text, or information, about Edison's life from Lesson 2.12. Elicit one or two ideas from the class, then students continue in pairs. Elicit ideas and discuss with the class.

Answers

1. Answers depend on students, but possibly:

   Make your own luck – she escaped from Austria, presumably learnt a new language to be successful.

   Make the most of your abilities – don't get stuck into one situation.

   Women can achieve as much as men.

2. Obvious connections are:

   • both were inventors;

   • both did many different things in their lives;

   • both produced inventions in the field of communications;

- Edison invented the machine which started the motion picture industry; Hedwig was a motion picture actress;
- however, Hedwig invented something which people didn't want at the time.

Closure

Use Exercise F.

Knowledge quiz: Grammar auction game

Objectives

By the end of this lesson, students should be able to:
- review target grammar from the theme;
- discriminate between correct and incorrect forms;
- discuss and explain decisions in a group.

Methodology note

Grammar auctions are great fun, but with a large or noisy class you will need to make sure you keep the students under control!

You can use toy money from a Monopoly game, for example, or use coloured counters to represent different denominations. If you do not use toy money or counters, you will need to keep a careful check of how much money each group is spending. Use the board to keep track: draw columns with the name of each group at the top. Make a note of the amount for each successful bid and the remaining balance. If you like, you can ask a student to be your assistant to do this.

It's a good idea to use an electronic projection of the sentences, so that students can refer to them as the auction goes on.

You may find there are too many sentences for one lesson, so do half of them in this lesson and leave the others for another time.

The most important thing is for the teacher to keep a straight face throughout and not to give any indication as to which sentences are correct until the very end!

The activity could easily be adapted – for example, you can use other sentences, vocabulary definitions or even spellings.

Introduction

Explain the idea of a grammar auction. If you like, you can also spend a few minutes revising some vocabulary from the sentences for the auction.

Give students some phrases to use:

I am sure this sentence is correct.

I don't think this one is right.

Let's bid for this one.

Grammar auction

1. Divide the class into groups of five or six students. Name each group A, B, C, etc., or get students to come up with more imaginative team names!

2. In their groups, students decide which sentences are correct or incorrect. Monitor and help with vocabulary if necessary, but do not give any further help.

3. The teacher is the auctioneer. Make sure students are clear on the rules for bidding. Remind them that they should only bid for sentences which they think are correct. Ask students for bids for the first sentence. Make a note of which group wins the sentence. You can either tell the class at this point if the sentence was in fact correct or not, or leave this until the end.

4. Continue with the remaining sentences.

Closure

Announce the winning group. Give feedback by eliciting how to correct the incorrect sentences.

Answers

1. Humans have ~~being~~ able to communicate since they first learnt to speak.	*been*
2. As you probably know, the Sumerians invented writing thousands of years.	*... ago*
3. In Ancient Egypt, messages with couriers were not very fast or ~~not~~ very secure.	
4. New businesses should offer better products customers.	*... customers better products*
5. Successful companies supply customers ~~of~~ benefits.	*with*
6. Telegraph offices delivered telegrams to people's homes.	*correct*
7. The employment agency found ~~for~~ me a good job.	
8. Berners-Lee realized that every document needed an address, so you find it on another computer.	*so you could find it ...*
9. In the second phase of the Internet, it became a marketing tool.	*correct*
10. Although etailers use the virtual infrastructure of the Internet, they have to use the real infrastructure of postal delivery to get goods to customers.	*correct*
11. Statistics show that around 80 per cent of blind people in the world ~~is~~ unemployed.	*are*
12. Braille ~~played~~ with an awl when he hit his eye.	*was playing*
13. While Braille was studying at the institute, a soldier came to teach night writing.	*correct*
14. Give me a call when you pick up this message.	*correct*
15. In 1928, Alexander Fleming was studying a bacteria that ~~it~~ causes food poisoning.	
16. He left some slides overnight and, next morning, found that there was not bacteria on them.	*correct*
17. He realized that a mould ~~grew~~ on the slides.	*was growing* (or possibly, *had grown*)
18. Friedrich Kekule was studying the structure of carbon compounds when he ~~was having~~ a day-dream.	*had*
19. In his dream, he ~~was seeing~~ a snake with its own tail in its mouth.	*saw*
20. His dream led to the discovery that the structure of benzene was a ring of carbon atoms.	*correct*
21. I've forgotten what ~~was I~~ going to say.	*I was*
22. You were going to ~~telling~~ us about the accident.	*tell*
23. Edison saved a little boy from hit by a train.	*being hit*
24. He was selling newspapers when the boy fell onto the tracks.	*correct*
25. Jumping down, Edison pulled the boy back onto the platform.	*correct*
26. Inventing things ~~it~~ was Edison's first love.	
27. Edison's deafness was probably hereditary since his father also suffered from the disability.	*correct*
28. Hedwig Kiesler married Fritz Mandl who was an industrialist ~~produced~~ guns for Hitler.	*producing*
29. Hedy Lamarr's invention was years ahead ~~for~~ its time.	*of*
30. After firing a torpedo, sailors control ~~them~~ with radio signals.	*it*

Writing: Communication inventions

2

2.16 Vocabulary for writing: Types of competition

Objectives

By the end of this lesson, students should be able to:

- demonstrate understanding of and be able to spell target vocabulary for the section;
- demonstrate understanding of three types of competition as described by Smitalova and Sujan (1991).

Introduction

Check understanding of the word *competition* in its everyday meaning(s) as well as the business context.

Elicit other forms of the word:

compete (v)

competitive (adj)

competitor (n)

Students discuss the following questions in pairs or small groups:

Is competition a good or a bad thing for business?

Is it good to be a competitive person? Why (not)?

What do you think 'cut-throat' competition means?

A Developing critical thinking

Exploit the visuals and set the task. Students discuss in pairs or small groups. Elicit ideas. Students may also mention food chains or webs. Tell students in the next exercise they will find out the link between the three animals and marketing.

Answers

Answers depend on students but here are some ideas:

1. Rabbits and sheep are in competition for the grass, foxes eat rabbits but they do not eat sheep unless they are very young.
2. a. There will be less grass for the rabbits so the rabbit population will fall; perhaps the fox population will fall too.
   b. There will be less grass for the sheep. There will be more rabbits for the foxes to eat therefore the fox population will increase.
   c. There will be more rabbits and therefore less grass for the sheep.

B Understanding structure in context

Tell students to read the first paragraph only. Ask: *What is the link between the three animals and marketing?*

(*Three different types of competition:*

1. *sheep and rabbits are similar to two businesses competing for the same market;*
2. *a fox killing a rabbit is similar to one product 'killing' another;*
3. *sheep and foxes are similar to two products that do not compete with each other.*)

Then ask: *What is the rest of the article about?*

(*A theory by Smitalova and Sujan about competition in marketing.*)

Now set the task. Encourage students to read through the complete article first before writing answers. Students complete individually then compare answers in pairs. Monitor. Show the completed version of the text on an electronic projection so that students can check their answers. Ask students which ones they had problems with, and discuss.

Ask: *How many different types of competition are there, according to Smitalova and Sujan? (six)*

Why does the article only mention three? (because these are the most common)

Methodology note

Note the reference to customer *benefits* in the text. In the listening section of this theme, students learnt that three key principles of business are:

- benefits;
- personnel;
- infrastructure.

If students worked on the listening section, you can revise this point here. If not, you can simply mention that *customer benefits that meet customer wants* is a key business principle.

Answers

Sheep, rabbits and foxes in the marketplace

Some researchers in marketing compare interactions in the commercial market with interactions in the animal kingdom. Sometimes two or more products compete for the same market, like sheep and rabbits compete for grass. Sometimes one product kills another product, in the way that foxes eat rabbits. Sometimes two products live side by side, but do not compete, like sheep and foxes, which only very occasionally kill ⑦ In this article, we look at competitive interactions in the modern commercial market, according to Smitalova and Sujan (1991). New products usually enter an old market. For example, a new type of mobile phone, Product A, must compete in the existing mobile phone market, which already contains ⑧ So Product A needs to take market share from the existing products. In this situation, each product loses some sales to the others. Even the new product suffers because it loses potential sales, that is sales which are lost ③ According to the 1991 paper, this is Type 1 competition. In this type, each company has a similar marketing strategy which is simply ① If a company brands its existing product with different benefits, e.g., cheaper or faster, it may be able to recover lost sales.

Sometimes, a new product offers much better benefits than existing ones, which leads to ② This happened with CDs, which very quickly replaced ④ In the 1991 analysis, this is Type 5 competition. The cassette companies could not react to the competition, which led to ⑨ Sometimes, the manufacturers of competing products adopt a new marketing strategy. They say to customers, in effect, 'We do something different.' In other words, they rebrand their product as, for example, a luxury item rather than something which is used ⑤ As a result, the product does not compete anymore, which to some extent happened ⑩ CD sales declined rapidly after MP3 players became widely available. However, CDs were rebranded as quality items. They are still popular with some people because of their sound reproduction, which is ⑥ This, according to Smitalova and Sujan, is Type 6 competition. The two products compete at first, and then one moves into a different market.

The 1991 paper lists three other types of competition but these are the most common types – see Table 1.

Smitalova, K. and Sujan, S. (1991) *A Mathematical Treatment of Dynamical Models in Biological Science*, London: Prentice Hall.

Methodology note

This activity focuses on *which* clauses. These have not been formally presented in writing sections, but have been focused on in other skills. If you wish, ask students to find and copy into a table some or all of the *which* clauses to show the common structural patterns.

which	adverb (before verbs)		adverb (after *be*)	extra information
which	only very occasionally	kill		new-born lambs.
	already	contains		Products B, C, D, etc.
		are lost		because of the competition.
		is	simply	'We do the same thing, but better.'
		leads to		a rapid decline in sales of the old products.
	very quickly	replaced		cassettes in the recorded music market.
		led to		their disappearance from the market.
		is used		every day.
	to some extent	happened		with CDs and MP3 players.
		is	clearly	much better than MP3s.

There is further practice of *which* in Lesson 2.17.

C Transferring information to a table

Set the task and go over the examples. Students complete the table individually then compare answers. Show the completed table on an electronic projection so that students can compare with their own. Discuss any differences and/or problems.

Answers

Table 1: Some competition types

type	markets	effect on sales	strategy	example
1	both products in same market	each product takes sales from other	'we do the same thing but better'	different mobile phone companies
5	both products in same market	product A takes all or most of the sales of product B	'we do same thing *much* better'	CDs and cassettes
6	products in different markets	none – products do not compete	'we do something different'	CDs and MP3 players

D Understanding vocabulary in context

This activity could be done before Exercise B, if you prefer. If you are short of time, elicit answers in class and ask students to write sentences for homework.

Otherwise, ask students to find and identify the part of speech for each word then set the task for individual completion. Monitor. Ask some students to read out one or two of their sentences for students to compare with their own.

Target words:

market share (noun phrase)

existing (*adj*)

suffers (*v*)

potential (*adj*)

marketing strategy (noun phrase)

brands (*n*)

recover (*v*)

analysis (*n*)

react (*v*)

manufacturers (*n*)

rebrand (*v*)

declined (*v*)

Answers

Answers depend on students.

Closure

As a class discussion, or in pairs or groups, ask students to discuss:

Which products have 'eaten' others over the last 20 years?

Possible answers:

mobile phone and fixed line

e-mail and fax machine

DVD and video cassette

ipod and cassette / CD players

phone / e-mail and telegrams

computers and adding machines / tills / calculators

2.17 Real-time writing: The battle of the pens

Objectives

By the end of this lesson, students should:

- know more about the effect of competition on sales;
- demonstrate understanding of the organization of a discussion-type essay;
- have added information in order to complete an essay.

Note: This lesson contains exercises on editing and inserting information into the main text. Therefore it will probably be more successful if students can use computers for the writing activities.

Introduction

Revise the three most common types of competition as described by Smitalova and Sujan.

Use an electronic projection to show the table from the previous lesson (2.16, Exercise C) with blanked-out information. In pairs students try to remember all the missing information. Elicit answers and add the information to the table.

A Preparing to write

Students read the assignment handout. Students will probably know ballpoint pens as 'biros', which in fact is the name of the inventor, as students will learn during the lesson.

1. Students discuss possible topics in pairs. Do not elicit answers.

2. Students check their ideas by reading the introductory paragraph. Confirm the correct answers after students have finished reading.

Answers

Invention of the fountain pen
Invention of the ballpoint pen
Sales figures for both
Competitive relationships

B Previewing vocabulary

1. Link this activity to the previous one by saying that, as students know, this lesson is about pens; the fountain pen and the ballpoint pen. In this activity, they will learn the vocabulary connected with the two items. Set the task. Students complete individually then compare answers in pairs. Show completed diagrams on an electronic projection for students to self-check their answers.

2. Students discuss the verbs in pairs. Elicit answers. Don't worry too much at this stage if students are not completely certain of the meanings (especially *smudge*) as they will become clearer during the lesson.

Answers

1.

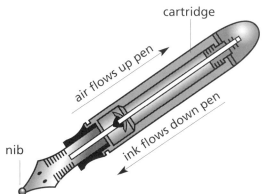

Figure 1: fountain pen

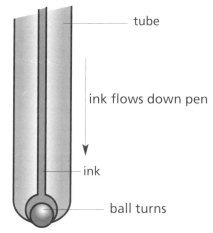

Figure 2: ballpoint pen

2. Possible answers:

refill – You used to refill fountain pens; now you change the cartridge.

leak – Fountain pens, and sometimes biros, leak – the ink comes out.

flow – Ink flows down the nib or the tube on to the paper.

smudge – Ink is spread accidentally on the page – by touching with the finger or hand, perhaps.

C Previewing grammar

1. Set the task. Decide if you want the students to write out the full sentences correctly, or simply to edit the mistakes. When students have finished, use an electronic projection to show the correct sentences so that students can compare and check their work. Highlight the following:

   • use of present simple to explain diagrams
   • *the* + *pen* / *cartridge* (because we are talking about the pen in the diagram / pens in general)
   • *ink, air* do not need *the* because they are uncountable nouns

2. Set the task. Students complete individually then compare answers in pairs. If students find it difficult, write some prompts on the board as a guide. Or, with students' pens down, elicit and write the sentences on the board. Then erase so that students use their memory to help them write the sentences. Use an electronic projection to show the correct answers.

Answers

1. As the nib moves across the paper, ink flows down the pen from the cartridge. At the same time, air flows up the pen.

2. As the ball moves across the paper, it picks up ink from the tube and leaves it on the paper.

D Gathering data

1. Ask students to focus on the notes only (do NOT read the essay or graph on the opposite page yet). Check understanding of some of the abbreviations and symbols used:

   W. = Waterman

   imp. = important

   Write the following questions on the board for students to ask and answer in pairs:

   Who invented each pen?

   What nationality was each inventor?

   What problems did each inventor have?

   When was each pen invented?

   Now focus students' attention on the graph. Ask questions:

   When were sales of fountain pens at their highest? And lowest?

   What about ballpoint pens?

   What happened to fountain pen sales in the late 1960s? (They fell steeply.)

   What about ballpoint pen sales? (They rose steeply / steadily.)

   Why were ballpoint pens so successful? (cheap, easy to use, convenient, etc.)

2. Explain that the *printed* information in the notes is already included in the model essay. The *handwritten* notes are 'extra' and need to be incorporated into the text. Students should read the essay, find the existing information and add the new. Obviously the new information should be written in full sentences or phrases. Use an electronic projection to give an example of how to add new information to the essay. Students complete individually. Monitor and give help where necessary. You can use an electronic projection to show the version of the essay with the extra information added so far at this point, or leave until after D3 or D4.

3. Set the task. Students complete individually.

4. At this point, if you have not already done so, you will need to revise the Smitalova and Sujan model from Lesson 2.16.

   Ask students: *Why did sales of the fountain pen increase in 1974? (It was rebranded as a luxury item – see table.)*

   You can use one of the following approaches for dealing with the writing of the final paragraph:

   - Students complete the paragraph individually or work on it in pairs.

   - Give prompts for each sentence of the paragraph. Students complete individually then compare answers in pairs.

   - Show the model paragraph, with students' pens down. Highlight some of the grammar, conjunctions and phrases used. Then remove the text. Students rewrite the paragraph from prompts or from memory.

   - Elicit the paragraph sentence by sentence and write on the board, once again with students' pens down. The paragraph you end up with may not be exactly the same as the model paragraph. Erase the text. Students rewrite from memory or from prompts.

   Monitor during the writing phases and give help where necessary.

Answers

Please see opposite page.

Closure

Give feedback on students' written work. Show the full version of the model answer if you have not already done so. Highlight any features you think are useful for your class to focus on, e.g.,

- tenses;

- conjunctions;

- organization of text;

- useful phrases.

Model answer:

What effect did the invention of the ballpoint pen have on sales of the fountain pen? Describe with reference to the analysis of competition by Smitalova and Sujan.

In this essay, I will describe the invention of the fountain pen and the ballpoint pen. I will then give details of the global sales of each product. Finally, I will analyze the competitive relationships between the two products, as explained by Smitalova and Sujan (1991).

The *first practical* fountain pen was invented by *an American called* Lewis Waterman, *improving on an existing product*. In 1883, Waterman, *who was an insurance salesman*, wanted a client to sign an important contract *and he bought a new fountain pen for the purpose*. However, as the client was signing, the pen leaked and destroyed the contract. Waterman set out to make a better pen, experimenting with many different designs *in his brother's workshop*. Finally, he produced a design which worked. *As the nib moves on the paper, the ink flows down the pen and air flows up the pen*. Waterman obtained a patent in 1884 *and began to make hand-made pens the following year*.

The ballpoint pen was invented by a *Hungarian called* Ladislo Biro. In the 1930s, he was working as a proofreader, checking manuscripts from writers and making corrections on them. He used a fountain pen *but he faced problems*. Firstly, the ink took a long time to dry so he often smudged his corrections. *Secondly, the pen did not hold very much ink, so he had to keep refilling it.* Biro decided to make a better pen, asking his brother Georg, *who was a chemist*, to make a thicker ink. However, the thicker ink did not flow through a normal nib so Biro decided to put a small ball in the tip of the pen, producing a pen which wrote reliably and did not leak. *As the pen moves along the paper, the ball turns, picks up ink and leaves it on the paper.* Biro obtained a patent in 1938 *and eventually began manufacturing the pens in 1943*.

Ballpoint pens became widely available in 1951. From then until 1956, sales of fountain pens continued to rise, reaching a peak of 45 million per annum in that year. Then, from 1956 to 1974, sales of fountain pens declined as sales of ballpoint pens rose. The manufacturers of fountain pens reacted by dropping the price of their product. However, their market share continued to go down. *By 1973, the average price of a fountain pen was 72 cents, but sales did not improve* and the product was facing extinction. Then, in 1973, sales of fountain pens began to recover. By 2007, they were back to 17 million per annum. In the same year, the sales of ballpoint pens reached more than 5 billion. *By 2011, the figure was 14 billion per annum.*

According to Smitalova and Sujan (1991), there are six possible types of competition between two products. We can identify three stages in the competition between fountain pens and ballpoint pens. During the first stage, from 1951 to 1956, the newly-invented ballpoint took sales away from fountain pens and vice versa. This was competition type 1. Each product suffered from the existence of the other product. In the second stage, *from about 1956 to 1974, the products moved into competition type 5. One product, the fountain pen, suffered while the other, the ballpoint, was not affected. Finally, in 1974, the manufacturers of fountain pens moved their product to competition type 6. They stopped competing with the ballpoint pen. They rebranded their product as a luxury item, raising the price and changing the marketing strategy. Nowadays, people use ballpoint pens for one kind of purpose and fountain pens for another. As a result, sales of fountain pens began to rise again, although they never reached the levels of the 1950s.*

Objectives

By the end of this lesson, students should be able to:

• use a variety of ways to add extra information to the basic SVO sentence pattern.

Introduction

Revise the information about the fountain pen and the ballpoint pen from the previous lesson (2.17) or go straight into Exercise A.

A Reviewing vocabulary and grammar

Set the task. Students complete individually then compare answers in pairs. Elicit answers, explaining why the use of a particular tense is correct in each case.

Answers

What effect *did* the invention of the ballpoint pen have on sales *of* the fountain pen?

In this essay, I *will* describe the invention *of* the fountain pen and the ballpoint pen. I *will then* give details of the global sales of *each* product. Finally, I will *analyze* the *competitive* relationships between *the* two products, *as is* explained by Smitalova and Sujan (1991).

B Identifying a key skill

1. Check students understand the task and ask them to discuss the questions in pairs. Do not elicit answers at this point.

2. Refer students to the Skills Check. Go through each example sentence and elicit the SVO basic sentence. Then use an electronic projection to elicit and highlight the answers for B1.

Optional activity

Students' books closed. Write the SVO sentences from the Skills Check on the board. Write the extra information separately. Ask students to rewrite the sentences adding the extra information.

Methodology note

Students should be very familiar by now, if they have followed the *Progressive Skills in English* course, with the basic SVO pattern of the English language. If not, explain that S = subject, V = verb and O = object. You can also refer them back to earlier grammar lessons with further explanations and practice of this pattern.

Answers

The basic SVO is *The biro was invented by Ladislo Biro.*

Extra information: *in 1938 / Hungarian / with the help of his brother Georg, who was a chemist*

C Practising the key skill

Check students understand the task and go over the example. If necessary, do another sentence (answer) with the class as a further example.

Set the task for individual completion or students can work in pairs. Elicit answers, preferably using an electronic projection. There may be more than one way of completing some of the sentences, so accept anything reasonable.

Answers

1. The first component of knowing a word is meaning, *which is the dictionary definition of the word.*

2. Two researchers *called Lloyd and Margaret Peterson* conducted an experiment into memory recall *in 1959.*

3. Acme Engineering is located in Causton, *which has a population of 10,000.*

4. The company, *which employs 14 people*, occupies premises of 5,000 square metres.

5. There is a major motorway close to Bellport, *which links the city to London.*

6. When heat energy reaches the Earth, some of it is absorbed, *or taken in*, by the land.

7. Some is reflected, *or sent back*, by the clouds.

8. Most scientists believe that gases in the air *such as carbon dioxide* cause the greenhouse effect.

9. According to Sachs and Gallup, *who conducted a survey of 150 countries in 1991*, economic performance is largely the result of geography.

10. The UK is a member of the EU, *which comprises 27 countries and represents a market of 500 million people.*

Closure

Display a version of the sentences from Exercise C (see below) and ask students to cross out words until the basic SVO/C is left. Obviously, the information which was added can go, but further cuts can be made.

Sentences for display:

1. The first component of knowing a word is meaning, which is the dictionary definition of the word.
2. Two researchers called Lloyd and Margaret Peterson conducted an experiment into memory recall in 1959.
3. Acme Engineering is located in Causton, which has a population of 10,000.
4. The company, which employs 14 people, occupies premises of 5,000 square metres.
5. There is a major motorway close to Bellport, which links the city to London.
6. When heat energy reaches the Earth, some of it is absorbed, or taken in, by the land.
7. Some is reflected, or sent back, by the clouds.
8. Most scientists believe that gases in the air such as carbon dioxide cause the greenhouse effect.
9. According to Sachs and Gallup, who conducted a survey of 150 countries in 1991, economic performance is largely the result of geography.
10. The UK is a member of the EU, which comprises 27 countries and represents a market of 500 million people.

   Model answer:

1. The ~~first~~ component of knowing ~~a word~~ is meaning, ~~which is the dictionary definition of the word.~~
2. ~~Two~~ researchers ~~called Lloyd and Margaret Peterson~~ conducted an experiment ~~into memory recall in 1959.~~
3. Acme Engineering is located ~~in Causton~~, ~~which has a population of 10,000.~~
4. The company, ~~which employs 14 people~~, occupies premises ~~of 5,000 square metres.~~
5. There is a ~~major~~ motorway close to Bellport, ~~which links the city to London.~~
6. When ~~heat~~ energy reaches the Earth, some ~~of it~~ is absorbed, ~~or taken in, by the land.~~
7. Some is reflected, ~~or sent back, by the clouds.~~

8. ~~Most~~ scientists believe that gases ~~in the air such as carbon dioxide~~ cause the ~~greenhouse~~ effect.
9. ~~According to Sachs and Gallup, who conducted a survey of 150 countries in 1991,~~ economic performance is ~~largely~~ the result ~~of geography.~~
10. The UK is a member ~~of the EU, which comprises 27 countries and represents a market of 500 million people.~~

2.19 Grammar for writing: Joining sentences with participles (1)

Objectives

By the end of this lesson, students should be able to:
- spell participles correctly;
- use participles to join clauses with the same subject.

Note: This lesson is a continuation of the grammar for joining sentences with participles. The activities in this lesson assume that students have worked on those from Lesson 2.13, Grammar for reading, in the previous section of this theme. If students did not do this lesson, start by studying the tables from Lesson 2.13. If there is time, do some of the items from the exercises.

Introduction

Ask students to look back at the essay in Lesson 2.17. Get them to find and underline all the verbs ending in ~*ing*. Ask them what the word is doing in the sentence in each case, but do not confirm or correct.

On the next page are the sentences with ~*ing* verbs. Focus students' attention on the italicized words. This usage is the focus of this lesson. Notes below show the other usages.

Waterman set out to make a better pen, *experimenting* with many different ideas.	in this lesson
In the 1930s, he was working as a proofreader, *checking* manuscripts from writers and *making* corrections on them.	*was working* = at a particular time in the past = past continuous other usage is dealt with in this lesson
Biro decided to make a better pen, *asking* his brother, Georg, to make a thicker ink.	in this lesson
However, the thicker ink did not flow through a normal nib so Biro decided to put a small ball in the tip of the pen, *producing* a pen which wrote reliably and did not leak.	in this lesson
From then until 1956, sales of fountain pens continued to rise, *reaching* a peak of 45 million per annum in that year.	in this lesson
The manufacturers of fountain pens reacted by dropping the price of their product.	*dropping* = gerund after a preposition
However, their market share continued to go down, and the product was facing extinction.	*was facing* = at a particular time in the past = past continuous

Grammar box 9

Revise the information about joining sentences with participles in the tables in Grammar for reading, Lesson 2.14 (see note above).

Set the task: students discuss the questions in pairs. Elicit answers. Elicit the two short sentences that have been joined:

Waterman set out to make a better pen.

Waterman experimented with many different ideas.

Show how the past simple form *experimented* has changed to *experimenting* in the second clause of the joined sentence. Explain that although the form has changed, the meaning of the verb is still past.

Elicit the subject, verb and object in each clause of the joined sentence. See table at the bottom of the page. Point out that we only need the subject, *Waterman*, once.

Answers

1. There are two clauses: when more than one finite verb appears in a single sentence, we have clauses – each clause has a finite verb.

2. *Waterman* is the subject of both clauses.

3. *set out, experimenting*

4. past simple, present participle

5. You need a comma after the first clause.

Methodology note

You must make sure that students understand that, despite its name, *present* participle, the participle here refers to the past because it takes its time from the time of the main verb in the sentences.

A Forming the present participle

1. Set the task. This should be very easy for the students but tell them to make sure they use accurate spelling. After a minute or two, write the answers on the board so that students can compare their spelling with the board.

2. Tell students they are going to learn some spelling rules for participles. Set the task. Students work in pairs. They may not be sure about some of the rules or be able to find examples for all of them. This does not matter. Elicit answers, making sure students can see the connection between the rules and the example participles.

sentence 1 / clause 1				sentence 2 / clause 2		
S	V	O		S	V	O
Waterman	set out to make	a better pen	.	He	experimented with	many different ideas.
			,	-	experimenting with	

Answers

1.

a. write	*writing*
b. put	putting
c. make	making
d. try	trying
e. speak	speaking
f. lie	lying
g. dry	drying
h. set	setting
i. begin	beginning
j. offer	offering
k. prefer	preferring
l. know	knowing

2.

a. take off final *e*	yes, *writing*, *making*
b. change final *ie* to *y*	yes, *lying* also *dying*
c. change *y* to *ie*	no, see *trying*
d. with one-syllable verbs, double the final consonant letter after a single vowel letter	*putting*, *setting* but not with *w*, *x* or *y* – *know*, *fix*, *buy*
e. with multi-syllable verbs, double the final consonant letter after a single vowel letter	only if the final syllable is stressed

B Joining with a present participle

Remind students that to join sentences with a participle, the subjects must be the same. Go over the two examples, showing that the second pair of sentences cannot be joined because the subjects are different. Students complete the remaining sentences individually, then compare answers in pairs. Monitor and make a note of any common errors.

Elicit correct answers or use an electronic projection to show the correct answers and leave students to self-check. Go over any sentences students had difficulty with. Highlight places where commas are used.

Answers

1. The pen leaked, destroying the contract.
2. (cannot be joined – different subjects)
3. Biro checked manuscripts, making corrections on them.
4. Acme Engineering makes car components, selling 75 per cent of its finished goods to customers in Britain.
5. A major motorway runs near Bellport, linking the city to London.
6. (cannot be joined – different subjects)
7. People can send a text message to Freedom Fone, getting a call back from the organization.

Closure

Dictate some of the words from the lesson, including a few participles.

2.20 Applying new writing skills: MP3 players and CDs

Objectives

By the end of this lesson, students should be able to:

• organize research notes and ideas in preparation for the written task;

• add extra information to a second draft;

• use target vocabulary, language, discourse structure from the section in order to produce a description essay about the effect of competition on CD sales.

Note: In this lesson, students will write the first draft of an essay based on only the research at the bottom of the page. Then, in order to practise the new sub-skills from this section, they will be given further information to add in a second draft. This is a slightly different approach from other writing lessons and will therefore need careful setting up.

Introduction

Discuss some ideas in answer to the question on the assignment handout: *What effect did the invention of the MP3 player have on sales of CDs?*

Further questions for discussion:

Do you have an MP3 player? How many songs are on it? How often do you download music?

Do you have a CD player? How often do you use it? How many CDs do you have? How often do you buy CDs?

A Thinking and organizing

Give students time to study all the information and if necessary to check back with Lesson 2.17.

Students complete the writing plan individually then compare notes in pairs. Elicit answers.

Answers

	Writing plan
Para 1	Introduction
Para 2	History of CD
Para 3	History of MP3
Para 4	Competition between CDs and MP3s
Para 5	Analysis of competition

B Writing and editing

1. Tell students they will write a first draft of the essay in this activity. Ask a few questions to check understanding of the three pieces of information at the bottom of the page. Monitor while students are writing their first draft and give help where necessary.

2. Follow the usual procedure.

3. Follow the usual procedure.

C Rewriting

1. Remind students about the work they did on adding extra information in Lesson 2.18 and joining sentences in Lesson 2.19. Explain that they need to write a second draft of the essay now, adding extra information. Do an example with the class if necessary.

2. The essay can be completed in class or for homework. If done in class, monitor and give help where necessary. Make a note of common errors. Give feedback on errors at a suitable point.

Answers

No model answer on this occasion as there are so many ways that students can use the information.

Closure

Present the following scenario for students to discuss in pairs or small groups:

You are the managing director of a chain of CD shops. Sales of CDs are falling steadily. How can you save the chain of shops from going out of business?

Students may suggest ideas such as:

Sell a wider range of items, such as computer games, MP3 players, etc.

Market CDs as:

- *good presents for birthdays, etc. (sell cards and offer a gift-wrap service);*
- *high quality sound – sell the best quality you can get;*
- *in-car music – at present, very few vehicles have in-car MP3 players, particularly older cars.*

Portfolio: Communication aids for the vision-impaired

Objectives

By the end of this lesson, students will have:

- worked independently to produce presentations in speech and/or writing about some ways modern technology assists people with visual impairments;
- used vocabulary, grammar, sub-skills and knowledge from the theme in integrated skills activities.

Note: The Portfolio, as usual, brings together all the main elements of the theme in one activity. In particular, in this lesson, you will have opportunities to revise the following information and concepts:

- from the listening section:
  two of the three key business principles – *benefits and infrastructure*
- from the speaking section:
  communication disabilities
- from the reading section:
  living with and overcoming disabilities
- from the writing section:
  how things work – expressing the present simple

However, if your students have not studied one or more of the sections, it will be enough to give a brief explanation of the relevant information.

Research, note-taking and other preparation may have to be set as assignments. The presentations can then be given at a later date in class.

Introduction

Briefly discuss some of the ways in which modern technology has helped people with disabilities.

A Activating ideas

Revise / teach the meaning of *vision-impaired*. Students discuss the questions in pairs. Monitor and give help if students are not sure of the correct vocabulary. Elicit ideas. Check understanding of the phrase *colour-blind* (but be aware that some students in the class are likely to be colour-blind and may be sensitive about it).

Answers

1. Login with cursor, eye test, colour-blindness test (people who are not colour-blind on this combination should see the number 26).

2. Possible points: can't find the correct key on the keyboard, can't see the cursor on the screen, can't read the text because it's too small or because the contrast is wrong for a colour-blind person. (Students may have other ideas.)

B Gathering and recording information

1. When students have finished reading the assignment handout, check understanding and clarify some of the points. Students choose which area they wish to research. Students should highlight it and mark up the important points in the assignment. Divide the class into groups according to the area they have chosen. Elicit possible headings for students' notes. Elicit phrases to type into a search engine in order to find relevant articles. This will usually be *accessibility for vision-impaired* or similar. Students can of course do research in their own language.

    Set a deadline or a time limit for the research to be completed. The research may have to be done as a home assignment. If the research is done in class, monitor and give help where necessary.

2. Divide the class into pairs or groups. Students make suggestions to improve each other's notes and make comments about interesting or unusual facts.

    Remind students about the work they have done in Lesson 1.8 about sharing research. Point out that this is a good opportunity to practise those phrases.

C Preparing a presentation

This activity will partly depend on whether students are working individually or in pairs or groups for the presentations. However, at this point students should practise saying sentences for the talk and prepare slides and/or visuals if possible. Monitor and give help where necessary. If they are working in pairs or groups, students should decide who is going to say what, and the order of each speaker.

D Listening to a presentation

Check students understand the task and remind them that the 'listening' students should make notes to answer the questions on the handout. Monitor while students are giving their presentations and check the 'listening' students are making notes.

When the presentations are finished you can:

- give feedback on the presentations;
- discuss answers to the questions – this can be done as a whole-class activity or students can discuss in small groups.

E Writing

Remind students to follow the usual procedure for writing activities. They have already researched most of the information, so now they should: organize notes, write a first draft, edit and then rewrite. During the editing stage, students can show their work to other students for feedback.

Once again this is a very flexible exercise. Choose one of the following procedures:

- You could allow individual students to choose one of the writing activities.

- You could select one activity yourself for the whole class to work on.

- Elicit ideas for how to approach each activity, then take a vote on which activity the class should work on.

- You could allocate different activities to individuals or groups according to their levels of ability (for example, the poster activity may be easier for students whose writing ability is less fluent).

- As usual the activity can be set in class or for homework.

Closure

Give feedback on oral or written presentations if you have not already done so. Discuss further some of the points raised in the lesson. Ask students how computers can make communication easier for people with other disabilities, e.g., partial paralysis.

Theme 3

Media and advertising

- The case against television

- The hidden persuaders

- Conventions in narrative fiction

- Reality TV – real or fiction?

Listening: The case against television

3.1 Vocabulary for listening: Violence in stories for children

Objectives

By the end of this lesson, students should be able to:

- recognize new vocabulary for the section in isolation and in context;
- develop understanding of new vocabulary for the section;
- demonstrate understanding of the function of fairy tales.

Note: It is important to move fairly quickly through the introduction activities and Exercise A. As long as students have a rough idea of the story of Little Red Riding Hood, that will be sufficient to understand the lecture extract.

Introduction

Tell students that in this lesson they are going to find out some information about *fairy tales / stories*. Check students understand this phrase. In fact, many of the stories do not actually have fairies in them but students will need to use this phrase for Internet research. Ask students to discuss some of the characteristics (conventions) of fairy tales. After a few minutes elicit ideas, for example:

- *traditional (origins often 200 or 300 years old, or even older)*
- *often have a moral – good against evil, etc.*
- *usually have a happy ending*
- *often read aloud but also spoken to children from memory*
- *many variations*
- *fantastic characters, including witches, giants, talking animals, hero or heroine, beautiful young girl, ugly wicked stepmother, etc.*
- *places: castles, palaces, woods, cottage*
- *characters are very simple and are either good or bad*
- *often have magic*
- *often violent*

(The above activity could also be done as **Closure** at the end of the lesson.)

Explain the aim is not to find out about children's stories from different cultures, but to learn about:

1. the purpose of the stories;
2. the reasons why modern publishers, teachers, parents, etc., are sometimes unhappy about telling traditional fairy stories to children.

A Activating knowledge

1. To ensure that students can answer the questions about the illustrations, briefly elicit / teach some of the vocabulary in the visuals: *wolf, cloak* or *cape, hood, wood* or *forest, basket, disguise, nightdress.*

   Students discuss the questions in pairs or small groups, but tell them it does not matter if they do not know the answers. Students do not have to tell the complete story of Little Red Riding Hood as this would probably take up far too much lesson time – a few sentences is enough. After a few minutes, elicit answers.

2. Students discuss the question in pairs. Elicit ideas.

Answers

1. The fairy tale is called *Little Red Riding Hood*. This is the name of the little girl in the story because she always wears a red cloak with a hood.

   Basic story: Little Red Riding Hood's grandmother is ill. LRRH's mother gives her a basket of food to take to her. She lives in a cottage in the woods. On the way to the cottage, LRRH meets a wolf disguised as a man. He asks her where she's going and LRRH tells him. The wolf runs quickly to the cottage. When he gets there he eats LRRH's grandmother and then dresses up in her nightdress. LRRH arrives at the cottage and is suspicious of the wolf.

   She says: What big ears you have, Grandmother!

   The wolf replies: All the better to hear you with!

   LRRH: What big eyes you have!

   Wolf: All the better to see you with!

   LRRH: What a big mouth you have!

   Wolf: All the better to eat you with!

   LRRH escapes at this point and brings a woodcutter back to the cottage. He cuts the wolf open and out pops Grandmother!

2. Answers depend on students.

B Understanding vocabulary in context

1. Give students time to read through the questions. Play 🎧 **3.1** and elicit answers.

2. Give students time to read the words in the list. Some words may have been discussed in the previous activity, B1, and students will probably know the meanings of some of the words anyway. Play 🎧 **3.2**. Students complete the task individually, then compare answers in pairs. Elicit answers and correct pronunciation if necessary (but you do not need to practise pronunciation extensively). Tell students not to worry about the words they are not sure about as the next activity (B3) will help.

3. Give students time to read the sentences and complete any answers they think they know.

4. Play 🎧 **3.3**. Elicit correct answers.

Answers

1. a. It has become less violent.

   b. Probably because society thinks it is wrong now to have stories about people and animals being hurt.

   c. Be careful of men.

   d. Children: Don't speak to strangers. / Adults: Supervise your children.

   e. Hansel and Gretel; Goldilocks

2. Answers depend on students.

3. See transcript for 🎧 **3.3** below.

Transcripts
🎧 3.1

Presenter: 3.1. Theme 3: Media and advertising
              Lesson 3.1. Vocabulary for listening: Violence
              in stories for children

              Exercise B1. Listen to part of a talk about
              fairy tales. Answer the questions.

Lecturer: So, as we have heard, psychologists say that
              young children need to experience fear. Fairy
              tales, like Little Red Riding Hood, bring fear into
              the child's life. Fairy tales were very violent,
              originally. People were eaten, burnt in an oven,
              poisoned. The violence is often against children
              or young people – think of Hansel and Gretel,
              and Goldilocks. People are aggressive. Even
              animals are aggressive – the Father Bear in the
              Goldilocks story deals with Goldilocks with
              aggression. In the 18th century, many fairy tales
              ended with the violent act. Initially, in the Little
              Red Riding Hood story, the weak people died –
              the girl and the old lady – and the wolf went
              free. Later, the girl is rescued but the old lady
              and the wolf die.

Nowadays, extreme violence is banned in fairy tales – people are not allowed to be hurt. Even animals are safe from harm. The violence and aggression have been toned down in recent years. So, in Little Red Riding Hood now, the old lady is put in a cupboard, the girl is rescued and the wolf escapes. Some people say that the message of this fairy tale has also changed, as a result. Originally, it was a story with an important message for young women. It said: *Be careful of men. They may not be what they seem to be.* They may be wolves. Now the message of the story for children is much simpler. It is just: *Don't speak to strangers.* Perhaps there is a message for adults, incidentally. *Always supervise your children when they are young. Do not send them off on their own to do chores for you.* Some people say this is dumbing down – in other words, taking a complex idea and making it so simple that it is not useful.

🎧 3.2

Presenter: 3.2. Exercise B2. Listen to part of the talk
              again. Number each word from the list on
              the right as you hear it.

              [REPEAT OF SCRIPT FROM 🎧 3.1]

🎧 3.3

Presenter: 3.3. Exercise B4. Listen and check your
              answers.

Lecturer: a. Young children need to experience fear.
              b. Fairy tales were very violent, originally.
              c. The violence is often against children or
                 young people.
              d. The Father Bear in the Goldilocks story deals
                 with Goldilocks with aggression.
              e. Initially, in the Little Red Riding Hood story,
                 the weak people died.
              f. Nowadays, extreme violence is banned in fairy
                 tales.
              g. The violence and aggression have been toned
                 down in recent years.
              h. Some people say that the message has
                 changed, as a result.
              i. Now the message of the story for children is:
                 Don't speak to strangers.
              j. Perhaps there is a message for adults too,
                 incidentally.
              k. *Always supervise your children when they are
                 young.*
              l. Some people say this is dumbing down – in
                 other words, taking a complex idea and making
                 it so simple that it is not useful.

Optional activity

- You could switch B2 and B3 around if you prefer.

- If you wish you can write the answers for B2 on the board in the wrong order (and perhaps add one or two extra words as 'distractors'). Either elicit the pronunciation of each word or pronounce each word yourself for the students in order to help with recognition when you play ◉ 3.2. Play ◉ 3.2; students number each word in the word list in the order they hear them.

C Developing critical thinking
Students discuss in pairs. Elicit ideas.

Closure
Choose one of the following:
- Use feedback from Exercise C.
- Use the 'characteristics' discussion from the introduction if you have not already done so.
- Ask students about the violence in other fairy·tales they may know, e.g., Hansel and Gretel, Goldilocks, Snow White.

3.2 Real-time listening: Violence on television

Objectives

By the end of this lesson, students should be able to:
- use existing skills to follow a media studies lecture about the effect of violence on television on young children;
- demonstrate understanding of the lecture through using PowerPoint slide headings for notes;
- recognize new vocabulary in context.

Introduction
Choose one of the following:
- Show (carefully selected!) visuals of violence, e.g., photos or TV news clips of demonstrations, football hooligans, bomb damage. Use them to revise vocabulary such as *violent, aggressive*, etc.
- Exploit the visuals on the right-hand page. Use them to revise vocabulary and/or to discuss the following questions:
  What types of programme are shown in the visuals?
  Which ones are suitable for children?
  Does it depend on the child's age / if there is an adult with them?

- Write the following adjectives on the board and elicit the noun forms:

adjectives	nouns
violent	*violence*
aggressive	*aggression*

Write the following gapped sentences on the board and elicit answers:
He's a very ... person. (violent / aggressive)
I didn't enjoy the movie. It was too ... (violent)
Explain that *violent / violence* can be used for people or things. *Aggressive / aggression* is generally only used for people and animals.

A Activating ideas
1. Set the task. Play ◉ 3.4; pause after each statement and elicit who is probably speaking. There may be more than one answer. Elicit and check understanding of phrases such as *getting under my feet*.
2. Refer students to the transcript. In pairs, students discuss their reaction to each statement. Elicit ideas.
3. Refer students to the handout about the lecture. Students briefly discuss the question and their opinion or answer. Students should make a note – this will be returned to at the end of the lesson (students may change their minds after listening).

Transcript
◉ 3.4

Presenter:	3.4. Lesson 3.2. Real-time listening: Violence on television
	Exercise A1. Listen to statements about television from adults and children.
Teacher:	Violent television produces violent children. I see it every day at school.
Dad:	When the kids are watching television, they're not getting under my feet.
Mum:	I think my children learn a lot from television.
Child:	I'm not allowed to watch the best programmes. All my friends are.
Adult:	Some children are just naturally violent. I have to deal with it on a daily basis, in the centre of town.
Teenager:	Obviously, children know the difference between TV and the real world.

Answers
1. teacher; dad; mum; child; adult; teenager
2./3. Answers depend on students.

It is not the normal practice of this course to ask students to guess who is speaking, as this has no parallel with normal listening in real life. However, in this case, the idea is that students use the opinion to identify the speaker, to some extent, and therefore become aware of the different opinions.

B Preparing for a lecture

Set the task and go over the examples. Point out that these are all examples of *signpost language*, phrases that guide and help you to understand the lecture. Students discuss the remaining phrases in pairs. Elicit ideas. Make sure students understand the following phrases in particular: *counter-arguments, issue, incidentally*. Elicit ideas but do not confirm now; leave until after students have listened to the complete lecture.

Answers

These are the answers but **elicit after Exercise C**.

Let's start with some facts.	facts
Nobody can deny that ...	opinion of speaker
According to research ...	person, place, time, details of research
Just think about that for a minute.	reminder of a key point
Now, I accept that ...	accepting another point of view – this is the key skill for Lesson 3.3
Clearly, ...	an obvious point
So that's the first point.	the speaker will now move on to the second point
It's true that ...	accepting another point of view
What should we do about this issue?	suggestions for a solution
We must consider the counter-arguments.	the counter-arguments
Some people say ...	a point of view – probably not the speaker's
Incidentally, ...	an extra piece of information

C Understanding a lecture

Give students time to read through the slides. Check the vocabulary in particular: *behaviour, stranger, unsupervised*. Tell students to listen for the correct pronunciation of the three names on the final slide (avoid pronouncing the names for them in advance in order to encourage independence).

Check students understand there are two parts to the task:

- adding notes;
- notes of arguments against each point.

Set the task using one of the following options.

- More able classes and to encourage more independence: Play DVD 3.A all the way through without pauses. Students make notes individually then compare answers in pairs.
- Less able classes: Play DVD 3.A. Pause after each section. Elicit answers for the relevant PowerPoint slide before moving on to the next section.
- All classes: Show the completed slides using an electronic projection for students to check their answers. Talk through any variations students may have and discuss if they are acceptable.

At a suitable point either replay all of DVD 3.A or any extracts students had difficulty with. Students can follow the transcript at the same time, if you wish. You can also ask students to check their ideas for Exercise B (above) at this point.

1. This is revision of the sub-skill from Theme 2 listening: using slide headings to take notes. However, even if your students didn't do that sub-skill, this is a fairly straightforward activity.

2. The introduction to the lecture is not particularly clear. This is deliberate, in order to introduce students to lecturers who do not always deliver completely coherent lectures! You can play the lecture on DVD 3.A, pause after the introduction and discuss what she says before continuing with the rest of the lecture, if you wish.

Answers

Model answers:

Violent TV and young children

○ children watch a lot of television
                        - US 28 h.p.w.
○ children see a lot of TV violence
                - 8,000 murders by 12
○ children become violent
        - predict violent response from
                        adults by 8   **1**

BUT children have to experience
fear, e.g., fairy tales = violent

- but told by parents, who
  mediate = tone down
- not unvarying, alone
- TV <u>shows</u> violence, fairy
  tales talk about it

Violent TV and young children

○ children are visual learners

○ children 'model' behaviour

- copy hero/superhero who uses
  violence
- children model in playground,
  use later to resolve conflict   **2**

BUT not show people dying
        but message = 'violence has no victim'

- teaching kids bad behaviour
- stop children watching certain progs

Violent TV and young children

○ TV is like a stranger in
  your house

○ children shouldn't watch
  unsupervised

    - not use as childminder   **3**

BUT if children don't see progs = not able to socialize at
    school
    people want to conform, more powerful in ch. and teens
    but ch. who spend more than ave. on violent TV = less
    popular! + more likely to commit agg. acts / get into
    trouble
        H. and M. (94)

Transcript

🌐 3.5 DVD 3.A

Lecturer: Today, we're going to look at television – well, not look at it, actually. Talk about it. Looking at it could be a problem, as we shall see. In particular, we are going to talk about children's television – at least, children's television in the United States and Britain. Television is a powerful force. I think everybody agrees about that. But a powerful force for what? Let's see what people say. Now, I'm not here to tell you what I think, but it will probably become obvious as we go along.

Let's start with some facts. Firstly, children all over the world watch a lot of television. For example, in the US, a young child spends an average of 28 hours per week watching television. That's four hours a day, of course, which is a very high proportion of their free time. The second fact is this. Nobody can deny that children see a lot of violence on television. Researchers have calculated that a 12-year-old American child has witnessed over 8,000 fictional murders on television, and probably quite a few real ones as well, on news programmes. Yes, that's right. Eight *thousand*. According to research by Huesmann and others, reported in the book *Aggressive Behavior* – it's on your reading list – children become so used to seeing aggression as a response to conflict, that they *predict* that an adult will respond to conflict with aggression. Oh, I should say, that is by the age of eight. Just think about that for a minute. Parents keep telling them not to fight, and saying things like 'Violence solves nothing,' and then the children go and watch television and see that it is the only solution in most cases.

In fact, children's programmes are actually more violent than adult programmes. That's quite astonishing, isn't it? Research suggests there is five times more violence during children's programmes than during prime-time TV. So children watch a lot of television and see a lot of violence. This brings us to a simple proposition. Watching TV violence is a bad thing and has bad consequences. If children see a lot of violence, you expect them to behave violently, don't you? But is that proposition actually correct? Now, I accept that children have to experience fear, and learn how to deal with it. Clearly, this is why we have fairy tales, which are full of murders, kidnappings and violent acts. I agree that these stories are just as violent as kids' TV programmes. Just think of Hansel and Gretel, who push the witch into the bread oven and kill her. Or Little Red Riding Hood, in which Grandma is eaten by the wolf and then cut from his stomach, in some versions of the story at least. Fairy tales are very old and presumably perform a useful function in education, so this is a very powerful argument.

But we must take into account several factors. Firstly, children are visual learners, and television is a visual medium. It actually *shows* the violence, whereas fairy tales *talk* about it. There is a big difference. Also, most fairy tales are initially told to a child by a parent. So the parent has a chance to mediate the experience for the child – in other words, to tone it down, if they think the child will not be able to cope with the events as written. Actually, that's an interesting

word – *mediate*. It comes from *media*, of course. The parent is the medium by which the child receives the story, and he or she can change the story if necessary. But television is a very different medium. It is unvarying. It does not change to suit the viewer, even if the viewer is eight years old, alone with the television in the sitting room and terrified.

OK. So, that's the first point. Children are visual learners. Secondly, and it is related to the first point, children model behaviour of other people – in other words, they copy what they see. They copy the hero in a television programme, and the problem is, that hero often uses violence to resolve a conflict. Comic book superheroes do not have great intellectual powers. You have probably noticed. Superman is not a PhD in Psychology. The X Men do not have degrees in Philosophy or Economics. They do not solve a problem by thinking about it. They use violence – in many cases, ridiculous, excessive violence, like throwing a train at a villain or creating an earthquake. Children model behaviour – it is what they do – and they model some of their behaviour in the playground on their cartoon heroes and superheroes. When they are older, they use real violence to resolve conflict.

Television executives, of course, deny being responsible for real-life violence in society. Sometimes they say: *It's true that there is violence in some of our children's programmes. But we do not show people* dying *in our programmes for children.* It's true. In most cases, when a baddie is hit by a train or blown up by a booby-trap mine, he flies through the air, and then gets up and runs away. But what message does this send to the child, watching on his or her own? This says: *Violence solves the problem, but it does not really hurt the victim.* In many ways, this is worse than showing the real effects of being hit by a train. Just moving away from our subject for a moment, a well-known news reporter in Britain, Kate Adie, recently made the point that if news programmes showed the real effect of war, rather than distant shots of bombs falling and exploding, people would see the true horror of war and be much more careful about starting conflicts. Anyway, what was I talking about? Ah, yes. Violence causes pain – but you wouldn't know it from watching children's television.

What should we do about this issue? Dr Jerome Singer is a professor of Psychology at Yale University. He makes a very interesting point. He says that television is like a stranger in your house. This stranger is teaching your kids all sorts of bad behaviour while you are in another room, or distracted by daily chores. Would you invite a real stranger into your house and leave them alone with your children? Perhaps you should have the same attitude to unsupervised television. Actually, he also makes the point that this stranger in the corner is trying to sell your kids junk food and high-sugar-content sweets while you are not there, but that's another matter entirely. So I guess what Dr Singer is saying is that we should stop children watching certain types of programme, and we should not use television as an unpaid childminder. We shouldn't let young children watch TV unsupervised. I have two children and I remember letting them watch television on their own when they were very young. I really regret doing that now, but anyway ...

Of course, we must consider the counter-arguments. Some people say if we don't allow our children to watch popular TV programmes – by popular, I mean violent – then they will not be able to socialize with their friends. Again, it's a powerful argument. We know that generally people want to conform, and this impulse is even more powerful in children and teenagers. But actually, research shows that children who spend a higher than average amount of time watching violent programmes are *less* popular than other children. This finding again comes from the Huesmann research – it's on your handout. Huesmann and Miller (1994). Incidentally, they also found that those same children – the ones who watch a higher than average amount of violent programmes – are more likely to commit aggressive acts. They are also more likely to get into trouble with the authorities.

OK, finally ... We've talked of ideas and theories. What about the research studies? You can look up all the details for yourselves, but, basically, the vast majority concluded that violent television promotes violence. In fact, according to the American Medical Association, out of 3,000 studies, 2,888 come to this conclusion. For example, Berkovitz carried out a laboratory experiment with university students in 1969. The study involved participants watching violent films to see if they acted more violently than the control group. Parke et. al. worked with young offenders in an institution. That was in 1977. The result was similar to Berkovitz. Williams did a study with 6- to 11-year-olds in Canada. This is an interesting study, actually. The researcher looked at the impact of television on a community which did not have television before. The introduction of TV led to a significant increase in aggression in the community. And on the other side? Well, nothing really, although there is one well-known study – this was Charlton et. al., 1999 – which looked at the introduction of television on the island of St Helena. There, results were not significant. There was no increase in aggression.

OK. So that's it from me. Over to you. Any questions?

D Developing critical thinking

Set the two questions for discussion in pairs or small groups. After a few minutes, elicit ideas. Help students with forming questions correctly. Of course, you won't have definite answers for most of the questions raised by the students, but if there is time some possible answers can be discussed.

Answers

2. Answers depend on students but here are some possible questions:

How can we stop TV-makers showing violent programmes?

Why doesn't the government do something about this problem?

What is the most vulnerable (important) age for children for violence on TV?

When is it acceptable for children to watch TV unsupervised?

How can we educate parents about this problem / issue?

Closure

Use Exercise D.

3.3 Learning new listening skills: The concessive argument structure

Objectives

By the end of this lesson, students should be able to:
- recognize intrusive vowel sounds /ɪ/, /w/, /j/;
- recognize phrases for concession in a lecture.

Introduction

Write the title of the lesson on the board:

The concessive argument structure

Say that this title appears to be difficult to understand but if you break it down into each word, it becomes easy.

Revise or elicit the meaning of the word *concessive*; teaching the other forms of the word may also help with the meaning: *concede (v), concession (n) concessive (adj)*.

Elicit synonyms for *concede* and write on the board:

concede = admit, accept, allow

Elicit the antonyms and add to the board:

opposites = refuse, deny, disagree

Now look at the word *argument*. Remind students that in academic English, this simply means your opinion or point of view.

Finally, *structure*. In a lecture context, this means how the lecture is organized, or the order in which information is presented.

So in this lesson, students will learn about how lecturers accept different opinions from their own.

A Recognizing sounds in context

1. Tell students that when we speak in English, we often join words together. In writing, words are separate; in speaking, they are not. Write the following on the board:

   There's an orange car on the road outside. (writing)

   "There'sanorange caron theroadoutside." (speaking)

   Ask students when we join words and elicit the answer (when there are two vowel sounds or a vowel and a consonant together). Find examples in the sentence on the board.

   Tell students we sometimes even add sounds when there are two vowel sounds together. Refer students to the Pronunciation Check. Give them time to read the information, then check understanding. Ask students to listen to ⊕ **3.6** and mark the sentences for the extra sound. Play ⊕ **3.6**, then elicit answers.

2. Set the task. Students complete individually then compare answers in pairs.

3. Play ⊕ **3.9**. Students compare answers once again. Then show answers on an electronic projection (i.e., the sentences marked up with the intrusive sounds) for students to self-check.

Answers

1. a twelve-year-/r/-old; Grandma /r/ is eaten; used to /w/ aggression; you /w/ expect the /j/ average child; be /j/ able to cope

2./3.

a. But we must take into *account* several factors.	into – /w/ – account
b. Fairy tales are *initially* told to children.	are – /r/ – initially
c. Young children *see* a lot of violence.	see – /j/ – a
d. Of course, there *are* counter-*arguments*.	there – /r/ – are; counter – /r/ – arguments
e. There was no *increase* in aggression.	no – /w/ – increase
f. They often have trouble with the *authorities*.	the – /j/ – authorities

Transcripts
⊕ 3.6

Presenter: 3.6. Lesson 3.3. Learning new listening skills: The concessive argument structure

Exercise A3. Listen and check your ideas.

Lecturer:	a. But we must take into account several factors.
	b. Fairy tales are initially told to a child by a parent.
	c. Nobody can deny that young children see a lot of violence.
	d. Of course, there are counter-arguments.
	e. There was no increase in aggression.
	f. These children are more likely to get into trouble with the authorities.

⊕ 3.9

Presenter: 3.9. Pronunciation Check. Listen to the pronunciation of each phrase. Can you hear the extra sound?

Voice: a twelve-year-old
              Grandma is eaten
              used to aggression
              you expect the average child
              be able to cope

Language note

Some students may say that the letter *r* is already there in, e.g., *year-old*. The letter is, but the sound is not. It only appears if a vowel sound follows.

B Identifying a new skill

Make sure students understand the following, which shows the usage of the various key words here:

Speakers may concede*, by giving the* counter-argument*.*

These are concessions*.*

The whole argument structure is concessive*.*

1. Give students time to read the slide. Play ⊕ **3.7**, then elicit the answer.

2. Refer students to the Skills Check. Work through the check with the students, then play ⊕ **3.10**. Feed back, eliciting some of the expressions.

Transcripts
⊕ 3.7

Presenter: 3.7. Exercise B1. Listen to part of the lecture again. How does the lecturer introduce the counter-argument?

Lecturer: *[fade in]* Watching TV violence is a bad thing and has bad consequences. If children see a lot of violence, you expect them to behave violently, don't you? But is that proposition actually correct?

Now, I accept that children have to experience fear, and learn how to deal with it. Clearly, this is why we have fairy tales, which are full of murders, kidnappings and violent acts. I agree that these stories are just as violent as kids' TV programmes. Just think of Hansel and Gretel, who push the witch into the bread oven and kill her. Or Little Red Riding Hood, in which Grandma is eaten by the wolf and then cut from his stomach, in some versions of the story at least. Fairy tales are very old and presumably perform a useful function in education, so this is a very powerful argument.

But we must take into account several factors. *[fade out]*

🌐 3.10

Presenter: **3.10. Skills Check. Listen. What other words and phrases can you use in place of each word in italics?**

Voice: I accept that children have to experience fear.
It's true that children have to learn how to deal with fear.
Clearly, this is why we have fairy tales.
I agree that these stories are just as violent as kids' TV programmes.
It's a fact that Hansel and Gretel are violent.
Obviously there is violence in Little Red Riding Hood.
I realize that fairy tales perform a useful function in education.
Of course, this is a very powerful argument.

Answers
Skills Check

I	*accept*	that …
	agree	
	realize	
	understand	

It is	*true*	that …
	a fact	
	correct	

Clearly, …
Of course, …
Obviously, …

C   Practising the new skill

Check students understand the task. Give them time to read the three lecture topics. In pairs or small groups, students can quickly brainstorm as much information as they can about each topic.

Remind students to listen out for the phrases from the Skills Check. Play 🌐 **3.8**. Pause after

each lecture (or play the three extracts straight through) and elicit answers.
Replay 🌐 **3.8** with students following the transcript.

Optional activities

Choose one of the following:

- Once you have elicited the answers, replay each extract. Pause after each concessionary sentence and elicit the exact phrases the lecturer used.
- Refer students to the transcript. Students find and underline the concessive statements.

Answers

Lecture	Speaker's argument	Counter-arguments
1	friendship = face to face	online serves a purpose
		nice to exchange info around the world
		benefit from virtual relationships
2	you must balance your work and your social life	have to keep up with work
		not get behind with projects
		work = 1st a lot of time
3	be careful about green decisions – things are complex	can make big difference with small changes
		turn down thermo, etc.
		save energy

Transcript
🌐 3.8

Presenter: **3.8. Exercise C. Listen to sections from three lectures. What's the lecturer's argument in each case? What counter-arguments does he or she concede?**

Lecture 1: Friendship in the 21st century

Lecturer 1:   I'm here today to talk about friendship. Clearly, it's as old as human life on Earth. But there is evidence that it is changing for this new generation. Friendship used to mean meeting people, talking to them face to face, doing things together. Surely that is real friendship? Well, not according to some sociologists. They say that virtual friends are as real as physical friends. In fact, research in America suggests that some children do not distinguish between the two kinds of friend at all. I am not sure that this is a good thing. In my view, having friends involves meeting people face to face.

OK. I accept that online acquaintances serve a purpose. I agree that it is very nice to be able to exchange information with people in different towns, even different countries and continents. Obviously, a lot of people get a lot of benefit from virtual relationships. But people who you only meet online are not friends in the true sense of the word. Friendship means meeting people, talking to them face to face, doing things together.

Lecture 2: Time management

Lecturer 2: We've talked a lot about time management today. Let me end with a key point. It's called the Work–Life Balance. It means simply, you must balance your work and your social life. Now, of course, you have to keep up-to-date with your current work. Clearly, you must not get behind with projects and assignments because it is so much harder to manage your time if you have previous work to do as well as current. And I accept that work comes first a lot of the time.

But you must make sure you save enough of your time and your energy for your friends and your family. If you don't, you will find one day you have a wonderful job and a terrible life.

Lecture 3: Going green

Lecturer 3: I want to finish talking about environmental projects with a personal plea. Be careful about making so-called green decisions. The environment is a very complex place. It's absolutely true that we can make a big difference if every one of us makes a number of small changes to the way we live. It's right to turn down the thermostat on your central heating. Of course, you should save energy by switching off lights when you leave a room, and not leaving appliances on standby for hours and hours. But sometimes things are more complex than they seem. For example, growing tomatoes in Spain and shipping them to the UK uses less energy than growing them in greenhouses in the UK. So buying local produce may not be the greenest option.

Closure
Choose one of the following:
- Replay 🎧 **3.8** and have students follow the transcript if you have not already done so.
- Discuss some of the points made in the lecture extracts. For example, you could write some questions on the board for students to discuss in small groups:

  Do you switch off lights when you leave a room?

  How many items do you leave on stand-by?

  Are you prepared to make small changes to save energy?

Objectives

By the end of this lesson, students should be able to:
- recognize sentence patterns for verbs + gerund;
- recognize sentence patterns for verbs followed by *that*;
- use the above sentence patterns to predict information when listening.

Introduction
Write the first verb from each group below on the board. Ask students what the two groups are. Keep adding verbs until students start to tell you, but do not confirm or correct. As students begin to work it out, say a verb and then ask students which list it should go in.

Group 1

promise	
intend	
refuse	
have /hæf/	
forget	to do
remember	
need	
prefer	
remember	
try	
offer	

Group 2

want	
expect	
tell	
ask	
remind	someone to do
force	
persuade	
encourage	
teach	
help	
allow	

Point out that today you are going to look at two more common patterns with verbs.

Grammar box 10

Students study the information in the tables. Ask students to explain the main difference between the sentences in the two tables. (In the second table, the verbs need an object between the verb and the gerund, just as in Group 2 in the introduction with verbs that take the infinitive.)

A Hearing the gerund

Set the task and play the example. Then play ⊕ **3.12**; pause after each item but do not elicit answers. When all the items have been listened to, students complete individually then compare answers in pairs. Replay ⊕ **3.12** and pause after each sentence to elicit the answer.

Optional activity

After completion of Exercise A, say each sentence from the transcript, pausing after the first verb for students to complete:

T: *I remember ...*

Ss: *... using the television as a childminder.*

Answers

2 doing
   making
7 producing
5 seeing
4 stopping
6 telling
1 using
3 watching
   writing

Transcript
⊕ 3.12

Presenter:	3.12. Exercise A. Listen to some sentences. Number the gerund you hear in each case.
Voice 1:	I remember using the television as a childminder.
Voice 2:	I regret doing it now.
Voice 3:	Have you finished reading the article about TV habits?
Voice 4:	How can we prevent children watching too much television?
Voice 5:	My lecturer suggested controlling TV for young children.
Voice 6:	Dr Singer proposed stopping young children from watching TV on their own.
Voice 7:	Do you mind your children seeing violence on TV?
Voice 8:	I really resent people telling me how to bring up my children.
Voice 9:	The TV executive defended producing violent cartoons for children.

Grammar box 11

Give students time to study the table and the information. Check students understand the function of each verb in the first clause of the sentences. Tell students these verbs with *that* help them to predict the rest of the sentence.

B Recognizing the function

Give students time to read through the list of functions. Give explanations or examples where necessary, keeping in mind the activity itself will help with clarification.

Play ⊕ **3.14**. Students complete individually then compare answers in pairs. Elicit answers; there may be debate about some of them, for example, 6 and 8. Replay any sentences students had difficulty with.

Answers

7 conceding
1 predicting
5 reporting speech
8 expressing possibility
3 expressing statistical fact
6 expressing strong possibility
2 expressing assumption
4 expressing observable fact
9 expressing old idea

Transcript
⊕ 3.14

Presenter:	3.14. Exercise B. Listen to some sentences. Number the function of the sentence in each case.
Voice:	1. I predict that the problem will get worse. 2. I imagine that you have all seen violent children's programmes. 3. Researchers have calculated that children spend more time watching television than attending school. 4. Newton demonstrated that each force has an equal and opposite force. 5. Dr Singer said that TV should be treated as a stranger. 6. Doctors suspect that the disease started in chickens. 7. I recognize that many programmes are educational. 8. The results suggested that there was a serious problem. 9. People thought that the Earth was flat.

C Predicting the next word – gerund or *that*

Set the task and go over the example. Point out that they are going to hear the same verbs from earlier in the lesson, but they must immediately say what they expect to hear next. Play ⦿ **3.15**, then elicit answers.

Answers

1. that	9. that
2. gerund	10. gerund
3. that	11. that
4. that	12. gerund
5. gerund	13. that
6. that	14. gerund
7. gerund	15. that
8. that	16. that

Transcript
⦿ 3.15

Presenter: 3.15. Exercise C. Listen to the start of some sentences. What do you expect to hear next – gerund or *that*?

Voices: 1. I realize …
                 2. The lecturer dislikes …
                 3. Doctors suspect …
                 4. Dr Singer said …
                 5. Have you finished …?
                 6. People thought …
                 7. How can we prevent children …?
                 8. I imagine …
                 9. I predict …
                 10. Do you mind your children …?
                 11. Researchers have calculated …
                 12. I really resent people …
                 13. I recognize …
                 14. I remember …
                 15. Newton demonstrated …
                 16. The results suggested …

Closure
This time, tell the students they are going to hear verbs from five patterns. Write them on the board, with numbers.

1. + *to do*
2. + object + *to do*
3. + gerund
4. + object + gerund
5. + *that*

Students must shout the number(s) as you say the verb. Some verbs can be followed by two or more structures, sometimes with a change in meaning, e.g., *remember to do vs remember doing*. Accept an alternative answer if students can justify it.

3.5 Applying new listening skills: Let's ban television!

Objectives

By the end of this lesson, students should be able to:
- identify concessionary points in a lecture;
- make notes of arguments and counter-arguments plus supporting evidence from a lecture;
- apply new knowledge to self.

Introduction
Revise some of the points discussed and factual information from the lecture which students watched in Lesson 3.2, *Does violent TV produce violent children?*

Explain that in this lesson students will hear the argument for banning TV completely.

1	2	3	4	5
to do	object + *to do*	gerund	object + gerund	*that*
want	want	are used to	spend	accept
have /hæf/	expect	keep	stop	suggest
intend	tell	deny	recall	predict
refuse	ask	stop	remember	believe
forget	remind	remember		understand
prefer	force	hate		
try	persuade			
offer	encourage			
	help			
	allow			

A Reviewing vocabulary

Remind students that they need to listen for concession – counter-arguments – when a speaker is giving a point of view. Students are going to hear the stressed syllable from some of the words that introduce concessions, and they must try to identify the full word or phrase in each case.

Play the first one as an example, then set for individual work and play the rest of ⊘ **3.16**.

Elicit the answers, getting students to pronounce each word or phrase with the correct stress.

Answers

2 a'gree

6 'clearly

8 co'rrect

7 ho'wever

5 'obviously

1 of 'course

3 'realize

4 under'stand

Transcript
⊘ 3.16

Presenter:	3.16. Lesson 3.5. Applying new listening skills: Let's ban television!
	Exercise A. Listen to the stressed syllables from each word or phrase. Number the correct word in each case.
Voice:	1. cour
	2. gree
	3. rea
	4. stand
	5. ob
	6. clear
	7. ev
	8. rect

B Activating ideas

Ask students to study the assignment. Check understanding:

Who is giving the talk?

What's his job?

What's the talk about?

What does elimination *mean?*

Set the question; students discuss in pairs. Keep students on track – they should try to consider the case for banning TV only. They will have the opportunity later to put the other side, why TV should not be banned. Elicit ideas but do not confirm or correct.

Answers

Answers depend on students.

C Preparing for a lecture

Students read all the information. Remind students about *concession* and *counter-arguments* and refer to earlier lessons in this section if necessary. In pairs, students discuss the question about the ways of organizing notes for the talk. Elicit answers.

Answers

A concessionary lecture will contain arguments for and against each point. Therefore the best note format is probably the *table* with plus and minus columns.

D Following a lecture

1. This activity checks that students have the correct idea about how to organize their notes. Play DVD 3.B, pausing after the introduction if you wish, to check understanding. Also students could make some predictions at this point about the rest of the lecture. Play the first part of the lecture. Students make notes individually then compare answers. You could do Exercise E at this point, **before** giving students the correct model notes. Use an electronic projection to show the model notes (below). Discuss any differences or problems students had with their own notes and replay DVD 3.B if necessary.

2. Students should now be well prepared to take notes for the rest of the lecture. Play DVD 3.C then repeat the procedure for D1. Discuss some of the phrases the lecturer uses in order to show concession.

Answers

Model notes (see opposite).

Transcripts
⊘ 3.17 DVD 3.B

Guest speaker:	I'm here today to ask for the impossible. I want you all to stop watching television. I'm not asking this because television programmes are bad, although that is a small part of the argument. I'm asking this because *television* is bad – bad for physical health, bad for mental health, bad for critical thinking and bad for good government. Where does this idea come

argument	points	concessions
one	TV = simple messages	TV = world in living room
	repeated again and again	occas. inspires children
	small section with recap	progs about other countries, nat. world, etc.
	900 hrs at school, 1,500 hrs watching TV	
	BUT information v. limited	
	information turned into slogans	
	20,000 ads per year watched in US; know brands but can't name trees, etc.	
	TV stops us going out to see the world	
	75 per cent US not have passport	
	progs = dumbing down	
two	small number control TV	democratic countries = regulators
	6 comps. = nearly all TV in US and round the world	laws to ensure competition, balance
	BUT TV comps. more powerful	
	people don't look for balance	
three	effect on minds and bodies	golden age – TV brought fam. together, people watched same progs. discussed them, etc.
	mind:	
	medium = addictive	
	sedative, channel hop, keep watching, no control, angry if can't have it	
	watching = solitary	
	BUT now many TVs, people watch diff progs in diff rooms	
	66% in US = 3 or more TVs	
	1,680 mins watch TV, 3.5 mins talk to kids	
	54% US prefer TV to dad	
four	TV = no democ. potential	ordinary people on TV, opinions
	BUT cannot make progs	community TV
	BUT nobody watches	

from? In 1978, a man called Jerry Mander wrote a book called *Four Arguments for the Elimination of Television*. Let's have a look at each of those arguments.

OK. So … What's the first argument against television? It is that television reduces everything to very simple messages. Television is not a good medium for complex ideas. You need books for that. So instead, it gives us very simple ideas and repeats them again and again. There is only a small number of programmes which convey real information about the world, but those programmes are split into many small sections, with adverts in between, and, at the beginning of each section, the previous sections are quickly recapped. This is not the way to put across complex ideas. AC Nielsen, an organization that monitors television output, estimates that an average American child spends 900 hours a year at school, and 1,500 hours watching television. Incidentally, most of the statistics in this lecture are from Nielsen. Check them out on Nielsen.com. Anyway, I accept that television brings the world into your living room. I realize that television occasionally inspires children to

learn something, do something, become something. And of course there are programmes about other countries, about the natural world and about history. But in most cases, the information is very limited.

Mander said that information is turned into repeated slogans. For example, foreign countries are 'exotic or scary'. Animals are 'furry or scary'. History is a few very famous events, particularly the Second World War, because they have lots of film of that historic event. On average, people in the United States see 20,000 adverts a year. People can recognize thousands of brands but only a few countries on the world map, a few plants, birds and trees. Television brings the world into our living rooms but it stops us having the time to go out and experience it for ourselves. Americans may think they know about the world because they have seen it on TV, but researchers have calculated that more than 75 per cent of Americans don't even own a passport. In the end, most people only know the world that is brought to them by television. Celebrity and sport, mindless quiz shows and reality shows – which aren't anything like reality

– are more important than the environment and politics. Of course, people need to relax, and television is a wonderful way of unwinding. But the quality of programmes is getting worse and worse – we call it 'dumbing down' in Britain … and we'll come back to this later.

🌐 3.18 DVD 3.C

Guest speaker: The second argument concerns the control of television. The medium reaches millions of people in each country, but only a small number of people in each case – perhaps only one person – controls *all* of the broadcast output. That puts him – it is always a man – in the position of a dictator. According to freepress.net, six companies own nearly all of the television output in the United States. In many cases, they own the complete production and broadcasting process. The same six companies own large percentages of television output in many other countries in the Western world. Obviously, democratic countries have regulators who try to control the controllers. I agree that there are often laws which try to ensure some competition and some balance in news reporting. But television companies and their owners have become more powerful in many cases than the lawmakers in many countries. People watch Fox News – they don't look for news balance on a number of different channels.

The third argument involves the effect of television upon individual minds and bodies. Firstly, minds. The medium is addictive. According to psychologists, there are a number of measures of *dependency*, a mental health condition. If a person reports that two of the measures apply to them for a particular item – like drugs, or alcohol, or gambling – they are suffering from a clinical condition. They are dependent on the item. Just think about your use of television. Firstly, do you use it as a sedative – to wind down at the end of a stressful day? Secondly, do you use it indiscriminately – do you plan your viewing, or do you channel hop? Do you find there is nothing interesting on, but keep watching anyway? Thirdly, do you have control over your viewing – or do you just do it? The fourth measure is: Do you feel angry that you have wasted your time watching it? Number 5: Are you upset if you are not able to watch – because the hotel room doesn't have a television, for example? As I said, if you answered yes to two or more of those, you are dependent on television.

The problem is, watching television is largely a solitary occupation. I realize that, in a golden age, television brought the family together in one room. Everyone sat down together and watched the same programme, discussed it, laughed or cried at it. My parents recall watching television with their parents. But now many houses have three, four, five televisions. For example, 66 per cent of Americans have three or more televisions so, in most cases, each person is on their own, in a different room, watching a different, probably pointless programme. Research shows that, on average, parents spend 1,680 minutes a week watching television, and 3.5 minutes having meaningful conversations with their children. This must have an effect on

the relationship between children and parents. And research indicates that it does. In a recent survey, 54 per cent of American children said they preferred the TV to their father.

So that's minds. What about bodies? Well, during their 28 hours per week watching television, children see a lot of adverts. Let's just think about one horrific statistic. In an average four-hour programme of Saturday morning cartoons, American children see 200 adverts for junk food. Is this why 11 per cent of 6- to 17-year-olds in the US are now obese – double the figure 20 years ago? Oh, and of course, all those beautiful people on television have a bad effect too. Seventy-five per cent of American women think that they are too fat. Of course, if they only eat the junk food from the adverts, it might be true.

Finally, the fourth argument claims that television has no *democratic* potential. In other words, it is impossible for ordinary people to become involved. Obviously, ordinary people are *on* television all the time now, as participants, in silly quiz shows and talent contests. Of course, they are asked their opinions in the street, and they are interviewed after a crime or an accident. But they cannot contribute to the *making* of programmes, or the decision-making on the content of programmes. I realize that there is community television in some areas but this is a tiny, tiny percentage of the total output, which nobody watches anyway.

OK. So, to sum up … Mander had four arguments against television. He believed that television reduces everything to simple messages in a complex world. He thought that a small number of people controlled television and therefore could control people. He said that television was bad for minds and bad for bodies. And finally, he maintained that television was bad for democracy – the people could not get involved. What do you think? Thank you very much.

Optional activity

- When all the notes have been checked, ask students to restate each point in their own words. This could be done as a group activity:

  S1: makes point

  S2: makes counter-point

  S3: makes additional point

- Probably the lectures are becoming too long to listen to a second or third time in one lesson. However, at least play an extract with students following the transcript, or set this as a home assignment.

E Checking understanding of facts

1. Set the task, preferably before giving the model answers for Exercise D. In this way students can further check their notes are correct before feedback. Students complete individually then compare answers in pairs.

2. Play ⊕ **3.19**, then elicit answers. Discuss with the class any information they found surprising and ask students to consider if the information is similar or very different in their own country/ies.

Transcript and Answers
⊕ 3.19

Presenter:	3.19. Exercise E2. Listen and check.
Voice:	a. AC Neilsen estimates that an American child spend 900 hours a year at school and 1,500 hours watching television.
	b. On average, people in the States see 20,000 adverts a year.
	c. Researchers have calculated that 75 per cent of Americans don't own a passport.
	d. Only six companies own the majority of television output in the United States, and in large parts of the Western world.
	e. Sixty-six per cent of Americans have three or more televisions.
	f. On average, an American parent spends 1,680 minutes a week watching television and 3.5 minutes having a meaningful conversation with their children.
	g. In a survey, 54 per cent of American children said they preferred television to their father.
	h. In the average four-hour programme of Saturday morning cartoons, children see 200 adverts for junk food.
	i. In the US, 11 per cent of 7- to 17-year-olds are obese.
	j. Seventy-five per cent of American women believe they are too fat.

F Developing critical thinking

Students discuss in pairs or small groups. Elicit ideas.

Answers

Answers depend on students.

Closure
Use one of the following:

- Use the discussion in Exercise F.
- Students spend a few minutes studying the transcript. Ask them to find examples of target vocabulary and grammar from this discussion.
- Set a home assignment. Students write a short essay on whether TV should be banned or not.

Speaking: The hidden persuaders

3.6 Vocabulary for speaking: Selling a product

Objectives

By the end of this lesson, students should be able to:
- demonstrate understanding of meanings of target vocabulary;
- pronounce target vocabulary in isolation and in context;
- use knowledge about selling products in order to complete tasks.

Introduction

Write the title of the lesson on the board. Elicit that the phrase can have two meanings:

1. selling items in a shop, etc.;
2. advertising or marketing an item or service.

Find out how many students in the class are interested in working in advertising or marketing or have studied or worked in this area.

A   Understanding new vocabulary in context

1. Give students a minute to read the assignment handout. Students discuss the question in pairs. Elicit ideas.
2. Go over the advertising brief and check understanding. However, don't go into too much detail about the meanings of new vocabulary as this should become clear when students listen to the conversation.

   Set the task and play ⊚ **3.20**. Students complete information individually, then compare answers again. Elicit answers, preferably using an electronic projection to display the completed table. Check understanding of the following:

   endorsement vs slogan

   competition, audience – these words can have different meanings in different contexts

Answers

Advertising Brief: 343/79	
Product	the ZX Drive
Main selling point	value for money
Personality	Elliot Horn
Endorsement	*'I always drive Hitoshi'*
Slogan	*'Get in the open air … fast!'*
Audience	young men, sporty women
Special offer	Buy before 31ˢᵗ July and we pay the VAT.
Competition	test drive to enter; win a brand new ZX
Release date	1ˢᵗ August

Transcript
⊚ 3.20

Presenter:	3.20. Lesson 3.6. Vocabulary for speaking: Selling a product
	Exercise A2. Listen to a group of students doing the first choice in the assignment. Complete the advertising brief.
Student A:	So, how are we going to sell this product?
Student B:	We could use a star from the movies … or is that too expensive?
Student C:	Yes, I think so. What about a TV personality, someone from sports television – Elliot Horn?
Student A:	OK. Do we ask him to present the advert?
Student B:	No, just to endorse it. You know, he says: 'I always drive Hitoshi,' or something like that.
Student C:	Is that the slogan?
Student B:	No, that's the endorsement. We need something catchy for the slogan.
Student C:	Yes, something that will appeal to the target market. What is the audience, by the way?
Student B:	It says here: 'Young men' … and sporty women, perhaps?
Student A:	OK. It's a convertible, right? And a sports car? So what about 'Get in the open air … fast!'
Student B:	Maybe … Shall we have a special offer of some sort?
Student A:	There's one already. The manufacturers will pay the VAT if you order before 31ˢᵗ July.
Student C:	That's fantastic!
Student A:	But we should have a competition, too. Maybe get them to register for a test drive to enter, then we get their names and e-mail addresses for future marketing.
Student C:	What's the prize? A brand new ZX, I suppose.
Student B:	The car will be released on 1ˢᵗ August, by the way.
Student C:	So what's the main selling point?
Student B:	Value for money. It's a sports car but they say it does 80 kilometres to the litre.
Student A:	They're exaggerating, of course.
Student B:	Yes, but the tests show that it's very economical.

B Recognizing vowel sounds and stress within words

1. Students work in pairs, helping each other with the pronunciation of new words. Make sure students tick words with the same vowel sounds.
2. Play ⏺ **3.21** so that students can check their answers and hear the words correctly pronounced. Note that students will only hear words with the same vowel sounds, not every word in each row. Elicit answers and practise pronunciation.

Optional activity

Ask students to give you a full sentence for some of the target vocabulary in the activity. This can be their own ideas completely, or students can recall the way the word was used in the conversation.

Answers

See table below.

Transcript
⏺ 3.21

Presenter:	3.21. Exercise B2. Listen and check.
Voice:	a. endorse, order, audience, August, money, sports
	b. appeal, release, litre, competition, e-mail, need
	c. slogan, show, product, offer, suppose, economical
	d. exaggerate, catchy, value, star, personality, address

Methodology note

Notice that, on this occasion, the stressed syllable of the words is not indicated. So students must first work out the stressed syllable in each case, and then decide if it matches the target sound. Make sure students are stressing the correct syllable in each case.

C Practising new vocabulary in context

1. Before you set the task, and with the conversation extracts covered, elicit from students some of the different forms of making suggestions. Write a list on the board:

   Let's … (go to a movie tonight)

   How about … (having spaghetti bolognese this evening)?

   Shall we … (ask about this at our next tutorial)?

   Set the task, pointing out that each extract is either making a suggestion or asking for a suggestion. Students complete individually, then compare answers in pairs.
2. Play ⏺ **3.22** so that students can check their answers.
3. Replay ⏺ **3.22**. Pause after each line for repetition and drilling. Focus on intonation used for suggestions and stressed words. Students practise in pairs. Monitor and give feedback.

Transcript and Answers
⏺ 3.22

Presenter:	3.22. Exercise C2. Listen and check.
Voice A:	So, how are we going to sell this product?
Voice B:	We could use a star from the movies.
Voice A:	Do we ask him to present the advert?
Voice B:	No, just to endorse it.
Voice A:	We need something catchy for the slogan.
Voice B:	Yes, something that will appeal to the target market.
Voice A:	Shall we have a special offer of some sort?
Voice B:	There's one already.
Voice A:	We should have a competition, too.
Voice B:	What's the prize?
Voice A:	What's the main selling point?
Voice B:	I think it's 'value for money'.

D Producing new vocabulary

Divide the class into groups of four or five. Set the task. In Exercise A, students studied an advertising brief for a car. Explain that, this time, students will look at marketing a brand of yoghurt. Briefly discuss any TV or magazine yoghurt adverts students may know. Ask a few questions:

a. end**or**se	order ✓	audience ✓	August ✓	money	sports ✓
b. app**ea**l	release ✓	litre ✓	competition	e-mail ✓	need ✓
c. sl**o**gan	show ✓	product	offer	suppose ✓	economical
d. ex**a**ggerate	catchy ✓	value ✓	star	personality ✓	address

- *What are the brands called?* (e.g., Activia, Ski, Muller, etc.)
- *What are their slogans?* (e.g., 'lead a Muller life' – a pun on 'lead a fuller life')
- *What's the main selling point?* (good for health, low-fat, low price, etc.)

Refer students back to the advertising brief for the car, but ask them now to apply this to the yoghurt. Explain there are no 'correct' answers; students must design their own competition, slogan, etc. They must complete all the headings, as in Exercise A. Remind students to use some of the suggestion phrases from Exercise C.

Monitor and make notes of common errors during the activity. Ask one or two people to report on their group's discussions. The class decides which group had the best slogan, competition, etc.

Give feedback on common errors you noted during the group work.

Closure
Use your feedback for Exercise D.

3.7 Real-time speaking: Jingles, tag lines, punchlines and other tricks

Objectives

By the end of this lesson, students should be able to:
- use existing skills to give a marketing presentation about advertising methods;
- pronounce target vocabulary in context.

Introduction
Use Exercise A.

A Reviewing vocabulary

Check students remember the meanings of the verbs, perhaps by eliciting the sentences they were used in in the previous lesson.

Set the task. Students work in pairs. Elicit answers, practising pronunciation as you do so.

Point out the following patterns:
- In two-syllable verbs, the stress is usually on the second syllable.

- In nouns ending ~*tion* / ~*ment* the stress is on the penultimate syllable.

Optional activity

Students make a new sentence from each of the nouns or verbs.

Answers

verbs	nouns
'advertise	ad / 'advert / ad'vertisement / 'advertiser
a'ppeal	a'ppeal
com'pete	compe'tition / com'petitor
en'dorse	en'dorsement
ex'aggerate	exagge'ration
pre'sent	presen'tation
pro'duce	pro'duct(ion) / pro'ducer
re'lease	re'lease
'register	regi'stration

B Gathering information

1. Students study the assignment information. Ask: *What is the purpose of the assignment?* Elicit that it is to learn about advertising methods. Focus on the question in the handout: *How do advertisers try to sell their products?* Ask students to discuss the question in pairs. Monitor and make a note of any mispronounced words. Elicit ideas, but don't worry if students did not have many suggestions. Tell students they will be able to answer the question more fully by the end of the lesson. Practise correct pronunciation of any mispronounced words you noticed when monitoring.

2. Refer students to the table and ask them to study it for a minute. Ask questions to check understanding:

   What is the first method?

   What do ads with this method contain?

   Why does this sort of ad work?

   What current TV ads use this method?

   Now set the task. Students should suggest ideas for:
   - *people / actors in the ad*
   - *setting, clothes*
   - *graphics*

- *props*
- *what the actors (or voiceover) should say*

Students discuss in pairs. With certain classes, you could also ask students to act out the ad. Monitor and give help where necessary with pronunciation or phrases students might need. After a few minutes, ask students to describe their ad to the rest of the class. Practise correct pronunciation of any mispronounced words you noticed when monitoring.

3. Check students understand the task. Play 🎧 **3.23**. Students complete notes individually, then compare answers in pairs. Show the completed notes using an electronic projection. Go over any answers students had difficulty with.

Answers

Answers depend on students, but here are some ideas:

1. competitions, offers, exaggerations, endorsements

2. people; beautiful (famous?) woman, maybe a handsome man too

   setting; glamorous location, e.g., penthouse, by the sea, on a yacht, etc.

3. See table below.

Transcript
🎧 3.23

Presenter:	3.23. Lesson 3.7. Real-time speaking: Jingles, tag lines, punchlines and other tricks
	Exercise B3. Listen to some students and complete the information about the second method.
Tutor:	So, I hope you all know about TV ads now, and you've got lots of examples of TV advertising to share with us today. Joe, could you start us off with one of the methods?
Joe:	OK. Um. I worked with Sarah on this research. We chose BOGOF, which is Buy One, Get One Free.
Student 1:	Sorry. I don't understand.
Joe:	What I'm saying is, it's the first letter of each one. Buy One, Get One Free.
Student 1:	Oh, I see.
Joe:	So, customers who buy a packet of biscuits, for example, get another packet free.
Sarah:	The advertisers who use this method usually start with the normal price, then give the offer. They emphasize the value for money.
Student 2:	So what's the science behind this method?
Sarah:	I'm just coming to that. Apparently, people don't want cheap products. They want expensive products cheaply.
Student 3:	Did you find any good examples of BOGOF on TV at the moment? We couldn't find any.
Sarah:	Sorry. Can I deal with that in a second? So they pay full price for one product and get the second one free. And, um … ah. I've forgotten what I was going to say.
Student 3:	You were going to give us examples on TV at the moment.
Sarah:	Oh, yes. There's an advert which uses BOGOF for Superbuy supermarkets. Twenty products which are basics are in the promotion, like bread and milk.
Student 2:	But going back to Joe's example for a minute. BOGOF is the same as half price, isn't it? You get two of them for the price of one. So why don't they just say 'Get these biscuits half price'?
Joe:	Yes, I wondered about that too. So I did a bit more research. Psychologists say that the word *free* is very powerful, more powerful than *half price*.
Student 3:	So BOGOF sells more products than 'Get one half price'?
Joe:	Yes. Apparently, it does.
Student 3:	That's weird.
Joe:	Not really. As Sarah has said, people want something for nothing.
Student 3:	I still think they're the same thing.
Joe:	Perhaps you're right.
Student 4:	I don't know if this is relevant, but I read that supermarkets use BOGOF with products that are loss-leaders.
Tutor:	Yes, that's a good point.
Student 5:	Sorry I'm late!
Tutor:	That's OK. We're talking about adverts that use BOGOF. We've discussed customers who want free things. The example is the Superbuys campaign.
Student 5:	Right. Has anyone mentioned that BOGOF products are often loss-leaders?
Tutor:	Yes, we've just talked about that.
Joe:	That's it, really.
Sarah:	Yes. That's what we found.

method	contents of the ad	science behind the ad	current TV example
the big lie (= not true)	exaggerated claims, e.g., this product will make you richer, more attractive, etc.	people believe big promises more than little ones; people believe what they want to believe	Youth4U – anti-ageing cream
BOGOF (= buy one, get one free)	*the ad usually gives the normal price, then the offer; it emphasizes value for money*	*people want an expensive product cheaply; people want something for nothing*	*Superbuys = 20 products on offer*

C Studying a model

1. Explain that this is a revision activity. Set the task and check understanding of one or two functions, for example: *clarify, explain that you are lost*. Leave the other functions for students to work out for themselves in the activity. Students complete individually, then compare answers in pairs. Elicit answers.

   Deal with any new words or phrases from the transcript, for example, *loss-leader*.

2. Remind students it is important to use polite intonation patterns for these expressions, as well as the correct word stress. Play ◉ **3.24**; pause after each phrase for students to repeat chorally and individually.

3. Set the task, reminding students again to use polite intonation patterns. Divide the class into pairs. Students practise the extracts. Monitor and give feedback. Practise any phrases students had difficulty pronouncing correctly.

Answers

1.

introduce the presentation	I worked with *Sarah on this research.*
	We chose *BOGOF, which means Buy One, Get One Free.*
ask for clarification	Sorry. I don't understand. *Is it a word?*
	I still don't get what you mean.
clarify	What I'm saying is, *it's the first letter of each word. Buy One, Get One Free.*
introduce research	Apparently, *people don't want cheap products.*
ask people to wait	I'm just coming to that.
	Sorry. Can I deal with that in a second?
explain that you are lost	And, um, ah. I've forgotten what I was going to say.
help the speaker	You were going to *give us examples on TV at the moment.*

Transcript

◉ 3.24

Presenter:	**3.24. Exercise C2. Listen to some expressions from the extracts. Repeat, copying the stress and intonation.**
Voice:	I worked with Sarah on this research. We chose BOGOF, which means Buy One, Get One Free. Sorry. I don't understand. Is it a word? I still don't get what you mean. What I'm saying is, it's the first letter of each word. Buy One, Get One Free. Apparently, people don't want cheap products. I'm just coming to that. Sorry. Can I deal with that in a second? And, um, ah. I've forgotten what I was going to say. You were going to give us examples on TV at the moment.

D Producing a model

1. There are six different advertising methods for students to choose from on pages 164–176. Students can choose a method for research (but make sure there are a reasonable number of students for each method). Divide the class into pairs of students who have chosen the same method. Set the task. If students cannot think of a current TV ad for their method, they can select a classic one, or a radio, Internet or even magazine ad.

2. Re-divide the class into small groups. Make sure all the students in each group have researched different methods. Remind students to try to use some of the expressions from Exercise C where appropriate. Students take turns to explain their ad methods. Monitor and give feedback.

Closure

Use your feedback for Exercise D.

Everyday English: Complaining

Objectives

By the end of this lesson, students should be able to:

• use appropriate language and phonology for complaining in everyday situations;

• select the correct tense for use in key phrases.

Methodology note

With a more able class, you can deal with problems with complaints – i.e., when the complaint is not dealt with satisfactorily. This can be highlighted in Exercise B – asking students to give alternative endings. Then in the role play at the end, they can decide whether to end with the complaint resolved or not.

Introduction

Write the title of the lesson on the board and elicit the meaning. Elicit the noun – *complaint*. Also teach the phrase *make a complaint*. Write the following phrases on the board and ask students to discuss a possible context for each:

- *She's always complaining.* (About a person, possibly a friend, who is very negative.)

- *The food was terrible, but I didn't like to complain.* (About a meal in a restaurant, or someone's house. The person did not say anything about the bad food.)

- *I've no complaints about the weather, but the hotel was very noisy.* (On return from a holiday – good weather, but the hotel wasn't so good.)

A Activating ideas

Exploit the visuals with the conversations covered. Elicit one or two possible complaints for each situation, for example:

- Hotel room: too noisy, dirty, small, etc.
- Restaurant: cold food, food not what you ordered, etc.
- Shop: item broken or damaged, clothes too small / big, etc.

Elicit possible resolutions, but do not correct or confirm as several are dealt with in the next exercise.

B Studying the models

1. Set the task and ask students to cover the conversations. Play 🎧 **3.25**. Students discuss answers. Elicit answers.

2. Set the task. Point out to students that the missing words are all verbs, so this is good revision of tenses. Students should try to complete some of the missing words before you play 🎧 **3.25** again. Highlight the grammar of some sentences and discuss the tenses used.

3. Play 🎧 **3.25** a third time. Pause after each sentence (or select sentences) for repetition. Make sure students use polite intonation for both complaining and responding to the complaint. Then students practise in pairs. Monitor and make a note of errors. Give feedback.

Transcript
🎧 3.25

Presenter:	**3.25. Everyday English: Complaining**
	Exercise B1. Listen to the conversations below. What is the complaint in each case?
	Conversation 1.
Voice A:	Hello, reception.
Voice B:	Ah, yes. This is Mr Adams in Room 306.
Voice A:	Yes, Mr Adams. How may I help you?
Voice B:	I'm afraid the air conditioning isn't working.
Voice A:	Have you tried changing the thermostat?
Voice B:	Yes, it doesn't do anything.
Voice A:	OK. I'll send someone up.
Voice B:	Thank you.
Presenter:	**Conversation 2.**
Voice A:	Excuse me.
Voice B:	Yes, madam?
Voice A:	Well, we have been waiting a long time.
Voice B:	I'm sorry. Have you ordered yet?
Voice A:	No. We haven't even seen the menu.
Voice B:	OK. Sorry. Here you are.
Voice A:	Thanks.
Voice B:	Now, what would you like?
Voice A:	Could you give us a moment?
Voice B:	Oh, yes. Sorry.
Presenter:	**Conversation 3.**
Voice A:	Can I help you?
Voice B:	I hope so. I bought this iPod here a few days ago but when I unpacked it, I found the screen was cracked. See?
Voice A:	Oh, dear. OK, so have you got the receipt?
Voice B:	No, I think I've lost it.
Voice A:	Well, we can replace the item but I'm afraid we can't give you a refund.
Voice B:	No, that's OK. I want a replacement.
Voice A:	Right. Just give me a moment. I'll get the form.
Voice B:	Thanks.

Methodology note

1. Exercises B2 and B3: In these activities, you can either deal with one conversation at a time, give feedback, practise, then move on to the next conversation. Or you can play all three conversations one after the other, then do all the feedback and practice.

2. Conversation 3: In the UK, you can nearly always get a refund for an item bought in a shop if you return it within 28 days for

whatever reason, as long as you have the receipt. After that date, or without a receipt, the shop will replace the item or give you a voucher to spend in the shop.

However, in many countries, unlike the UK, you cannot return an item simply because you decide you don't like it or if it doesn't fit.

3. Many people say that the British don't like complaining. This is perhaps reflected in the intonation used for complaining. It tends to be quite tentative. British people will often begin a complaint with *I'm sorry, but / I'm afraid that …* Therefore, it is important for students to understand the importance of remaining polite when they complain.

C Building vocabulary

Set the task and go over the first one as an example (e.g., *I'm sorry, but my bed is broken*). Students discuss each problem in pairs. After a few minutes, elicit ideas. Ask students to make each problem into a complaint, for example:

I bought these yoghurts this morning, but they're past their sell-by date.

The towels are missing from my bathroom.

Drill some of the sentences.

Answers

Possible answers – there are many others:

D Practising the model

Set the task. If necessary, demonstrate with a more able student. Students work in pairs. Monitor and make a note of common errors. Give feedback. For consolidation, students can write a conversation.

Closure

Use your feedback for Exercise D.

3.8 Learning new speaking skills: Linking to a previous speaker

Objectives

By the end of this lesson, students should be able to:
- use intrusive sounds in connected speech;
- link to a previous speaker in a discussion.

Introduction

Revise some vocabulary in preparation for the lesson, for example:

BOGOF   loss-leader

products   relevant

promotion (getting something to sell by, e.g., special price, competition, endorsement)

	hotel	restaurant	product
a. broken	toilet, bed, light	glass, plate	any part, or whole item
b. blocked	toilet, sink		
c. cold	room	food	
d. damaged	any item in room		anything!
e. dirty	sheets	plate, glass, knife, fork, spoon	
f. faulty	TV or any electrical item in the room		anything electrical, electronic
g. missing	light bulb		instructions, cable
h. overcooked		food	
i. past its sell-by date			food
j. scratched			CD, TV screen
k. wrong	key	bill, order	colour, model, etc.
l. not working	TV, toilet		anything electrical, electronic

A Saying vowels

1. If students did Lesson 3.3, they will be familiar with the concept of intrusive sounds. If so, you can remind them about the activities they did. Now refer students to the Pronunciation Check. When students have finished reading, play 🎧 **3.28** of the example sentences. Then replay for repetition.

2. Set the task. Students complete individually, then compare answers in pairs. Do not elicit.

3. Play 🎧 **3.26** so that students can check. Play 🎧 **3.26** again; pause after each sentence for repetition. At this point, you can confirm the answers for Exercise 2.

Transcripts
🎧 3.28

Presenter:	**3.28. Pronunciation Check. Listen and copy the intrusive sounds.**
Voice:	They are all in the promotion. They are all in the promotion. Have you all looked at the examples? Have you all looked at the examples?

🎧 3.26

Presenter:	**3.26. Learning new speaking skills: Linking to a previous speaker**
	Exercise A3. Listen, check and practise.
Voice:	a. BOGOF products are often loss-leaders. b. I worked with Sarah on this research. c. It's on TV at the moment. d. So I did a bit more research. e. The word *free* is very powerful. f. You get two of them.

Answers

a. BOGOF products are /r/ often loss-leaders.

b. I worked with Sarah /r/ on this research.

c. It's on TV /j/ at the moment.

d. So /w/ I did a bit more research.

e. The word *free* /j/ is very powerful.

f. You get two /w/ of them.

B Identifying a key skill

Remind students about the tutorial they listened to in the previous lesson. It would be useful to replay the tutorial again and ask students to follow the transcript as well. You will probably need to keep referring to the conversation and transcript throughout the Skills Check.

1. Ask students to read the Skills Check. Check understanding of words by eliciting synonyms, for example: *refer* = mention or speak about something, *relevant* = connected.

Ask students to find and underline the relevant phrases in the transcript of the tutorial. In this way, they can see how the phrases are used in context.

Go over the information about pronouncing long sentences. Explain that stressed words are said slowly and loudly. Other words in a sentence are unstressed and spoken more quickly. Pauses in the correct places in a sentence will help students to say longer sentences.

Play 🎧 **3.29** for the Skills Check. Pause after each sentence. Elicit the sentence and discuss the stressed words and the pauses.

2. Set the task. Students can discuss in pairs which words they think are stressed and where the pauses are. Elicit answers and/or play the tutorial again for students to check their answers. Practise pronunciation of the italicized sentences by asking students to repeat (from another playing of 🎧 **3.23** or model the sentences yourself).

3. Students practise the extracts in pairs (they will need to change roles for each extract). Monitor and give feedback.

Transcript
🎧 3.29

Presenter:	**3.29. Skills Check. Listen to some sentences with linking expressions.**
Voice:	As Joe has said, advertisers sometimes use bribes. Taking up Sarah's point, tag lines are very important. Going back to Joe's point, jingles sell products. Returning to Sarah's point, people believe big lies. I don't know if this is relevant, but the word *free* is very powerful. I'm not sure if this is related, but advertisers use bribes a lot to sell children's products. Has anyone mentioned that viral advertising is very important nowadays?

Answers

Possible answers:

2. Joe:	Customers who buy a packet of biscuits get another packet free.
Sarah:	Superbuys is using BOGOF at the moment.

Mark:	*But / going back to **Joe's** point, / BOGOF is the same as **half price**, / isn't it?*
Mark:	So BOGOF sells more than half price?
Joe:	Yes. Apparently, it does.
Mark:	That's weird.
Joe:	Not really. *As Sarah has said, / people want **something** / for **nothing**.*
Debbie:	*I don't know if this is **relevant**, / but / I read that BOGOF products / are often **loss-leaders**.*
Tutor:	Yes, that's a good point.
Pierre:	Sorry, I'm late.
Tutor:	That's OK. We're talking about BOGOF.
Pierre:	Right. */ Has anyone mentioned / that BOGOF products / are often / **loss-leaders**?*
Tutor:	Yes, we've just talked about that.

C Practising the new skill

Go over the example, explaining there is more than one possibility for each answer.

There are various ways this drill can be carried out:

• Teacher–class: Play ⊚ **3.27**. Pause after each sentence. Elicit different possible answers from individual students round the class. Drill one or two of the answers.

• Teacher–S1, S2: Play ⊚ **3.27**. Pause after each sentence. S1 turns to a partner and gives an answer. Play the next sentence. Pause. S2 turns to a partner and gives an answer.

• Give out copies of the transcript. In pairs, students practise adding a linking phrase to each sentence. Monitor and give feedback.

Transcript
⊚ 3.27

5. The Ogallala Aquifer will be dry in 200 years.
6. Aural learners need to talk about information.
7. Fleming was studying bacteria at the time.
8. Rote learning is useful for lists of things.
9. British sign language is different from American sign language.
10. The Indian government may privatize water supply.

Closure

Test how well students can remember the phrases from the lesson. With books closed, give the headings (function) of each set of phrases in the Skills Check. Students tell you what the examples were. For example:

T: *Agreeing with a previous speaker.*

Ss: *As Joe has said … / Taking up Sarah's point …*

3.9 Grammar for speaking: Noun phrases with relative clauses

Objectives

By the end of this lesson, students should be able to:

• form sentences with relative clauses using *who* and *which*;

• pronounce long sentences using pauses in appropriate places.

Introduction

Revise some of the 'marketing' vocabulary which will be needed for this lesson, for example:

endorse a product

jingle

slogan

punchline

Grammar box 12

Give students time to read through all the information and the example sentences. Ask:

What does O/C mean?

What does BOGOF mean?

What do we call words such as which *and* who *in these sentences?* (relative pronouns)

How many words are in the object clauses of the sentences in the table?

Elicit answers to the questions below the table.

Play 🔊 **3.30**. Elicit the pauses, preferably using an electronic projection to show the sentences in the table.

Answers

We use *who* for a person or people. We use *which* for thing(s). In other words, these relative pronouns can have singular or plural nouns.

The basic SVO is: *We are talking about adverts / Adverts are targeted at people.*

Transcript
🔊 3.30

Presenter:	3.30. Lesson 3.9. Grammar for speaking: Noun phrases with relative clauses
	Grammar box 12. Listen to the sentences. Where do the speakers pause?
Voice:	We are talking about adverts which use BOGOF. Adverts are targeted at people who might buy the product.

1. Relative pronouns have been mentioned already for comprehension – in Level 3, Lesson 5.4 Grammar for listening.

2. We look at relative clauses in the object / complement first because these are easier – students don't have to 'delay' the main verb, for example, *The students who studied BOGOF products in Superbuys ... decided ...* Relative clauses with new subject + deleted object, e.g., *We're talking about adverts which supermarkets use them* are covered in the next theme.

A Adding extra information about objects and complements

1. Check students understand the task. Students complete individually, then compare answers in pairs. Monitor, but do not elicit answers.

2. Set for individual work and pairwork checking. Monitor, but do not confirm or correct.

3. Play 🔊 **3.31** once so that students can check their answers. Play 🔊 **3.31** again, pausing after each sentence for students to repeat. Allow students to practise in pairs if you wish.

Students look at the first half of each sentence in the Course Book. The second half should be covered and also their answers to Exercise A2. Students try to remember the complete sentence.

Transcript
🔊 3.31

Presenter:	3.31. Exercise A. Listen and check.
Voice:	a. There are many ads which use BOGOF. b. A jingle is a tune which is memorable. c. A tag line is a slogan which contains the name of the product. d. A big name is a person who is famous for movies, sport or television. e. A big name ad contains a personality who endorses the product. f. A bribe is money which encourages someone to do something. g. A punchline is an ending which is funny and makes people laugh. h. Ads with punchlines have a set-up which prepares people for a particular ending. i. A narrative is a story which is usually in many episodes. j. People may like the characters who appear in narrative ads.

Answers

1. There are <u>many ads</u> / which use <u>BOGOF</u>.

2. A jingle is a <u>tune</u> / which is <u>memorable</u>.

3. A tag line is a <u>slogan</u> / which contains the <u>name</u> of the product.

4. A big name is a <u>person</u> / who is <u>famous</u> for movies, sport or television.

5. A big name ad contains a <u>personality</u> / who <u>endorses</u> the product.

6. A bribe is <u>money</u> / which <u>encourages</u> someone to do something.

7. A punchline is an <u>ending</u> / which is <u>funny</u> and makes people <u>laugh</u>.

8. Ads with punchlines have a <u>set-up</u> / which <u>prepares</u> people for a particular <u>ending</u>.

9. A narrative is a <u>story</u> / which is usually in many <u>episodes</u>.

10. People may like the <u>characters</u> / who appear in <u>narrative</u> ads.

Grammar box 13

Students read the information in the table.

Play 🔊 **3.32**. Elicit answers.

Answers

Customers who buy a packet of biscuits / get another packet free.

Twenty products which are basics / are in the promotion.

Transcript
🌐 3.32

Presenter:	3.32. Grammar box 13. Listen to the sentences. Where does the speaker pause?
Voice:	Customers who buy a packet of biscuits get another packet free.
Twenty products which are basics are in the promotion.

B Adding extra information about subjects

1. Give students time to read through the sentences. Set the task. Students complete individually, then compare answers in pairs. Do not elicit at this point.

2. Play 🌐 **3.33**. Students check their answers. Ask students if there are any answers they are still not sure of and replay the relevant sentence(s). Then confirm the correct answer. Don't spend too long on this as answers will become much clearer during the repetition activity.

   Replay 🌐 **3.33**. Pause after each line for students to repeat. Alternatively, model the sentences yourself and use *backchaining (with the normal price > start the advert > start the advert with the normal price)* to help with the length of the sentences.

3. As well as practising pausing in long sentences, remind students about joining words (linkage), removing sounds (suppression or elision) and intrusive sounds in phrases such as:

   … start the /ʲ/ advert …

   People who /w/ are /r/ aural learners…

   water which is used for /r/ irrigation

   You can also remind students about schwa sounds in unstressed words.

   [Optional activity]

   Elicit the two basic sentences for each long sentence:

   a. Many / some advertisers use BOGOF. They start the advert with the normal price.

b. Some people are aural learners. They need to hear new information.

c. Many / some farmers in the States use irrigation. They are worried about the future.

d. A third of the water is used for irrigation. It comes from the Ogallala Aquifer.

e. Some people apologize a lot. They give a reason for their actions.

Elicit what changes have been made in order to form the long sentences with the relative clause.

Transcript
🌐 3.33

Presenter:	3.33. Exercise B2. Listen and check your ideas.
Voices:	a. Advertisers who use BOGOF start the advert with the normal price.
b. People who are aural learners need to hear new information.
c. Farmers in the States who use irrigation are worried about the future.
d. A third of the water which is used for irrigation comes from the Ogallala Aquifer.
e. People who apologize a lot often give a reason for their actions.

Answers

a. Advertisers who use <u>BOGOF</u> / <u>start</u> the advert / with the <u>normal</u> <u>price</u>.

b. People who are <u>aural learners</u> / <u>need</u> to <u>hear</u> / <u>new information</u>.

c. <u>Farmers</u> in the <u>States</u> who <u>use irrigation</u> / are <u>worried</u> about the <u>future</u>.

d. A <u>third</u> of the <u>water</u> which is <u>used</u> for <u>irrigation</u> / comes from the <u>Ogallala Aquifer</u>.

e. People who <u>apologize</u> a lot / often give a <u>reason</u> / for their <u>actions</u>.

Closure

Give some sentence openers and ask students to complete the sentence with something logical. For example:

People who live in hot countries …	*often have a rest in the afternoon.*
Animals which don't eat meat …	*are called herbivores.*
Cars which run on biofuel …	*are only slightly greener than petrol engine cars.*
Celebrities who appear on adverts …	*earn a lot of money.*
Advertisers who tell lies …	*can be taken to court.*

Objectives

By the end of this lesson, students should be able to:

- research and present information about marketing methods used in the movie industry;
- use sub-skills from the section to take part in a focus group discussion;
- present their findings from the mock focus group session.

Introduction

Use Exercise A.

A Previewing vocabulary

1. Set the task. Students can use dictionaries if they wish. Elicit answers.
2. Again, students can use dictionaries if they wish. Elicit answers.
3. Students mark the stress in each word individually. Say each word for the students so they can check their ideas. Elicit answers. Practise pronunciation of each word.

Optional activity

Ask students to make a full sentence with each word.

Answers

1.–3.

a. dis'gusting (*adj*)	de'licious (*adj*)
b. 'eye-catching (*adj*)	dull (*adj*)
c. in'triguing (*adj*)	'obvious (*adj*)
d. live 'action (*n*)	car'toon (*n*)
e. 'series (*n*)	'one-off (*n*)
f. un'known (*adj*)	'famous (*adj*)

B Researching information

1. Set the task, telling students not to worry if they do not understand the words for the methods at this point. Give students two or three minutes to read all the information.

Check understanding of the phrase *focus group*.

2. Students choose – or you can allocate – one set of methods for research. Divide the class into pairs of students who have chosen the same set of methods. Students should help each other to understand the research, and, where possible, to think of examples for each method. Monitor and give help where necessary.

3. Students prepare some sentences to use in the group work activity which follows. Remind them about the grammar from Lesson 3.9 and encourage them to make longer sentences where possible. Students practise pronunciation of sentences in their pairs, helping each other as much as possible. Students can write out sentences in full if they wish, but warn students they will not be able to read them aloud in the following discussion.

C Taking part in a discussion

Ask students to look back at Lesson 3.8 and remind themselves about phrases for linking back to a previous speaker. Tell students to try to use some of these phrases if and when appropriate. You could also remind students about other sub-skills and phrases from previous themes if you wish.

Finally, remind students to wait for suitable pauses before expressing an opinion or asking for clarification, etc.

1. Re-divide the class into groups of three or six, making sure there are representatives for each set of methods. At this stage, students should find out about all nine methods and make notes. Monitor and make notes of:

   - common errors;
   - where students missed opportunities to use target language;
   - where students used target language appropriately;
   - using turn-taking (in)appropriately.

2. During this phase, students should move on to ranking the methods in order, according to effectiveness of 'selling'. Tell students there is no 'right' answer. Monitor as before. Stop the activity when half the groups have finished ranking the methods. Ask each group to report their order and write each list on the board for ease of comparison. Discuss the results:

Were any of the ranking lists the same or similar? Why has this happened?

What were the differences between the rankings?

Should movie makers use more than one method at a time for each film?

Give feedback on the notes you made while monitoring.

3. Use the question for a whole-class discussion or students can discuss it in their groups from Exercises C1 and C2. Alternatively, you could leave this question until the end of the lesson, if you prefer.

   If necessary, you can prompt students with the ideas in the Answers.

Answers

1./2. Answers depend on students.

3. Answers depend on students as this asks for a personal opinion, but you might mention in feedback that many people have doubts about the value of focus groups. Firstly, it is difficult to extrapolate from a small number of people to a whole target market. Secondly, focus groups are often entertained by the advertisers (or other interested party) and may be subject therefore to 'demand effect', giving the moderator of the group the answer they think he/she wants to hear.

D Taking part in a discussion

1. Set the task and tell students this should be a very short presentation.

   Set a maximum time limit of two minutes. Students should make notes. They can then practise making sentences from their notes with a partner.

2. Divide the class into small groups. Students take turns to give their presentations. Monitor and give feedback.

Methodology note

Exercise D could be set as a written assignment to consolidate the lesson, or students could make notes and prepare their presentations as a home assignment. They can then give their presentations in another lesson.

E Developing critical thinking

Students discuss in pairs or small groups. After a couple of minutes, elicit ideas. Ask students which methods they have *not* used, and get them to explain.

Answers

Answers depend on students.

Closure

Use Exercise E, or give feedback on students' performance in the various speaking activities if you haven't already done so.

Reading: Conventions in narrative fiction

3

Objectives

By the end of this lesson, students should be able to:
- demonstrate understanding of vocabulary for the section;
- use new vocabulary to talk about narratives, including some of the conventions;
- demonstrate understanding of links between storytelling and cultural conventions.

Introduction

Exploit the visuals of the two movie posters. Elicit the title of each movie and ask students if they have seen any of them. Here are a few facts about each movie that you could elicit or discuss with the students:

Lord of the Rings: The Fellowship of the Ring: a fantasy adventure based on the first book in J. R. R. Tolkien's trilogy. Starred Elijah Wood and Sir Ian McKellan.

Harry Potter and the Deathly Hallows: based on the last book in J. K. Rowling's series of books about a young wizard. Played by Daniel Radcliffe.

A   Activating ideas

Set the task. Students work in pairs then elicit answers. Students may want to add other words they know that are not in the list: *horror, adventure, revenge,* etc.

Ask students what they think happens in each film – or what actually happens if they have seen it.

Answers

Lord of the Rings
Genre: adventure, fantasy
Characters: hero, villain

Harry Potter
Genre: adventure, fantasy
Characters: hero, villain, victim

B   Understanding words in context

1. The link between the text about Bartlett and the movie posters in the previous exercise may not be immediately apparent. The point is that the stories in the movies follow the conventions that Bartlett describes.

   Set the task. Students complete individually, then compare answers in pairs. Elicit answers and give further explanations of new vocabulary if necessary. Make sure students have changed the form of each target word where necessary.

2. In this activity, students are introduced to the reference codes necessary for academic texts. Students discuss the meanings of the bold words using the phrases in the box. Elicit answers. You don't need to give explanations of what exactly *ibid.* and *pp.* stand for.

3. Tell students we can often form adjectives from nouns by adding the suffix ~*al*. Set the task. Elicit answers.

Optional activity

Write the following nouns from the text on the board. Elicit ones which can be changed into adjectives by adding ~*al*:

psychologist (psychology) – *psychological*

experiment – *experimental*

tribe – *tribal*

part – *partial* (note the spelling *ial* and change in pronunciation of the *t* – /ʃ/)

but:

code – adjective is *coded* or even *codified*

memory – no – *memorable*

Answers

1. **Bartlett** Sir Frederic Charles (1886–1969): British psychologist who studied memory. Bartlett's most famous experiment was conducted in 1928. He asked a group of participants who were not Native Americans to read a *fictional* narrative from that culture called 'The War of the Ghosts'. The story of a *conflict* between two tribes was entirely logical in the original culture but, for the participants, there were strange *characters* and illogical parts. He asked the participants

to repeat the story several times, after a few days and eventually after a few months. He found that they reconstructed the *narrative*, leaving out the strange parts, and turning it into a story with the pattern of stories from their own culture.

Bartlett concluded that stories are controlled by patterns, or **codes**, so understanding a story involves decoding. 'A story,' he said, 'is at once labelled as being of this or that type … The form, plan, type, or scheme of a story is … the most persistent factor of all' (Bartlett, 1928). In other words, stories have to follow certain **conventions**. If they do not **conform** to this code, they will be changed in the memory so that they do fit. 'In fact all incoming material, if it is to be dealt with in any manner, must be somehow labelled' (ibid.). Bartlett called these labels '**schema**', and pointed out that they are cultural.

References

Bartlett, F. C. (1928) 'An experiment upon repeated reproduction', *Journal* of General Psychology Vol 1: pp. 54–63.

* This **synopsis** by courtesy of *Journal of General Psychology*, © 1928.

2. a. copyright   ©
    b. pages   pp.
    c. journal   Vol(ume) = in the sense of *part of a series*
    d. author   (Bartlett)
    e. date of work   (1928)
    f. from the same author and same work   (ibid.)

3. fictional
    original
    logical
    illogical
    cultural

C   Understanding the text

Set the task. Students discuss each statement in pairs. Elicit answers.

Answers

1. The participants in the experiment were Native Americans.	false – they were from a different culture, which is why they found the story hard to understand, Bartlett concluded
2. *Conflict* is another word for *war*.	true – story is called *War of the Ghosts* and it is about a conflict
3. The participants retold the story, using schema from their own culture.	true – this is what Bartlett concluded
4. Conventions are rules.	true – social or cultural rules
5. *Labelled*, in this context, means 'put into a genre'.	true – it says things must be labelled as being of this or that type, which in this case, means genre
6. According to Bartlett, we label fiction when, for example, we see a poster for a film.	true – all incoming material

Closure

Return to the two movie posters from Exercise A. Remind students they were able to tell you at the beginning of the lesson what they thought each movie was about.

Discuss with the class if, therefore, they agree with Bartlett's theory or not.

Point out that we will hear a lot more about this theory in this theme.

3.12 Real-time reading: Conflict, stages and characters

Objectives

By the end of this lesson, students should be able to:

• use co-text and research questions in order to understand a text about media conventions in narrative;

• deal with new vocabulary in a text;

• understand the use of a References section to show all the sources used to construct an academic text.

Introduction

Revise the information about Bartlett and his theory of 'schema' from the previous lesson (3.11).

Ask students to:

- describe his experiment;
- explain Bartlett's theory about schema.

A Preparing to read

Ask students to focus on the assignment handout. Point out it is from the School of Language and Literature. This will give students a broad idea of the content of the lesson to follow. Explain that this is an example of schema theory, because you know something about the kind of information you will read if it is part of an academic course in language and literature.

Remind students about the point of research questions if necessary.

Students work on the research questions in pairs. Elicit ideas.

Answers

Research questions

- Defining terms: What is narrative?
- Defining terms: What are conventions?
- What are the conventions of fiction films?
- What are the conventions of novels? *(Note that research will show these are the same as fiction films for the purposes of this section.)*
- How do conventions assist audience understanding?

B Understanding the text

1. Revise some vocabulary from Lesson 3.11 relevant to the article: *decoding narrative (= understanding a story), conflict, conventions,* etc). Set the question for discussion in pairs. Write the beginning of the following sentence on the board for students to complete as their answer:

    Conventions are important in narrative fiction because … (they help the audience to understand the film / novel).

2. Before you set the task, ask students to read the list of names. Have they heard of any of the people before? What do students know about each person already?

    For example, on this course students have learnt a lot about Aristotle, including dates (384–322 BCE); philosophy (learning by doing, three types of friendship), etc. They have just heard about Bartlett. Students may not have heard of the others.

    Set the task. Give students several minutes to read through the article and make notes individually. Encourage students to try to deal with new words in context, or use a dictionary rather than asking you for explanations. Tell students you will help with new words later. Then students compare answers in pairs and help each other with new vocabulary.

    Elicit answers and use an electronic projection to display the model notes on the board.

3. Students reread the text, then discuss the answers in pairs. After a few minutes' discussion, ask students to make notes for each question. Elicit answers and show model notes using an electronic projection. Go over any answers or vocabulary students had difficulty with.

4. Students discuss in pairs. Students should now be able to answer all their original research questions.

5. Students rearrange the phrases into the correct order in pairs (if possible, provide students with the phrases written on pieces of paper so that they can 'drag and drop' them into the correct position). Write the correct sentence on the board for students to compare with their own version.

Answers

1. Answers depend on students.
2.

Aristotle	*all dramatic narrative is conflict*
Lévi-Strauss	*narratives have binary opposition*
Todorov	*all narratives have three stages*
Propp	*main characters perform roles defined by convention*
Bartlett	*people need a schema to understand a narrative*

3.		
	a. What types of conflict are there, according to Aristotle?	within a person, or opposing principles
	b. What are possible binary oppositions, according to Lévi-Strauss?	good *vs* evil, right *vs* wrong, strength *vs* weakness, youth *vs* age
	c. What are the three stages of narratives, according to Todorov?	equilibrium, disequilibrium, restored equilibrium
	d. What are the main roles in a narrative, according to Propp?	hero or protagonist, villain or antagonist, victim, donor, helper, princess, false hero
	e. How do we use schema in everyday life, according to Bartlett?	we use it to understand

4. Answers depend on students.
5. Conventions in narrative fiction help the audience to understand what to expect in terms of basic ideas, story and characters.

2.

		1	2
a.	encountered	seen and dealt with ✓	met a person
b.	originated	created	happened for the first time ✓
c.	emerging	coming out of a difficult time ✓	appearing
d.	established	made clear ✓	fixed
e.	strict	having lots of rules	very clear, cannot be changed ✓
f.	stable	not liable to be changed easily ✓	place for horses
g.	idyllic	very happy ✓	very beautiful
h.	critic	a reviewer of art or literature ✓	person who says bad things about behaviour
i.	distinguish	show bravery or judgement	mark the difference ✓
j.	stock	unchanging ✓	supply of goods

C Understanding new words in context

1. Set the task, making sure students understand the synonyms are *in the text*. Students complete individually, then compare answers in pairs. Elicit answers.
2. Check students understand the task. Students complete individually, then compare answers in pairs. Elicit answers. Elicit the part of speech for each word as used in the text.

Answers

1. a. conflict   *struggle*
   b. binary   *two opposite parts*
   c. equilibrium   *order*
   d. disequilibrium   *disorder*
   e. protagonist   *hero*
   f. antagonist   *villain*

D Transferring information to the real world

You can do this as pairwork or discussion in groups. Monitor to make sure students use some of the target vocabulary and describe the films in academic terms, rather than just say whether they enjoyed them or not. Finally, ask students to write a brief description of a film using the three questions as a guide. This could be set as a home assignment.

Optional activity

If the class is keen on the topic, you could ask them to try to watch a particular film on TV or at the cinema over the next few days. Ask them to answer the questions about it in the next lesson.

Answers

Answers depend on students.

Closure
Use Exercise D.

Objectives

By the end of this lesson, students should be able to:
• record sources of information from reading research.

Introduction
Use Exercise A.

A Reviewing vocabulary

1. Set the task. You can either tell students not to look back at previous lessons, or you may decide to allow this. Students work individually, then compare answers. Write the correct answers on the board so that students can self-check. Go over any words students had forgotten.

2. Revise / elicit the meaning of *binary* in this context. Set the task. Students discuss in pairs. Elicit answers. Point out that pairs a–f are nouns, pairs g and h are adjectives. Highlight words with similar endings: *strength, wealth, youth; weakness, ugliness; imaginary, reactionary*.

Answers

1. a. conflict
   b. struggle
   c. convention
   d. character
   e. protagonist
   f. antagonist
   g. equilibrium
   h. victim
2. a. good and evil
   b. strength and weakness
   c. youth and age
   d. wealth and poverty
   e. knowledge and ignorance
   f. beauty and ugliness
   g. real and imaginary
   h. progressive and reactionary / old-fashioned

B Identifying a new skill

1. Write *recording sources* on the board. Check understanding of the phrase in this context (both words can have different meanings). Students study the Skills Check and the cards.

2. Students discuss the questions in pairs. Elicit answers.

Answers

2. The first card shows the information for a book and the second card the information for a journal article. You clearly can't record book or journal information, e.g., page numbers for Internet articles, but categories on the cards that haven't been used are needed for Internet articles, i.e., *retrieved* and *full URL*.

Methodology notes

1. It is very important to record sources while you are actually doing reading research, although it is boring to do so. Point out that it is difficult, if not impossible, to go back and check sources later.

2. The conventions of compiling references are fully detailed in the writing section of this theme.

C Practising the new skill

1. Set the task. Students complete individually. Monitor and give help where necessary. Students compare answers in pairs. Show completed cards on an electronic projection so that students can compare with their own.

2. Tell students these are typical of resources for this kind of topic. They are not, however, authentic so students shouldn't waste time on the Internet trying to find them!

   Set the task and repeat the procedure for Exercise C1.

Answers

1. **Note:** These are real works.

book / ~~journal / Internet~~	
author(s)	Lacey. N. (?)
date	2000
title	Narrative and Genre
pub. place	London
publisher	Palgrave Macmillan
journal	
volume	
page nos	
retrieved	
full URL	

book / ~~journal / Internet~~	
author(s)	Lévi-Strauss, C. (M?)
date	1990
title	The Naked Man
pub. place	Chicago
publisher	University of Chicago Press
journal	
volume	
page nos	
retrieved	
full URL	

book / ~~journal / Internet~~	
author(s)	Todorov, T. (M?)
date	1969
title	Grammaire du Décameron
pub. place	The Hague
publisher	Mouton
journal	
volume	
page nos	
retrieved	
full URL	

2. **Note:** These are not real works.

book / ~~journal / Internet~~	
author(s)	Nelson, A. (M)
date	2010
title	Studying narrative
pub. place	New York
publisher	Taylor Press
journal	
volume	
page nos	
retrieved	
full URL	

book / ~~journal / Internet~~	
author(s)	Hughes, A. (F) and Dean, B. (M)
date	2006
title	Conflict in film
pub. place	London
publisher	Jones and Miller
journal	
volume	
page nos	
retrieved	
full URL	

~~book /~~ journal ~~/ Internet~~	
author(s)	Andrews, B. (M)
date	2009
title	Schema in fictional narrative
pub. place	
publisher	
journal	Media today
volume	23
page nos	26–30
retrieved	
full URL	

book / journal / Internet	
author(s)	
date	
title	*Todorov and Propp – convention in narrative*
pub. place	
publisher	
journal	
volume	
page nos	
retrieved	*20/12/12*
full URL	*http://mediastudiesonline/todandpropp.html*

Closure

If possible, take in real books and journals. (They do not have to be about media.) Take in stocks of index cards. Students record the information on index cards.

3.14 Grammar for reading: Understanding participle clauses (2)

Objectives

By the end of this lesson, students should be able to:

- identify sentences with participle clauses in a text;
- identify the 'missing' subject of participle clauses using past participles.

Note: Before you start this lesson, you may want to revise:

1. Understanding participle clauses (1) from Lesson 2.14
2. past passive verb forms

Introduction

Write some verbs with irregular past participles on the board and get students to write the past participle in each case, e.g.,

take	*taken*
bring	*brought*
teach	*taught*
leave	*left*
see	*seen*
break	*broken*
find	*found*

write	*written*
begin	*begun*
win	*won*
tell	*told*

Feed back, getting the correct words with the correct spelling on the board.

Grammar box 14

Students study the sentences in the table then discuss the questions in pairs. Do not elicit answers. Students read the information under the tables. Now elicit answers. Use an electronic projection to show how the subjects link back to the subject or object respectively of the two first clauses.

Answers

The forms are similar (apart from SVO and SVC in the first clauses).

They are different because, in sentence 1, the second clause is about the subject. In sentence 2, the second clause is about the object.

A Recognizing participle clauses

Break the activity down into two stages. First students find and underline the sentences with participle clauses. Check students have the correct five. Then, in pairs, ask students to discuss the subject of each one, and decide on the original verb. Remind students that each verb will be a passive one. Elicit answers.

Answers

The narrative begins with **a state of equilibrium**, or order, **established** in the early scenes.	S = equilibrium V = is established
An **event** occurs, **unnoticed** at first perhaps, which eventually turns the characters' lives upside down.	S = event V = is unnoticed
In most fiction, the main characters perform **roles**, **defined** by convention …	S = roles V = are defined
Another central character is the **victim**, who is **threatened** by the antagonist …	S = victim V = is threatened
Many narratives have **a female character, called** the *princess* by Propp (ibid.).	S = a female character V = is called

You might want to remind students of these structures which were examined in Lesson 2.14.

Supporting these two central characters, other stock characters appear = other stock characters support …

Stepping into an unknown world, **we** need convention to guide us. = we step into …

You might have to remind students about the idea of stock characters, from Propp.

B Predicting the next information after a past participle

Note that all the second clauses in this activity have the same subject as the first clause.

Set the task. Students complete individually. Elicit answers. Now elicit a full sentence for each second clause:

1. He / James Bond was tied to a radiator.
2. She was dressed in white.
3. They were lost and frightened.
4. It was loaded and ready to fire.
5. He / She was hidden in the shadows.

Answers

1. James Bond was in a locked room, tied …	3	and frightened.
2. Cynthia arrived at the church, dressed …	4	and ready to fire.
3. The two children wandered through the wood, lost …	5	in the shadows.
4. The gun was on the desk, loaded …	2	in white.
5. The spy was waiting in a shop doorway, hidden …	1	to a radiator.

C Understanding sentences with participles

Note that all the second clauses in this activity have the same subject as the object of the first clause. Set the task. Students complete individually. Once again, elicit the full sentence for the second clause, e.g.

1. It / The horse was tied to a fence post.

The verbs here are all past passive, but, in fact, any passive verb can be converted to past participle in clause joining. For example:

This process is (it is) called photosynthesis.

Recently, Pluto has ceased to be a full planet, (it has been) reclassified as a celestial object.

Answers

1. The sheriff found his horse, *tied* to a fence post.
2. Malcolm looked at the photograph of his brother, *taken* many years before in France.
3. The soldiers arrived at the town, *captured* from the enemy the previous day.
4. The aliens inspected the humans, *brought* from all over the planet Earth by their spaceships.
5. The thief was delighted when he saw the window, *broken* some time before by a child's ball.

D Finding the subject of participle clauses

Set the task. Explain to students the need to consider the context of the sentence when choosing the answer. For example, in sentence 1, the three nouns and possible subjects are: *Collins, the camp,* or *the forest.* However, only a person can be injured so the answer must be *Collins.* Students complete individually, then compare answers in pairs. You may need to go round and help with vocabulary, or tell students they can use their dictionaries. Elicit answers.

Answers

1. Collins – the only possible noun that could be 'injured and broken in spirit'
2. Stewart – Marlon couldn't leave if he was locked in the basement
3. The natives – one person could not be 'assembled', as it applies to groups
4. Sophie – because of 'herself' later in the sentence
5. The gun – Kit and Billy cannot be 'loaded with one final bullet'

Methodology note

Strange as it may seem, it was once considered that grammar could, and indeed should, ignore semantics. We know now that it is only possible to recover the referent of a word or phrase if we understand the meaning of the sentence.

Closure

Ask students to think of a sentence to continue the story for some of the items in Exercise D. For example:

Collins returned to the camp in the centre of the forest, injured and broken in spirit. He washed his cuts in a stream, drank some water and then lay down in his tent.

Sophie looked up at the young man nervously, scared of making a fool of herself. 'Sorry. My English isn't very good. Could you repeat that, please?'

Point out that we can do this because of schema and the conventions of fictional narrative.

3.15 Applying new reading skills: Genre and plots

Objectives

By the end of this lesson, students should be able to:

- use new reading sub-skills, grammar and vocabulary in order to understand statements and supporting evidence;
- demonstrate understanding of a webpage text about genre and plot in movies and novels.

Introduction

Use Exercise A.

A   Activating ideas

1./2. Ask students to list:

- the common binary oppositions, according to Lévi-Strauss;
- the three stages of all fictional narratives, according to Todorov;
- the common stock characters, according to Propp.

Elicit answers and write them on the board, then get students to self-check by looking back at the text in 3.12.

Answers

1./2. Answers depend on students.

B   Preparing to read

Set the task and explain that students must think of research questions. Revise / elicit the meaning of the word *plot* in this context. Give students a minute to read the assignment handout then they can work on research questions in pairs. Elicit ideas for the questions (but do not elicit answers yet!). Then point out that students have to decide whether to talk about a film or novel.

Answers

Defining terms: What is Booker's thesis? (and possibly: What are *plots*? What is *genre*?)

To what extent is Booker's thesis true with regard to … (my chosen genre of films or novels)

C   Understanding the text

1. Set for individual work and pairwork checking. Only give students a few moments before feeding back.

2. Give students time to read through the sentences. Tell them not to worry about words such as *equilibrium* and *hubris* as these are explained in the text. Set the task. Make sure students realize that the superscript numbers refer to the references. Point out this is a common way of referencing on the web. Students complete individually, then compare answers in pairs. Elicit answers, allowing time for extra discussion and explanation where necessary.

Answers

a. Adventure, comedy and sci-fi / fantasy are the most popular film genres.	wordpress.com
b. Romance is the most popular novel genre.	bookmarket.com
c. Humans require schema to make sense of something new.	Bartlett
d. There are seven basic plots in fictional narrative.	Booker
e. All authors have used the same images.	Johnson
f. Fairy tales do not all conform to particular basic plots.	the Opies
g. All comedies contain movement from ignorance to knowledge.	Aristotle
h. All narratives end with a return to equilibrium.	Todorov
i. Hubris is the most common theme in tragedies.	Booker
j. The princess is a common character in fictional narrative.	Propp

D Applying information from the text

Go through the questions, checking understanding, and make sure students remember what the Proppian character types are. If necessary, students can look back at the text in Lesson 3.12.

Answers

If students know the actual films, they may be able to give more information about each point but the idea here is not to know the answer, but to deduce possibilities.

See table below.

E Completing the assignment

This can be done as a discussion in class or set as a written home assignment. Set the task by talking about one or two current films the students may have seen, deciding on the genre and discussing which of the seven plots, if any, apply.

Closure

Use feedback on Exercise E. Ask students to complete source index cards at home for the information in this article.

	Possible genre(s)	Plot	Possible characters	Restored equilibrium?	Actual title
a.	Romance or comedy	Comedy	heroes – the children; princess – the mother	the parents remarry	*The Parent Trap*
b.	Drama – biopic	Man against the Monster	hero – the mother; villain – the CEO of the power company	the single mother wins	*Erin Brockovich*
c.	Romance	Rags to Riches	hero – the man; princess – the waitress	they get married	*It Could Happen to You*
d.	Fantasy (with animation)	The Quest	donor – the wizard; hero – Frodo; villain – Sauron	he returns home after destroying the ring	*Lord of the Rings: The Fellowship of the Ring*
e.	Drama	Tragedy	hero – Bud Fox – could be a false hero, too!; villain – his boss	the hero turns against his boss and saves his father's company	*Wall Street*
f.	Adventure (with animation)	Voyage and Return	princess – the daughter; hero – Jack Sparrow	Jack returns home with the daughter	*Pirates of the Caribbean: The Curse of the Black Pearl*

Knowledge quiz: Advertising, television and narrative fiction

Objectives

By the end of this lesson, students will have:
- reviewed core knowledge from the theme;
- recycled the vocabulary from the theme.

Introduction

Tell students they are going to do a vocabulary and knowledge quiz on the first three sections of the theme. If you like, while you are waiting for everyone in the class to arrive, students can spend a few minutes looking back over the listening, speaking and reading sections, especially the vocabulary lists, to remind themselves of the target words.

Methodology note

See the notes in the Introduction for further ideas on how to do the quiz. As usual, the focus should be more on content than using correct grammar.

Exercise 1

Divide the class into two teams: A and B. Tell Team A to answer all the odd numbered questions: 1, 3, 5, etc., and Team B should answer all the even numbers: 2, 4, 6, etc.

When you give feedback, give one point to each team for a correct answer. If the team gives an incorrect answer, the other team can have a go. If they get it correct, they get two bonus points.

Keep a running score on the board for each team.

Answers

a. What is an *endorsement*?	d	A joke – it is the funny ending.
b. What do you see on a *billboard*?	j	A product from a particular maker which many people recognize.
c. Who has *copyright* of a piece of fiction?	b	An advertisement, often for a film.
d. What has a *punchline*?	a	A statement from a celebrity or personality from sport or television saying they use the product.
e. Why do supermarkets use *loss-leaders*?	g	Conflict, stages, plots, genre, characters.
f. What happens in a *reconciliation*?	i	Outer space, or perhaps another dimension.
g. What are some of the *conventions* of narrative fiction?	f	People who were in conflict reach agreement.
h. When should you write *(ibid.)*?	c	The writer, because he/she owns the right to reproduce it.
i. Where do *aliens* come from, according to fiction?	e	To get people into their shop to buy other products.
j. What is a *brand*?	h	When you are quoting again from the same work.

Exercise 2

Decide if you want students to use dictionaries or not. Students complete the vocabulary quiz in pairs. The pair who finishes first and with the most correct answers are the winners. For feedback, focus on the most difficult words only and briefly practise pronunciation if you have time.

Answers

a. fiction	h	accurate
b. code	k	allow
c. villain	b	decode
d. good	l	deny
e. ignorance	m	Earth man
f. antagonist	d	evil
g. famous	c	hero
h. exaggerated	e	knowledge
i. sequel	o	live action
j. forgettable	j	memorable
k. ban	a	non-fiction
l. admit	i	prequel
m. alien	f	protagonist
n. friend	n	stranger
o. CGI	g	unknown

Exercise 3

Divide the class back into two teams again. Once again, allocate odd and even numbers as for Exercise A. When students have completed their five words, regroup the class into pairs, one student from Team A, the other from Team B. Students 'swap' answers so that each student finishes with the answers to all ten questions.

For feedback, show correct answers on the board with an electronic projection.

Answers

a. story	d	acceptance
b. authorities	c	aggression
c. violence	e	at first
d. concession	o	by the way
e. initially	n	catchy tune
f. synopsis	k	destroy
g. genre	j	do
h. argument	l	follow
i. experience	i	go through
j. commit	b	government
k. eliminate	m	meaning
l. conform	a	narrative
m. message	h	proposition
n. jingle	f	summary
o. incidentally	g	type

Closure

Tell students to learn the information or vocabulary for any of the answers they got wrong in class.

Writing: Reality TV – real or fiction?

Objectives

By the end of this lesson, students should be able to:

- demonstrate understanding of and be able to spell target vocabulary on the topic of media studies;
- demonstrate understanding of a media studies text extract about the genre of reality TV, which contains quotations and references.

General note

In this section, for the first time in the course, the students work on a single piece of work. This is in order to prepare them for producing longer pieces of writing.

Introduction

Write the title of the lesson on the board: *Drama or reality?*

Check understanding of the word *reality* in the context of TV programmes. If students are not sure what *reality TV* programmes are, you can give examples of programmes they will probably know, such as *Big Brother, X Factor*, etc. Ask them what the name is of each in their language / country.

Ask students which drama and reality programmes they have watched recently or watch regularly.

A Activating ideas

1. Ask students to study the TV schedule. Ask a few questions to check understanding:

   How many channels are shown?

   What time is Cold Case on?

   What time does Family Guy finish?

   Set the question, explaining that students will have to guess the answers from the programme titles.

   Students discuss the question in pairs. Elicit ideas.

2. Ask one or two questions to check understanding of the pie chart:

   What does Figure 1 show? (the number of people who watch each type of programme)

What's the most popular type of TV programme? (drama)

Students discuss the question in pairs. Elicit answers. Ask students if they notice any genres that are missing. (Quiz programmes are not mentioned.)

Answers

1. Drama: Desperate Housewives, Brothers & Sisters, Cold Case, Shark

   Reality: Extreme Makeover, America's Next Top Model

2. Students may be surprised that news / documentaries have a very small percentage, and that reality TV has such a large one.

Methodology note

This activity revises vocabulary for different types of TV programme and checks understanding of the word *reality*. However, this has probably become an 'international word' so may not need a lot of checking. In addition, there is much more information about the genre in the following lessons in this section.

B Understanding sentences

Exploit the heading of the text and discuss what the text is going to be about. You should be able to elicit that drama is still number one in terms of popularity, despite the popularity of newer genres such as reality TV.

Set the task, explaining that it is a useful editing activity which will help students with their writing. Point out that the words missing are either function words – *in, on, at* – or are clear from the context, e.g., *two*. Students complete individually, then compare answers in pairs. Monitor and give help where necessary, but avoid answering too many questions about vocabulary if possible, as this will be dealt with in the next activity. If students find the task difficult, write the missing words on the board in random order. If students are still struggling, you can indicate the positions for the missing words. With this extra information, students should be able to complete the task.

Show the complete text using an electronic projection so that students can compare and correct their own work.

Answers

Missing words in bold.

This is the clear message from the media *authority* Nielsen.com in **its** latest figures. During the last year, the largest TV *audiences* were for drama, which took, **on** average, 44 per cent of *viewers*. It seems that the majority of Americans still prefer to watch *actors* rather **than** members of the public. Clearly, drama is a very large genre and contains many sub-genres, such as *soap operas*, crime thrillers and science fiction, but all have **two** things in common – actors and a *script*.

In second place in the Nielsen survey is reality TV, up three per cent from the previous year, despite many rude comments **from** *critics*, both inside and outside the television industry. For example, Barry Langberg, a Los Angeles *lawyer*, **who** represented an unhappy couple from a reality *show*, is *cited* as saying:

'Something like this is done for no other reason than to *embarrass* people or humiliate them **or** scare them. The *producers* don't care **about** human feelings … **They** only care about money.'[1]

The reality genre also has sub-genres with **a** wide variety of *settings*. Some series are filmed *on location*, like a desert island, some **are** filmed at private houses and others take place in a *studio*. But in all cases, the format is similar, with *contestants* from the general public taking part in a *contest* and gradually **being** eliminated, often, as Mr Langberg says, with embarrassment or *humiliation*.

C **Understanding vocabulary in sentences**

1. Tell students they are now going to work on the vocabulary in the text. Set the task. Students complete individually then compare answers. Elicit answers. Students may need further explanation for the words *embarrass* (= make someone feel ashamed, nervous, uncomfortable) and *humiliation* (= feel stupid, weak, ashamed, angry), which have very similar meanings.

2. Set the task and go over the example. Students complete definitions for the remaining words individually. Show the answers on an electronic projection. Elicit any variations students have in their own definitions and discuss if they are acceptable or not.

   Ask questions to further check understanding of the text:

What are the sub-genres of drama / reality TV?

What is similar about the format of reality TV shows? (they humiliate / embarrass the contestants)

Optional activity

Ask students to find and underline all the examples of passive verbs in the text. This will help to prepare them for the grammar lesson: joining clauses with passive verbs.

Answers

1. a. a drama which continues for many months or years — soap opera

   b. reported — cited

   c. words for actors in a play — script

   d. competition — contest

   e. programme — show

   f. to make people feel ashamed of themselves — embarrass

   g. feeling that you have made a fool of yourself — humiliation

   h. not in a studio — on location

2.

authority	a person who knows a lot in a particular field
audience	people who watch an entertainment of any sort (in this case, television)
viewers	people who watch television
actors	people who act in plays on stage, in movies or on television
critics	people who comment on things – in this case negatively, but the word can also refer to people who say nice things
lawyer	a person who works in the law in some capacity
producers	people who are in charge of television programmes or movies
settings	places where programmes are set, e.g., in a house
studio	a place where TV programmes are recorded
contestants	people who take part in a contest

D Developing critical thinking

The purpose of the questions here is not only to practise the target vocabulary, but for students to start to consider some of the ethical issues involved in making TV programmes. Therefore, the target output from the students should hopefully include sentences such as:

I wouldn't like to appear in a reality show. I don't think it's right to humiliate people.

I don't want to be famous.

TV producers should make better quality programmes.

Methodology note

In the Portfolio, students will have the opportunity to debate and write about the ethical issues in reality TV programmes in more detail.

Closure

Use the discussion in Exercise D.

3.17 Real-time writing: Reality TV – volume and conventions

Objectives

By the end of this lesson, students should be able to:

- know more about the reasons for the popularity of reality TV;
- demonstrate understanding of the organization of a discussion or outline essay;
- use *statement + supporting evidence* paragraph structure in order to produce the first two paragraphs of a media studies essay.

General note

As mentioned at the beginning of Lesson 3.16, this section does not follow the same pattern as previous writing sections. Students work on the first half of the essay in this lesson, and will complete the second half in Lesson 3.20. This is so students have the opportunity to produce an essay of a similar length to the minimum they will be required to do on a university course.

Introduction

Dictate some of the words from Lesson 3.16 as a spelling test. Revise the meanings of the words you have selected for the spelling test.

Write the title of the lesson on the board: *Reality TV – volume and conventions.*

Explain that, in this context, *volume* means *total amount*.

If students did the reading section of this theme, elicit the meaning of *convention* in this context. If not, explain briefly that it means the rules or patterns that you find in a particular piece of work – novel, play, film or television programme.

Language note

Students now know three meanings of the word *volume*:

1. amount of liquid a container holds or can hold

2. an edition of a regular journal

3. total amount of anything

Use this to point out the importance of understanding the meaning of a word in context, and the need to recognize that familiar words can have different meanings from the one(s) known. This will happen increasingly as the students meet more complex texts.

A Activating ideas

Check understanding of the following:

- the noun *reality* comes from the adjective *real*, but the pronunciation of the verb changes
- the adjective *scripted* comes from the noun *script* (see Lesson 3.16)
- features (*v*) = includes or makes a feature, i.e., a big thing of

Check students understand the task. Students discuss the items in pairs. Elicit ideas and establish that for some items there is no 'right' answer.

Answers

✓ It's dramatic.

✓ It's humorous. (sometimes)

✓ It has real-life situations. (sometimes, e.g., *Motorway Cops*, etc., but not *Big Brother* – this is invented reality)

✓ It features ordinary people.

✓ It features celebrities.

✓ It's very popular all around the world.

B   Preparing to write

1. Focus students' attention on the assignment handout. Ask them to read the information. Check / elicit the meaning of the word *franchise* – sold as a branded product so that the owners of the format get money, but the buyers can localize.

   Elicit answers to the question about statistics. Follow up by checking the reference for each statistic, for example:

   How big was the regular audience of Big Brother? (5 million)

   What is the reference for this fact? (channel4.com)

   Point out that the word *popular* does not have an objective meaning, so these statistics prove different kinds of popularity – see Answers.

   You might mention that it is very easy to make statements like 'It's very popular', but in the academic world you must then define what you mean and prove it.

   Check students understand the assignment task. In pairs, students discuss possible reasons for the popularity of reality TV. Elicit a few ideas.

   Focus on the word *outline*. This means explain, or list with details.

2. a. Students read the introduction then discuss the question in pairs. Elicit ideas.

   b. Set the task. Students write the new introduction individually. Monitor and give help where necessary. After a few minutes, students can compare their version of the introduction with a partner. Ask some pairs to tell you any similarities or differences they had. Finally, show the model introduction using an electronic projection. Highlight the way that some sentences have been combined so that there is less repetition.

Answers

1. The statistics show different measures of popularity:

   • audience statistics for one show

   • number of countries with the genre

   • percentages for regular viewing

   • number of people wishing to take part

2. a. Good because it says what the essay will do and in what order; bad because it is very repetitive in terms of words and structure.

   b. Model answer:
   Reality TV, which started in the UK and the United States about 20 years ago, has become one of the most popular genres on television around the world. In this essay, I will consider four reasons for the popularity. Firstly, I will look at the volume of the genre on television around the world. Secondly, I will discuss the similarity between reality TV and narrative fiction. Next, I will consider reality TV in relation to psychological needs. Finally, I will examine the issue of the range of reality TV programmes, from music contests to survival games.

C   Noticing the paragraph structure

1. Give students time to read through the first set of notes: *1. volume*. Check understanding of abbreviations in the notes and any new vocabulary. Students discuss the question in pairs, then elicit answers.

2. Set the task. Avoid explaining the meaning of the subsections before students do the task as the meaning will become clear during the activity. Point out that the paragraph starts with a signpost sentence – *There are a number of reasons …*

   Students complete individually then compare answers. Elicit answers, giving further explanation where necessary. Emphasize that this way of organizing sentences in a paragraph is a very good model for students to follow in their own writing.

Answers

1. *There is (such) a large volume of reality TV on the schedules, the audience often has little choice of viewing.*

2. 4 Direct quotation

   1 Statement

   2 Supporting evidence

   3 Related statement

   5 Reported speech

Division of paragraph:

introduction	There are a number of reasons for the popularity of reality TV.
statement	Firstly, the genre is now a major part of the schedules, so the volume of reality TV means that the audience often has little choice of viewing.
supporting evidence	Figures from Nielsen Media show that the genre accounts for 60 per cent of all programmes made around the world. (nielsenmedia.com, 2010).
related statement	Television companies make a lot of reality TV because it is very cheap to produce.
direct quotation	'Reality TV requires no actors, no scripts and no expensive settings,' says Wow TV CEO, Andrea Gibson (Gibson, 2011). 'Some programmes take place in one studio, made to look like a house or a school.'
reported speech	Eric Johannson of *Treasure Quest* agrees, pointing out that it does not cost as much to produce reality TV as drama or documentary, even if it involves taking everyone to a remote island and location filming (Johannson, 2011).

D Preparing to write

Give students time to study the notes. Once again, check understanding of abbreviations used and any new vocabulary. You will also need to check that students understand the (fictional) names of two reality shows are mentioned: *Private School (PS)* and *Treasure Quest (TQ)*. You could briefly discuss with the class what they think the format of these shows is. Set the task. Students complete individually then compare in pairs.

Show answers using an electronic projection so that students can compare their versions. Discuss any differences students may have had and accept any logical variations.

Answers

1. The main statement here is that …	audiences like reality TV because it is similar to fiction.
2. Aristotle said that …	the basis of all narrative fiction is conflict.
3. Conflict in reality TV comes from …	the situation or the selection of contestants.
4. Producers of *Treasure Quest* set up some of the dangers to …	increase the conflict.
5. 'Stuck-up Stephanie' was the villain …	in Series 1 of *Private School*.

E Writing the paragraph

Set the task and go over the paragraph structure from Exercise C. If necessary, elicit the first sentence (the statement) and write it on the board, showing students how the notes build into a complete sentence. Repeat with the next sentence (the supporting evidence), if necessary.

Students complete the rest of the paragraph individually. Monitor, giving help where necessary, and make a note of common errors.

Use an electronic projection to show the complete model answer.

Highlight how the model answer follows the paragraph structure from Exercise C. Tell students that, as in this paragraph, it is possible to have more than one related statement or quotation.

Allow students time to study the model answer and ask you about variations from their own work.

Answers

Model answer:

statement	Secondly, audiences like reality TV because it is similar to fiction in terms of its conventions.
supporting evidence	Although it is based in real life, it presents conflict between participants, which is the basis of all narrative fiction, according to Aristotle (Belfiore, 2000).
related statement	Sometimes, the conflict is part of the set-up of the programme, for example, in *Treasure Quest*, where contestants have to struggle against nature.
related statement	Sometimes, the conflict is created by the producers in their selection of contestants, in a programme such as *Private School*.
quotation	Television critic Miles Morton claims: 'Producers like some binary opposition in the *Private School* staffroom or on *Treasure Quest* island.'
reported speech	He gives examples of a rich girl and a poor boy, or a progressive teacher and a reactionary (Morton, 2011).
reported speech	Barbara Hughes goes further, pointing out that one contestant often becomes a 'villain', who the audience want to destroy.
quotation	She cites an example of 'Stuck-up Stephanie', who appeared in Series 1 of *Private School* (Hughes, 2010).

Methodology notes

1. There are several variations on the above approach, including:

   - Students' pens down. Elicit the complete paragraph and write it on the board. Then erase all of it (or leave key words as prompts). Students rewrite the paragraph.

   - An alternative to the above idea is to show the model paragraph for two minutes. Students are not allowed to write anything during this time. After two minutes, remove the model paragraph; students rewrite it.

   - To focus on the correct order for the structure of the paragraph as shown in Exercise C, you could do the paragraph as a jigsaw reading: cut up the subsections for students to organize in the correct order. Then remove the strips of paper; students write the paragraph.

   - Other alternatives include doing the paragraph as a gapped text, a wall dictation, or supplying the text with errors for students to correct, or with missing information for students to supply in the correct place.

2. You can use a process writing approach for this activity. Students write a first draft of the paragraph, show it to their partner to check readability, edit their work and then write a second draft.

Closure

Use feedback for Exercise E.

Para 2

1	There are a number of reasons for the popularity of reality TV.
2	Firstly, the genre is now a major part of the schedules, so the volume of reality TV means that the audience often has little choice of viewing.
3	Figures from Nielsen Media show that the genre accounts for 60 per cent of all programmes made around the world (nielsenmedia.com, 2010).
4	Television companies make a lot of reality TV because it is very cheap to produce.
5	'Reality TV requires no actors, no scripts and no expensive settings,' says Wow TV CEO, Andrea Gibson (Gibson, 2011).
6	'Some programmes take place in one studio, made to look like a house or a school.'
7	Eric Johannson of *Treasure Quest* agrees, pointing out that it does not cost as much to produce reality TV as drama or documentary, even if it involves taking everyone to a remote island and location filming (Johannson, 2011).

Para 3

1	Secondly, audiences like reality TV because it is similar to fiction in terms of its conventions.
2	Although it is based in real life, it presents conflict between participants, which is the basis of all narrative fiction, according to Aristotle (Belfiore, 2000).
3	Sometimes, the conflict is part of the set-up of the programme, for example, in *Treasure Quest*, where contestants have to struggle against nature.
4	Sometimes, the conflict is created by the producers in their selection of contestants, in a programme such as *Private School*.
5	Television critic Miles Morton claims: 'Producers like some binary opposition in the *Private School* staffroom or on *Treasure Quest* island.'
6	He gives examples of a rich girl and a poor boy, or a progressive teacher and a reactionary (Morton, 2011).
7	Barbara Hughes goes further, pointing out that one contestant often becomes a 'villain', who the audience want to destroy.
8	She cites an example of 'Stuck-up Stephanie', who appeared in Series 1 of *Private School* (Hughes, 2010).

3.18 Learning new writing skills: Giving evidence for statements

Objectives

By the end of this lesson, students should be able to:
- use evidence (including statistics, quotations and reported speech) in order to support statements;
- produce short paragraphs linking statements and evidence.

Introduction

Ask students to read through the model answers for the introduction and paragraphs 1 and 2 of the essay from Lesson 3.17. Many of the examples in this lesson are from the essay so this will provide students with a context.

A   Reviewing vocabulary

Set the task and go over the example. Students complete individually then compare answers in pairs. Show correct answers on an electronic projection. Discuss any differences with the students' versions of each sentence.

If your students are likely to find the task difficult, follow this procedure. With students' pens down, show the answer for each sentence on an electronic projection and allow students to study for one or two minutes. Highlight grammar and/or word order. Remove the electronic projection. Students now attempt the exercise.

Answers

1. In this essay, I will consider reasons for the popularity of reality TV. (why)	*In this essay, I will consider why reality TV is (so) popular.*
2. The volume of reality TV means the audience often has little choice of viewing. (because of)	*The audience often has little choice of viewing because of the volume of reality TV.*
3. Reality TV is very cheap to produce so television companies make a lot of programmes. (cost / leads)	*The low cost of reality TV leads to television companies making a lot of programmes.*
4. The genre requires no actors or scripts. (needed)	*No actors or scripts are needed for the genre.*
5. Audiences like reality TV because it is similar to fiction. (similarity)	*Audiences like reality TV because of its similarity to fiction.*
6. Sometimes the producers create conflict in their selection of contestants. (results in)	*Sometimes the (producers') selection of contestants results in conflict.*

B   Identifying a key skill

Briefly revise some of the information students learnt about reality TV in the previous lesson (the examples in the Skills Check are based on this).

Remind students about the activity they did on paragraph structure in Lesson 3.17, Exercise C. Tell them that, in this lesson, they will learn more about this paragraph structure.

Tell students that if they make a statement of fact in an academic essay, they must explain why the statement is correct. They must give evidence.

Give students plenty of time to study the information in the Skills Check. Check understanding of the word *authority* in this context (= expert or specialist). Focus on the questions in Exercise B and ask students to discuss in pairs for a minute. Elicit answers.

Answers

The statement = statistics

The related statement = a quotation and reported speech

C Practising a new skill

1. Set the task. (All the statements are taken from previous themes in the course, but you may need to quickly revise some of the vocabulary or concepts.) Students complete individually, then compare answers in pairs. Elicit answers.

2. Elicit or give students some phrases to help them if you feel it is necessary:
   - *According to …*
   - *As X says …*
   - *The graph shows …*
   - *Research by X indicates …*

   Monitor while students complete the activity. Show model answers using an electronic projection and discuss any variations students had in their own answers.

Academic note

The evidence given comes from a range of sources. In this case, all the sources are acceptable, e.g., The Waterman Pen Company is an authority on numbers of pens sold at a particular time. The original research quoted – *writer's survey* – is acceptable in theory because it is primary research, but readers would look closely at the research to see how valid results are for extrapolation.

Evaluating a source is covered in the next theme, but with a more able group you could discuss here why each of these is an authority in a particular field, or whether you might have any doubts about the evidence.

Answers

1.

a. Global warming is caused by greenhouse gases.	Atmospheric CO_2 has risen in line with average world temperatures (World Meteorological Organization).
b. Recruitment of new employees will be easy in Causton.	Unemployment rate in the area is 20 per cent (UK government figures).
c. Most decisions for teenagers in my culture are made by their parents.	93 per cent (writer's survey of ten families)
d. Mobile phones have not had any effect on cultural values in rural areas.	official (UNESCO, Africa)
e. Economic performance is linked to geography.	survey of 150 countries (World Bank)
f. Sales dropped to 5 million per annum in 1975.	graph (The Waterman Pen Company)

2. Possible answers:

   A survey of ten families revealed that …

   As the graph from The Waterman Pen Company shows, …

   According to information from the World Meteorological Organization, …

   A UNESCO official in Africa says …

   The World Bank survey of 150 countries indicates that …

   An unemployment rate of 20 per cent in the area means that … (UK government figures)

Closure

Spend a few minutes looking back at the model answers for the essay in Lesson 3.17 and show how the paragraph structure, sources and quotations relate to the information in this lesson.

3.19 Grammar for writing: Joining sentences with participles (2)

Objectives

By the end of this lesson, students should be able to:

- spell past participles correctly;
- use past participles to join clauses with the same subject.

Introduction

Ask students to look back at the essay in Lesson 3.17. Get them to find and underline all the verbs ending in ~ing. Ask them what the word is doing in the sentence in each case, but do not confirm or correct.

Remind students that they learnt to understand sentences with past participles in the reading section.

Grammar box 15

Elicit the two basic sentences for the example sentence and write them on the board:

- *We flew everyone to an island.*
- *It was located in the South Pacific.*

Students discuss the questions in pairs. Elicit answers.

Answers

1. two – *We flew everyone to an island / located in the South Pacific.*
2. first clause = *We*; second clause = *an island*
3. first = *flew*; second = *is / was located*
4. first = past simple; second = past participle

A   Forming the past participle

1. Elicit that the past simple and past participle forms are the same with regular verbs. The only problem is spelling, which is slightly harder than it seems at first. Set the task. Students complete individually. Write the correct past participles on the board so that students can check their spellings.
2. Students discuss in pairs. Elicit answers.

Answers

1. a. believe   believed
   b. describe   described
   c. play   played
   d. ban   banned
   e. die   died
   f. try   tried
   g. offer   offered
   h. stop   stopped
   i. regret   regretted

2.

a. take off final *e*	✓ *believe, describe*
b. change final *ie* to *y*	✗ *die*
c. change final *y* to *ie*	✓ after a consonant, e.g., *try*
	✗ not after a vowel, e.g., *play*
d. with one-syllable verbs, double the final consonant letter after a single vowel letter	✓ *ban, stop*
e. with multi-syllable verbs, double the final consonant letter after a single vowel letter	✓ only if the final syllable is stressed, e.g., *regret*
	✗ *offer*

B   Joining with the past participle

Before setting the task, you can, if you wish, elicit the passive sentence first. For example: *it was written in about 1590, decisions are taken in families,* etc. Go over the example for the joined sentences. Students complete individually, then compare answers in pairs. Monitor. Show correct answers using an electronic projection so that students can correct their own sentences. Give further explanation of any sentences students had difficulty with. Note that writers sometimes do not use commas at all, and some use them when the information does not define the object of the previous sentence but rather adds some extra information.

Answers

1. Shakespeare's first play was called *Henry VI*, it was written in about 1590.
2. This study identifies the key decisions taken by people in families.
3. The study involved 1,000 participants chosen from six different age groups.
4. The company sells computer chips made by companies in Japan.
5. Most scientists believe in global warming, caused by greenhouse gases in the atmosphere.
6. The pen used a new ink invented by Biro's brother, Georg.

C Completing sentences with past participles

Elicit some possible endings for some of the sentences. Point out that this is partly a general knowledge quiz! You might like to put students into pairs or groups to decide on an ending, but then each student must write the sentence. Monitor and give help where necessary. Make a note of common errors. Ask students to read out one or two of their completed sentences (or they can write them on the board). Go over any common errors you noted.

Answers

Possible answers:

1. People in many countries know the tragedy, *Romeo and Juliet*, written …	*by William Shakespeare / in the 17th century.*
2. In the 16th century, colonists began to travel to America, discovered …	*by Columbus / in 1492.*
3. The highest mountain on Earth is Everest, conquered …	*by Sir Edmund Hillary / in 1953.*
4. One of the wonders of the Ancient World is the Great Pyramid of Giza, built …	*by the Ancient Egyptians / 500 years ago.*
5. Long-distance communication was revolutionized by the telephone, invented …	*by Alexander Graham Bell / in the 19th century.*
6. The United Kingdom and France are now linked by a tunnel, drilled …	*under the Channel.*
7. Learning by doing is a theory, proposed …	*by Aristotle.*
8. The atmosphere releases nitrogen, dissolved …	*in rain.*

Closure

Ask students to write out the second clause of the sentences in Exercise C as full passive sentences.

Answers

1. *Romeo and Juliet* was written by William Shakespeare / in the 17th century.
2. America was discovered by Columbus / in 1492.
3. Everest was conquered by Sir Edmund Hillary / in 1953.
4. The Great Pyramid of Giza was built by the Ancient Egyptians / 500 years ago.
5. The telephone was invented by Alexander Graham Bell / in the 19th century.
6. A tunnel was drilled under the Channel.
7. The theory was proposed by Aristotle.
8. The nitrogen is dissolved in rain.

3.20 Applying new writing skills: Reality TV – psychological needs and range

Objectives

By the end of this lesson, students should be able to:

- organize notes from given research into statements and evidence;
- write two paragraphs for completion of the essay in Lesson 3.17;
- use supporting evidence with references accurately to support statements;
- use target vocabulary, language and discourse structure from the section in order to produce an outline-type parallel essay about the genre of soaps.

Introduction

Dictate some infinitives and ask students to write the past participle in each case. Mix up regular verbs with spelling issues and irregular verbs, e.g.,

take stop

write try

offer send

refer allow

A Reviewing sentence and paragraph structure

1. This activity will revise and provide the background for the rest of the lesson, as well as focus on set phrases for writing. Set the task. Students should not look back at the original introduction in Lesson 3.17, as the introduction on page 96 is based on the revised introduction from Lesson 3.17, Exercise B2. Students complete individually. Show the completed text on an electronic

projection so that students can correct their own work. Highlight areas where students made mistakes, for example with prepositions in each phase.

2. Elicit the statements and supporting evidence (or students can discuss in pairs). Allow students to self-check. See the optional activity below for an alternative methodology.

Answers

1. Reality TV, which started in the UK and the United States about 20 years ago, has become one of the most popular genres on television around the world. In this essay, I will consider *the reasons for* this popularity. Firstly, I will look at *the extent of* the genre on television around the world. Secondly, I will discuss *the similarities between* reality TV and narrative fiction. Next, I will consider *the relation(ship) between* reality TV and the psychological needs of the audience. Finally, I will examine *the issue of* the range of reality TV programmes, from popular music contests to survival games.

2. Self-check – students refer to original paragraphs in Lesson 3.17.

B **Thinking, organizing and writing**

Before you set the task, check understanding of the topic for paragraphs 4 and 5. Focus on the definitions of the three words (opposite Exercise B) and explain these are three of the psychological needs that will help to complete paragraph 4. Give students time to read the definitions. Check understanding and allow time for a brief discussion: *Do students agree that reality TV satisfies these three needs? In what way?*

Now move on to the instructions for the main task. Check students understand where the relevant source material is and what they have to do with it.

Students can discuss the information in source material in pairs or small groups, but the first writing draft should be done individually.

Answers

There are so many ways that students may choose to deal with the source materials that on this occasion, the answers depend on the students.

C **Editing and rewriting**

1. Remind students of things to check for: *spelling, correct tenses,* etc. Monitor and give help where necessary.

2. The final version can be written in class or set for homework. If done in class, monitor and make a note of common errors. Give feedback on students' common writing errors to the whole class.

D **Writing the references**

If students did the reading section of this theme, refer them back to the references under the text in Lesson 3.15. Point out that the references here are written following the APA (American Psychological Association) conventions, which is a common system in many universities, although they should check what their university / faculty uses.

Ask students for the order of information:

<u>for a book:</u>
surname + initial + date + book title + city of publication + publisher

<u>for a journal article:</u>
surname + initial + date + article title + journal + volume no. + issue no. + page nos

<u>for an Internet article:</u>
full address including http + retrieval date

Ask students when we use:

commas	after the surname, after the name of the book
full stops	after the initial of the first name
colons	between city of publication and publisher
brackets	around the date of publication
italics	for title of book (not article)

Set for individual work. Monitor and assist.

E **Writing a parallel essay**

Ask students to think of some possible reasons in pairs or groups. Set for homework if you think the class is good enough to manage. Take in at some future date and display the best answers.

Closure

Feed back on brainstorm for Exercise E.

Answers

Possible reasons:

Soap operas are fiction – people like fiction.

They go on for a long time, so people become very involved with the characters.

There are heroes and villains.

It is escapism.

They might begin to see the people as real because they 'live' with them for so long.

They see people coping with the same sort of problems which they have in their own lives, so perhaps learn life lessons.

Portfolio: Media debate

Objectives

> By the end of this lesson, students will have:
> - worked independently to produce presentations in speech and writing about television programmes;
> - used vocabulary, grammar, sub-skills and knowledge from the theme in integrated skills activities.

Note: The Portfolio, as usual, brings together all of the main elements of the theme in one activity. In particular, in this lesson, you will have opportunities to revise the following information and concepts:

- From the listening section:
  o the idea that perhaps we should protect children from violence on TV, and the structure of concessive argument
- From the speaking section:
  o the idea the television programmes are used to sell products rather than inform and educate the public
- From the reading section:
  o vocabulary and theory related to the conventions of fiction which relates to reality television because it is, in fact, manufactured reality, or fictionalized reality; the fact that you must find evidence for statements and that evidence should come from an authority in the field

- From the writing section:
  o vocabulary and theory related to reality television

However, if your students have not studied one or more of the sections, it will be enough to give them a brief explanation of the relevant information. Research, note-taking and other preparations may have to be set as assignments. The presentations can then be given at a later date in class.

Introduction

Ask students to make a list of the main genres on television, and then to tick any which they like watching. Feed back to get a general idea of which are the most popular genres with your class.

For students who haven't studied the reading section, make sure you teach *reality TV* and some of the main ideas about the genre – that it involves real people, but they are put into conflict situations, and that humiliation is often involved; check the meaning of *humiliation*.

A Activating ideas

Give students time to read the opinions and then check understanding with comprehension questions:

How do people make fools of themselves on reality programmes?

What were freak shows in the Middle Ages?

What does Jenny mean by 'voting for' and 'voting off'?

What does the advertising executive mean about a clear demographic?

Ask students which ones they agree or disagree with and record the results to get a feel for the consensus.

B Gathering and recording information

Tell students they are going to have a debate. This is an organized discussion with people speaking for a fixed length of time either in favour of or against a statement, which is called the *motion*. Elicit the motion in this case: 'This house believes that: Television programmes that involve humiliation of contestants should be banned.' After the speeches (and sometimes questions from the audience), the audience votes on whether they are for or against the motion.

Point out that in an academic debate, you sometimes have to argue for something you disagree with, just so you can see the arguments on both sides – the argument and counter-argument.

Set the task. Allow students to choose, but when they have chosen, label students A (for) or B (against). Students work individually and list some points for or against the motion, depending on whether they are A or B. Monitor and offer help where necessary.

Point out that they must now do some research to find support for their statements, or indeed, new statements from people who have researched the topic already. Remind them of the importance of recording sources and refer them to the index cards if they did the reading section of this theme.

C Preparing a presentation

Form groups of As and Bs. If the class is large, then you can have several groups of As and several groups of Bs. In their groups, they check their points and add to their lists. They then collaborate on writing a two-minute speech in favour of or against the motion. Get them to divide up the presentation between themselves. Make sure they are referring to the sources of their supporting evidence: *As White says ...,* *Cameron pointed out in her article ...* Ideally, they should give the references on a slide at the end of the presentation.

D Listening to a debate

With a large group, have a number of debates going on in different parts of the room, but make sure that each debate has an audience. The audience is composed of people who have done their debate or are about to do it. At the end of the two speeches, members of the audience can ask questions. Then the audience votes on who won that particular debate.

E Writing

Remind students to follow the usual procedure for writing activities. During the editing stage, ask them to show their essay to other students for feedback. Set for individual work. Take in at a later date and display the best essays.

Closure

Feed back on general points you noticed during the debates.

Theme 4

Living life to the full

- Life systems

- A sporting life

- Learning for leisure

- Living longer, living better

Listening: Life systems

4.1 Vocabulary for listening: Cells, tissues and organs

Objectives

By the end of this lesson, students should be able to:
- recognize new vocabulary for the section in isolation and in context;
- develop understanding of new vocabulary for the section;
- demonstrate understanding of some basic elements of physiology of the human organism.

Introduction

With Course Books closed, ask students to make a list of at least ten words for parts of the body. Do not elicit now, but leave until after Exercise A. Then ask students to go back to their lists and (1) check for correct words, spelling, etc., and (2) see if they have any additional words in their lists.

A   Activating knowledge

1. Most of the words in this activity should be revision for the students. Set the task, making sure students understand they should write the number only, not the word. Play ⊕ 4.1. Do not elicit answers.

2. Set the task for pairwork. Students should try to remember the correct word for each number. Elicit answers or use an electronic projection to show the correctly labelled diagram. Spend a few minutes checking pronunciation of 'difficult' words such as *thigh, shoulder, elbow*. Also point out spelling of words such as *thigh, wrist, knee*, etc.

Transcript
⊕ 4.1

Presenter:	4.1. Theme 4: Living life to the full Lesson 4.1. Vocabulary for listening: Cells, tissues and organs
	Exercise A1. Listen and write the number of each word in the correct place on the diagram.
Voice:	1. ankle
	2. arm
	3. chest

4. elbow
5. foot
6. hand
7. hip
8. knee
9. neck
10. ribs
11. shoulder
12. thigh
13. wrist
14. head

Answers

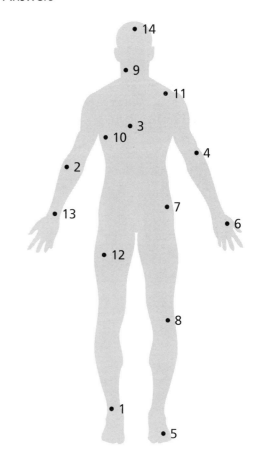

B   Understanding new words from illustrations and definitions

Ask students to study the figure and its title. Explain that the diagrams for the cell and the tissues are shown many hundreds of times larger than in 'real life'. Set the task. Students complete individually then compare answers in pairs. Elicit answers, helping with the pronunciation of target words if necessary. However, you do not need to practise pronunciation at this point. Elicit words for other organs the students may know already, e.g., *heart, brain*, etc.

Answers

1. group of cells which act in a particular way	tissue
2. group of molecules; the smallest unit of life	cell
3. group of organs working together to achieve a particular objective, like converting food into energy	organ system
4. organ systems working together in one body	organism
5. tissues which perform a particular function, like breaking down food	organ

C Understanding new words in context

Check or teach the meaning of *physiology* (= the functions / processes of the body). Set the task and give students time to read through the words in the list. Play ⊕ **4.2**, pausing for students to write the number. When all ten incomplete sentences have been played, students can compare answers in pairs.

Play ⊕ **4.3** of the complete sentences so that students can check their answers. Go over any words where students are still not sure about the meaning.

Answers

- breathe.
2 cells.
8 digestion.
5 electricity.
1 body.
- form.
3 functions.
6 heart.
4 purpose.
7 systems.

Transcripts
⊕ 4.2

Presenter: **4.2. Exercise C1. Listen to part of a lecture about physiology. When the lecturer stops, number the next word.**

Lecturer:
1. OK. So first let's look at the levels of organization that make up the human …
2. At the lowest level, we have the cell. This is the smallest unit of life and every part of the body is composed of …

3. These cells can take in nutrients, convert nutrients to energy or carry out specialized …
4. Cells are grouped into tissues. Each kind of tissue is designed for a particular …
5. For example, muscular tissue is able to contract while nervous tissue conducts …
6. At the next level, some tissues combine to achieve a particular objective. These tissues are called organs. For example, the stomach, the lungs and the …
7. At an even higher level of organization, we have organ …
8. In each system, different organs work together – for example, the mouth, the stomach, the small intestine and the large intestine all play a role in …
9. The highest level is a group of organs working …
10. Groups of organs in the same body are called organisms. For example, humans, animals and …

 4.3

Presenter: **4.3. Exercise C2. Listen and check your answers.**

1. OK. So first, let's look at the levels of organization that make up the human body.
2. At the lowest level, we have the cell. This is the smallest unit of life and every part of the body is composed of cells.
3. These cells can take in nutrients, convert nutrients to energy or carry out specialized functions.
4. Cells are grouped into tissues. Each kind of tissue is designed for a particular purpose.
5. For example, muscular tissue is able to contract, while nervous tissue conducts electricity.
6. At the next level, some tissues combine to achieve a particular objective. These tissues are called organs. For example, the stomach, the lungs and the heart.
7. At an even higher level of organization, we have organ systems.
8. In each system, different organs work together – for example, the mouth, the stomach, the small intestine and the large intestine all play a role in digestion.
9. The highest level is a group of organs working together.
10. Groups of organs in the same body are called organisms. For example, humans, animals and plants.

Closure

Choose one of the following:

- Refer students to the transcript. Ask students to find and underline all the verbs used to describe how the body functions or works. Elicit answers and make a list on the board. Then elicit a synonym where possible:

make up = form, comprise

is composed of = is made of, is formed from

take in = receive

convert = change

carry out = do

are grouped into = are arranged

is designed for

combine

work together = do, perform

play a role = have a function

- Ask students to complete the following table of the levels of organization of the human body:

level	item
highest	organism, e.g., humans, animals, plants, fish, etc.
	organ systems working together, e.g., moving the body
	an organ system, e.g., digestion
	organs, e.g., heart, lungs, stomach, etc.
lowest	cells

4.2 Real-time listening: Organ systems

Objectives

By the end of this lesson, students should be able to:

- use existing skills to follow a physiology lecture about some of the systems of the body;
- demonstrate understanding of the lecture through adding notes to diagrams provided;
- recognize new vocabulary in context.

Introduction

Revise the vocabulary and information from Lesson 4.1. For example, you could write the following questions on the board for students to discuss in pairs:

What is the lowest level of organization of the human body? (the cell)

What are some of the functions of cells? (they can take in nutrients / convert nutrients to energy)

What is the function of muscular tissue? (it can contract)

What is the function of nervous tissue? (it conducts electricity)

What happens at the next level? (tissues combine to form organs, e.g., the stomach, lungs, heart)

Which organs work together in the digestion system? (stomach, small and large intestines)

What do we call a group of organs working together in one body? (organism)

As an alternative, you could ask students to complete the table suggested in the Closure of the previous lesson (4.1). Even if students have done it before, they could try to replicate it from memory on this occasion.

A Activating ideas

Set the task and tell students it does not matter if they cannot answer the questions at this stage. Students discuss questions in pairs. Elicit a few ideas but do not confirm or correct.

Answers

Answers depend on students.

Methodology note

Ideally, for Exercises B2 and B3, students should listen and check answers. However, it is probably not practical to deal with the DVD *and* a CD. Therefore the teacher should provide the models on this occasion.

B Understanding an introduction

1. This activity focuses on students recognizing 'difficult' multi-syllable words in context. Give students time to read the phrases in the box. An optional activity is for students to look up the meanings in a dictionary before they watch the DVD. You could also pronounce the words for the students if you wish.

   Play DVD 4.A. Elicit answers and replay any sections where students missed the target word.

2. Set this as a pairwork activity. Then say each word so that students can check their answers.

3. Set the task. Students complete individually then compare answers in pairs. Read out the completed text as a final checking activity. This will also give students the opportunity to hear the target words in context once again.

Methodology note

The lecturer in this case is deliberately not very organized. This is because students will have to deal with the fractured text produced by some lecturers. Mention this to students and point out the reason for asking them to listen to this kind of speech.

Answers

2. a'ssociated

'breathing

circu'latory

com'ponents

di'gestion

'function

interre'lated

'muscular

'nutrient

physi'ology

'skeletal

'systems

3. In this lecture, which is part of the core course in *physiology*, the lecturer will talk about six human body *systems*, including the *skeletal*, muscular and *circulatory* systems. He will describe the *function* of each system, mention some of the *components*, and explain how the systems are *interrelated*.

Transcript

🌐 4.4 DVD 4.A

Right. What I'm going to do in this session is firstly, the skeleton – the bones and so on that keep us upright. Secondly, I'm going to mention the way the muscles enable the bones to move, and then, thirdly, the nervous system which sends messages to the muscles from the brain. So that's the skeletal system, the muscular system and the nervous system. Next, the digestive system – the stomach, and so on. Of course, it's this system that supplies the nutrients to enable the other systems to work, to grow and to repair. OK. Where was I? Let's

see. Skeleton, muscles, nerves, digestion – ah, yes, right. What comes next is the respiratory system – the mouth and nose – breathing, if you like, although I'm going to point out that it's a bit more than that. Then finally, we have the circulatory system, based on the heart, which sends the blood around the body.

Ⓒ Understanding a lecture

1. Set the task, reminding students about what information they will hear according to the introduction (above). Explain that you will pause the DVD after each section so that students can write and compare answers. Students will have to guess the spelling of some words if they are not sure. In order to encourage prediction, elicit a few ideas for the functions of each system, but do not confirm or correct.

   Play DVD 4.B until the end of part 1. Monitor to check students are completing the task correctly. They can use dictionaries to check spelling.

   Repeat the procedure with the remaining sections. Elicit answers orally. (Tell students they will see the completed diagrams with notes after Exercise C2 below.)

2. Before students draw arrows on the diagrams, ask them to discuss the relationships in pairs. Then students can draw the arrows. Show the diagram with the arrows (see Answers below) using an electronic projection so that students can compare the completed version with their own.

Optional activities

- Replay DVD 4.B (the whole thing if there is time, otherwise one or two extracts). Students can follow the transcript at the same time.
- Replay a section of DVD 4.B. Ask students to tick words they hear that are shown on the relevant diagram. For example, section 1, students look at the skeletal system diagram and tick the words *skull, ribs, pelvis, spine*, etc.

Answers

1.

skeletal system	muscular system
supports body; protects organs; makes red blood cells	*enables body to move*
nervous system	digestive system
interfaces with external environment; gets messages and sends messages	*converts food into nutrients*
respiratory system	circulatory system
exchanges oxygen and CO_2 with cells, blood and air in lungs	*moves blood round body; supplies nutrients and oxygen to other systems*

2. Arrows should be drawn and labelled as follows:

The digestive system	gives nutrients to	the circulatory system.
The respiratory system	gives oxygen to	the circulatory system.
The circulatory system	gives nutrients and oxygen to	all the other systems.
The muscular system	is attached to	the skeletal system.
The muscular system	is controlled by	the nervous system.

Transcript

🌐 4.5 DVD 4.B

Lecturer:

Right, so … let's consider the first system. The skeleton. What the skeleton does, basically, is keep us upright. It also gives the body its basic form, its basic shape. The human *skeletal system* is made up of 206 bones. The structure forms a strong internal framework for the body, which protects the organs involved in the other human body systems. It provides the basic strength for the rest of the body. Did you know bone can be four times as strong as concrete? Anyway, the main bones are, of course, the skull, which contains the brain, the ribs which protect most of the main organs – the heart, the lungs, the liver, the kidneys, and so on – and the pelvis, or hips, to give the bones their common name. Oh, and of course, the spine – the bones which run down the back. The spine, or vertebral column, comprises 33 bones or vertebrae. Just going back to the function of the skeleton for a moment … Bones don't only provide strength. They also store important minerals and vitamins. The bones meet at joints – for example, the hip joint and the shoulder joint, which are ball and socket joints. They give maximum movement, up, down, left, right. Then there are the knee joints and elbow joints, for example. They are hinge joints, like on a door. Oh, and I forgot to say – bones make red blood cells, too.

The next system is the *muscular system*. The muscles are attached to the skeletal bones and, basically, the primary function is to enable the body to move. Muscle tissue has the unique ability to contract. However, and this is quite interesting, it cannot then expand to its former position by itself. That's strange, isn't it? It contracts, but then it needs another muscle to work in opposition, to pull it back to its original position. These groups are called antagonistic pairs, and are the basis for human movement. *Antagonistic* … it comes from *antagonist*,

clearly. Like the person in a story who opposes the hero, the protagonist. Sorry, perhaps you don't know anything about literature. Still, you get the basic idea. I understand we have a lot of people from Sports Science on this course. Well, for you, important muscles in the arms are the biceps and triceps. Across the stomach we have the abdominal muscles – from *abdomen*, of course. These are sometimes called *abs* for short. We also have the important muscles in the back of the thigh, which are often called the hamstrings. Oh, and of course, the Achilles tendon in the back of the ankle. Athletes often injure that part of their body. Now, what was I talking about? Right, the muscles are attached to the bones in pairs. Each one can only contract, but when one contracts, the other expands and vice versa. But how do we make the muscles contract? That's the next system. Oh, um, did I mention, there are over 600 muscles in the human body? And you have to learn them all. No, only joking!

It is the central nervous system that controls muscle contraction. The system is two-way. What I mean by that is, the system gathers information from nerves throughout the body and takes it to the brain through the spinal column. It uses electrical impulses. The brain is the primary processing centre for the body. If the decision is taken to react to a particular stimulus, the brain sends the necessary impulses to the muscles – electricity again. The main parts of the nervous system are the nerves, as I've just said, the brain, obviously, and the spinal cord, which runs down the spine. We can see now why the skull and the spine are so important. They protect key parts of the central nervous system. So we could say that it's the nervous system that interfaces with the external environment. I mean, it gets messages *from* the environment and it tells the body to move *through* the environment. For example, it senses heat with the nerves in the fingers and tells the hand to move away.

Right, so we have seen that the skeletal system provides the basic structure for the body and the muscular system is attached to the skeletal system. The muscles need instructions to move and they come from the central nervous system. But what provides the body with the necessary energy to do things, and the nutrients to enable the body to grow and repair? Well, the *digestive system* is responsible for converting foods into usable substances along the digestive tract. These substances are then absorbed into the blood. We take food in through the mouth and down the oesophagus in the neck and chest. The food is broken down in the stomach and then absorbed into the blood stream through the walls of the intestines. But, and this is very important, at this stage, the nutrients are in the blood, they are *not* in the muscles and nerves and so on. We'll see how they get there in a few minutes.

Right, so we have supplied the blood with nutrients, but, in fact, the body cannot use those nutrients without oxygen. So we need another system. What we need is the respiratory system. Now, some people think that respiration is the same as breathing but that's not true. Respiration is not just about taking in air and giving out CO_2. It's the exchange of oxygen and carbon dioxide between cells, the blood and air in the lungs. It's the lungs which suck in air using strong muscles between the ribs ... Oh, I should have talked about those muscles on the way through! They are called the *diaphragm* and they sit under the lungs. They move up and down to contract and expand the chest cavity, and that movement pulls air in and pushes carbon dioxide out. Sorry about that. Can you add the diaphragm to the muscular system?

Oh dear, I see we are nearly out of time. So, very quickly, the last system for today. We've seen that nutrients enter the blood from the digestive system, and oxygen enters the blood from the respiratory system, but of course all this is pointless if the blood just sits there and doesn't move. We need a system to move the blood around the body. We need ... the circulatory system. It was an English physician, William Harvey, who discovered this system in the 17th century. The blood is pumped out of the heart through the arteries to the skeletal system, the muscular system, the nervous system, the digestive system and the respiratory system. The nutrients and oxygen leave the blood and enter the cells of the organs and then the blood returns to the heart through the veins.

That's enough for now. There are other systems and I'd like you to research those before the next lecture. The details are on the handout. OK. Thanks very much. In the next lecture, we'll be looking at what happens when something goes wrong with one of the systems. Oh, and I meant to point out that we have tutorials on Wednesday. I'm going to ask you questions about the systems we've talked about today, so have a look at your notes between now and then.

D **Showing comprehension**

This activity can be done in several different ways, either individually or in pairs. It revises question forms as well as further checking of comprehension. Once the correct questions have been elicited, students can practise asking and answering in pairs. The correct questions can be written in class or for a home assignment as consolidation.

Answers

Model questions:

1. What is the function of the skeletal system?	*It supports the body and protects the organs.*
2. How many bones are there in the human body?	*206.*
3. What is an example of a ball and socket joint?	*The shoulder or the hip.*
4. What kind of joint is the knee joint?	*A hinge joint.*
5. What is the function of the muscular system?	*It allows the body to move.*
6. How many muscles are there in the human body?	*Over 600.*
7. Why do muscles come in pairs?	*Because muscles can only contract.*
8. How does the central nervous system work?	*It uses electricity.*
9. Which system converts food into usable nutrients?	*The digestive system.*
10. Why does the body need the respiratory system?	*Because the body can't use nutrients without oxygen.*
11. Who discovered the circulation of the blood?	*William Harvey.*
12. What is the difference between arteries and veins?	*Arteries take blood away from the heart, veins take it back to the heart.*

E **Developing critical thinking**

This activity focuses on study skills. In pairs or groups, students think of different ways to remember the names of the different parts of the body. After a few minutes, elicit ideas.

Answers

The set of words for each system can be written on a different file card.

Write the words alphabetically.

Make copies of the diagrams without labels, try to write all the labels.

Identify all the words which are the same in most languages (i.e., the Greek-based words).

Write the words in order from top of the body to the feet (if relevant), e.g., skull, shoulder bone, ribs, etc.

Write the words in order of usage in the system (if relevant), e.g., mouth, oesophagus, stomach, etc.

Closure
Divide the class into groups of six students. Number each student from 1 to 6. Each student takes it in turns to explain the body system with the corresponding number, its functions and how it relates to the other systems.

> **4.3 Learning new listening skills: Additional information in lectures**

> **Objectives**
>
> By the end of this lesson, students should be able to:
> * predict pronunciation of new words;
> * recognize phrases for adding new information in a lecture.

Introduction
Write some words on the board from the previous lessons where the spelling does not help with the pronunciation. For example:

heart	blood
tissue	breathe
shoulder	thigh
nutrient	organism
digestion	physiology
interrelated	

Point to each word and elicit the pronunciation. Use this activity to move smoothly into Exercise A.

A Predicting the sound of new words

1. Give students time to read the Pronunciation Check. Then ask:

   *Why should you check pronunciation of words **before** a lecture?* (So you recognize them when you hear them in context – it will help you to understand the lecture.)

2. Ask students to cover the right-hand column with the phonemics. Students try to guess the pronunciation of each word. Do not confirm or correct. Then set the task. Students can work in pairs.

3. Elicit the pronunciation of (a) *bronchi*. Play 🔊 4.6. Pause after (a). Did students use the correct pronunciation? Repeat the procedure for each item. You do not need to practise or correct the pronunciation of each word, nor do students need to learn all the words.

   Tell students it is important for them to have a good dictionary with phonemic script so that they can check pronunciation in future.

Answers

a. bronchi	j	/ˈbræki:/
b. colon	a	/ˈbrɒŋki:/
c. larynx	g	/serəˈbeləm/
d. nasal	b	/ˈkəʊlən/
e. sciatic	c	/ˈlærɪŋks/
f. pharynx	d	/ˈneɪzl/
g. cerebellum	f	/ˈfærɪŋks/
h. trachea	e	/saɪˈætɪk/
i. trapezius	h	/trəˈki:ə/
j. brachi	i	/trəˈpi:zi:əs/

Transcript
🌐 4.6

Presenter:	4.6. Lesson 4.3. Learning new listening skills: Additional information in lectures Exercise A3. Listen to the correct pronunciation and check your ideas.
Voice:	a. bronchi b. colon c. larynx d. nasal e. sciatic f. pharynx g. cerebellum h. trachea i. trapezius j. brachi

B Identifying a new skill

1. Give students time to study the notes and think about the answer to the question. They should be focusing on the word *diaphragm* which is out of line, and the arrow pointing back to the main list. Do not elicit answers.

2. Students read the Skills Check. Elicit the answer to B1. Set the task. Play ⊚ 4.8. Students make a note individually of the additional information in each case. Then students compare answers in pairs. Elicit answers. Ask students to listen again to the CD and say if they notice anything about how each introductory phrase is pronounced. Play ⊚ 4.8 again. Students should be able to tell you that the phrases are spoken more quickly than the additional information.

Answers

The notes are like that because the lecturer gave the information about the diaphragm out of order.

Transcript
⊕ 4.8

Presenter:	4.8. Skills Check. Listen. What has the lecturer forgotten in each case?
Lecturer 1:	1. I forgot to say that Harvey discovered the circulation of the blood in the 17th century. 2. Did I mention that Harvey was English? 3. I should have told you about white blood cells. 4. I meant to point out that arteries are normally bigger than veins. 5. Just going back to the skeletal system for a minute, the bones in the lower part of the spine are joined together. 6. Can you go back and add that there are special heart muscles?

C Practising a new skill

Before you set the task, divide the class into small groups. Ask them to brainstorm the three lecture topics and think of any vocabulary or information connected with each topic. Set a time limit of two minutes. After the time is up, ask some of the students to report to the rest of the class on any ideas they had.

Now set the task. Play ⊚ 4.7. You can deal with each lecture one at a time, giving feedback before moving onto the next lecture, or play all the lectures and give feedback on the three at the end.

Give feedback by showing the completed notes on an electronic projection. Play ⊚ 4.7 again, pausing after each point where the extra information is given so that the relationship between what the lecturer says and the notes becomes clear.

Optional activity

An alternative activity for less able classes, or if you are short of time, is to give students the notes for each lecture minus the additional information. Students listen to each extract and add the additional information.

Answers
Studies on the effects of TV violence

Berkovitz (1969) – lab exp. – uni. students – watched violent films

Parke et al. **(1977)** young off –

Williams (early 70s) imp. of TV on comm. – sign inc. in aggression

Charlton et al. (1999) – intro TV on St Helena not sig.

The history of the Internet

Tim Berners-Lee – Br. in Switz. – sci. look at each other's docs – **1990**

every doc = add.

invented http = **hypertext transfer protocol hypertext = Ted Nelson, 1960s = connect docs so you can jump from one to another**

also inv. browser = look at docs on another comp.

Pakistan and Chile

	Pakistan	Chile
pop		
total pop	185 million	10% = **17.3 million**
density	177 p km²	20 p km²
urban:rural	**34:66**	**87:13**
land		
area	803,000 km²	**756,000 km²**
agric	30%	21%
nat. water	perm lakes / riv. – Indus	perm. lakes / riv – Loa

Transcript
⊕ 4.7

Presenter:	4.7. Exercise C. Listen and make notes. Add extra information in the correct place. Lecture 1: Studies of the effects of TV violence
Lecturer 1:	I'd like you to do some work on research studies into violent television. I'll give you some references to start you off and then I'd like you

to find at least three more. OK, so in order, then, we have Berkovitz, 1969. He carried out a laboratory experiment with university students. The study involved participants watching violent films to see if they acted more violently than the control group. Parke et. al. worked with young offenders in an institution. The result was similar to Berkovitz. And on the other side? Well, nothing really, although there is one well-known study – this was Charlton et. al., 1999 – which looked at the introduction of television on the island of St Helena. Their results were not significant. There was no increase in aggression. Did I mention the date for Parke et. al.? It was 1977. Oh, and sorry. I forgot to say that Williams did a study with 6- to 11-year-olds in Canada. This is an interesting study, actually. The researcher looked at the impact of television on a community which did not have television before. It was in the early 70s – you'll have to find the exact date. The introduction of TV led to a significant increase in aggression in the community.

Presenter: **Lecture 2: The history of the Internet**

Lecturer 2: So where have we got to? Right ... The late '70s. By then, we had most of the parts for the Internet in place. But an important piece was missing. The big breakthrough was made by Tim Berners-Lee, a British scientist working in Switzerland. He wanted all the scientists in his laboratory to be able to look at each other's documents. He realized that every document needed an address so you could find the document on another computer. So Berners-Lee invented a way of addressing documents. He called the address *http – hypertext transfer protocol*. Berners-Lee also invented a simple program, called a browser. This program allowed the user of one computer to look at documents on another computer. And, hey presto – we had the Internet. Sorry, I see some of you are looking a little blank. I should have explained *hypertext*, shouldn't I? The ht in http. Berners-Lee knew about hypertext but you didn't! The idea of hypertext was invented by a man called Ted Nelson in the 1960s. It is a way of connecting documents so you can jump from one to another. And while we're going back over this, I meant to point out that this was in 1990. The Berners-Lee breakthrough, I mean.

Presenter: **Lecture 3: A comparison of Chile and Pakistan**

Lecturer 3: Let's look at population now. As before, I'm going to look at three sub-areas under this heading: the total population, the density and the urban:rural split. Pakistan has a large population, but Chile's is quite small. The population of Pakistan is 185 million, whereas Chile's population is about ten per cent of that size. Pakistan has a much higher density of population than Chile – 177 people per square kilometre against 20 per square kilometre. Um. Sorry. Did I mention the actual population of Chile? It's 17.3 million.

Next, land. As you know, we consider area, percentage of agricultural land and availability of natural water, that is, lakes and rivers. Both countries are large. In fact, they are almost about the same size. Pakistan has an area of 803,000 square kilometres whilst Chile is

slightly smaller. Both countries have quite a high percentage of agricultural land. Pakistan has 30 per cent agricultural land and Chile has 21 per cent. Just going to back to area, Chile is 756,000 square kilometres. Where was I? Oh, yes, natural water. Both countries have permanent lakes and rivers. The most important river in Pakistan is the Indus, while the most important river in Chile is the Loa.

Ah ... I forgot to give you the urban:rural split, didn't I? I think I did. Well, the population of Pakistan is more rural than the population of Chile. The split in Pakistan is 34 to 66, whereas in Chile it is 87 to 13.

Closure
Ask students to study the transcript for each lecture extract (you can replay 🔊 **4.7** as well if you wish).

4.4 Grammar for listening: Cleft and pseudo-cleft sentences

Objectives

By the end of this lesson, students should be able to:
- identify cleft sentences in spoken discourse;
- demonstrate understanding of the function of cleft sentences for emphasizing important information.

Introduction
Revise information about Harvey from Lesson 4.2.

Grammar box 16
Give students time to read all the information and study the sentences in the tables. Set the task (identifying the SVO/A). Elicit answers. Elicit the 'basic' sentence for each cleft and pseudo-cleft sentence:

I'm going to talk about each system.

The skeletal system supports the body.

Harvey experimented with fish and snakes.

Next week we will look at sports injuries.

The brain controls the nervous system.

Harvey discovered the circulation of the blood.

Play 🔊 **4.9**. Elicit answers to the question.

The first table contains examples of *cleft sentences*. The second table contains examples of *pseudo-cleft* sentences. It is up to you whether you want students to learn these grammatical terms or not.

Point out that while students need to be able to recognize the sentences when listening, they do not need to learn how to say or write them at this stage. You don't need to go into the grammar in detail; the important thing is for students to recognize that when they hear a cleft sentence, some important information will follow.

Answers

There is a pause after *is/was* in sentences 1–3 (cleft sentences) but not in sentences 4–6 (pseudo-cleft sentences).

Transcript
🎧 4.9

Presenter:	4.9. Lesson 4.4. Grammar for listening: Cleft and pseudo-cleft sentences
	Grammar box 16. Listen to the sentences. Does the speaker pause in any of the sentences?
Voice:	What I'm going to do first is [PAUSE] talk about each system. What the skeletal system does is [PAUSE] support the body. What Harvey did was [PAUSE] experiment with fish and snakes. It will be next week that we look at sports injuries. It is the brain which controls the nervous system. It was Harvey who discovered the circulation of the blood.

A Recognizing cleft sentences

1. Set the task and play the examples on 🎧 **4.10**. Elicit answers to the question in the Course Book: *How do you know?* Play the remaining beginnings of questions / statements on 🎧 **4.10**. Do not elicit answers.

2. Play 🎧 **4.11** with the complete questions. Students check their answers. Replay any items students had difficulty with. If there's time, allow students to read the transcript, or show it on an electronic projection.

A lot of vocabulary from the previous lesson in this section is recycled here. You may want to use the opportunity to revise some of the target words.

Answers

1. There is a higher start for questions – mid-range start for cleft; the order of information after *What* is different in cleft sentences – i.e., *What* + verb / auxiliary = question; *What* + subject = cleft.

Transcript
🎧 4.10

Presenter:	4.10. Exercise A1. Listen to the beginning of some questions or statements.
Voice:	a. What is … b. What we'll look at … c. What Alcmaeon did … d. What doctors … e. What were … f. What can … g. What did … h. What I'm going to … i. What Kendrew … j. What was … k. What Schwann … l. What the arteries …

Transcript and Answers
🎧 4.11

Presenter:	4.11. Exercise A2. Listen to the whole of each question or statement and check your answers.
Voice:	a. What is the solution? b. What we'll look at first is the digestive system. c. What Alcmaeon did was distinguish between veins and arteries in 520 BCE. d. What doctors are hoping for is more research during the next ten years. e. What were we talking about? f. What can we do about the problem? g. What did Aristotle say about the heart? h. What I'm going to concentrate on next week is the functions of the cells. i. What Kendrew described in 1960 was the structure of the oxygen-carrying protein in muscles. j. What was the date of the first heart transplant? k. What Schwann discovered in 1836 was the first animal enzyme. l. What the arteries do is take oxygenated blood from the heart.

B Understanding cleft sentences

1. Set the task. Make sure students understand they are focusing on the statements in the transcript and not the questions. Go over the example.

2. Students complete individually then compare answers in pairs. Show the completed table using an electronic projection so that students can compare correct answers with their own. Go over any answers students had difficulty with.

Answers

See table below.

C Understanding pseudo-cleft sentences

1. Set the task. Give students time to read through the sentence endings. Elicit the fact that all the endings are about the invention of the telephone. Play ⊕ **4.12**, and pause if necessary while students choose the best way to complete each sentence. Do not elicit answers or allow students to shout out.

2. Play the complete sentences on ⊕ **4.13** so that students can check their answers. Go over any sentences students had difficulty with.

With students' books closed, say the first half of each sentence; students recall and say the sentence ending:

T: *It will be next week …*

Ss: *… that we look at the history of the telephone.*

You could do this as a pairwork activity. S1 looks at the transcript and reads out the sentence beginnings. S2 has the Course Book closed, listens to the beginning of the sentence and completes it.

Answers

e	that Bell invented the telephone.
f	that the telegraph declined in popularity.
a	that we look at the history of the telephone.
c	which began high-speed communication.
d	which Bell invented.
b	who invented the telephone.

Transcripts
⊕ 4.12

Presenter:	4.12. Exercise C1. Listen to the beginning of some pseudo-cleft sentences. Letter the logical way to complete each sentence.
Voice:	a. It will be next week … b. It was a man called Bell … c. It was the invention of the telephone … d. It was the telephone … e. It was in 1879 … f. It was after the invention of the telephone …

	S	V	O	A
b.	*We*	*'ll look at*	*the digestive system*	*first.*
c.	Alcmaeon	distinguished between	veins and arteries	in 520 BCE.
d.	Doctors	are hoping for	more research	during the next ten years.
h.	I	'll concentrate on	the function of the cells	next week.
i.	Kendrew	described	the structure of the oxygen-carrying protein in muscles	in 1960.
k.	Schwann	discovered	the first animal enzyme	in 1836.
l.	The arteries	take	oxygenated blood	from the heart.

4.13. Exercise C2. Listen to the whole sentence in each case and check your answers.

Voice:
a. It will be next week that we look at the history of the telephone.
b. It was a man called Bell who invented the telephone.
c. It was the invention of the telephone which really began high-speed communication.
d. It was the telephone which Bell invented.
e. It was in 1879 that Bell invented the telephone.
f. It was after the invention of the telephone that the telegraph declined in popularity.

Closure

Write the beginnings of some cleft sentences and pseudo-cleft sentences on the board and ask students to think of some different ideas for completing them. (Don't worry too much if the grammar isn't 100 per cent correct. The main idea is to understand the purpose of these kinds of sentences, rather than produce them correctly.)

It was a teacher who …

It was my car that …

It was last weekend that …

What I'm doing next weekend is …

What my father did …

4.5 Applying new listening skills: The PRICE of sports injuries

Objectives

By the end of this lesson, students should be able to:

• identify additional information in a lecture;

• make notes of sports injuries and treatments in a lecture;

• recognize that strategies are needed for dealing with poorly presented lectures.

Methodology note

As usual we have provided what we hope is a carefully-scaffolded lesson for practising listening to a lecture. However, as an alternative, with students' books closed, you could simply set the two questions in the lecture handout and play 🎧 4.14. This would give students a feel for the real-life situation, where they would have minimal guidance.

Introduction

Focus students' attention on the lesson title: *The PRICE of sports injuries*. Elicit ideas for what this means. Ask students why *PRICE* is in capital letters (suggests it is an acronym).

A Preparing for a lecture

1. Set the task, making sure students understand they should not worry about exact meaning at this stage. However, the lecture title, *Dealing with sports injuries*, tells the students that the words on the handout are all connected with injuries. Similarly, the words on the diagram will be parts of the body. Students discuss possible pronunciation of each word in pairs. Do not confirm or correct ideas at this stage – do that after students have listened to the introduction to the lecture.

2. Play DVD 4.C. Elicit meanings (where possible – not all words are explained here) and pronunciations of the target words from Exercise A1. Don't worry if students are not completely clear on the meanings at this point, as they are dealt with in more detail during the main part of the lecture.

Optional activity

If students enjoy working with phonemic script, they could even use it to write down what they think the pronunciation is for each of the target words in Exercise A1.

Answers

strains /streɪnz/

sprains /spreɪnz/

bruises /bruːzəz/

contusions /kəntjuːʒnz/

compression /kəmpreʃn/

elevation /elɪveɪʃn/

joint /dʒɔɪnt/

trauma /trɔːmə/

inflammation /ɪnfləmeɪʃn/

swelling /swelɪŋ/

Transcript

🔊 4.14 DVD 4.C

Presenter:	**Lesson 4.5. Applying new listening skills: The PRICE of sports injuries**
Lecturer:	Welcome, everybody. This session is on dealing with sports injuries. So today we are going to look at fascinating issues like the difference between strains and sprains, and bruises and contusions. You'll know all about those by the end of today. We'll also talk here about compression and elevation, but they're not injuries. They're treatments.
	OK. Let's start by looking at this photograph. *[points in direction of screen]* What has happened here? She has hurt her leg, but what has she done, exactly? Fallen over? Twisted her ankle? Pulled a muscle? We say all these things, don't we? But what do we mean by 'twisted an ankle' or 'pulled a muscle'? These expressions don't tell us about the actual injury. To understand that, we need to look inside the body.
	Now, I hope you remember your Core Physiology course, but just in case you've forgotten everything already ... let's quickly look at this illustration. What have we got here? Yes, the knee joint. Let's make sure that we can recognize the important parts of this joint – and any joint, in fact. So first, we have bones, of course. These give strength and support to the body. But we must connect the bones together. How do we do that? We use ligaments. Ligaments connect bone to bone. To put it simply, they stop the bones from pulling apart. But ligaments don't *move* the bones. What we need to move the bones are muscles. In this case, the muscles make the knee bend and straighten. So here, we have some muscles. But muscles don't connect directly to bone. We need another kind of tissue, which is called tendon. Tendons connect muscle to bone. Right, so here we have the muscle again, and this is the tendon, connecting the muscle to the bone.
	OK. Now, let's start the lecture proper. What we're going to talk about is, first, the common causes of injury and then, the basic treatment. As far as causes are concerned, there are two basic types of injury – trauma and overuse. So what we need to do is look at each of those in turn. Now, after all kinds of traumatic injury, there is always inflammation and swelling, so what I'm going to do is look at trauma – the minor types and then the major types, then what I'll do is discuss inflammation and swelling. What are they and why are they important? Then, with regards to treatment, there is a very useful acronym, PRICE – that's P-R-I-C-E – which helps us remember the basic actions. So causes of sports injury and the price of treatment, if you like. Oh, and physiotherapy. Very important kind of treatment nowadays.

B Following a lecture

1. Go over the headings on the first slide. Encourage students to predict possible injuries for each heading. With a monolingual class, ideas could be discussed in L1. Students should copy the headings as a basis for making notes. Remind students to:

   • add 'extra' information;

   • guess spellings – correct them after the lecture.

   Set the task and play DVD 4.D. Students complete notes individually then compare answers in pairs. Elicit answers, preferably using an electronic projection. Discuss with students where they had to go back and add information that was presented in the wrong order. Check the meanings of all the highlighted words. Give students time to correct their spelling of new or difficult words in their notes.

2. Go over the headings on the second slide and ask students to try to predict the treatments (it does not matter if they cannot think of anything). They might be able to suggest that *R* means *rest*. Play DVD 4.E and repeat the procedure for Exercise B1.

3. Students discuss in pairs. If students find the questions difficult, replay the second part of the lecture. Elicit answers.

> **Optional activities**

• If you prefer, set Exercises B1 and B2 together and play the whole of DVD 4.E. Then give feedback on the two sets of notes together. This would be an effective strategy for more able classes.

• Replay a section of DVD 4.E with students following the transcript.

• Ask students to focus on a section of the transcript, then have them find and underline examples of one of the following: *passive verbs, cleft sentences, target vocabulary, signpost phrases.*

Answers

1./2. Sports injuries

types	
trauma	= wound, shock common in contact sports, e.g., football
minor	bruise **or contusion** strain = muscles torn sprain = ligaments displaced (bone to bone) tendon, e.g., Achilles – mainly happens through overuse
major	**fractures in bones** **hairline or complete break**
inflammation	**inflame = get hot; Lan Zhou 2010 – IGF-1 – helps to heal**
swelling	**swell = get bigger – fluid leaks into tissue**
overuse	all sports RSI = repet. strain inj., e.g., tennis elbow muscle tear – actually how muscles grow! but muscle needs rest
treatment	
P	protection = stop!
R	rest – don't stress injury
I	ice = anaesthetic + reduce swelling
C	**compression = squeezing – wrap in bandage but not too tight**
E	elevation = raising above heart
physiotherapy	prepare body esp. injury for return to training
	Extra point – Hyperbaric chamber – raises pressure + oxygen = speeds up healing – 1/3 or 1/2

3.

a. IGF-1? — a chemical which increases the speed of muscle regeneration

b. RSI? — repetitive strain injury – from repeating the same action

c. tennis elbow? — a kind of RSI – problem with the elbow

d. an anaesthetic? — a painkiller

e. a compression bandage? — a bandage that squeezes the affected area

f. physiotherapy? — a way of preparing people to return to training or competition

Transcripts

🌐 4.15 DVD 4.D

Lecturer: Right. So let's begin. Types of sports injuries. We can divide sports injuries into two types. The first is the result of trauma. The second is the result of overuse. Let's look in detail at the first kind and then I'll just say a few words about the second kind.

OK. Trauma. *Trauma* means 'a wound or shock produced by sudden physical injury'. Traumatic injuries are most common in contact sports. That is, sports where the athletes are supposed to come into contact with each other. So football is a contact sport and so is rugby, but tennis and basketball aren't. If the players come into contact with each other in basketball, for example, one or both of them will be disciplined by the referee.

Now, under trauma, we need to distinguish between minor items and major items. The first minor item is the bruise, which is the colouring of the skin after an injury. You know what happens. You bang your knee and, sometime later, it changes colour. It goes blue or purple.

This change of colour is caused by blood leaking from damaged cells. So that's the first kind of minor injury.

The second minor item is called a strain – that's *strain* … Oh, by the way, I should have said, we don't use the word *bruise* in physiology. We call this colouring of the skin a contusion. Contusion.

Now, where was I? Ah yes. The second minor item is a *strain* with a *t* and the third one is called a *sprain* with a *p*. So strain and sprain. Yes, I know. It's annoying that they are so similar in pronunciation but it is important to distinguish between these two. In a *strain*, it's the muscles that are affected. Strains happen when the muscle is torn. In a *sprain*, it's the ligaments that are damaged. They can get damaged in traumatic injuries by being displaced – I mean moved – out of alignment. And that's what we call a *sprain*. How can you remember the difference between a strain and a sprain? Well, just think of *muscle* strain and *ligament* sprain.

The fourth kind of minor injury is related to the tendons. Do you remember that tendons connect muscle to … bone? That's it. There is one very well-known tendon in the back of the foot, in the heel. It's called the Achilles tendon. It's named after the Greek hero, Achilles, because the story goes that it was the only part of his body that could be injured. But that's not important really. Damage to the tendons is quite common in sport, although it mainly happens through overuse – so we'll come on to that in a minute.

What we need to look at now is inflammation and swelling. In all cases of traumatic injury, the body responds in the same way. The dead or damaged cells release chemicals. These chemicals carry messages to the body's immune system – that's the system that protects the body – and the immune system sends cells to repair the damage. The result of this is … you've guessed it – inflammation and swelling. So, we can see that inflammation and swelling are natural parts of the healing process. However, and this is very important for sports scientists so listen carefully – too much inflammation or swelling can slow down healing.

Did I talk about *major* trauma? No, I don't think I did. OK, so *major* trauma involves fractures in bones. A *hairline* fracture is, as the name implies, very small, the width of a human hair. There is no displacement of the pieces of bone. A complete fracture means the bone is broken in two or more parts.

Now, one more thing to say about inflammation and swelling. Inflammation and swelling happen at the same time, but they are not the same. Inflammation means getting hot or inflamed. As you know, the site of an injury always gets hot. Swelling, on the other hand – or foot, of course – means getting bigger, which you are also familiar with after an injury. Fluid leaks into the tissue and it swells. Now, back to inflammation. It was Lan Zhou in 2010 who conducted a study of inflammation – it's cited on your handout – Lan Zhou, 2010. The professor found that inflamed cells produce *insulin-like growth factor*

1 … don't worry about the full name, it's always called IGF-1. Now IGF-1 is a chemical that increases the speed of muscle regeneration. In other words, it helps the muscle to grow again. It also helps to heal damaged tissue. So can you see the importance of this research? It's clear from the work of Lan Zhou that inflammation should be *managed* but not removed altogether. We need some inflammation …

Ah, just going back to fractures for a minute. I think I forgot to ask a crucial question. What's the difference between a fracture and a break? The answer is – they are the same thing. It's a bit like contusion and bruise. One is the medical term, the other is the common word.

OK. So that's the first type of injury – *traumatic*, mainly from contact sports. The second type is *overuse* injury and it can happen in all sports, contact and non-contact. In fact, some people are saying now that overuse injuries are far too common, and are the result of sportspeople playing too much sport, or training too much or both. But that's not relevant to this lecture. The most common overuse injury for sportspeople is RSI, or repetitive strain injury, which, obviously, results from an athlete repeatedly using the same joint or set of muscles. For example, a tennis player will use the elbow joint on one arm all the time which is why injury to that joint is sometimes called 'tennis elbow'. One official name though is *tendinitis*, which of course refers to the tendon. The tendon becomes inflamed because very, very small tears in the muscle do not repair properly.

Which brings us on to the second main overuse injury – major muscle tears. This can happen, for example, in weightlifting. However, there is a strange point about muscle tears. They are actually the way the muscle grows. If you use a muscle a lot, it tears a little. It's sometimes called a micro-injury. Then, if you rest the muscle, it repairs itself, but in the process, it grows bigger, so next time it can deal with the load that you put on it. The problem comes if you do not give the muscle enough time to repair the micro-injury and then you develop a real injury. So remember that. It's tearing muscles slightly which makes them grow.

OK. So, we have seen a little about the types of sports injuries. Clearly, trainers and coaches should do everything they can to reduce the risk of injury during training and in matches themselves. But I'm not here to talk to you about this now. I'm more interested today in the treatment.

4.16 [DVD] 4.E

Lecturer: Obviously, there are specialist treatments for each individual injury and companies make a lot of money selling special creams and bandages and pills and so on, but they all work on some general principles. These principles are sometimes given the acronym PRICE – we'll see why.

Firstly, the P stands for *protection*. This means 'stop playing as soon as you notice the injury' to prevent making the damage worse. If possible, don't put any weight on the injured part. Sounds easy, but of course a lot of athletes are encouraged to play through the pain and carry on even if their leg is falling off. This is just stupid. It's pain that warns you to stop! If you ignore it, you will injure your body more, maybe much more.

R is pretty simple. It stands for *rest*. What your body needs after an injury is to stop using the hand or arm or leg or whatever. In most cases, the body will recover from a sports injury by itself, if it is given enough time without stressing the injured area.

I is for *ice*, which can be a bag of frozen peas or a specialist cold pack. Cold serves two purposes. Firstly it is a mild anaesthetic so it reduces the pain, but, more importantly, it reduces the amount of swelling, which is caused by blood rushing to the injured area. The ice reduces blood flow, which is a good thing for a short time, but you should never leave ice on for more than 20 minutes. You could damage the area more than the original injury. In fact, there is quite a lot of uncertainty about ice treatment. Read the article by Macauley from the *Clinical Journal of Sport Medicine*, 2001 – it's in your reading pack.

Finally, what does E mean? It's *elevation*, or raising. Once again, it is a way of reducing blood flow to the injury, and basically you must just get the affected part higher than the heart. So for an injured ankle, the patient can rest in bed with the foot on a cushion or pillow. It's a little harder for an injured arm, but most sporting injuries happen to feet, ankles, legs and hips.

Hang on. I've missed one out. Just going back for a minute, C is *compression*, or squeezing. This also reduces swelling and we can achieve it by wrapping the affected area in a bandage – particularly a compression bandage. But, just as with ice, we have to be a little careful. If the patient experiences throbbing around the area, the bandage is too tight. The blood cannot flow properly and bring the repair cells to the affected area. So unwrap the bandage and rewrap with less compression.

Right. I think I've done them all now. But there is another huge area of treatment for sports injuries that will interest many of you here. Physiotherapy. PRICE is clearly an initial treatment, to ensure that the injury repairs as quickly as possible. But there is another element to getting the athlete back into training and competition – rehabilitation. The aim of physiotherapy is to prepare the body, particularly the injured part, for full use again, and to try to ensure that the injury does not recur.

I mentioned specialist treatments earlier. Some of these are controversial because they are owned by companies which, of course, want to make money from them, but some are accepted now by the majority of sports scientists, at least. For example, the hyperbaric chamber. *Hyperbaric* means 'high weight' or 'high pressure'. The chamber is big enough to take one person or even two or three. The injured patient gets inside and the chamber is then sealed from the atmosphere. The pressure inside is raised. In addition, the patient puts on breathing apparatus so that they are inhaling pure oxygen. Blood supply is reduced by the pressure, which reduces swelling, but more oxygen reaches the damaged tissue which means that healing is speeded up. Some people claim that recovery can be cut by a third or even a half by these chambers. That's sports scientists, by the way, not just the manufacturers of hyperbaric chambers. On your handout you have a reference to one endorsement for this treatment in the *Sports Injury Bulletin*.

Right, so, to sum up. What we have looked at today are the types of sports injury – trauma and overuse, and the basic treatment – PRICE and physiotherapy. Next time, we'll look at a few case studies to see how these general points apply in real life. Thank you.

C Developing critical thinking

Elicit some reasons why a lecture might be difficult to follow, for example:

* Difficult subject matter / content.
* Lecturer speaks too quickly / quietly / with an unfamiliar accent – point out that you can get used to a voice so next time it might be easier.
* Information not presented clearly / logically.
* Student unprepared for lecture.
* English / listening skills not developed enough.

Use the elicited reasons above to move smoothly into the activity. Students discuss the questions in pairs. Elicit ideas.

Answers

Model answers on the next page.

Closure

Do one of the optional activities suggested in Exercise B or use the discussion in Exercise C.

Check the meaning of key words from the lesson, as follows:

strain *and* sprain?	Strains are muscle tears. Sprains are ligament tears.
ligaments *and* tendons?	Ligaments join bone to bone. Tendons join muscle to bone.
fracture *and* break?	There is no difference – *fracture* is the medical term.
bruise *and* contusion?	There is no difference – *contusion* is the medical term.
inflammation *and* swelling?	Inflammation is heat. Swelling is increase in size.
trauma *and* overuse	Trauma happens suddenly. Overuse happens over time.

1. What would you do this time?

• blame yourself and your poor English?	*not a good idea; it will not help you to do better next time*
• accept that sometimes lecturers do not give perfect lectures?	*this is certainly true*
• ask to copy someone's notes?	*not a good idea – he/she may not have taken accurate notes*
• discuss the lecture with several other students?	*a good idea; several people should be able to agree on the important contents of the lecture*
• ask the lecturer for help?	*a good idea, but it is often difficult; if extra English classes are possible, you could ask to go to these*

2. What will you do next time?

• do more preparation?	*very good idea – the more you prepare, the more likely you are to understand*
• listen carefully to the introduction?	*very good idea – introductions are excellent ways of helping you understand the organization of a lecture – and, even more importantly, help you to get back into a lecture if you get lost*
• record it and listen several times?	*not a very good idea; most lectures only have a few important points and, in most cases, you will not have time to listen again and again just to get those points*

Speaking: A sporting life

4

4.6 Vocabulary for speaking: Mental and physical conditions

Objectives

By the end of this lesson, students should be able to:
- demonstrate understanding of meanings of target vocabulary;
- pronounce target vocabulary in isolation and in context;
- demonstrate understanding of information about mental and physical problems for sportspeople.

Introduction
Use Exercise A.

A   Activating ideas

Students discuss the questions in pairs. Elicit a few ideas:

What's wrong with the young women?
- *I think the one on the left has a cold / flu.*
- *I think she's got a cold because she's blowing her nose.*
- *She looks unwell / depressed / worried, etc.*

What should they do?
- *Take paracetamol.*
- *Go to bed.*
- *Stay at home so they don't pass on germs / bugs.*
- *Drink plenty of water / fluids.*
- *See a doctor / psychologist / counsellor.*
- *Talk to a friend.*

Methodology note

Avoid getting into the teaching of too many expressions for symptoms of colds and flu. They aren't really relevant for this section. Some language for talking about symptoms is presented in Everyday English in this theme.

B   Understanding new vocabulary in context

1. Set the task. Students will probably know the meanings of enough of the words (*cold, flu, asthma, depression*) in order to be able to attempt the task. If not, tell them not to worry, they can complete the task after the listening. Students should also work out possible pronunciations for each word; again, these can be checked when listening.

   Elicit one or two ideas for the two possible groups of words, but do not confirm or correct.

2. Set the task. Briefly discuss what the role of a sports psychologist might be. Play ♪ **4.17**, then elicit answers for Exercise B1.

   Ask a few follow-up questions if you wish:
   - *What are the main physical factors for athletes?*
   - *What kind of problem is asthma?*
   - *What are the advantages and disadvantages of obsession in a sports person?*
   - *What's a 'top athlete'?*

3. Set the task. Students discuss the sentences and missing words in pairs. Encourage students to have a go at the pronunciation of words they are not sure about; more pronunciation of target words is given later in the lesson.

4. Play ♪ **4.18** so that students can check their answers. Give further explanation of any words students had difficulty with.

5. Set the task. Point out that the **bold** words often have another meaning in everyday use. Students should think about the meaning in this context. Encourage students to discuss ideas in pairs; this will increase the amount of speaking practice for the lesson. After a few minutes, elicit answers.

Optional activities

- Allow students to study the transcript at a suitable point. You could also replay the interview with students following the transcript.

- Students could practise an extract from the transcript in pairs.

Answers

1. Group 1: *anxiety, depression, neurosis, obsession (mental difficulties)*

   Group 2: *asthma, cold, fatigue, flu, breathing difficulties (physical difficulties)*

   Note: Some students may point out that some physical symptoms may be a result of mental difficulties, e.g., *fatigue* or *breathing difficulties*.

2. See 1.

3. a. When you **go down with** a cold or *flu*, you get tired easily.

   b. *Fatigue* is a **symptom** of a physical problem.

   c. Many sportspeople have *asthma*, which is a respiratory **condition**.

   d. During an **attack**, people with asthma experience *breathing difficulties*.

   e. Top athletes often have an *obsession* with their sport. They think about it all the time and **train** hard because they are obsessed.

   f. Sometimes obsession is bad because it leads to *anxiety* – worrying about your **performance**.

   g. Sometimes, you become so obsessive that you **experience** *neurosis*.

4. See 3.

5.

go down with	catch, get
symptom	sign
condition	problem
attack	sudden case of a particular condition
train	exercise in a particular way or for a particular activity
performance	how well you do
experience	feel, have, suffer from

Transcripts

🌐 4.17

Presenter: 4.17. Lesson 4.6. Vocabulary for speaking: Mental and physical conditions

Exercise B2. Listen to an interview with a sports psychologist. Check your answers to Exercise A.

Interviewer: Hi. Welcome to Sports Hour. To start with today, I'm talking to Emma Gibson, who's a sports psychologist. Welcome, Emma.

Sports psychologist: Thank you. Nice to be here.

Interviewer: OK, so your job is to help sportspeople to perform better, right?

Sports psychologist: Yes, that's part of my job, certainly.

Interviewer: What factors can affect the performance of a sportsperson?

Sports psychologist: Well, we can divide the factors into mental and physical.

Interviewer: What does *mental* mean?

Sports psychologist: 'To do with the brain'. And *physical* means 'to do with the body'.

Interviewer: So can mental factors affect performance?

Sports psychologist: Yes, indeed. Most people think that only physical factors are important, things like colds and flu.

Interviewer: Why do we think that? Because when you have a cold or flu, you get tired easily?

Sports psychologist: Yes, that's right, so that affects your performance, but there is also fatigue, which is extreme tiredness.

Interviewer: Is fatigue a physical condition in itself?

Sports psychologist: Well, yes and no. Fatigue is a symptom of a physical condition. It might be something very simple like lack of sleep or something more serious like heart problems.

Interviewer: Right. So that's physical conditions.

Sports psychologist: Yes – but I must just mention asthma. It's very common now, at least in the West. Many sportspeople have asthma, which is a respiratory problem.

Interviewer: What are the symptoms of asthma?

Sports psychologist: Well, during an attack, people experience shortness of breath. They can't breathe properly.

Interviewer: OK. So we've got colds and flu, fatigue and asthma. What about mental conditions?

Sports psychologist: Well, this is interesting. Mental conditions are probably more important than physical conditions for the top sportsperson.

Interviewer: In what way are mental conditions more important?

Sports psychologist: Well, top athletes often have an obsession with their sport. They think about it all the time.

Interviewer: Isn't that a good thing?

Sports psychologist: It can be. It depends. Sometimes it is good because it means they train harder and perform better. Sometimes obsession is bad because it leads to depression or anxiety – you know, worrying about your performance – your last performance and the next one. Sometimes, you become so obsessive that it causes neurosis.

Interviewer: And what does that mean?

Sports psychologist: Well, neurosis covers a huge range of mental conditions, including unpleasant or disturbing thoughts, aggression, fear and perfectionism – you know, everything has to be absolutely perfect.

Interviewer: And that's bad?

Sports psychologist: Yes. Because it is impossible for anything to be *absolutely perfect*, so you will always disappoint yourself. And you will suffer from depression.

🌐 4.18

Presenter: 4.18. Exercise B4. Listen and check your answers.

Sports psychologist:
a. When you go down with a cold or flu, you get tired easily.
b. Fatigue is a symptom of a physical problem.
c. Many sportspeople have asthma, which is a respiratory condition.
d. During an attack, people with asthma experience breathing difficulties.
e. Top athletes often have an obsession with their sport. They think about it all the time and train hard because they are obsessed.
f. Sometimes obsession is bad because it leads to anxiety – worrying about your performance.
g. Sometimes, you become so obsessive that you experience neurosis.

C Understanding new words in context

1. Check students understand the task, then go over an example (*aggression*). Students complete individually then compare answers in pairs.

2. Play 🌐 **4.19** so students can check the pronunciation and their answers. Go over any that students had difficulty with.

3. Play 🌐 **4.20** and practise the pronunciation of each word. You can do this while students follow the phonemics for each word in their books or you can ask students to close their books.

Methodology note

There are several words here where the spelling does not help with pronunciation, or where the pronunciation is hard because of clusters, e.g.,

anxiety – x = /z/ but anxious – x = /ʃ/

asthma – cluster

fatigue – i = /iː/

neurosis – eu = /j ʊə/

At a suitable point, you could replay 🌐 **4.17** of the interview so that students can hear the pronunciation of the target words again in context.

Answers

1.

1. /əˈɡreʃn/	aˈggression
2. /əˈɡresɪv/	aˈggressive
3. /æŋˈzaɪətiː/	anˈxiety
4. /ˈæŋkʃəs/	ˈanxious
5. /ˈæsmə/	ˈasthma
6. /æsˈmætɪk/	asthˈmatic
7. /dɪˈprest/	deˈpressed
8. /dɪˈpreʃn/	deˈpression
9. /fəˈtiːɡ/	faˈtigue
10. /fəˈtiːɡd/	faˈtigued
11. /njʊəˈrəʊsɪs/	neuˈrosis
12. /njʊəˈrɒtɪk/	neuˈrotic
13. /əbˈseʃn/	obˈsession
14. /əbˈsesɪv/	obˈsessive
15. /ˈbreθ/	breath
16. /ˈbriːð/	breathe

Transcripts

🌐 4.19

Voice:
1. aggression
2. aggressive
3. anxiety
4. anxious
5. asthma
6. asthmatic
7. depressed
8. depression
9. fatigue
10. fatigued
11. neurosis
12. neurotic
13. obsession
14. obsessive
15. breath
16. breathe

🌐 4.20

Presenter: 4.20. Exercise C3. Listen again and repeat.

[REPEAT OF SCRIPT FROM 🌐 4.19]

Closure

Allocate one or two words from the lesson to each student. Ask them to think of a good sentence for their word(s) but they shouldn't write it down. Quickly divide the class into small groups (of students already sitting near each other). Each student says the word they were given, and then gives the sentence. The other students listen and correct pronunciation if necessary.

S1: *aggressive*. Some football fans are very aggressive at matches.

Methodology note

Either allocate the words orally or write all the words down on separate pieces of paper before the lesson. Put all the pieces of paper in a bag. Each student then takes a piece of paper with a word on it.

Objectives

By the end of this lesson, students should be able to:
• use existing skills to give a talk about a physical factor that affects sports performance;
• pronounce target vocabulary in context.

Introduction

Show some of the words from the previous lesson in phonemic script. Ask students to recognize them. Correct pronunciation and check students can explain the meaning or give you a synonym for each word.

A Gathering information

1. Elicit and revise the meanings of *physical factors* and *performance*. Students discuss the handout question in pairs. Elicit a few ideas.

2. Set the task, explaining that students should focus on *how* the information is presented. (Students will have an opportunity to understand *what* information is presented in the next activity.) Give students time to read through the list of presentation points. Discuss one or two of the points, e.g., *he/she speaks loudly*. Why is this sometimes a good thing and sometimes a bad thing?

   Play DVD 4.F. Students discuss the list of points in pairs. Elicit answers. Discuss why the first presentation about mental fatigue is poor.

   • Clearly unprepared (not sure of sources, research information, etc.).
   • Too much hesitation.
   • Too informal (short sentences, slang, etc.).

   Remind students to try to include the techniques the good presenter used in their own presentations later in the lesson.

3. Students will now watch the presentations again and focus on the information given. Students study the notes; they may be able to complete some of the information already. Students should guess the spelling of difficult names (sources). Play DVD 4.F again. Students complete the table individually then compare answers in pairs. Show the completed notes using an electronic projection so that students can check their answers and finalize

spelling of difficult names. Go over any answers students had difficulty with.

Answers

factor	symptoms	research	source
fatigue	*feeling tired during exe; giving up exe. because tired*	*exe. after diff. cognitive task = "exe. more diff." so thinking exe. changes perception of phy. exe.*	*Marcora, Staiano and Manning (2009) Journ. of App. Physio.*
asthma	*inability to breathe properly in severe cases, fatal*	*certain sports affect asth. more than others – swimming rarely brings on attacks; majority of asth. can prevent attacks during exe. if medic. taken beforehand.*	*Fitch and Godfrey (1976) Journ. of the Am. Med. Assoc.*

Transcript
🌐 4.21 DVD 4.F

Presenter:	**4.21. Lesson 4.7. Real-time speaking: Physical factors in sport**
Student 1:	Right. Umm. OK. Er ... fatigue. Um. Fatigue means ... well... tired. Really, really tired. So when you are doing exercise, sometimes you give up. You stop doing it – the exercise, I mean. Um ... because you're tired. And maybe you don't really feel like it. That's it really.
Tutor:	OK. So, those are the symptoms. What about the research?
Student 1:	Oh, yes, right. Research. Um. If people do a cognitive task – *cognitive* means 'thinking', right?
Tutor:	Yes. 'Connected with thinking'.
Student 1:	OK. Where was I? Um, yes, if they do that before a physical task, er, then they think the physical task is ... um ... harder.
Tutor:	And why do they think that?
Student 1:	Um. I don't really know. Oh yeah. I think maybe it changes their view.
Tutor:	OK. So it changes their perception. Now, what's your source?
Student 1:	Oh, yeah. Um ... some people called – um – Marcora, Stai – um – ano and er someone.
Tutor:	Manning. And when was that?
Student 1:	In 2009.
Tutor:	What were they writing in?
Student 1:	English?
Tutor:	No, I mean the name of the book or the journal …
Student 1:	Um, let me check. Yeah. *The Journal of Applied Psychology.*
Tutor:	Psychology?
Student 1:	Oh, no. Physiology.
Student 2:	I researched asthma, which is an illness of the respiratory system. The symptoms of asthma are an inability to breathe properly. In severe cases, the illness can be fatal. Physical exertion can bring on an attack.

Student 3:	So what you're saying is, it could be dangerous for people with asthma to do sport.
Student 1:	Well, to some extent. But it's possible that certain sports affect asthmatics more than others. For example, Fitch and Godfrey, writing in the *Journal of the American Medical Association*, 1976, found that swimming very rarely brings on an asthma attack.
Student 4:	In other words, asthmatics should only take part in swimming?
Student 1:	No, I'm not saying that. The point is that asthma is controllable in most cases.
Student 3:	Are you saying that the majority of asthmatics can control the illness with medication?
Student 1:	Yes, exactly. In fact, I think there are several top athletes who are asthmatic.
Student 2:	What's your source? *[laughter]*

B Practising a model

Explain the sentences on the left are not academic (sophisticated) enough for a presentation. Set the task and go over the example. Students work in pairs. Monitor and give help where necessary. Elicit complete sentences. Give some oral practice by drilling phrases from each sentence, building up to the complete long sentence, for example:

I looked at fatigue ...

> *... as a factor ...*

>> *... in sporting performance.*

I looked at fatigue as a factor in sporting performance.

The full sentences can be set for written consolidation in class if there is time, or for homework if not.

Answers

1. I looked at fatigue as a factor in sporting performance.
2. Fatigue is a feeling of extreme tiredness or weakness.
3. The symptom of fatigue is athletes giving up doing physical exercise.
4. The athletes have done a cognitive or thinking task before exercising.
5. Three researchers called Marcora, Staiano and Manning did research into the factor.
6. They found that athletes who have completed difficult, thinking tasks perceive physical activity as harder.
7. The research was reported in the *Journal of Applied Physiology* in 2009.

C Producing the model

1. Students select which presentation they want to work on. Then divide the class into pairs or small groups according to the presentation they have chosen. Remind students they must refer to sources. Students help each other in the usual way to prepare and practise their presentations. Monitor and give help where necessary.

2. Go through the points for giving a presentation and add any of your own you think students need to improve. Alternatively, tell students to select one aspect about presenting that they would like to improve or focus on in this lesson.

   Go through the points for the listening students, and elicit examples of phrases and questions to use.

   Re-divide the class into small groups with equal numbers for each presentation. Students take turns to give their presentations. (This could also be done in pairs.) Monitor and make a note of common errors. Give feedback, especially on how students referred to sources in their presentations.

Optional activity

You can replay the DVD of the second presentation before you set the activities here if you wish. This will give students another chance to notice key elements and have a good model in their head before doing their own presentations. However, students should try to use their own words rather than simply copy every phrase or sentence when they do their own presentation.

Closure

Give feedback on the presentations if you haven't already done so.

Model presentation

I looked at fatigue. Fatigue is extreme tiredness. The symptom of fatigue is athletes giving up doing physical exercise because they have done a cognitive task before. According to three researchers called Marcora, Staiano and Manning, athletes who have completed difficult *thinking* tasks perceive *physical* activity as harder. The research was reported in the *Journal of Applied Physiology* in 2009.

Objectives

By the end of this lesson, students should be able to:

- use appropriate language when talking about illness and physical fitness.

Introduction

Ask students:

Have you been to a doctor recently? Why did you go? What treatment did the doctor give you? What medication?

Are you a member of a sports club? Why did you join?

A Activating ideas

Set the task. Students discuss the question in pairs. Elicit ideas.

Answers

They are all common health problems for students.

B Studying the models

1. Make sure students have covered the conversations. Set the task and play 🌐 **4.22**. Students discuss answers. Elicit answers. Ask students any key words they heard which helped them match to the picture.

2. Set the task, pointing out that all the missing words are verbs. Students complete individually then compare answers in pairs. Play 🌐 **4.22** again so students can check their answers. Allow students to ask you if they are still not sure of any answers but it should not be necessary to go over every one again.

Spend a few minutes on highlighting and practising one or more of the following:

- questions (there is deliberately a wide range of forms used in the questions so that they can be used for revision of tenses) – remind students about different intonation patterns for closed and open questions;

- responses – describing pain / health problems.

Answers

1. photo 3

2. photo 2

3. photo 4

4. photo 1

Transcript and Answers

🌐 4.22

Presenter:	4.22. Everyday English: Talking about health problems
	Exercise B1. Listen and match each conversation to a photograph above.
	Conversation 1.
Voice A:	What seems to be the trouble?
Voice B:	Well my throat is really sore. And I think I've got a temperature.
Voice A:	Mm. I'm just going to feel your glands. Mm. OK. It's nothing too serious. Just strep throat.
Voice B:	Oh right. My friend had that recently.
Voice A:	Yes. It's very infectious. I'll write a prescription for some antibiotics.
Presenter:	**Conversation 2.**
Voice A:	Are you feeling alright?
Voice B:	Not really. I've got a really bad headache. Feel sick too.
Voice A:	You look terrible. And you're very hot.
Voice B:	Yeah? But I can't stop shivering. I really don't feel too good.
Voice A:	OK, I'm going to call the health centre.
Presenter:	**Conversation 3.**
Voice A:	What is the matter?
Voice B:	Nothing really. Just feeling a bit stressed.
Voice A:	Oh. Do you want to talk about it?
Voice B:	Well, my student loan hasn't come yet. I've got two essays to finish and I can't sleep.
Voice A:	OK … well … let's go and get some fresh air. Then you can tell me all about it.
Presenter:	**Conversation 4.**
Voice A:	Have you ever had TB?
Voice B:	I don't think so. What is it?
Voice A:	Tuberculosis. It's a respiratory disease.
Voice B:	Oh, right. No, I have never had it.
Voice A:	Are you currently taking any medication?

C Practising the models

1. Select one or two conversations for intensive drilling and controlled practice. Then set the task. Students work in pairs to add more lines to the conversations. Monitor and give help where necessary.

2. Monitor while students practise in pairs. Make a note of common errors. Give feedback. Ask some pairs of students to read out their conversations for the rest of the class so they can hear different variations.

3. Discuss the questions as a class.

You can have all the students working on all four conversations or you could allocate one or two conversations to each pair.

D Building vocabulary

Set the task without giving too much explanation – allow students to show you how much they already know. Students work in pairs to complete the sentences.

Elicit answers. Point out some of the problem areas: We don't usually say …

- I've got an arm / leg / foot / hand, etc., ache.*
- I've got a pain in my throat.
- My back is paining me.

Instead we say …

- I've got a pain in my arm. / My arm aches.
- I've got a sore throat. / My throat hurts.
- My back is hurting me. / I've got a pain in my back. / I've got backache. / My back aches.

*This is not a grammatical error, it is simply collocation.

Answers

1. I've got (a/n) … ache.	head / back / tooth
2. I've got a pain in my …	neck / arm / leg
3. I've got (a/n) …	temperature / sore throat / indigestion
4. I've … myself.	cut / burnt / hurt
5. I'm feeling …	ill / hot / cold / sick / exhausted / better / dizzy

Closure

Copy the table below onto the board and elicit the verbs / nouns as a summary of the activity.

verb	noun
burn (yourself)	a burn
cut (yourself)	a cut
hurt (yourself)	-
ache	an ache
-	a pain

4.8 Learning new speaking skills: Summarizing and reacting to summaries

Objectives

By the end of this lesson, students should be able to:

- identify sense groups in long spoken sentences;
- use appropriate pauses and intonation in long spoken sentences;
- use phrases for summarizing at appropriate points in a tutorial discussion.

Note: In preparation for the final activity in this lesson, you might want to ask students to read and revise information about the topics below. Do this at the end of the preceding lesson.

- BOGOF (Theme 3)
- Braille (Theme 2)
- Ogallala Aquifer (Theme 1)

Alternatively, spend a few minutes revising them as an activity for the introduction.

Introduction

If you wish, replay the second presentation from DVD 4.F. Revise the topics above.

A Using sense groups

1. Give students time to study the information and the examples in the Pronunciation Check. Elicit from the students the position in each sentence where the pause should happen. It is usually after a noun. However, in these examples there is also a pause after an adverb (*properly*) and an adjective (*fatal*). Elicit places where a speaker would **not** normally pause, for example, after articles, prepositions, subject pronouns and between auxiliary + verb which forms a tense (*has done, was doing, didn't do,* etc.).

   Of course, all speakers hesitate at times so students will hear pauses in all sorts of places but in these cases, there will probably be a hesitation device, like *um* or *er*.

   Play ◉ 4.24 once so that students can simply listen to the sentences. Then replay, pausing for repetition.

2. Set the task for marking up the sentences. Students discuss possible sense groups in pairs.

Elicit answers and point out that it is possible to have variations. For example, a confident speaker will have longer sense groups (by joining two shorter sense groups together):

It's possible / that certain sports / affect asthmatics / more than others. (less confident speaker)

It's possible that certain sports / affect asthmatics more than others. (more confident speaker)

Also, for some phrases there may be more than one choice of where to pause:

It's possible that / certain sports ...

It's possible / that certain sports ...

Drill the sense groups and sentences, then let students practise in pairs. Monitor and give feedback.

Answers

For less able students:

It's possible / that certain sports / affect asthmatics / more than others. // For example, / Fitch and Godfrey / 1976, / writing in the *Journal / of the American Medical Association*, / found / that swimming / very rarely / brings on / an asthma attack.

Transcript
🌓 4.24

Presenter:	4.24. Pronunciation Check. Listen and repeat.
Voice:	It's possible that certain sports affect asthmatics more than others. For example, Fitch and Godfrey 1976, writing in the *Journal of the American Medical Association*, found that swimming very rarely brings on an asthma attack.

B Identifying a new skill

1. Give students time to read the questions about the extracts. Play 🌓 **4.23**. Students can discuss the answers in pairs. Do not elicit.

2. Give students time to read through the Skills Check. Explain that summarizing is really another way of clarifying or checking information. (If necessary, refer back to other examples of clarifying that you know students are familiar with.)

   Play 🌓 **4.25**. Pause after each item for students to repeat. Check for appropriate

intonation patterns, stressed words and pauses. Highlight in particular the following:

Well, to some extent (pause after *well*, and intonation)

The point is (stress on *point*)

So, what you're saying is ...? In other words ... (pause at end of each phrase)

Transcripts
🌓 4.23

Presenter:	4.23. Lesson 4.8. Learning new speaking skills: Summarizing and reacting to summaries
	Exercise B1. Listen to three extracts from the discussion in 4.7.
	Extract 1.
Student 1:	Physical exertion can bring on an attack.
Student 2:	So what you're saying is, it could be dangerous for people with asthma to do sport?
Student 1:	Well, to some extent.
Presenter:	Extract 2.
Student 2:	In other words, asthmatics should only take part in swimming?
Student 1:	No, I'm not saying that. The point is that asthma is controllable in most cases.
Presenter:	Extract 3.
Student 2:	Are you saying that the majority of asthmatics can control the illness with medication?
Student 1:	Yeah, exactly.

🌓 4.25

Presenter:	4.25. Skills Check. Listen and repeat the expressions above. Copy the stress and intonation.
Voice:	So what you're saying is, exercise is a good thing? Are you saying that exercise is a bad thing? In other words, everyone should do exercise? Yes, that's right. Well, to some extent. No, that's not really the point. The point is, we should do the right kind of exercise.

Answers

The male speaker is trying to summarize.

The female speaker is reacting to the summaries.

C Practising the new skill

Give students time to read through the example conversation. Drill the sentences from the conversation. Select three pairs of students. Each pair demonstrates a different version of the conversation (as given in the example in the Course Book) to the rest of the class. Divide the class into pairs. Students practise the example conversation and choose which of S1's three responses to give.

Set the task for more practice using the resources at the back of the Course Book. Briefly revise the topics covered in earlier themes:

- BOGOF (Theme 3)
- Braille (Theme 2)
- Ogallala Aquifer (Theme 1)

If your students did not do the relevant section or lesson, you might want to leave that resource out.

Give students time to read through the resources. Check understanding and revise the meaning of difficult words. Monitor while students are working in pairs. Give feedback.

Closure
Use your feedback for Exercise C.

4.9 Grammar for speaking: Review of modals

Objectives

By the end of this lesson, students should be able to:

- use the modal verbs *must* and *don't have to* to talk about obligation;
- use the modal verbs *can, may, might* and *could* for possibility;
- use the modal verb *should* to give advice;
- pronounce unstressed *was* and *were* in past continuous sentences;
- pronounce *must / mustn't* correctly.

Introduction
Use the Grammar box tasks.

Grammar box 17
Make sure students know what a *modal* verb is; ask them to look and find examples in the table:

must

can

should

have to

might

Other modal verbs students might mention include:

would

could

will

may

Elicit some of the formal characteristics of modals:

- The form does not change to agree with the subject (*I / he / she / we + must / can*, etc.).
- The verb pattern is modal + infinitive without *to*.
- There are passive infinitives as well as active (see Table 1).
- There is no continuous form.
- No auxiliary needed for questions or negatives (*Can I help you? I can't see without my glasses*).
- Inversion used to make questions (*Should I do this?*).

The exception to these rules is *don't have to* – see Language note on the next page.

Set the task for matching the modal meanings with the sentences in the table. Students discuss in pairs, then elicit answers. (As usual all the sentences are taken from the preceding lessons in the section. You can spend a minute or two revising the context and ideas for each sentence if you wish.) Point out that modals can have other meanings (or *notions*) such as ability – *I can play the piano*, but in this lesson we are looking mainly at *possibility, obligation* and *advice*.

Note that *can* in this example means it is a possibility because of the nature of the illness.

Play ⊚ **4.26** of the sentences in the table. Elicit answers to the question about verb stress. Confirm that the infinitive is usually stressed rather than the modal. In fact, the modal is said with so little stress and so much assimilation into the infinitive that it is often not even heard by non-native speakers. However, we often stress the modal *must* in order to emphasize the obligation (*We **must** remember to lock the door when we leave!*).

Play ⊚ **4.26** again, pausing so that students can repeat each sentence. As well as stressing the correct word, check students are pronouncing consonant clusters correctly.

Transcript
🔊 4.26

Presenter: 4.26. Lesson 4.9. Grammar for speaking: Review of modals

Grammar box 17. Listen to the sentences in the table. Which part of the verb is stressed in each case?

Voice:
1. We must support statements in essays.
2. People's ideas mustn't be quoted without a reference.
3. Asthma can be fatal.
4. People with flu should avoid exercise.
5. Asthmatics don't have to stop all sport.
6. Fatigue might be caused by lack of sleep.

Language note

The form *to have to* is often regarded as a modal, because it is used where *must* cannot be used:

obligation	I must do it.	
lack of obligation	I don't must do it. ✗	I don't have to do it.
past obligation	I musted do it. ✗	I had to do it.
future obligation	I will must do it. ✗	I will have to do it.

However, in many ways the form can be regarded as a normal verb:

agreement with subject:	I have to, he has to …
negatives with auxiliary:	I don't have to …
questions with auxiliary:	Do you have to …?

You probably don't need to explain any of this for students of this genre, as *have to* is rarely used to express obligation in academic texts. It features around 400 times per million words, compared with *must / should* which occur six times as often. (Source: Biber et al., 1999)

A — Changing statements to laws or rules

1. Point out the heading for the exercise *changing statements to laws or rules*. Also, explain that the sentences are all on the topic of rules for writing academic essays. Check students understand the task and go over the example. Exploit Table 1, pointing out that the other modals can be substituted instead of *must*. You can either ask students to discuss the correct sentences in pairs or to write the sentences individually.

2. Play 🔊 **4.27** so that students can check their answers. Elicit answers to the question about pronunciation. Then refer students to Table 1 again. Highlight the pronunciation of *must* + infinitive, showing that the letter *t* is not pronounced if followed by a consonant.

Show the correct answers using an electronic projection and highlight the following:

- *must(n't)* + infinitive without *to* in each sentence;
- #3 has two negatives, *mustn't* and *without* (therefore the sentence means: *Writers must include information from other people with a reference*);
- #4 and #5 are passive verbs.

3. Play 🔊 **4.28**, pausing after each sentence for students to repeat. Make sure they copy the rhythm of the sentences and are pronouncing the consonant clusters correctly (i.e., without adding vowel sounds between each consonant in phrases such as *must be, mustn't*, etc.).

Answers

a. Academic essays must include a list of references.
b. References must follow conventions, for example, brackets for dates.
c. You mustn't include other people's words without a reference.
d. Page numbers must be given for direct quotes.
e. In most cases, personal opinions mustn't be included.
f. Wikipedia mustn't be used as a source.

Language note

Note that *(should)n't* could also be used in all these cases, because these are not the law of the land, just the rules of academia.

Transcript
🔊 4.27

Presenter: 4.27. Exercise A2. Listen and check your answers. How does the speaker say the modal in each case?

Voice:
a. Academic essays must include a list of references.
b. References must follow conventions, for example, brackets for dates.
c. You mustn't include other people's words without a reference.

d. Page numbers must be given for direct quotes.
e. In most cases, personal opinions mustn't be included.
f. Wikipedia mustn't be used as a source.

🌐 4.28

[REPEAT OF SCRIPT FROM 🌐 4.27]

B Talking about possibility

Go through Figure 1: Degrees of possibility. Point out that there is very little difference in meaning between *may* and *might* and the meaning also depends on the stress and intonation of the speaker.

1. Play 🌐 **4.29** of the example of the mini-dialogue. Practise the mini-dialogue with the class. Point out that you can completely disagree with the statement if you wish, but you must be polite.

2. Students continue in pairs. Monitor and give feedback.

Transcript and Answers
🌐 4.29

Presenter: 4.29. Exercise B1. Listen and repeat the examples.

Student 1:   Nuclear power is the future for energy supply.
Student 2:   Well, it might be the future. But more solar power could be used instead.

Student 1:   Lack of clean water is the greatest world problem.
Student 2:   Well, it could be the greatest, but food might be a bigger problem.

C Giving advice

Set the task and go over the examples. Drill the example sentences. If necessary, elicit a few ideas for the other topics. Then set the task for pair- or small group work. Monitor. Give feedback. Students can write some sentences for consolidation.

Answers

Answers depend on students but here are some ideas:

a. energy supply:
   renewable energy / insulation

b. clean water:
   aquifers / desalination

c. global warming:
   reduce carbon emissions / reduce air and road travel

d. economic progress:
   help developing countries / trade

e. violent children:
   stop violent TV programmes / education about violence

f. helping poor countries:
   put conditions on loans or aid

g. crime:
   help addicts to get off drugs

h. road accidents:
   driver education / safer roads

Closure
Feed back on Exercise C. Try to reach a consensus on the best ideas.

4.10 Applying new speaking skills: Psychological factors in sport

Objectives

By the end of this lesson, students should be able to:

• research and present information about psychological factors affecting sporting performance;

• use sub-skills from the section to take part in a seminar-type discussion.

Introduction
Choose one of the following:

• Use the photographs to revise vocabulary from the previous lesson. Ask students to describe the people, using *aggressive, anxious, depressed, angry,* etc.

• Replay DVD 4.F of the second presentation from Lesson 4.7.

A Preparing to research

Divide the class into small groups to discuss each point. Monitor and give help where necessary. After a few minutes, ask a spokesperson for each group to report back to the class on some of their ideas. Do not confirm or correct.

Answers

Answers depend on students.

B Researching information

Spend a couple of minutes reminding students about the 'good and bad' presentations from Lesson 4.7 (or replay `DVD` 4.F as suggested in the introduction). Elicit the features of a good presentation, including using more sophisticated sentences.

1. Set the task. Give students time to read the information in the assignment handout. Allow students to read all the resources quickly so that they can decide which topic to work on.

2. Once students have chosen their topics, put them into groups so that they work with others with the **same** topic. Remind students to read the notes and discuss with their group any new words or anything they don't understand. They should also practise pronunciation of words and sentences. Tell students how long the presentation should be and if necessary set a strict time limit, e.g., three minutes. On the other hand, if your students are reticent, you might need to set a minimum time! Monitor and give help where necessary.

Methodology notes

1. If the resources are available, students can make PowerPoint slides or other visuals to accompany their presentations at this point. They could also research further information to add to their presentations.

2. When students are discussing, you can remind them of some of the following, or write them up on the board / display them on an electronic projection:

Clarifying:
Do you mean ...?
No, sorry. I mean ...
Did you say ...?
Yes, sorry. I meant to say ...

Raising an objection:
They should / could ... instead.

Dealing with an objection:
But that would ...
Yes, I think you're right.

Saying you are lost:
Where was I?

What was I saying?
I've forgotten what I was going to say.

Helping a speaker:
You were talking about ...
You were going to tell us about ...

Saying you can't help:
Sorry. I can't remember.
I've forgotten, too.

Agreeing with a previous speaker:
As Joe has said ...
Taking up Sarah's point ...

Referring to a previous point:
Going back to Joe's point ...
Returning to Sarah's point ...

Expressing uncertainty about relevance:
I don't know if this is relevant, but ...

Expressing uncertainty about previous contributions: *I'm not sure if someone has made this point ... Has anyone mentioned ...?*

C Presenting and discussing

Tell students which presentation sub-skills you want them to work on besides the ones mentioned in the Course Book for this activity. (You can refer back to previous speaking lessons if you wish.) For example:

- eye contact;
- speed and volume of delivery;
- sticking to a time limit;
- introduction / conclusion, etc.

Re-divide the class into groups with students for each topic. Make sure listening students take an active part while each presentation is happening by following the instructions in the Course Book.

Monitor and give feedback on:

- common errors;
- where students missed opportunities to use target language;
- where students used target language appropriately;
- using turn-taking (in)appropriately.

Closure

Use your feedback stage for closure. Alternatively, have a discussion about the different psychological factors and perhaps ask students which are the most important ones.

Reading: Learning for leisure

4.11 Vocabulary for reading: Shorter working week, longer life!

Objectives

By the end of this lesson, students should be able to:

- demonstrate understanding of vocabulary for the section;
- use new vocabulary to understand figures and paragraphs about shorter working week and longer life expectancy;
- use new vocabulary to discuss implications of shorter working week and longer life expectancy.

Introduction

Select two or three of the questions below. Write them on the board for students to discuss in pairs.

- *How many hours a week do you work?* (if relevant)
- *How many hours a week does your father / mother / brother / sister work?*
- *How many hours is the average working week in your country?*
- *Are working hours controlled by the government?*
- *How much free time do you have?*
- *Do people in your country have more free time than they did 20 years ago?*

After a few minutes, elicit some of the students' ideas.

A Reading line graphs

Ask students to focus on the two figures (graphs). Check understanding of:

- the titles;
- the period covered;
- the word *trend* (from *Progressive Skills*, Level 1, Theme 5).

Set the task for discussion in pairs. Elicit answers. Point out that only the first question has a definitive answer. The second question requires ideas and the third a prediction based on the angle of the line. Several answers may well lead to further discussion of the points raised. This is fine and should lead smoothly into the text topic for Exercise B.

Optional activity

The graphs could be used as the basis for an IELTS-type written activity (IELTS Academic Module Writing Task 1). The skill for the writing section for this theme is also about describing graphs.

Answers

	Figure 1	Figure 2
1.	falling steeply until about 1970 then rising slightly	rising steeply although there was a fall in the 1870s (perhaps due to the American Civil War)
2.	laws, personal decisions not to work so many hours – or, more recently, to work more hours	medical advances, more healthy living, clean water
3.	about 42.5	about 90 or 95

B Understanding new vocabulary in context

Explain that the first text goes with Figure 1 (Average weekly hours) and the second paragraph goes with Figure 2 (Life expectancy). Ask students to read through the two paragraphs before you set the task. Check understanding of the words *working class, leisure, labour force.*

1. Set the task. Students complete individually then compare answers in pairs. Elicit answers and give further explanation of the meanings of the vocabulary where necessary. Deal also with the following phrases that arise in this section:

   raise the question = make people think about

   take into account = realize that this is an important factor

2. Ask students to discuss the question in pairs for a minute. Then elicit ideas. Students' answers could stimulate a lot of discussion about the implications. If so, you can move smoothly onto the next activity.

Answers

1. Figures show that average working hours in developed countries have fallen steadily for the last 200 years (Figure 1). *The impetus* for

this change has mainly been the rise in power of the working class in these countries, *campaigning* throughout the period. Many countries now have *state-controlled* hours which provide considerable leisure time in a week. Most people in the developed world now work a maximum of 40 hours a week, largely in *sedentary* office jobs. However, there are *indications* that the trend may be changing. Research shows a slight increase in working hours in recent years.

Many countries now provide for retirement after a particular age with state pensions, paid for by contributions from the current labour force. However, the official retirement age in many countries does not *reflect* the recent rise in *longevity*, particularly in the developed world (see Figure 2). In the 1950s, people only had two or three years of life expectancy after *retiring,* so pensions were only paid for a short period. Nowadays, on average, a person will receive an old-age pension for about 20 years. This raises the question of how society will cope. Very few people suggest *abolishing* state pension payments, but *radical* proposals *are* needed to take into account the *significant* rise in life expectancy.

2. The main points are, perhaps:

    Para 1 – Average working hours have dropped significantly, but the trend may have reversed.

    Para 2 – People are living longer but governments can't afford to pay pensions.

C   Developing critical thinking

Some ideas for answers to the questions may have arisen naturally during the lesson. If so, remind students of these before setting the task. If not, elicit one or two ideas for each question. Make sure students understand the words *implications* and *radical proposals*. Then divide the class into pairs or groups for further discussion. After a few minutes, elicit ideas.

Answers

Answers depend on students but here are some ideas:

1. Social and economic implications

    Para 1 (shorter working hours)

    Lower working hours = more leisure time

    Reversal of trend because …

Officially lower hours but many 'high flyers' and salaried workers work longer hours.

High unemployment therefore people in work feel they have to prove themselves by working (unpaid) overtime.

Para 2 (life expectancy)

Living longer = more leisure time.

Need pensions for longer (state cannot afford this).

More care needed for elderly; live longer with diseases, get more / different diseases.

2. Radical proposals – some are not acceptable, morally, perhaps!

    People pay more into private pensions for longer.

    Labour force pays much higher tax to fund pensions.

    People work for much longer.

    People do not receive pensions until they are 70 years old, or older. Perhaps even a sliding scale, based on the rise in longevity.

    State doesn't pay for health care for the elderly. Must pay for themselves, or family pay.

Closure

The following questions can be discussed in pairs or groups:

Why are people living longer?

How long will you live?

How long will your children and grandchildren live?

At what age do people receive pensions in your country?

4.12 Real-time reading: Learning for 21st-century life

Objectives

By the end of this lesson, students should be able to:

- use context and research questions in order to understand a text about modern educational philosophy;
- deal with new vocabulary in a text about the role of state education;
- identify relevant points in a text in order to complete research.

Introduction

Use Exercise A.

A Preparing to read

Give students time to study the information for the assignment. Check understanding of the words *obedient* and *well-balanced*. Elicit the noun and verb forms from the adjective *obedient – obedience, obey*.

1. Remind students of the importance of research questions before writing an essay. In this case, the questions will help students to predict the text. Students write questions individually, then compare answers in pairs. Elicit questions, and write the relevant ones on the board. (See also Optional activity below.)

2. Students discuss the questions in pairs. Elicit ideas.

3. Elicit a few ideas from the class in answer to the question. If the students are interested in the idea, build up a spidergram on the board; you can come back to this when they have read the article. Start with *literacy, numeracy, information technology* ... and perhaps suggest something radical like *flexibility* – because people will have to do several different kinds of jobs in their lifetime. Students make notes individually then compare answers in pairs.

Optional activity

This is an adaptation for Exercise A1.

Write the following possible research questions on the board. Students discuss which ones are relevant for the assignment.

a. *What is the aim of state education in my country?*

b. *When do children start school?*

c. *What subjects do children study?*

d. *How many hours a week do children study?*

e. *What jobs do most people do in my country?*

f. *What is the literacy level in my country?*

g. *How many children go on to university?*

(a, c and e are relevant)

Answers

1. Possible research questions include:

What is the aim of state education in my country?

What subjects do children study?

What jobs do most people do in my country?

2. Statements from Ministry of Education, the state education curriculum, statements from educationalists, statements from students about success / failure of education to help them in later life, statement from industry about what they want in new employees.

3. Answers depend on students.

B Understanding the text

1. Focus students' attention on the title of the article. Ask students to predict the main point of the article (*the education system is still based on an old approach*).

Set the task. Encourage students to read through the sentence beginnings first, then look through the text for the answers. Students complete individually in writing then compare answers in pairs. Show correct answers using an electronic projection so that students can self-check. Go over any answers students had difficulty with. In particular, focus on the quotation from Gough and check students understand the main point he is making. (See Methodology notes and Exercise D.)

2. Students discuss the question in pairs. Elicit answers.

Methodology notes

- Make sure students understand that this is one possible research text in preparation for writing the assignment. Students do not have to write the assignment (unless you choose to set this as a homework assignment at the end of the lesson). If they were really doing the assignment, they would have to read several more articles and get other points of view.

- Before you set Exercise B1, encourage students to use context to predict the content. In this text students should read the title, the introduction and the topic sentences before studying in detail. They could also look at the list of references below the text. You might also ask students how much they know about the British education system already, e.g., age of starting Primary School, leaving age, etc.

- Gough mentions the Victorian workhouse. This was an institution for the homeless poor in which, for example, a married couple and any children were separated. The conditions were terrible and similar to being in prison. Working-class people of the time were afraid of being put in one.

Answers

1. Possible endings:

a. State education in Britain may have started because ...	*the working class had poor literacy and numeracy.*
b. Some people say that obedience, learnt at school, prepared people for ...	*the army.*
c. It could be argued that long, boring schooldays prepared people for ...	*long, boring work days.*
d. After 1944, state education followed in some ways Plato's ideas of ...	*three types of people therefore three types of school.*
e. The national curriculum since 1988 has concentrated on ...	*'old' subjects like history and the sciences.*
f. Gough thinks that state education based on the national curriculum ...	*does not prepare children for life in the 21st century.*
g. Gough thinks state education should produce ...	*self-starters.*

2. The last three points are particularly valuable to answer the assignment question.

C Understanding vocabulary in context

Set the task. Students discuss the matching activity in pairs. Elicit answers. Elicit nouns that can follow each verb, for example:

state   facts, your name, etc.

abolish   smoking, child labour, etc.

lack   ideas, confidence, etc.

respect   politicians, your parents, etc.

promote   a product, an idea, etc.

abandon   an idea, an animal, etc.

afford   a new car, a bigger flat, etc.

require   a signature, qualifications, etc.

Spend a few minutes eliciting the meaning of several more words from the text, if you wish.

Answers

1. state	*say*
2. abolish	*get rid of*
3. lack	*not have*
4. provide	*give*
5. promote	*push*
6. abandon	*give up on*
7. afford	*have money for*
8. require	*make (force)*

D Developing critical thinking

Ask students to read the Gough quote again. Elicit one or two ideas for a curriculum. For example, Gough says we need free thinkers and entrepreneurs. This suggests the curriculum should include *critical thinking*, *business studies*, etc.

Students continue to discuss ideas in pairs or small groups. After a few minutes, elicit ideas.

Ask students to find the other subjects mentioned in the text and discuss if they have a place in Gough's ideal school (e.g., obedience, patriotism, literacy, environmental science, etc.).

Methodology note

Encourage students to consider that the curriculum is not just about *what* is taught, but *how*. Gough is probably not against the subject of literacy, for example, but would wish to see it approached in a more flexible way.

Students may wish to consider the following point. If children are prepared for a life of obedience, does that discourage free thinkers, entrepreneurs and risk-takers?

Answers

This one really does depend on students and on the culture they come from.

Closure

Refer students back to the spidergram on the board, if you made one, and ask if they want to change or add anything. Set the assignment as a written task for a home assignment, if you wish.

Objectives

By the end of this lesson, students should be able to:
- recognize key points in a text;
- record sources.

Introduction

Spend a couple of minutes revising the information from the text in Lesson 4.12. Refer students to the newspaper headlines. Ask what problem each headline is about (*literacy, numeracy, obedience, history / geography / culture of own country*). You may need to explain that Britain used to have national service, where all young men spent between 18 months and two years in the army. Clearly, this taught them obedience to authority at least.

A Reviewing vocabulary

Set the task. Students complete individually then compare answers in pairs. Elicit answers. Go over any that students had difficulty with.

Answers

1. Some people say that a major role for schools is to teach children *obedience*.
2. We should continually review the subjects on the *curriculum*.
3. Some children can do abstract subjects and some cannot. This was the *supposition*.
4. After some years, this idea of different types of school was *abandoned*.
5. UK state education is not suited to the needs of the modern world, according to some *educationalists*.
6. Many theorists believe that it is the 21st-century world that school subjects should *reflect*.
7. The first aim of any education system should be *literacy*.
8. The second aim should be *numeracy*.
9. There is a sensible argument that schools should try to produce good *citizens*.
10. Many people now work less and have far more *leisure*.
11. Medical advances are responsible for the huge increase in *longevity*.
12. Every country in the world is going to have to look again at the official age of *retirement*.

B Identifying and practising a new skill (1)

1. Students read Skills Check 1. Check students understand the link between the topic sentence and the key point.
2. Set the task. Students complete individually. Monitor to make sure students have the right idea. Elicit answers, preferably using an electronic projection.

Answers

2. Possible answers (although, as it suggests in the rubric, this is to some extent a matter of opinion):

para	topic	key words or sentences
intro	introduction	none
1	start of education in Britain	1870: no requirement to be free
		1891: fees abolished
		(role of education) = obedience, literacy, numeracy
		respect for authority
2	state school prepared working class for lives in factories / the army	patriotism, obedience
		learning did not involve thinking but following instructions
		work = little mental activity
3	compulsory secondary education	three kinds of children =
		abstract concepts
		more concrete explanations
		practical activities
4	influenced by Plato?	three classes =
		gold – ruling
		silver – auxiliaries
		copper – farmers, craftsmen
		very similar to different schools
		abandoned – schools for children of all levels of ability
5	all schools required to follow national curriculum	similar to early 19th century
		history, science, arts, language, morality
		no integrated subjects
		suit a Victorian factory worker
		brilliantly wrong for creating self-starters, etc.
6	tried to prepare children for later life	Victorian system was highly effective
		current curriculum does little to prepare for 21st-century life

C Identifying and practising a new skill (2)

1. Revise the work students did on recording sources in Theme 3 (or simply ask students to study Lesson 3.13 for a couple of minutes). Give students time to read Skills Check 2 from this lesson.

2. Give students time to read the task. Check students understand what to do. Students complete individually then compare answers in pairs. Show correct answers using an electronic projection so that students can compare with their own.

Answers

These depend on the key words the students chose, but they should really choose information mainly from the last two paragraphs, because the other paragraphs are about historical developments which have no bearing on the present. Para 5 begins with a date but students should notice the adverb *since* and the present perfect tense, which shows that the information here is still relevant to the present.

Closure

Ask students to complete some of the noun phrases from the text.

vast	majority
compulsory	education
state	schools / education
historic	role
labour	force
working	class
factory	work / workers
abstract	concepts
national	curriculum
leisure	time
risk-	takers
self-	starters
flexible	employees
creative	artists

Objectives

By the end of this lesson, students should be able to:
- distinguish between facts and possibility (hedging) in a text;
- identify a variety of hedging devices.

Introduction

Write a fact on the board, and ask students *Is this a fact?*

e.g., *The 1944 Education Act was strongly influenced by the ideas of Plato.*

Then hedge it by writing in front:

It is possible that ...

Point out to students that hedged or qualified statements have two parts – the hedge and the statement. If you don't recognize the hedge, you will think that the writer is stating a fact.

Grammar box 18

Ask students to study all the information in the first table. Highlight the verb of each example sentence. Elicit that there is no hedge, so these are facts, but point out that facts may be only *facts* according to the writer. Ask which one is not a real fact. (The last one is the writer's opinion.)

Ask students to study all the information in the second table. Highlight the hedging devices to show the range of possibilities for them. Ask students to identify the different kinds of hedges:

noun	argument
verb	seems
adverb	seemingly
adjective	possible

Point out that without the hedge, there is a simple statement of fact.

A Distinguishing between facts and possibilities

Set the task, explaining that the sentences are in the order in which they appear in the text. Students complete individually then compare answers in pairs. Elicit answers.

Answers

1. The working classes could still not afford to send their children to school.	writer's opinion
2. In 1891, fees for state schools were abolished.	fact – from research
3. State schools were designed to prepare children for lives in factories.	hedge – *it would seem that*
4. The state school day promoted patriotism and obedience.	fact – from research
5. Leisure time was very limited.	fact – from research
6. There are some children who can deal with abstract concepts.	hedge – *the supposition was that*
7. The national curriculum was a list of subjects that education ministers had studied at school.	hedge – *presumably*

B Recognizing hedging devices

Set the task. Students discuss in pairs. Elicit answers. Point out that in the writing section, students will get the opportunity to write sentences with hedging devices.

Answers

1. Some theorists believe / *think / argue / maintain* that ...

2. Many educationalists have argued / *suggested* that ...

3. The assumption / *belief / supposition* is that ...

4. It would appear / *seem* that ...

5. It is possible / *likely / probable* that ...

6. Presumably, / *Seemingly, / Arguably*, this is the reason for ...

Closure

Ask students to complete the sentences in Exercise B, orally, in different ways, from their own knowledge, or from research / ideas in this course.

Objectives

By the end of this lesson, students should be able to:

- use new reading sub-skills, grammar and vocabulary in order to understand statements and hedging;
- demonstrate understanding of a student essay about the role of state education.

Introduction

Ask students if they agree with the Henry Ford quote in the assignment handout.

A Preparing to read

Remind students about the information in the vocabulary lesson (4.11) regarding free time.

Ask students to discuss the questions in pairs. Then elicit a few ideas.

Answers

Answers depend on students, but students may raise some of the following points:

Why is free time a problem that you have to *live with*?

What skills / knowledge do people need to live with their free time?

(They may ask: *Why should state education help people with free time?* – but of course you cannot question the parameters of the assignment!)

B Understanding a text

Make sure students understand that in this lesson they will read an essay in answer to the assignment question and not a research text.

Set the task, checking students understand what to do. Students should work individually for at least five minutes. After this time, students can compare answers in pairs. Elicit answers and show the highlighted points using an electronic projection. Go over any answers students had difficulty with.

Answers

Model answers:

para	key points	source
1	no key words	
2	The average person has twice as much free time as work time during a working week.	BBC, 2007
3	they will also have, roughly, 20 years after they retire	ONS, 2010
4	in traditional subjects:	Mukherjee, 2011
	key skills related to work	
	new skills such as using IT	
	dealing with money	
	creativity	
5	value of exercise	NHS, 2011
6	teach children to be happy	Woolf, 2011
7	should stop looking at education as something which largely or wholly happens between the ages of 5 and 18	Mukherjee, 2011
8	to fund lifelong learning	Mukherjee, 2011
9	impetus from the consumers	Day, 1999

Methodology note

In order to make the lesson as realistic as possible, and to encourage independence, the text is presented as a whole, rather than being broken down into paragraphs or sections. Similarly, the number of exercises is kept to a minimum. If you think your class will struggle with this approach, however, you can do the following:

- Remind students to read the title, the introduction and the topic sentences before they start highlighting the main points.

- At a suitable point in the lesson, revise the sub-skills from Lesson 4.13. You could do this before students start reading the text. Alternatively, you could let students attempt the task, then revise the sub-skills if students have difficulty or have clearly forgotten to use them.

C Checking understanding

Students should attempt the task first without looking again at the text. This checks whether students noticed hedging during their earlier reading. Students complete individually from memory then compare answers with a partner. Finally, students check back with the text. Elicit answers and highlight the hedging devices used in the text.

Answers

1. We should continue to teach world knowledge at school.	strong – *good case*
2. People should learn key skills like literacy, numeracy and IT.	strong – *must remain / evidently of value*
3. Children should be taught to deal with money.	hedged – *may be valuable*
4. Children should be taught to be creative.	hedged – *arguable*
5. If you do not look after your body, you will suffer in later life.	hedged – *may / may not have*
6. Healthy living should be part of the school curriculum.	hedged – *could be argued*
7. Schools should teach children positive thinking.	hedged – *radical proposal*
8. School curricula should contain all the subjects, 'old' and 'new'.	hedged – *suggests then gives another solution*
9. Education should happen throughout life.	strong – *I believe*
10. Governments should provide opportunities for lifelong learning.	strong – *it is now time*
11. Teachers should educate children in the need to continue learning.	hedged – *some theorists believe*
12. Demand for lifelong learning will result in state provision.	hedged – *it is likely; perhaps*

Developing critical thinking

Students discuss in pairs or groups. Elicit some ideas.

Answers

Answers depend on students but the questions could stimulate discussion / argument.

Closure

Feed back on Exercise D.

Focus on noun phrases again, but this time spread the words around the board and ask students to make noun phrases. Other combinations are possible.

average	*person*
significant	*increase*
retirement	*age*
physical	*labour*
developed	*countries*
life	*expectancy*
traditional	*subjects*
key	*skills*
radical	*proposal*
psychological	*training*
healthy	*living*
lifelong	*learning*

Knowledge quiz: What? Where? Which? How? When?

Objectives

By the end of this lesson, students will have:
- reviewed core knowledge from Theme 4;
- recycled the vocabulary from Theme 4.

Introduction

Tell students they are going to do a knowledge and vocabulary quiz on this theme of the book. If you like, while you are waiting for everyone in the class to arrive, students can spend a few minutes looking back over the theme.

Methodology note

See notes in the Introduction for further ideas on how to do the quiz. As usual the focus should be more on content than using correct grammar.

Exercise 1

Divide the class into groups of three or four. Make sure the final column is covered (if you prefer, photocopy the quiz with the final column left blank for students to make notes). Students discuss the questions and make notes of their ideas. Do not elicit answers.

Exercise 2

Students match the questions and answers in their groups, or you could reorganize the students into pairs. Finally, elicit answers, preferably using an electronic projection.

Answers

See table on the next page.

Exercise 3

Tell students to cover the first column, or hand out another version of the quiz with only the answers. Elicit questions round the class, or put into groups to complete the activity.

Answers

Answers depend on students.

Closure

Tell students to learn the information or vocabulary for any of the answers they got wrong in class.

1. What is a *tissue*, in biology?	20	a teacher, a sports coach or a manager
2. What can *muscle tissue* do?	13	about 85
3. What does the *digestive system* do?	17	being able to read and write
4. Which system does the *spine* belong to?	2	contract but not expand
5. Which system is *asthma* a problem of?	3	converts food into nutrients
6. What did the English physician, *William Harvey*, discover in the 17th century?	1	a group of cells with the same function
7. How does the *nervous system* send messages around the body?	9	high temperature, severe aches and pains in joints and muscles, headache, fatigue
8. Where is the *Achilles tendon*?	19	in a school or university
9. What are some of the *symptoms* of flu?	8	in the heel
10. What is the difference between a *bruise* and a *contusion*?	14	it has more than doubled
11. When do you take *medication*?	7	it uses electricity
12. How do you behave if you are *neurotic*?	15	people in offices or professional drivers
13. What is the average *life expectancy* nowadays in the developed world?	16	something you think is true
14. What has happened to *longevity* in the last 150 years?	6	the circulation of the blood
15. What kinds of workers have *sedentary* jobs?	5	the respiratory system
16. What is a *supposition*?	4	the skeletal system
17. What is *literacy*?	10	there is none – one is the common term, the other is the medical term
18. If you provide the *impetus* for something, what do you do?	11	when you have an illness or a disease
19. Where do you find a *curriculum*?	18	you push people in a particular direction
20. What sort of person gives *feedback*?	12	you worry about everything

Writing: Living longer, living better

4.16 Vocabulary for writing: The changing beehive

Objectives

By the end of this lesson, students should be able to:

- demonstrate understanding of and be able to spell target vocabulary for the section;
- demonstrate understanding of changing demographics with regard to the ageing population.

Introduction

Elicit / teach the meaning of the noun *demography* (the study of human populations).

Discuss which faculties or departments study demography (Social Sciences, Sociology, Geography, Economics, Politics, etc.).

Why is it useful? (To predict and provide services for the future, e.g., housing, hospitals, teachers, etc.)

A Activating ideas

Check students understand the word *beehive*. Ask students to study the three figures. Ask one or two questions to check understanding:

What information is on the vertical axis? (ages, 0–80+)

What information is on the horizontal axis? (percentage of the population)

How has the shape changed? (In 1950 it was wider at the bottom. In 2050 it will be wider at the top.)

Now ask students to discuss the two questions in the Course Book in pairs. Elicit ideas. Feed back, pointing out that these are UN figures for the population of the world as a whole.

Answer

They show the percentage of men and women in each category for three points in time.

They indicate that the population is ageing.

B Understanding new vocabulary in context

1. Tell students to read through the definitions first before trying to find the missing words. Students complete individually then compare answers in pairs. Elicit answers.

2. Check students understand the task. Tell students not to worry too much about the meanings of any new words; the activity will help them to understand. Students complete individually then compare answers in pairs. Elicit answers.

Optional activity

- Ask students to explain the meanings of the words in italics. There are quite a lot of words in italics for students to explain. However, students may well know some of the words already. So, start by asking students to explain the familiar words, for example, *unemployed, retirement*, etc. Some words may also be the same or similar in the students' own language, e.g., *demographic*. Beware of the false friend *pension* for speakers of Latin languages.

- If students are likely to find the task difficult, give them the first letter of each word.

- Alternatively, choose one of the following three options:

  1. Allocate a few different words to different pairs or groups. Students work out the meaning from context or look up meanings in a dictionary. Students then regroup and explain their words to each other.

  2. Select a few words only for students to define. The remaining ones can be done for homework or another time.

  3. Provide a handout of the definitions. Students match words to the definitions.

Answers

Key terms

A graph which shows the *demographic* structure of a population is called a _beehive_ diagram, because it is shaped like an artificial home for bees. [e]

Women between 15 and 45 are considered to be of _child–bearing age_, although medical *innovations* mean birth can occur much later in life nowadays. [a]

The definition of _elderly_ has changed in the last 50 years. In the 1950s, this life period started at 60. [b]

Officially, people between 15 and 65 are considered to be in the _labour force_, even if they are *unemployed*. [d]

People below 15 and above 65 are considered to be _dependent_, because they usually receive *support* from the state, for example, child *benefit* to parents or old age *pension* after *retirement*. These people, by definition, are not in the labour force. [c]

C Describing a beehive diagram

1. Set the task. If you wish, you can elicit the answers orally first, and perhaps put notes or key words on the board as you go along. Explain that the answers to each question will form the basis of a complete paragraph describing the figure. Students then complete the task in writing individually. Monitor and give help where necessary, highlighting any problem areas. Students check and correct their own work.

2. Check students understand the task. Remind students about (or elicit) some of the differences between Figure 3 and Figure 1. Point out that Figure 3 is predicting the future (2050) so students need to use the

correct tense (*will* + infinitive). Students then complete the task in writing individually. Monitor and give help where necessary. Again, highlight any problem areas. Students check and correct their own work.

Answers

1. a. About 30 per cent of women were of child-bearing age in 1950.
   b. In 1950, about ten per cent of people were considered to be elderly.
   c. Approximately 40 per cent of men were in the labour force.
   d. About eight per cent of people were dependent.
2. Answers depend on students.

Closure
Discuss with the class some of the implications for society in the future based on the predictions of Figure 3. Alternatively, give a spelling test on some of the words from the lesson.

4.17 Real-time writing: Causes of population ageing

Objectives

By the end of this lesson, students should be able to:
- know more about the causes of population ageing;
- demonstrate understanding of the organization of an outline essay;
- use a figure and notes in order to complete the second paragraph of an essay.

Introduction
Revise the information shown in the beehive figures in the previous lesson.

Revise some of the vocabulary, especially *fertility, pregnancy, child-bearing, longevity, demographic*.

A Activating ideas

1. Give students a moment to study the assignment and think about the answer to the question. (Students should ignore all the references below the assignment for the

moment.) Elicit ideas. Prompt students by pointing out that the word *ageing* comes from the word *age*. You can also remind students about the beehive figures from Lesson 4.16, if you didn't do so in the introduction (above).

2. In pairs, students discuss the possible reasons for an ageing population. Elicit answers.

3. Set the task, making sure the right-hand page is covered. Students do not need to understand every word in the references, but they should notice that some words are repeated and that should give them a clue. Students discuss their ideas in pairs. Now ask students to uncover the right-hand page and check their ideas with the two figures. Elicit answers. Show how the word *fertility* appeared in the first two sources, and the word *longevity* appeared in the next two. Explain that *longevity* means the same as *life expectancy*. Briefly discuss how some of the points in Exercise B2 relate to the two main causes implied in the sources.

Elicit examples for *more*, *less* and *least developed* regions. *Developed* in this case means economically and socially.

Answers

1. Population ageing = a large percentage of the population is over 65 years old / the ratio of older people to younger is greater than it was 50 years ago.

2. You can make a case for all of them because the first two reduce the number of babies being born and the last three explain a greater number of older people.

3. Fertility rate, life expectancy.

B Gathering information

1. Check understanding of the title of the figure and the word *fertility*. Students will need plenty of time to study Figure 1 and the notes underneath. Make sure students cover the model answer. Ask students for their reactions to the figure:

   Are you surprised by any of the information? What in particular?

   Briefly check understanding of the notes under Figure 1, but don't spend too long on this as the meaning should become clearer as students work on the activities.

   Set the task. Students should write the answers in full sentences individually. Monitor and give help where necessary. Students compare answers in pairs. Do not elicit answers.

2. Students now uncover the text and compare their sentences with the model. If students' sentences are different, it does not mean they are incorrect. Allow a few students to read out one of their sentences and discuss with the class if it is an acceptable variation or not.

   Summarize some of the differences between the students' sentences and the model. For example, these could be:

   - vocabulary / phrases – *in the middle of the last century* instead of *in 1950*
   - signpost phrases – *with regard to the first factor*
   - referring to sources – *according to the research*

Answers

a. What was the world fertility rate in 1950?	On average, each woman had five children in 1950.
b. What has happened to the rate since 1950?	This average has fallen in the last 60 years to two children.
c. What is the current trend?	The rate is still falling.
d. What is the prediction until the middle of this century?	The research predicts that the rate will continue to fall until at least 2050.
e. What was the average for women in the least developed regions in 1950?	Women in the least developed regions, such as Africa and parts of Asia, had, on average, nearly seven children.
f. What was the equivalent figure in 2000?	By 2000, the average was five.
g. What happened between 1950 and 2000 in the more developed regions?	During the same period, fertility in the more developed regions fell from an average of three children per woman to under two.
h. What is the prediction for the least developed regions?	In the future, fertility in the least developed regions will fall significantly, according to the UN report, to under three by 2045–50.

Answers

Seemingly, there are two main reasons for this fall in fertility.	I
Firstly, the incidence of smaller families may be linked to urbanization.	I
In rural areas, large families are needed to work the land (Eshre Capri, 2010).	E
Secondly, the majority of women of child-bearing age now have full-time jobs.	E
It is possible that they postpone pregnancy until they have established a career.	P
They may also decide against having children altogether (ibid.).	P
It is worth noting that, in the more developed regions, a slight rise has occurred in fertility in the last five years (Fig. 1).	I
This rise is predicted to continue until at least 2050.	P
The increase will take the average to two children per woman.	P
There is a good argument that the rise is due to employment stability for spouses.	E
It may also be linked to social security benefits during pregnancy (Adsera, 2004).	E
A similar trend might appear in less developed countries as their economies improve.	P

C   Noticing the discourse structure

Set the task, checking that students are looking at the correct paragraphs. Students complete individually then compare answers in pairs. Elicit answers. Explain that students should use similar patterns when completing the writing task in Exercise D.

D   Completing the essay

Give students time to read the instructions for the essay. Use the board to consolidate the information:

Essay: Population ageing

Part 1: First factor – fertility

Part 2: Second factor – life expectancy / longevity

Remember! Refer to Figure 2 + notes, sources.

Add any other points you want students to focus on.

Set the task for class or homework. If set in class, monitor and give help where necessary. Make a note of common errors. Follow the usual TOWER procedure (see Introduction, page 11).

Answers

Model answer:

Turning to the second factor, life expectancy, longevity has risen in the period 1950 to 2010 and is predicted to continue to rise until at least 2050 (see Fig. 2). There are some variations according to region. In the 1950s, life expectancy in the more developed regions, such as Western Europe and Japan, was around 67. By 2000, it was around 72. During the same period, life expectancy in the least developed regions rose from an average of 35 to 50. In the future, life expectancy in the least developed regions is predicted to rise dramatically, to over 65 by 2045–50. The UN report on population ageing (UN, 2002) points out that although 'Great variations in life expectancy exist within the less developed regions ... these are expected to decrease' (UN, 2002, pp. 5–6). Seemingly, there are two main reasons for the rise in longevity. Firstly, it may be the result of medical innovation, such as the development of new drugs and surgical procedures (Lichtenberg, 2005). Secondly, research suggests that there has been an increase in spending on healthcare, which is linked to greater prosperity of countries (Suen, 2006).

Closure

If written work is done in class, give feedback. If set for a home assignment, elicit a possible first sentence and write it on the board for students to copy.

4.18 Learning new writing skills: Describing graphs – what and why

Objectives

By the end of this lesson, students should be able to:

- describe significant movements in a graph in a written paragraph;
- explain the reasons for movements in a graph in a written paragraph.

Introduction

Discuss the information in the two figures.

A Reviewing grammar

1. Students should read through the text first before starting to write in the answers. Students complete individually then compare answers in pairs. Elicit answers.

   Highlight the following:

   - nouns and noun phrases with **no** articles – plurals or uncountables talking about

   general items: *women, hours, Figure 1, on average, time use, household work, television viewing;*

   - phrases with *of* – *(**the** X of Y), **the** pattern of, **the** average number of*
   - phrases with *a* – *a week (meaning 'every')*
   - phrases with *the* – ***the** last, **the** same time*
   - countries – ***the** + USA, UK, UAE*, etc., but **not** *England, America*, etc.

2. The information in the Skills Check is revision. Make sure students read the information for point 1 only at this stage. After reading, ask students to find examples of some of the phrases in the text for Exercise A1, including the reference to the graph. (Students can underline or use highlighters.)

   Use the board to summarize the vocabulary:

   - *slight / gradual = a little*
   - *steady = regular*
   - *significant = large, important*
   - *steep / sharp = a lot*

   Ask students to find and underline the verbs in the text. Elicit the name of the form of each and why that tense has been used.

   Now spend a few minutes focusing on:

   - other vocabulary for describing graphs: *fall, rise, change;*
   - prepositions.

3. Set the task. Spend a few minutes discussing Figure 2 and the differences with Figure 1. Students complete individually then compare answers in pairs. Feed back as a class.

Methodology note

This exercise is as much about **not** putting in articles where they are not required as adding articles in the correct places. Point out how many nouns and noun phrases do not need an article.

Answers

1. According to a survey by the US government (NHTT, 2009), the pattern of time use for women in the United States has changed significantly over the last 50 years. For example, in 1995, they spent far less time on household work than in 1965, as can be seen in Figure 1. The average number of hours a week fell sharply from 27 to 16 during the period. At the same time, there was a steep

rise in television viewing, from 9 hours a week, on average, to 15.

3. Answers depend on students.

B Identifying a key skill

1. Set the task. Give help if necessary with any unknown vocabulary. Students discuss the question in pairs. Do not elicit.

2. Students read the second point in the Skills Check. Elicit answers to the question in Exercise B1 (the purpose of the text is to explain the movements in the graph). Use the board to highlight some of the key areas of the text:

   graph vocabulary: *gradual increase, significant rise, trend,* etc.

   key phrases for hedging, opinions, etc.: *It is probable that ... / may be ... / could explain ...*

Optional activity

Remind students about references and sources again if necessary.

Answers

The purpose of the paragraph is to explain why the movements in Figure 1 took place.

C Practising a new skill

1. Remind students what they wrote for Figure 2 about describing movements. Tell students they will now write a second paragraph explaining the movements. Elicit some possible explanations.

2. Students complete individually then compare answers in pairs. Feed back as a class.

Answers

1. Significant movements are: the rise in time spent on household work; the rise in recreation time; plateau in paid work.

2. Answers depend on students.

Closure

Give feedback on the writing activity. You could also discuss with students what other activities they would add to the figure for a more recent time period, e.g., computers and mobile phones.

Objectives

By the end of this lesson, students should be able to:
- select the correct tense form for describing the information in graphs;
- use a range of hedging devices for ideas, theories and research.

Introduction

Write the first two verb forms on the board. Ask students to tell you the difference – the first is fact, the second is possibility. Ask students to complete the table with the correct form after *may* in each case.

is	*may be*
shows	*may show*
is falling	*may be falling*
had	*may have had*
has fallen	*may have fallen*
will continue	*may continue*

Grammar box 19

Give students time to read the information in the first table. Set the task for individual completion. Elicit answers. Briefly remind students of the basic forms of each tense (without going into negatives and question forms).

Answers

S	V	other	usage	form
Research	*shows*	*the change ...*	general facts	present simple
The average	*is still falling.*		trend	present continuous
Each woman	*had*	*five children ...*	past facts	past simple
This average	*has fallen*	*recently.*	linking past and present	present perfect
It	*will continue*	*to fall ...*	predictions	future with will

Point out that all the verbs in the second table are *active*. Work through the example. Then set the task for the passive verbs. Students complete individually. Elicit answers. Revise the basic forms of passive verbs.

Answers

S	V	other	passive
Research	reveals	the problem.	The problem is revealed by research.
We	are finding	new stars every day.	New stars are being found every day.
Bell	invented	the telephone.	The telephone was invented by Bell.
Scientists	have discovered	new drugs.	New drugs have been discovered by scientists.
Engineers	will use	nanotechnology.	Nano-technology will be used by engineers.

A Choosing the correct tense form

1. Set the task. Students complete individually then compare answers in pairs. Elicit answers and give further explanation where necessary.

2. Set the task and go over the example. Students complete individually then compare answers in pairs. Elicit answers and give further explanation of passive verbs where necessary.

Answers

1. a. At one time, society *allowed* children to work in coal mines.

   b. Farms and factories *employed* the majority of people in the 19th century.

   c. Energy companies *are increasing* electricity prices at the moment because of the cost of oil.

   d. Many analysts *believe* that oil companies *will raise* prices to $200 a barrel.

   e. The British Government *introduced* paid holidays in 1936.

2. a. At one time, children were allowed to work in coal mines (by society).

   b. The majority of people in the 19th century were employed in farms and factories.

c. Electricity prices are being increased / raised (by energy companies) at the moment because of the cost of oil.

d. It is believed by many analysts that prices will be raised / increased by oil companies to $200 a barrel.

e. Paid holidays were introduced by the British Government in 1936.

Grammar box 20
If students did the reading section for this theme, you may wish to remind them of the work they did on hedging devices. Even if they didn't do this section, it would be useful at some point for students to read the information in Lesson 4.14. Students study the information in the table. Highlight the form used in each hedging device.

B Adding hedging devices

Check students understand the task. Students complete individually. Monitor and give help where necessary. Make a note of common errors. (Students will have different answers as there is more than one way the hedging devices can be fitted into the text.)

Answers

Answers depend on students but here is one possibility:

It seems that there are two main reasons for the rise in longevity. Firstly, research suggests that it is the result of medical innovation (Lichtenberg, 2005). It is probable that modern medicine deals with many illnesses of old age. Secondly, there has been an increase in spending on health care, which may be linked to greater prosperity of countries (Suen, 2006). There is a good argument that longevity will increase in developing areas as prosperity rises.

Closure
Use an electronic projection to show statements. Ask students to turn them into sentences with hedging devices:

Greenhouse gases cause global warming. (It is possible that greenhouse gases cause global warming.)

Better nutrition increases longevity.

By the end of this lesson, students should be able to:

- organize notes from given research and ideas in preparation for a written task;
- write an essay with reference to figures and research sources;
- use target vocabulary, language and discourse structure from the section in order to produce an evaluation-type essay about the social and economic implications of population ageing.

Introduction

Revise the causes of the ageing population, according to the United Nations: fertility and increased life expectancy. Tell students in this lesson they will look in more detail at the implications for society.

A Reviewing sentence patterns

Set the task, explaining that these are all different ways to explain the information in a figure. Students complete individually then compare answers in pairs. Show correct answers on an electronic projection so that students can correct their own work. Go over any problem areas. If you wish, get students to cover the first column and rewrite the sentence in the original way.

Answers

1. The average is lower than in 1990. *The average was*	*higher in 1990.*
2. The average is lower than 20 years ago. *The average has*	*fallen in the last 20 years.*
3. The trend continues at present. *The average is*	*still falling.*
4. There is a possibility that the average will fall further in the next five years. *The average might*	*fall further in the next five years.*
5. It is probable that the average will rise again in ten years' time. *The average will*	*probably rise again in ten years' time.*

B Thinking and organizing

1. This is an evaluation-type essay. After reading the assignment, ask students to discuss the questions in pairs. After a minute or two, elicit ideas.
2. Students study the figures. Elicit examples of *more developed regions*: North America, Europe, Japan, etc. Elicit examples of *less developed*: Africa, etc. Students discuss the questions in pairs. Elicit ideas.
3. Give students time to study the notes, and give help with understanding if necessary. (The quotes are important, but students do not really need to read the source and author details.) Discuss the questions with the class.

Answers

1. because people retire and require payments in pensions and possibly in higher health care
2. more developed regions; less developed regions
3. the first one; the second and third ones

C Writing, editing and rewriting

Set the task. Elicit an example for each point mentioned in the Course Book, and if necessary refer students back to the relevant lesson or page. Allow students to ask you about any of the points if necessary. Remind students at this point that they are writing a first draft of the essay. The essay can be completed in class or for homework. If done in class, monitor and give help where necessary. Make a note of common errors. Give feedback on errors at a suitable point.

Methodology note

Students could do further research for this writing activity if you wish. They could read more from the three sources given, or research their own information.

Answers

Model answer:

To what extent is population ageing a worldwide problem?

According to a United Nations report (UN, 2002), population ageing will affect the whole world in the next 40 years. The number of people over 65 will rise. This rise will increase the dependency ratio, which is the number of dependents as a percentage of workers. Dependents are normally defined as children under 15 and people over 65.

With regard to the rise in the number of elderly people, the UN research shows the change since 1950 (see Fig. 1). According to the research, the world figure was under 25 people per 100 children in 1950. The number has risen in the last 60 years and has now reached around 40 per 100 children. The figure is still rising and will reach 100 per 100 children by 2050.

There are some variations according to region. In the 1950s, in the least developed regions, such as Africa and parts of Asia, there were only around 10 elderly people per 100 children. By 2000, the average was slightly lower but it is rising now. During the same period in the more developed regions, the number of elderly people rose from around 40 per 100 children to around 100. In the future, the figure will rise significantly to over 220 per 100 children in 2050. As the UN report points out, 'Age-distribution changes in less developed regions have been slow, but will accelerate over the next 50 years.' (UN, 2002, p. 15)

It is worth noting that elderly people may not be dependent. Firstly, as Taeuber points out, 'not all ... old persons require support' because they are financially independent (Taeuber, 1992). Secondly, according to Morgan et al. (1991), 'older persons in many societies are providers of support to their adult children.' This suggests that some societies may benefit from their ageing populations. Thirdly, the UN report shows that a significant proportion of people over 65 continue to work, as can be seen in Figure 2 (UN, 2002). In more developed regions this is around ten per cent at present and is only falling slightly. In less developed regions, it is over 25 per cent, although the trend is down.

It is clear that population ageing is happening worldwide. However, this may not be as big a problem as it seems. Research suggests that many elderly people are not dependent, and therefore do not put pressure on the social security system of the state. Indeed, they may even contribute, directly or indirectly, to the support of children or people in the working population.

Objectives

By the end of this lesson, students will have:

- researched a variety of sources in order to complete tasks;
- worked independently to take part in a discussion and produce a written presentation about living longer;
- used vocabulary, grammar, sub-skills and knowledge from the theme in integrated skills activities.

Note: The Portfolio, as usual, brings together all the main elements of the theme in one activity. In particular, in this lesson, you will have opportunities to revise the following information and concepts:

- from the listening section: human body systems;
- from the speaking section: sports science and injuries;
- from the reading section: preparing for a life with more leisure time;
- from the writing section: people living longer.

However, if your students have not studied one or more of the sections, it will be enough to give a brief explanation of the relevant information.

Research, note-taking and other preparation may have to be set as assignments. The writing (and presentation, if you decide to do one) can then be given at a later date in class.

Introduction

Write questions on the board for the students to discuss in pairs, on the topic of old age. For example:

At what age do people become 'old'?

Is old age worse for women? Why (not)?

Is there less respect for older people nowadays?

A Activating ideas

1. Students study the photographs and discuss the question in pairs. Elicit ideas.

2. Before you set the task, elicit the title of the table and then elicit a few ideas for positive and negative aspects of ageing. Students complete individually then compare answers in pairs. Elicit answers. As you elicit answers for Exercises A1 and A2, you can revise some of the knowledge areas. Can students think of any other positive or negative aspects? For example, changing appearance (grey hair, wrinkles, etc.), may enjoy doing voluntary work, etc.

Answers

1. Answers depend on students but here are some ideas:
   - increased leisure time;
   - hobbies and active pursuits (but elderly people may have to be more careful because they may be more susceptible to sports injuries);
   - childcare (looking after grandchildren);
   - need for health care.

2.

positive aspects	negative aspects
They make a significant *contribution* to certain parts of the leisure industry because many take more holidays than younger people.	They sometimes need a great deal of *health* care because body systems fail or organs develop illnesses, like cancer.
They have learnt a huge number of *skills* which they can still use if given the opportunity.	They usually receive social *security* payments, e.g., old-age pensions.
They have acquired a vast amount of *knowledge* which they can share with the next generation.	They may suffer from *loneliness* because they have lost spouses, friends and relatives.
They often provide *childcare* for their grandchildren.	They may experience *boredom* because they don't know how to cope with leisure.
Some are financially *independent*, with their own homes and savings.	They may feel they have nothing further to *contribute* to society, so nothing to live for.

B Taking part in a discussion

Check students can remember the meaning of the word *stereotype*. Remind students of some of the language needed for the task for giving opinions, agreeing, disagreeing, etc.

Divide the class into pairs. Ask them to discuss the questions and note down a few ideas. Now re-divide the class into bigger groups and tell students to take their notes with them. Students should tell each other the ideas they came up with earlier in pairs. Students should compare ideas and add to them. Monitor. Finally, elicit a few ideas from the whole class and give feedback on their performance in the discussion.

Methodology note

If you prefer, you can set this task as individual presentations rather than a discussion. In this case, some time would need to be allowed for research and preparation.

Answers

Answers depend on students but here are some ideas:

1. Stereotypes include: grey hair, walking stick, old-fashioned clothes, glasses, hearing aids, forgetfulness, old-fashioned ideas, anger, very conservative views, etc.

2. Dangers: assume all old people are the same and therefore have nothing to contribute; are simply a burden on society; may hold back progress.

3. Avoid by showing wider range of elderly people in the media; educating people to live more widely, not just through their jobs; not forcing people to retire early, etc.

C Gathering information

Focus students' attention on the assignment handout. Ask them to read the quotation. Check students understand the vocabulary: *feeble, burden, ageism*. Ask students how the quotation relates to the points raised in the students' discussion in Exercise B.

Now ask students to focus on the assignment task questions. Notice how question 1 relates to the students' own country so students' answers should be more specific than the general points raised in the earlier activities. If you have students from the same country/ies, ask them to briefly discuss the question in order to brainstorm some ideas.

Focus on question 2 and once again ask students to brainstorm a few ideas.

1. Spend two or three minutes looking at the resources with the class. Elicit the basic topic of each source, for example, population ageing, health in old age, stereotypes, advantages / disadvantages of ageing, ageing in developed *vs* less developed countries, how the elderly contribute to society, etc. Remind students how to record sources. Monitor while students make notes and give help where necessary.

2./3. If you set these phases in class, monitor and give help where necessary.

Answers

Answers depend on students.

Closure

Give feedback on activities completed in class.

Theme 5

The past, present and future of food

- Agriculture through history

- Interfering with nature?

- Should man be a herbivore?

- GM: The future or the end?

5.1 Vocabulary for listening: Producing and protecting

Objectives

By the end of this lesson, students should be able to:

• recognize new vocabulary for the section in isolation and in context;

• develop understanding of new vocabulary for the section;

• demonstrate understanding of some of the issues with regard to organic farming.

Introduction

Write the following list of verbs on the board:

create, make, manufacture, construct, give, supply, deliver, grow, show

Ask students *Can you think of **one** synonym for all these verbs?* (produce)

Repeat with these verbs:

keep, look after, take care of, guard, watch over, shelter (protect)

Ask for some collocations with *produce* and *protect*:

produce – food, a meal, a film, crops, goods, evidence, etc.

protect – people, children, your skin, animals, your rights (*protect + against* – burglars, violence, fire, etc.)

Explain that today's lesson is all about protecting and producing crops.

A Activating knowledge

Students discuss the questions in pairs. If you wish, you can refer them to the first illustration. Elicit answers.

Answers

Plants need: water, sunlight, food (nutrients – N, K and P), air (oxygen, carbon dioxide)

B Understanding vocabulary in context

1. Ask students to read the radio programme information. Check understanding. Elicit ideas for the answer to the question.

2. Give students time to read the questions. Play 🔊 **5.1**. Students discuss the questions in pairs. Elicit answers.

3. Ask students to add *soil* (which they know) and *exhausted* (which needs explanation) to the word lists in their Course Books. Set the task. Students complete individually then compare answers in pairs. Replay 🔊 **5.1** so that students can check their ideas. Go over any answers students had difficulty with.

4. Set the task and go over the example. Play 🔊 **5.2**. (Do not elicit answers until all the items have been played.) Replay 🔊 **5.2** so that students can check their answers. Students compare answers in pairs. Go over any answers students had difficulty with.

Optional activity

After Exercise B3, elicit the stressed syllable of each word.

Answers

1. Answers depend on students at this stage.

2. a. organic

   b. Because it was the first form of farming, and perhaps we should return to it to look after the environment.

3. a. At one time, all farmers were *organic*.

   b. We know, of course, that plants need sunlight and water, but plants need *nutrients*, too.

   c. Nutrients exist naturally in *soil*.

   d. Eventually, the soil becomes *exhausted*.

   e. At one time, farmers put nutrients back organically, with animal *waste*, ...

   f. ... particularly *manure* from the cows and horses on the farm.

   g. Farmers must protect their crops from *pests*, like birds, insects and bacteria.

   h. From the earliest times, farmers have used natural *pesticides*, like sulphur, to destroy pests.

   i. Pests have been responsible for *famine*, with farms producing few or no food crops.

4.

6	environment.
3	farming.
7	fish.
10	future.
8	health.
4	laboratory.
2, 9	past.
5	pesticides.
-	rivers.
1	simple.

Transcripts

🌐 5.1

Presenter:	5.1. Theme 5: The past, present and future of food Lesson 5.1. Vocabulary for listening: Producing and protecting Exercise B2. Listen to the first part of Malcolm's talk.
Radio presenter:	Good morning. Welcome to this week's *Talking Point*. As always, we have someone in the studio this week who feels very strongly about a current issue. With his wife, Heather, Malcolm farms 10,000 hectares in Norfolk, which is in the east of England. Welcome, Malcolm.
Malcolm:	Thank you. Good morning.
Radio presenter:	Now, Malcolm, I understand that you are worried about where we are going with farming?
Malcolm:	Yes, indeed. I am very worried.
Radio presenter:	But we're not talking about the EU or supermarkets ...
Malcolm:	No, something much more important.
Radio presenter:	OK. Over to you then, Malcolm.
Malcolm:	Thank you. I need to start with a little bit of history. At one time, all farmers were organic. By that I mean that they only used natural products to help their plants grow and to protect them. Let's look at growth first. Now, we know, of course, that plants need sunlight and water, but plants need nutrients, too. The nutrients are chemicals like nitrogen, potassium and phosphorus. Nutrients exist naturally in soil, but the problem is, crops take nutrients out of the soil during the growing process. Eventually, the soil becomes exhausted. At this point, farmers must put nutrients back. At one time, farmers put nutrients back organically, with animal waste, particularly manure from the cows and horses on the farm. So that's growth. Now, what about protection? Farmers must protect their crops from pests, like birds, insects and bacteria. Birds and insects eat the crops, bacteria can give them diseases. From the earliest times, farmers have used natural pesticides like sulphur to destroy pests. It is a vital part of farming because certain pests can completely destroy a crop. On many occasions

in history, pests have been responsible for famine in a large area, with farms producing few or no food crops. For example, the Great Famine of the 1850s in Ireland, which was caused by bacteria, destroyed the complete potato crop of the country. This was the main food crop and, as a result, approximately one million people died through starvation.

OK, so that's the past. What about the present? Nowadays, most farmers use artificial fertilizers to help crops to grow. The fertilizers are made in a laboratory. They also use artificial pesticides to protect their crops. However, a small number of farmers, like Heather and me, have gone back to older ways. We are very afraid that artificial fertilizers and pesticides are running out of the soil and polluting the water system – I mean, the streams and rivers and finally the water supply to private houses. In the rivers and streams, they are damaging the environment, killing fish and aquatic plants. In our water supply, they are an enormous danger to public health.

Radio presenter:	Thank you, Malcolm. So what's your solution?

🌐 5.2

Presenter:	5.2. Exercise B4. Listen to the final part of Malcolm's talk. When he stops, number the next word or phrase.
Malcolm:	My solution is [PAUSE] simple. The future is going back to the [PAUSE] past. Farmers should return to organic [PAUSE] farming. They should stop using chemicals which are made in a [PAUSE] laboratory. They should use only natural fertilizers and natural [PAUSE] pesticides. If these chemicals escape from the farm, they do not damage the [PAUSE] environment. They do not pollute rivers and kill [PAUSE] fish. They do not endanger public [PAUSE] health. Organic farming is not only the [PAUSE] past. It is also the [PAUSE] future.

C Developing critical thinking

Students discuss in pairs or small groups. Elicit ideas.

Closure

Do the pairs of words below as a matching activity. You could say the first word, and students suggest a possible collocation:

T: *organic*

Ss: *vegetables* (or *fruit, meat, farming, farmer, agriculture*, etc.)

Alternatively, write all the words in the left-hand column on the board. Add the words from the second column in random order. Students find pairs of words.

organic	vegetables
exhausted	soil
essential	nutrients
natural	fertilizers
damage	the environment
pollute	rivers
kill	fish
endanger	health
protect	crops
destroy	bacteria

5.2 Real-time listening: Agriculture – the beginning of civilization

Objectives

By the end of this lesson, students should be able to:
- use existing skills to follow a lecture about the history of agriculture;
- demonstrate understanding of the lecture through adding notes to the handout provided;
- recognize new vocabulary in context.

Introduction

Exploit one or two of the illustrations on the opposite page. For example, crop rotation:

What crops does it show? (carrots, peas, cabbages [brassicas])

Why are the crops in a circle? (because each crop is replaced by a different one every year)

A Activating ideas

1. Check understanding of the word *civilization*. After reading the information in the lecture handout, students discuss the two paraphrases. Elicit answers.
2. Set the task for discussion in pairs. Students should be able to work out the meanings of any new words from the illustrations but they can resort to dictionaries if necessary.

Elicit answers and point out the following:
- *wild* is the opposite of *domesticated* in this context;
- a synonym for *gatherer* is *collector*;
- the pronunciation of *plough* (it does **not** rhyme with *through*, *though* or *rough*; the vowel sound is as in the word *now*).

3. It does not really matter if students cannot answer this question. It is just to generate interest in the subject matter. Elicit one or two ideas but do not confirm or correct.

Answers

1. a) is probably the better: *divided* here means 'split into small groups', **not** 'in conflict'
2.

A feast	11
A watering hole	10
A watermill	7
Crop rotation	9
Domesticated animals	5
Domesticated wheat	4
Hilly flanks (sides)	12
Hunter-gatherers	1
Planting rice	6
Ploughing with a horse	8
The Fertile Crescent	3
Wild grass	2

3. Answers depend on students.

Methodology note

Students do not need to learn all the words here. They simply need to understand them for this lesson.

B Understanding a lecture

1. Tell students you will pause the DVD after the introduction. Play DVD 5.A. Elicit answers.
2. Give students time to study the timeline handout for a few minutes. Remind students that most of the items in the *event* column are shown in the illustrations. Other new words and phrases will be explained in the lecture. Set the task and explain they should add extra information to the notes, including countries, other places and people. Play DVD 5.B. Students complete the notes individually then compare answers in pairs.

Show the correct version of the notes using an electronic projection so that students can compare with their own versions. Allow students to ask about any variations they may have. Replay any sections of the lecture students had difficulty with.

3. Remind students that in this part of the lecture they will hear some theories of how agriculture started. Go through each heading and relate to the illustrations where possible. Play DVD 5.C. Students complete the notes. When the DVD has finished, students can compare notes in pairs. Then follow the procedure explained in B2.

Methodology note

Depending on time, try to replay the DVD, or at least sections of it. Students can also follow the transcript.

Answers

1. Timeline then subheadings.
2. See page 240.
3. Model notes:

Origins of agriculture – theories

1. *Oasis*
   - *Pumpelly, 1908 in Rosen, 2007*
   - *climate change*
     – drier climate, people moved to oases, animals accepted humans = domestication
   - *people didn't move from oases, planted seeds*
   - *'makes sense but no evidence of climate change at the time'*

2. *Hilly flanks*
   - *Braidwood in Sutton and Anderson, 2009*
   - *people living in grassy land began to cultivate wheat*
   - *Turkey, Iran and Iraq*
   - *banks of the rivers*
   - *'sounds reasonable but no evidence'*

3. *Feasting*
   - *Hayden, 2002*
   - *feasts = display of power*
   - *leaders needed reliable source of food*
   - *'no evidence for or against'*

4. *Demographic*
   - *sources – reading pack*
   - *people became more sedentary, stayed, pop. grew*
   - *had to plant seeds and grow more food*
   - *'but why stop moving?'*

5. *Evolutionary*
   - *sources – reading pack*
   - *gradual protection of wild plants*
   - *understanding of diff. locations for diff. plants*
   - *'makes sense but still not really learnt this lesson'*

6. *Domestication*
   - *Daniel Quinn*
   - *people became domesticated, stayed, domesticated the area*
   - *'doesn't work for me – why did they become domesticated?'*

Transcripts
🌐 5.3 DVD 5.A

Presenter:	5.3. Lesson 5.2. Real-time listening: Agriculture – the beginning of civilization
Lecturer:	Agriculture is the name we give to the industry of farming. It has two main branches – producing crops and rearing animals for food. It has been happening for over 14,000 years, according to most sources. Today we are going to look briefly at the history of the industry, and then consider some of the theories of how agriculture started. In later lectures, we will review the *current* situation of agriculture, or 'agribusiness' as we should probably call it now, and, of course, the *future* of agriculture, which concerns all of us on this planet.

🌐 5.4 DVD 5.B

Lecturer:	Right, so, what I'm going to do first is take you on a quick trip through the history of agriculture. It all started about 14,000 years ago, as I said, in about 12000 BCE, in the area we now call Lebanon. This is part of an area now called the Fertile Crescent – basically, the Middle East. It was the cradle of agriculture – the place where it all started. Actually, perhaps I should have said, *one* place! Recent research suggests that agriculture started independently in many places at about the same time. But, anyway, at the moment, the only important thing is, it started! The local tribes started to harvest wild grasses. If that sounds strange, remember, wheat is just a kind of grass. I remember harvesting wild grass myself. When I was young, I used to pick wild grass and chew the kernel, the bit at the top. There was hardly anything in it, of course, because the grass was wild, but it's interesting to think that 14,000 years ago, people must have done the same thing and thought – hey, we can eat this! OK. So, getting back to the history ... Early people made flour from the seeds, but the yield – I mean, the amount of flour that they got

from each seed – was very, very low. *Yield* is a very important concept in agriculture, so make a note. Oh, of course, I should have said what was happening *before* agriculture started. Well, early man was a hunter-gatherer. In other words he, or in some tribes, she, hunted and killed wild animals for food, or gathered wild berries and fruits from the trees and bushes. Incidentally, when you are a hunter-gatherer, you spend all day hunting and gathering to get enough food to feed yourself and your family. Also, if the animals migrate each season to another area, you have to follow them. I want you to think about that when we consider the theories of the origins of agriculture.

OK. Jump forward to about 8500 BCE. It was then that people first began to grow crops such as barley, wheat, peas and lentils. We know this, of course, from the remains of food that has been found with the bones of early man. Oh, did I mention? … there is some evidence that rice was domesticated in China in about 11500 BCE. OK, let's get back to Lebanon. About 7000 BCE, people began to tame animals such as goats and sheep in Greece and other parts of the eastern Mediterranean. About 1,000 years after that – so where are we now, about 6000 BCE – cows and chickens were added to the list of domesticated animals … that was in Pakistan. It's strange, isn't it, to think of farmyard animals like sheep and cows as wild, but they certainly used to be.

OK. Where did I get to? Oh, yes, 6000 BCE. That's about 8,000 years ago. A thousand years later, in about 5000 BCE, the horse was domesticated, first in the area that we now call the Ukraine. Obviously, some people ate the meat of the domesticated horse – some people still do today – but horses were really much more important as work animals, to pull ploughs, for example, or to transport harvested crops. Actually, I've jumped the gun on the plough – that didn't appear until about 4000 BCE in the area we now call Iraq. That reminds me. I was in a village on the southern edge of the Sahara and I saw *camels* pulling ploughs. They are still using animals because tractors break down too often in the sand, and you can't get the spare parts. Anyway, where was I? Ah, yes – 5000 BCE.

Over the next 5,000 years, there were a lot of small improvements to agriculture, including irrigation and power supply – I mean windmills and watermills to grind corn. I'm not going to spend ages on that today because you have a project on Chinese agriculture and another on Arab agriculture later in the course. So what we'll do now is jump right forward to the Agricultural, or Agrarian, Revolution in 18th-century Britain.

Why is it called a revolution? Because it revolutionized the way people worked the land. Until about 1700, land all over the world was worked mainly by people, with the help, as I mentioned, of horses and other animals. Then, in 1701, a man called Jethro Tull decided to mechanize a basic part of farming. What he invented was the seed drill. This was a mechanical method of sowing seeds. Although it was more than 150 years before the method was widely adopted, it was the start of the

mechanization of agriculture. In 1786, for example, Andrew Meikle invented a mechanical threshing machine, which could thresh, or separate, the edible parts of cereal crops from the rest. There was also the steam plough, in the 1850s. It finally replaced horses in many places after about 7,000 years. Other inventions in the Agrarian Revolution were crop rotation and selective breeding, which we'll talk about in another lecture.

Just before we go back to look at theories, I must just mention one more revolution – the Green Revolution, which started in the early 1960s. Because the population of countries like India and China was rising so fast at the time, agriculturalists were terribly worried about famine. Many researchers around the world thought that millions of people were going to die of starvation in the near future because improvements in agriculture could not keep up with the increase in population. But a man called Norman Borlaug suggested an answer. He introduced a new variety of rice to India that had a much higher yield – remember that important word? – a much higher yield than the indigenous variety. It could produce ten times the crop in the best conditions. It was called 'Miracle Rice' by the people of Asia and started a revolution in yield that is still continuing to this day.

🌐 5.5 [DVD] 5.C

Lecturer:
So, we've had a brief overview of the history. But how did it all start, 14,000 years ago? Well, there are six main theories about why people moved from hunting and gathering to organized farming. Yes, sorry about that, six! But some, in my view, are much better than others. Here they are, in no particular order. We've got the Oasis theory, the Hilly Flanks theory – that's flanks, or sides – you'll see why in a minute. Next, the Feasting model. Feasting means having a lot of food at one meal. Then we have the Demographic theory – I'm sure you know about demographics. The fifth theory is the Evolutionary theory. And, finally, the Domestication theory. I expect you can guess what some of these theories involve, but let's look at each one in turn.

First, then, the Oasis theory. This was propounded by Raphael Pumpelly in 1908. It's described in Rosen, 2007, on your reference list. The theory argues that climate change caused the start of agriculture. He says that the climate in some areas became drier. When this happened, people moved to oases – or actually, more accurately, to watering holes. Because wild animals came to the watering hole to drink, people came into closer contact with them. Gradually, the animals accepted the humans, which in turn led to their domestication. At least, that's the theory. Also, because the people did not move from the oases or watering holes, they started to plant seeds. It makes sense to me, but it seems that this theory has not received much support, due to the lack of evidence of climatic change at the relevant time.

The second theory is the Hilly Flanks theory, put forward by Robert Braidwood. This is in Sutton and Anderson, 2009. Braidwood did not believe that there was a climatic change, as Pumpelly proposed. Instead, he thought that people living in grassy habitats began to cultivate the edible species such as wheat and barley. This occurred in the subtropical wooded hills of Turkey, Iran and Iraq on the flanks, or sides, of rivers – hence the Hilly Flanks theory. Although this theory sounds reasonable, Sutton and Anderson state that no evidence for it has been found.

A man called Brian Hayden – that's Hayden, 2002 on your list – proposed another theory, the Feasting model. He argues that leaders came to regard feasting as a display of power – in other words, they organized big meals for hundreds of people, to show how powerful they were. This led to agriculture because leaders had to have a reliable source of large amounts of food. It is difficult to evaluate this theory. There is no evidence for or against. I remember, though, when I lived in Arabia, it was clear that feasting was still very important. There was always too much food for the people invited to a meal – and in the case of rich people, that was often hundreds of people. In fact, I believe, in that culture, if the guests eat all the food, the host is ashamed. In Europe, of course, when people come to dinner, we like them to finish everything on their plate. Anyway, back to the point ...

Theory number 4 – Demographic theory ... or perhaps we should say *theories*, because there are several based on the same idea. You will see some sources in your Reading Pack. Basically, they all take the view that people became more sedentary and began to stay in the same place, so the population grew and they needed more food than the area supplied. So they had to plant seeds and grow more food themselves. In my view, these theories start from the wrong end. They suggest that people stopped moving and then started planting crops. But why did they stop moving? If we are to believe this theory, we must understand why people stopped moving. If you are a hunter-gatherer and the animals move away and the berries go out of season, surely you must follow them?

The fifth theory that has been suggested by several scholars is the Evolutionary theory. There are sources for this in your Reading Pack, too. The Evolutionary theory is the idea that agriculture began with the gradual protection of wild plants in order to preserve the resource. You know, they said to each other, 'We must look after these wild plants because we need them to produce fruit or berries next year.' Except of course, there was no spoken language at the time, but maybe they said it with sign language. This in turn led to an understanding of different locations for different plants. This theory gets my vote. If you use something every day, you begin to realize that it is important to protect it. I realize that we still haven't really learnt this lesson, but perhaps early man was closer to nature than us and therefore more protective ... which reminds me of one local council in Britain. They realized that a lot of visitors were coming to their town. They were coming, in fact, to see the old trees in the area. The problem was, there was nowhere for them to park. So the council cut down the trees to make a car park. Sorry. That's a silly story and probably not even true. So let's get back to the theories ...

The final theory is the Domestication theory propounded by Daniel Quinn, amongst others. Sorry, I haven't got the reference for him. You'll have to look it up. This theory suggests that people became more domesticated, staying in one area and beginning to domesticate that area. This involved looking after plants and taming the wild animals. Like the Demographic theory, this just doesn't work for me. Why did people become more domesticated? What was the impetus? Again, it seems to be the wrong way round. We need to explain why people became more domesticated in the first place.

So there we have the theories concerning the start of agriculture. Which do you think is most likely?

C Showing comprehension

Students can ask and answer in pairs. They can look at the transcript for any answers they are not sure of. Elicit answers and give further explanations where necessary.

Answers

1. hunted animals and gathered berries
2. the Fertile Crescent
3. cows and chickens
4. area now called Iraq
5. Tull
6. ten times the yield

D Developing critical thinking

Divide the class into small groups to discuss the question. After a few minutes, elicit ideas.

Answers

Answers depend on students but some seem far more likely than others. They should have noticed that the lecturer is most in favour of the Evolutionary theory – 'it gets my vote'.

Closure

Choose one of the following:

- Use the discussion in Exercise D.
- Recap on some of the vocabulary from the lesson. Tell students which vocabulary from the lesson you want them to learn.
- Tell students to close their books. Ask different students to tell you one piece of information from the lesson. (Each student should give you a new piece of information, so as you go round the class the task becomes harder.)

date	event	notes
pre-12 000 BCE	hunter-gatherers	killed animals, gathered berries, etc.
12 000 BCE	wild grasses harvested	Fertile Crescent = Lebanon; flour from seeds
11 500 BCE	rice domesticated	in China
8 500 BCE	barley, wheat grown	we know from remains of food
7 000 BCE	goats, sheep domesticated	Greece, E. Med.
6 000 BCE	cows and chickens domesticated	Pakistan
5 000 BCE	horses domesticated	Ukraine, ate meat but mainly for work
4 000 BCE	plough	Iraq
next 5,000 yrs	irrigation power sources	windmills, watermills
18th C	Agrarian Revolution	Britain
1701	seed drill	Tull, idea didn't take off for 150 yrs
1786	mechanical threshing machine	Meikle – separated edible parts of cereals
1850	steam plough	replaced horses in many places
early 1960s	Green Revolution	people worried about famine
1961	Borlaug – miracle rice	ten times the crop

5.3 Learning new listening skills: Dealing with digressions

Objectives

By the end of this lesson, students should be able to:
- identify the phonemic symbols for vowel sounds;
- recognize and deal with digression in a lecture.

Introduction

Give the definitions of some of the words in the box in Exercise A. Students find the correct word and attempt to say it correctly, e.g., opposite of *wild* = *domesticated*; grow crops on an area = *cultivate*.

A Reviewing vocabulary

1. Students discuss pronunciation of each word in pairs. Encourage them to attempt pronunciation even if they are not sure. Do not elicit answers.
2. Play ◉ **5.6**. Students listen and check their ideas. Replay and/or pause the CD if necessary.
3. Ask students to read the Pronunciation Check. Check understanding. Set the task for pairwork. Monitor and give help where necessary. Elicit answers.

Answers

/æ/	pat	'agriculture, 'famine, 'tractor
/e/	pet	do'mesticated, 'edible, 'mechanize
/ɪ/	pit	in'digenous, 'irrigate
/ʌ/	put	agri'cultural, 'cultivate
/ɑ:/	part	'harvest
/ɜ:/	per	'fertile, pre'serve
/i:/	Pete	ma'chine
/ɔ:/	port	re'source
/eɪ/	pay	irri'gation, star'vation
/aɪ/	pie	'climate

Transcript

◉ 5.6

Presenter: 5.6. Lesson 5.3. Learning new listening skills: Dealing with digressions

Exercise A2. Listen and check your ideas.

Voice: agriculture, agricultural, climate, cultivate, domesticated, edible, famine, fertile, harvest, indigenous, irrigate, irrigation, machine, mechanize, preserve, resource, starvation, tractor

B Identifying a new skill

1. Give students time to read the extract. Students discuss the question in pairs. Elicit ideas; students may suggest that the lecturer goes away from the main point. Tell students they will find out the word for this in the Skills Check.
2. After students have studied the Skills Check for a few minutes, elicit the word for going away from the main point: *digression*. Check students understand what to do about digressions in a lecture (ignore it for now, then find out about it later).

Methodology note

It is worth pointing out to students that although digressions are 'off the point', they do sometimes serve a useful purpose. They can inject humour or interest into the lecture, help illustrate a particular point, or help students to remember a particular point.

Answers

The lecturer is digressing.

C Practising a new skill

Go over the title for each lecture extract. If there is time, revise some vocabulary and information about each title (they are all from previous themes), for example, the locations of Qatar and Lebanon.

Set the task carefully. Play ◉ **5.7**. Play each extract one at a time and pause while students ask each other about the digression. If necessary, replay the extract. Elicit what students wrote down as notes, and check they understood each digression. Ask students what they thought about each digression, e.g., was it amusing / completely irrelevant / interesting / useful?

When all the extracts have been played, ask students to study the transcript and underline the digression phrases. If you wish, play 🔊 5.7 again with students following the transcript.

Transcript and Answers
🔊 5.7

Presenter: 5.7. Exercise C. Listen and make notes. When the lecturer digresses, write one or two words to help you remember.

Lecture 1: The development of Qatar and Lebanon

Lecturer 1: OK. Now we are going to compare two countries, using these areas and sub-areas. Both countries are located in the Middle East but Qatar is in the Gulf whereas Lebanon is in the eastern end of the Mediterranean Sea. Qatar is a peninsula, only bordered to the south by Saudi Arabia, while Lebanon is almost completely surrounded by Syria. I remember I once had to visit Qatar – that was over 35 years ago – and when I told people where I was going, none of my friends even knew where it was. I went back recently and it's incredible to see the progress that has been made in such a relatively short time. Lots of modern buildings and wide roads. I think perhaps the outlook has changed too. Anyway. Where was I? OK, Qatar in the Gulf, Lebanon on the Mediterranean. Does the location of these countries affect their human development?

Presenter: **Lecture 2: Long-distance communication: semaphore**

Lecturer 2: In 1793, a man called Claude Chappe invented the long-distance semaphore in France. The French government built a network of 556 relay stations all over the country. These were houses with arms on the roof. The arms could move to make different symbols. Urgent messages could travel at about 20 miles an hour now – faster and much more secure. That reminds me of a part from a French novel by Alexandre Dumas, *The Count of Monte Cristo*. He is falsely imprisoned for years and when he gets out, he takes revenge on all the people who falsely accused him. He destroys one man by bribing a semaphore station clerk to send a false message – something about Napoleon winning a battle or losing one – I can't remember which. So of course, this shows that semaphore wasn't completely secure. But getting back to the point, it was very difficult to intercept and stop a message from reaching its destination. It was in code, too, so even if you did intercept it, you couldn't understand it. But the system was very expensive, to build and to maintain. It was very expensive for the customers who wanted to use it, too. But Napoleon used it all the time to send urgent messages about troop movements – you know, how his armies were moving around the country.

Presenter: **Lecture 3: Children and violence on television**

Lecturer 3: Now, I accept that children have to experience fear, and learn how to deal with it. Clearly, this is why we have fairy tales, which are full of murders, kidnappings and violent acts. Fairy tales are very old and presumably perform a useful function in education, so this is a very powerful argument. But we must take into account several factors. Firstly, children are visual learners, and television is a visual medium. It actually *shows* the violence, whereas fairy tales *talk* about it. There is a big difference. I remember when I was a child of about eight, I had to watch a particular TV science fiction programme, with robots and aliens and green monsters with ten heads and so on from behind the sofa, or peeking through my hands because it was so scary. But I could read about the same sort of thing and it had no effect on me at all. Anyway. Why was I saying that? Oh yes, because fairy tales are not visual. Also, most fairy tales are initially told to children by a parent. So the parent has a chance to mediate the experience for the child – in other words, to tone it down, if they think the child will not be able to cope with the events as written. The parent is the medium by which the child receives the story, and they can change the story if necessary. But television is a very different medium. It is unvarying. It does not change to suit the viewer, even if the viewer is eight years old, alone with the television in the sitting room and terrified.

Presenter: **Lecture 4: The central nervous system**

Lecturer 4: It is the central nervous system which controls muscle contraction. The system is two-way. What I mean by that is, the system gathers information from nerves throughout the body and takes it to the brain through the spinal column. It uses electrical impulses. The brain is the primary processing centre for the body. If the decision is taken to react to a particular stimulus, the brain sends the necessary impulses to the muscles – electricity again. Which reminds me that when I was at school, I suppose in about Year 8 or 9, we had to do this experiment with frog's legs – don't worry, the animals were dead, and in fact, the legs were not even on the animal, they had been cut off. We touched them with the two ends of an electrical circuit and the legs twitched, which shows the effect of electricity on the muscle tissue even when the animal is dead. The girls all screamed, I remember, when the legs jumped – I think most of the boys did, too. Anyway, that's enough of that. Let's get back to the nervous system. The main parts are the nerves, as I've just said, the brain, obviously, and the spinal cord, which runs down the spine. We can see now why the skull and the spine are so important. They protect key parts of the central nervous system.

Closure
As this is the last theme of the course, spend a few minutes recapping some of the other listening sub-skills from previous themes.

By the end of this lesson, students should be able to:

- identify complex sentences in spoken discourse;
- predict information from either the main or the subordinate clause in complex sentences.

Introduction

Write the following sentences from the table on the board and ask students where you could divide each one. Ask them why they would divide each one there.

When I was young I used to pick wild grass.

Because the population was rising fast agriculturalists were afraid of famine.

Refer students to the table.

Grammar box 21

Explain that a *complex sentence* is a longer sentence with two parts to it; one part is main and one is subordinate. (This is different from a *compound* sentence, where the two parts are equal and joined by a co-ordinator, e.g., *and / but / or*.) Explain that it is obviously important to be able to understand longer sentences when listening to lectures, etc.

Ask students to study the explanation above the table and the example sentences in the table. Check understanding.

Play the first sentence on ⑨ **5.8** then pause. Try to elicit an answer. If students cannot answer, play the next sentence, and so on. If students can answer, do not confirm or correct but play the remaining sentences for students to check their ideas. Confirm the correct answer: that the speaker pauses after the subordinate clause. This gives students an opportunity for prediction. Set the task for restating the sentences. Elicit answers.

Methodology note

Speakers normally put a rise in intonation and pause at the end of a leading subordinate clause. Speakers sometimes pause before the end of a main clause, but this is not always the case, particularly with *when* and *if*.

For example:

When I was young [pause] I used to pick wild grass.

I used to pick wild grass [pause?] when I was young.

Answers

[for restating sentences]

I used to pick wild grass when I was young.

You must follow the animals if they migrate.

Agriculturalists were afraid of famine because the population was rising fast.

Scientists have found no evidence of this theory although it could be correct.

Transcript

⑨ 5.8

Presenter:	5.8. Lesson 5.4. Grammar for listening: Complex sentences (1)
	Grammar box 21. Listen to the examples. Where does the speaker pause in each case?
Voice:	When I was young, I used to pick wild grass. If the animals migrate, you must follow them. Because the population was rising fast, agriculturalists were afraid of famine. Although this theory could be correct, scientists have found no evidence.

A Identifying parts of complex sentences

Check students understand the task. Students complete individually then compare answers in pairs. Elicit answers, preferably using an electronic projection.

Answers

S	M
If you follow animals	you cannot establish towns.
Although the seed drill was invented in 1701	it wasn't used widely until the 1850s.

M	S
I saw camels pulling ploughs in a town south of the Sahara	when I worked there.
Many areas need irrigation	because there is not enough natural water.

B Predicting from the adverb and subordinate clause

1. Set the task and go over the example. Explain that students will hear the adverb and subordinate clause (refer back to the table if necessary). They must find the correct main clause in the list. Play ⑨ **5.9**; students write the number next to the

relevant answer. When all the items have been played, students can compare in pairs.

2. Play 🎧 **5.10** so that students can check their answers. Replay any sentences students had difficulty with.

Transcript and Answers
🎧 5.9

Presenter:	**5.9. Exercise B1. Listen to the first clause of some complex sentences. Find a suitable ending.**
Voice:	a. When you are a hunter-gatherer, … b. If you use something every day, … c. If guests eat all the food, … d. Because people stayed in one place, … e. Because there is a global shortage of fresh water, … f. Because Lebanon doesn't have any oil resources, … g. If the Sumerians wanted to communicate over a long distance, …

C Predicting from the main clause and adverb

1. Set the task and go over the example. Play 🎧 **5.11**. Play each main clause, pausing after each one. Students turn to a partner and suggest ways to finish. Ask one or two pairs to tell you their ideas.

2. Play 🎧 **5.12** if necessary as you go through the activity.

Transcripts and Answers
🎧 5.11

Presenter:	**5.11. Exercise C1. Listen to the main clause of some complex sentences. How could the speaker finish each one?**
Voice:	a. I'm not going to talk about Chinese agriculture very much because … b. The nerves in your fingers send a message to the brain if … c. There is much more agriculture in Lebanon than in Qatar because … d. In children's television programmes, people don't die when … e. It is possible that children become aggressive because … f. You shouldn't let young children watch television when …

🎧 5.12

Presenter:	**5.12. Exercise C2. Listen and check your ideas.**
Voice:	a. I'm not going to talk about Chinese agriculture very much because you are going to do a project on this. b. The nerves in your fingers send a message to the brain if they touch something hot or sharp. c. There is much more agriculture in Lebanon than in Qatar because it has more fertile land.

d. In children's television programmes, people don't die when they are blown up and shot.
e. It is possible that children become aggressive because they watch violent TV programmes.
f. You shouldn't let young children watch television when they are alone.

D Predicting the main or the subordinate clause

1. Play 🎧 **5.13**. Pause after each item. Students turn to their partner and suggest a possible ending.

2. Play 🎧 **5.14**. Pause after each complete sentence. Ask students if they had a similar idea or something different in Exercise D1. Highlight any grammar mistakes as you elicit.

Optional activity

Copy the main clauses on to a handout. Students can complete them in writing either in class or for homework.

Transcripts and Answers
🎧 5.13

Presenter:	**5.13. Exercise D1. Listen to the first clause of some sentences. When the speaker pauses, discuss possible endings to the sentence.**
Voice:	a. Parents often tone down fairy tales if … b. Muscles work in pairs because … c. When Napoleon had an urgent message for his army … d. Civilization started when … e. Sports injuries usually get better faster if … f. Although customers buy *products* … g. If you provide higher benefits …

🎧 5.14

Presenter:	**5.14. Exercise D2. Listen and check your ideas.**
Voice:	a. Parents often tone down fairy tales if they are very violent. b. Muscles work in pairs because they can only contract. c. When Napoleon had an urgent message for his army he sent it by semaphore. d. Civilization started when people stayed in the same place. e. Sports injuries usually get better faster if you rest. f. Although customers buy *products* they actually want benefits. g. If you provide higher benefits, some customers will pay more.

Closure

Check some of the vocabulary from the lesson, e.g.,

semaphore

violent

con'tract

migrate

famine

plough

shortage

seed

reservoir

nerves

5.5 Applying new listening skills: Same land, more yield

Objectives

By the end of this lesson, students should be able to:

• identify digressions in a lecture;

• make notes of problems and solutions to improve yield;

• begin to use strategies for dealing with digression in a lecture.

Introduction

Remind students that the topic of the section has been agriculture and food. Ask students to discuss in pairs if they eat food for *fuel* or *pleasure*. Follow-up points could include:

• What about hunter-gatherers? Did they eat for fuel or pleasure?

• When / why did people start thinking about food as pleasure and cooking as an art?

• How about people in the developing world?

A Reviewing vocabulary

Explain that it is important to understand colloquial expressions. There is not always a logic to the expression, but if you recognize it, you can concentrate on the next words.

1. Set for pairwork.

2. Play ⏺ **5.15**. Feed back orally.

Transcript and Answers

⏺ 5.15

Presenter:	5.15. Lesson 5.5. Applying new listening skills: Same land, more yield
	Exercise A2. Listen and check.
Voice:	a. It all started about 14,000 years ago in an area which we now call Lebanon.
	b. I've jumped the gun on the plough – that didn't appear until about 4000 BCE.
	c. Improvements in agriculture could not keep up with the increase in population.
	d. Here are the theories, in no particular order.
	e. But before we look at the theories, I must just mention the Green Revolution.
	f. Gradually, the animals accepted the humans, which, in turn, led to their domestication.
	g. The Evolutionary theory says that agriculture began with the gradual protection of wild plants to preserve the resource. This theory gets my vote.
	h. The Domestication theory suggests that people became domesticated and then stayed in one area. But this seems to be the wrong way round to me.

B Following a lecture

1. Students focus on the lecture handout. Elicit the meaning of the word *agronomy*.

   Agronomy = science of soils and plants (soil management, land cultivation and crop production). Elicit the word for the job: *agronomist*.

   Check understanding. Then give students time to read through the PowerPoint handout on page 165. Check the following vocabulary before you set the task: *nutrients, soil, pests*. Then students can discuss the question in the Course Book in pairs or small groups. Students can make a note of their ideas in pencil on the handout if they wish. After a few minutes, elicit ideas but do not confirm or correct.

2. Spend a few minutes revising how to follow digressions in a lecture; if necessary, refer students back to Lesson 5.3. Tell the students the lecture is quite long and they will hear it all the way through without stopping. (See Methodology note below.) Remind students to listen carefully to the introduction so that they can predict the organization of the lecture.

   Play DVD 5.D. Monitor while the DVD is playing to check where students are having problems making notes. Make sure students are making notes of any digressions.

Elicit answers using an electronic projection. Alternatively, show the completed notes and encourage students to ask you about any differences there are from their own answers. Replay any sections of the DVD students had difficulty with.

Answers

Possible solutions with possible extra notes: See opposite.

Transcript

🔊 5.16 DVD 5.D

| Lecturer: | This week we're going to look at developments in agriculture. For the whole of its long history, agriculture has been an industry that has constantly improved. Or, to put it another way, it has recognized problems and found solutions. The driving force for improvement for thousands of years has been a rising population. If you have more mouths to feed, you need more food. It's obvious. The industry has risen to that challenge time and time again – as we saw to some extent in the last lecture. Which reminds me ... I was reading a blog the other day and the guy was suggesting that the driving force behind agriculture has changed now. He reckoned the driving force now was profit, and now the stronger need is to make bigger and bigger profits from farming. We're not talking about agriculture anymore but 'agribusiness'. Although agriculture does not employ the majority of the population of a particular area anymore, it does make huge profits as a business. Sorry. That's enough of that! |
| | As I was saying, agriculture is about constant improvements. There have been literally |

thousands of improvements since the first person picked some wild grass and ate the seeds. But nearly all the improvements have been aimed at the same objective – more yield. There are three main ways to increase yield. Firstly, farmers have always tried to get more yield from a particular piece of land. Same land, more yield. Secondly, farmers have tried to get more yield from a particular crop. Same crop, more fruit, more berries, or bigger roots or stems. And thirdly – you've guessed it – farmers have tried to get more yield from a particular animal. Same animal, more meat or milk. Today, we're only going to look at the first way – same land, more yield. Because I'm going to ask *you* to research the other two ways.

Right, let's look at how we can get more yield from the same piece of land. Remember, we're talking about problems and solutions all the time. For the first solution, we need to go back to 3500 BCE. Plants need sunlight, which is probably why early agriculture developed in some of the sunniest parts of the world, the modern-day areas of Iraq, Syria and Egypt, for example. So what's the problem? Well, plants also need *water* to grow, obviously. And those same areas – Iraq, Syria, Egypt – are some of the driest areas on earth, with very little rainfall and hardly any natural rivers or lakes.

So the plants in these areas often did not get enough natural water to grow well. The solution? Irrigation. Throughout the centuries, different peoples have used different methods to irrigate their crops, to provide them with the water they need to grow well. For example, the Ancient Egyptians built reservoirs to retain water and to stop it running to the sea. They also built canals that were filled when the Nile flooded. Because they had to get the water from these canals on to the actual plants, they invented the *shaduf*. This was a pole with a bucket on one end and a heavy weight on the other. The Phoenicians, from what we now call Lebanon, used wells, tunnels and pumps powered by animals or people to bring water to their land. I remember when I lived in Oman in the Gulf, people in the villages on the edge of the desert were using water from a falaj system which brought water hundreds of miles underground from mountain streams. Nothing very strange about that, really, but the irrigation system was built by the Phoenicians hundreds of years before. Incredible. Anyway, irrigation is still needed all over the world, and farmers use systems such as sprinklers or trickle irrigators. This can be done automatically and electronically and so requires no labour and, in some cases, no attention at all once it is set up. Some irrigation systems even move automatically up and down the field to cover every part. So, problem? Not enough water. Solution? Irrigation.

So that's irrigation. Plants need sunlight and water, but – here's the next problem – they also need *nutrients*, like nitrogen, phosphorus and potassium. Although early farmers didn't know exactly what nutrients plants needed, they realized that growing plants on a particular piece of land destroyed the soil. If they farmed the same piece of land for several years, the yields went down. Eventually the soil was exhausted. For thousands of years, some tribes solved this problem by moving on to another

problem	solution
plants need sunlight	agriculture started in sunny areas
very little fresh water	retain rainfall in reservoirs, canals
must get water to plants	irrigation: canals, shadufs
plants need nutrients (N, P, K)	move to another piece of land
can't establish towns	leave fields fallow

Iraq, Syria, Egypt

water from flooding (Egypt)

shaduf = pole with bucket

nomadic

civilization = making a town

problem	solution
only 2/3 of land productive	grow peas, etc., every 3rd year
can't divide up large farms	fertilize land
no animal fertilizer	chemical fertilizer
crops can't absorb fertilizer	science improved
chemicals wash into rivers	return to traditional methods!

rotation

manure, guano

19th C

Bosch and Haber

pollute water

cow manure, etc.

problem	solution
organic products more expensive	customers willing to pay more?
pests destroy crops	pesticides inc. DDT
DDT 'causes cancer', etc.	ban DDT, use organic insecticide
malaria increases, etc.	allow controlled spraying

birds, insects

Sumerians = sulphur, Romans = salt

'Silent Spring', Carson

Head of WWF!

piece of land. They were nomadic, in other words, moving from one area to another, and perhaps eventually returning to a previous area. But this is not an efficient use of time. The solution creates a new problem. If you have to keep moving to new areas, you cannot establish towns and cities. In other words, you cannot start a civilization. Which reminds me of my Latin at school because *civis* in Latin is 'town', so *civilization* means something like 'making a town'. Incidentally, *agricola* is Latin for 'farmer' so that's two connections between the ancient world and modern English. I was hopeless at Latin at school so I don't know why I remember that!

Anyway, where was I? Oh, yes. Eventually, someone discovered that if they left the field 'fallow', or unused, for a year, it returned to being good for growing food crops. So the solution, in some areas, was a system in which each person had three strips of land. They grew crops on two of them – so they didn't starve – but left the third one fallow in *rotation*. That's an important word – *rotation*. Remember it. The solution created a new problem. If you leave one-third of your land fallow, you can only produce two-thirds of the potential crop on it. But some cultures solved the problem when they realized that certain crops actually put goodness back into the soil, for example, plants of the pea family. We know now why. Because some plants gather or fix nitrogen from the soil, they replace the nitrogen that other plants use up. Peas, of course, are edible, so with this kind of crop rotation all of the land produced food crops all of the time. Same land, more yield, year after year.

The system of crop rotation is still widely used all over the world today on small farms. But it leads to other problems. Because many farms are worked by huge machines nowadays, you cannot divide a field up into strips. Also, an agribusiness has a particular market for specific products, so it is not possible to change the crop every year. If your business is called Tomatoes Direct, you cannot become Peas Direct every third year. Farmers had to find a way to put nutrients back into the soil without planting different crops. In other words, they had to feed the crops with nitrogen and phosphorus and potassium and other important minerals. What do we call these chemicals, which improve the yield or the fertility of the land? Of course – *fertilizers*.

Actually, I've rather jumped the gun on fertilizer, because animal waste has been used for hundreds of years as a natural fertilizer. Animal waste is rich in nitrogen, so farmers spread this waste, or manure, on the land to improve the yield. Bird waste – called *guano* – was particularly successful in some areas of the world. But of course, if you do not have a local source of animal waste, there is a problem. In the early 19th century, chemists began to solve the problem. They started to experiment with the chemicals in manure. Justus von Liebig was one of these chemists. It was von Liebig who first created an artificial fertilizer but it was not successful. Although it contained useful nutrients, crops could not absorb them. Gradually, the science improved until, in the 1900s, two German chemists, Carl Bosch and

Fritz Haber, developed a cheap process for synthesising ammonia, which contains nitrogen. Which reminds me of an interesting piece of information that I came across the other day. Apparently, after the Second World War, the US government had a lot of ammonium nitrate, because it is the main substance in explosives. It also happens to be one of the best sources of nitrogen for crops. Agronomists persuaded the government to spread the chemical on farmland, and yields rose. Look up the story in Pollan, 2006 – it's on the net. I don't know if you realize, but the United Nations motto is 'We shall beat the swords into ploughs', meaning move from war to peaceful occupation. Perhaps we should add, 'And turn the bombs into crops.'

Anyway. What was I talking about? Oh, right. Artificial fertilizers. I should mention that many people feel these artificial fertilizers are damaging the environment. They wash out of the soil and pollute streams and rivers. So, as so often in the past, a solution leads to a new problem. Some farmers have kept traditional methods in order to produce better quality crops and not damage the environment. These traditional methods include crop rotation and the use of natural fertilizers like cow manure. This process is called *organic farming* and we'll talk a lot more about that later in the course. Unfortunately, crops from organic farming often cost more – solution leading to a problem again – so it is a question of whether the consumer is willing to pay more to protect the environment more.

So, where have we got to? We're talking about raising the yield of a particular piece of land, and we can do that with irrigation, crop rotation and with fertilizers, natural or artificial. But there is one final problem to deal with. Once the land is producing a good crop, how are we going to protect it from pests? Farmers call them pests, but of course we are just talking about other inhabitants of the environment – birds and insects, in the main. Pests are a big danger to agriculture. Birds or insects can completely strip a crop, so protection is needed. Early farmers used simple methods, such as scarecrows – models of people standing in fields – to scare off the birds, or they covered the crops in some way. But chemicals that deter or kill harmful creatures have a very long history. There is evidence that the Sumerians used insecticides in about 2500 BCE. The substance was sulphur, which was burnt to kill the creatures. Salt was used in Ancient Rome, and in Europe in 1600 CE, ants were attracted away from crops by honey and then killed with arsenic. But it was in the 1940s that the first mass use of pesticide occurred. The substance was called DDT, and it became extremely popular in the 1950s because it killed plant pests and insects that carried malaria, yellow fever, etc.

However, in 1962, a woman called Rachel Carson published a book called *Silent Spring* in which she described the dangers of DDT. She said the chemical was washing into rivers. When animals and birds drank from the polluted water, they became ill and sometimes died. DDT was banned in the USA shortly after. Pesticides are still widely used but they are much more targeted at specific pests, and now there are even organic insecticides that use natural ingredients so they do not harm animals or humans. Interestingly, some environmentalists are now calling for a return to DDT spraying on a large scale. Richard Liroff of the World Wildlife Fund said in 2005, 'If the alternatives to DDT aren't working, you've got to use it.' But others still feel that the dangers are too high, with insects that are basic to agriculture, like bees, being killed as well as harmful creatures.

i. Although Liebig's artificial fertilizer contained useful nutrients,	crops could not absorb them.
j. When animals and birds drank from the polluted water,	they became ill and sometimes died.
k. If the alternatives to DDT aren't working,	you've got to use it.

C Checking understanding of content

1. If you think students recognized at least two or three digressions (and made a few notes) then the activity can go ahead as it stands. If not, you will have to spend a few minutes preparing the class. You could do this by replaying the digressions on the DVD. When students have finished discussing the digressions, elicit answers. Ask students to read the relevant sections of the transcript for any answers they had problems with.

2. Make sure students are not looking at the transcript. Set the task. Students complete individually then compare answers in pairs. Elicit answers or show correct answers using an electronic projection.

Answers

a. If you have more mouths to feed,	you need more food.
b. Although agriculture does not employ the majority of the population in a particular area anymore,	it does make huge profits as a business.
c. Because the Ancient Egyptians had to get the water from the canals on to the plants,	they invented the shaduf.
d. Although early farmers didn't know exactly what nutrients plants needed,	they realized that growing plants on a particular piece of land destroyed the soil.
e. If they farmed the same piece of land for several years,	the yields went down.
f. If you have to keep moving to new areas,	you cannot establish towns and cities.
g. Because some plants gather, or fix, nitrogen from the soil,	they replace the nitrogen which other plants use up.
h. Because many farms are worked by huge machines nowadays,	you cannot divide a field up into strips.

D Understanding vocabulary in context

Students discuss the words in pairs. Elicit answers. You may also be able to elicit the sentences from the lecture which each word appeared in. Point out that it is important for students to be able to work out the meanings of new words from the context of the lecture. However, it is not necessary for students to learn these particular words.

Answers

absorb	take in
fallow	not being cultivated
guano	bird waste
insecticide	chemical which kills insects
manure	animal waste
nomadic	moving from place to place, perhaps following the seasons or animals

E Developing critical thinking

Students discuss in pairs or small groups. Elicit ideas.

Closure

Check some of the knowledge which students should have acquired during the listening section as a formal quiz or by flicking through the transcript and asking questions.

Speaking: Interfering with nature?

5.6 Vocabulary for speaking: Using genetics in farming

Objectives

By the end of this lesson, students should be able to:

- demonstrate understanding of meanings of target vocabulary;
- pronounce target vocabulary in isolation and in context;
- demonstrate understanding of some basic information about genetics and selective breeding.

Introduction

Focus on the title of the lesson: *Using genetics in farming*. Check students can pronounce the word *genetics*. Then write the following definition of *genetics* on the board:

genetics = the study of heredity and the variation of inherited characteristics

Elicit / teach the meanings of the words *heredity* and *inherited*. Elicit the verb *inherit*.

Write on the board:

- *heredity* = noun
- *inherited* = adjective / past participle
- *inherit* = verb

Check and practise pronunciation of these words.

Elicit examples of things you can *inherit*:

- physical characteristics from parents: eye colour, hair colour, height, etc.
- property and possessions: money, jewellery, a house, etc.

Write a second definition on the board:

X = a unit of heredity

Elicit what the letter *X* stands for: *gene*. Practise pronunciation of this word.

A Activating knowledge

Students discuss the statements in pairs. They may wish to qualify statements such as 'It is possible to make new kinds of animals *in a laboratory*.' Do not elicit answers now, but leave until students have listened to 🎧 **5.17** in Exercise B1.

Answers

See Exercise B.

B Understanding new vocabulary in context

1. Tell students they will listen to a conversation between a student and a tutor. The student is asking about genetics in farming. Set the task and play 🎧 **5.17**. Elicit answers.

2. Set the task. The word list is already quite full, but ask students to add the following **before** doing B2: *characteristic*, *code*, *defect*, *organism*. Divide the class into pairs to work, as follows:

   Student A: works on definitions a–h

   Student B: works on definitions i–n

3. Still in their pairs, Student A exchanges answers with Student B. Monitor to see which answers students are having difficulty with and give help with pronunciation of the target words where necessary. When most of the pairs have finished, elicit answers to the items students had difficulty with. (You shouldn't need to confirm every answer.)

Optional activity

At this point, or later in the lesson, students can act out an extract from the transcript.

In this lesson, students look at selective breeding in general. In the next lesson students will learn why selective breeding is important from a commercial viewpoint. Finally, if you are doing the whole course, students will discuss some of the ethical issues involved in this topic in the Portfolio.

Answers

A.
1.	It is possible to make new kinds of plants.	T
2.	It is possible to make new kinds of animals.	T
3.	Changes can only be done by scientists in a laboratory. – *can be done by farmers*	F

4. Some plants are more resistant to insects than others. T

5. You can combine different characteristics from two different plants, e.g., size and pest resistance. T

6. You cannot combine different characteristics from two different animals, e.g., size and shape. F

B2. and B3.

a. change	modify
b. based on a selection	selective
c. produce new plants or animals	breed
d. something you want	desirable
e. insect, etc., which damages a plant	pest
f. part of DNA code	gene
g. particular plant or animal	species
h. problem, something wrong	defect
i. stopping something happening	resistance
j. living thing	organism
k. instructions	code
l. visible sign or behaviour	characteristic
m. get from your parents	inherit
n. passing characteristics on	heredity

Transcript
🌐 5.17

Presenter: 5.17. Lesson 5.6. Vocabulary for speaking: Using genetics in farming

Exercise B1. Listen to a student talking to a tutor. Check your answers to Exercise A.

Tutor: Can farmers modify plant species – I mean, change them in certain ways?
Student: Yes. It's called selective breeding.
Tutor: And you do it in a laboratory?
Student: No. Farmers do it on their farms. They have been doing it for thousands of years.
Tutor: What can you breed for, selectively?
Student: Any desirable characteristics, anything you want. For example, size or shape or taste. Put two plants together with the same characteristic and the offspring will probably inherit that characteristic.
Tutor: What about pest resistance? I understand some plants do not suffer so badly from attacks by insects, for example.
Student: Yes, you can breed for that, too. The code for that characteristic is in every cell.
Tutor: OK. Here's a stupid idea. Can you breed from one plant which has large fruit and another one which is resistant to pests?
Student: Yes, and you will probably get large fruit which has pest resistance, because the characteristics are independent. Like blue eyes or green eyes and black hair or brown hair. It's heredity.
Tutor: So is it based on genetics?

Student: Yes, that's right. Each characteristic comes from a gene or a number of genes in the DNA. So you can breed a plant which has a gene for size and a gene for pest resistance, for example.
Tutor: Does it work with animal species, too?
Student: Yes. It works with all organisms.
Tutor: Because they all have a similar genetic code?
Student: Exactly.
Tutor: What if both plants or both animals have a genetic defect? All the offspring might have the same defect.
Student: Well, that could be a problem.

C Pronouncing vowels

1. Write the following two words on the board and elicit the stressed syllable in each: *genetic, species*. Elicit the pronunciation of the letter *e* in each word: /e/ and /iː/. Remind students that one letter can have more than one sound. Now set the task. Divide the class into pairs. Students identify the stressed vowel in each multi-syllable word and then discuss the pronunciation. Reassure them it does not matter if they are not sure at this point. Do not elicit answers.

2. Play 🌐 5.18 and ask students to repeat, then try to produce the sentences independently.

Answers
B1. and B2.

defect	/iː/
gene	/iː/
pest	/e/
selective	/e/
species	/iː/ (then /iː/ although some people say the second vowel as /ɪ/)
characteristic	/ɪ/
desirable	/aɪ/
inherit	/e/
resistance	/ɪ/
modify	/ɒ/
organism	/ɔː/
code	/əʊ/
modify	/ɒ/
produce (n)	/ɒ/
produce (v)	/uː/

Transcript
🌐 5.18

Presenter: 5.18. Exercise C2. Listen and practise some of the words in sentences.

Voice: 1. Farmers modify plant species.
2. It's called selective breeding.
3. Any desirable characteristic can be chosen.

4. Offspring inherit characteristics through the genes.
5. Some plants have more pest resistance than others.
6. All living organisms have a similar genetic code.
7. Sometimes parent plants have a genetic defect.
8. They may produce offspring with the same defect.

D Developing critical thinking

Ask *What are some disadvantages of selective breeding?* Find out if students can suggest any ideas of their own before you focus on the words in the box. Students may well try to express the ideas in the box, in which case you can refer them to the correct related phrase.

Go through any phrases in the box not discussed above, for meanings and how they are related to selective breeding. Say the words so that students can hear the correct pronunciation.

Students continue the discussion in pairs or small groups. After a few minutes, ask students if they are *against* selective breeding or *for* it.

Answers

Answers depend on students but here are some points against selective breeding that they might make:

If you breed selectively for size, the taste may not be as good.

We may lose traditional varieties of food so we have less choice.

Traditional varieties provide habitats for insects, etc. If we lose them we may have less biodiversity.

You may increase susceptibility to disease.

Selective breeding is expensive so might increase the cost of food.

It's better to rely on natural changes, rather than unnatural ones.

Closure

Use your feedback for the discussion in Exercise D. In your round-up, try to include as many of the target words from the lesson as possible.

Objectives

By the end of this lesson, students should be able to:

• use existing skills to give a talk about selective breeding and uniform food products;

• pronounce target vocabulary in context.

Introduction

Write the following questions on the board for students to discuss in pairs:

• *How much food do you waste every week?*

• *What sort of food do you throw away?*

• *Why should we try to avoid food waste?*

After a few minutes, elicit some of the students' ideas.

A Activating knowledge

Give students time to read the assignment and the slides. Students discuss the questions in pairs. Elicit ideas.

Answers

Each fruit or vegetable must have the same size and shape.

Each item must look 'beautiful', i.e., no ugly or misshapen fruit or vegetables, no marks or blemishes.

Supermarkets believe customers are reluctant to buy 'ugly' fruit.

Food of a uniform size is easier to pack, transport and display.

Methodology note

Some students from countries such as Italy, France and Spain may find it puzzling that in the UK and the USA such emphasis is put on cosmetic appearance of fruit and vegetables rather than taste. However, supermarkets are growing in power all over the world and the same trends may emerge in the future even in countries that currently prize local, 'natural' food.

B Studying a model

1. Give students time to study the slides on page 175. Check understanding of target vocabulary and also the symbols and short forms used for the notes.

2. Check students understand the task. If necessary, play [DVD] 5.E until the interruption by the second student and elicit answers for the first slide. Play the remainder of [DVD] 5.E. Students complete the notes individually then compare answers in pairs. Elicit answers, preferably using an electronic projection. Give further explanation of points or vocabulary if necessary. Replay the complete discussion or any sections students had difficulty with.

3. The information can be presented in many different ways but this is one suggestion. Divide the class into groups of five. Each student takes one slide and prepares sentences to explain it. Then students take it in turns to present the information for their slide so that each group gives the complete presentation. Monitor and give help where necessary during each phase. Make a note of common errors, then give feedback.

Answers

1. Answers depend on students.

2. Model annotations:

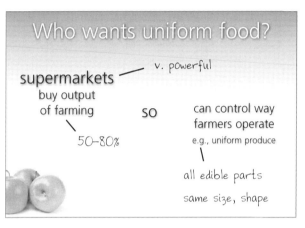

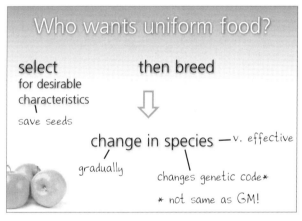

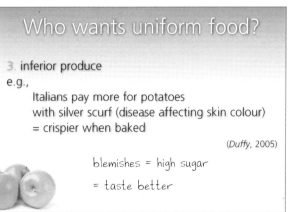

Transcript

5.19 [DVD] 5.E

Presenter:	**5.19. Lesson 5.7. Real-time speaking: The power of the supermarkets**
Student 1:	I'm going to talk about one effect of supermarkets on farmers and farming. As we all know, supermarkets are very powerful nowadays. They buy a very large proportion of the output of farming – between 50 and 80 per cent, depending on the country – so they can control the way that farmers operate. For example, they can demand a uniform product. In other words, all the edible parts are a similar size and shape. According to the website Waste 2, 2011, supermarkets maintain that uniform products appeal more to their customers. But uniformity leads to a lot of waste. It also means food is more expensive for farmers to produce. Let me explain. Uniformity is achieved by selective breeding …
Student 2:	Did you say the website was called Waste 2?
Student 1:	Yes, that's right. Waste 2 dot co dot uk.
Student 2:	Thanks.
Student 1:	OK. Where was I?
Student 3:	You were talking about selective … something.
Student 1:	Ah, yes. Selective breeding. Uniformity is achieved by selective breeding. When a farmer notices a desirable characteristic, he or she saves the seeds and breeds from the plants. The result of selective breeding is that the plant species gradually changes. Now, although selective breeding is very effective …
Student 2:	I don't understand. Does selective breeding change the genetic code of the plants?
Student 1:	Yes, it does.
Student 2:	So what you're saying is, selective breeding is the same as GM … genetic … um … modification?
Student 1:	No, not at all. When you breed plants selectively, the genetic changes occur naturally in the plants, whereas if you modify plants genetically, the changes are done artificially in a laboratory.
Student 3:	I don't know if this is relevant, but GM crops are banned in my country.
Student 1:	Yes, they are in mine, too. But as I said, plant breeding is not the same as GM. It's natural heredity. OK. Um. Sorry. I've forgotten what I was going to say.
Student 2:	I think you were going to give us some disadvantages. You said 'Breeding is .. .good …', or something.
Student 1:	Right, yes. Although selective breeding is very effective, it has some drawbacks. Firstly, the British Society of Plant Breeders or BSPB states that it is very time-consuming. Joliffe, writing in *Plant Breeding*, 2006, says it can take up to 12 years to develop a new breed. Because it takes a long time, it is very expensive for farmers.
Student 2:	Are you saying that it raises the cost of the products?
Student 1:	Yes, exactly. Secondly, there is a lot of waste with uniformity. If a fruit or vegetable does not conform to the uniform size or shape, it is thrown away. For example, Mather et. al., 2010, describe the problem in California. Hundreds of tons of edible fruit and vegetables are ploughed back into the soil because they are the wrong shape or the wrong colour.
Student 3:	Sorry. Do you mean *millions* of tons?
Student 1:	Yes, sorry. I meant to say *millions*. Finally, Duffy, 2005, argues that breeding for uniformity

actually gives us inferior produce. For example, the Italians actually pay more for potatoes with silver scurf, which is a disease affecting the skin colour of potatoes. When you bake them, they are crispier. Duffy also quotes a farmer as saying 'blemishes – that's marks – on melons, for example, are a sign of high sugar content. It means they taste better.'

Student 2:	So are you saying that supermarkets want uniform products but nobody else does?
Student 1:	I'm not sure. Certainly supermarkets want them and farmers don't want them. But what about customers?

C Revising discussion skills

1. Point out that the sentences contain points from Themes 1 to 4. Give students time to read through the extracts and complete any answers they know already. Play 🔊 **5.20**.

2. Play 🔊 **5.21** so that students can check their ideas / write in answers. Elicit answers.

3. Check students understand the task. If students are not sure what *functions* are, give examples such as *apologizing, offering, predicting*, etc. Set the task. Students complete individually then compare answers in pairs. Elicit answers. You may need to refer to the complete transcript in order to give a context to help with understanding.

4. Play 🔊 **5.22**, pausing after each item for repetition. As well as stress and intonation, make sure students pause appropriately in the following:

   e. *So what you're saying is [pause] plant breeding is the same as GM.*

   g. *I don't know if this is relevant, [pause] but GM crops are banned in my country.*

   h. *But, [pause] as I said just now, [pause] plant breeding is not the same as GM.*

Methodology note

This is a revision activity for discussion sub-skills. Students will have the opportunity to practise the functions and phrases in the last lesson of this section (5.10).

Answers

C3. a. 5; b. 3; c. 2; d. 1; e. 7; f. 6; g. 8; h. 4; i. 3; j. 2; k. 7; l. 6; m. 5; n. 9

Transcripts and Answers

🌐 5.20

Presenter:	5.20. Exercise C1. Listen to extracts from the presentation and discussion. Complete each phrase or sentence with one word in the space.
Student 1:	According to the website Waste 2, 2011, supermarkets claim that uniform products appeal more to their customers. But uniformity leads to a lot of waste and more expensive produce. Let me explain. Uniformity is achieved by selective breeding ...
Student 2:	Did you say the website was called Waste 2?
Student 1:	Yes, that's right. Waste 2 dot co dot uk. OK. Where was I?
Student 2:	You were talking about selective ... something.
Student 1:	The result of selective breeding is that the plant species gradually changes. Now, ...
Student 2:	I don't understand. Does selective breeding change the genetic code of the plants?
Student 1:	Yes, it does.
Student 2:	So what you're saying is ... plant breeding is the same as GM ... genetic ... um. .. modification?
Student 1:	No, not at all.
Student 2:	I don't know if this relevant, but GM crops are banned in my country.
Student 1:	Yes, they are in mine, too. But, as I said just now, plant breeding is not the same as GM. It's natural heredity. OK. Um. Sorry. I've forgotten what I was going to say.
Student 2:	You were going to give us some disadvantages. You said 'Although breeding is ... good ...', or something.
Student 1:	Because it takes a long time, plant breeding is very expensive for agribusinesses.
Student 2:	Are you saying that it raises the cost of the products?
Student 1:	Yes, that's exactly right. Secondly, there is a lot of waste with uniformity ... Hundreds of tons of edible fruit and vegetables are ploughed back into the soil because they are the wrong shape or colour.
Student 2:	Sorry. Do you mean *millions* of tons?
Student 1:	Yes, sorry. I meant to say *millions*.

🌐 5.21

Presenter:	5.21. Exercise C2. Listen again and check your answers.

[REPEAT OF SCRIPT FROM 🌐 5.20]

🌐 5.22

Presenter:	5.22. Exercise C4. Listen to the phrases and sentences in C1 and copy the stress and intonation.
Voice:	a. Did you say the website was called Waste 2?
	b. Where was I?
	c. You were talking about selective ... something.
	d. Does selective breeding change the genetic code of the plants?
	e. So what you're saying is, plant breeding is the same as GM.
	f. No, not at all.
	g. I don't know if this is relevant, but GM crops are banned in my country.
	h. But, as I said just now, plant breeding is not the same as GM.
	i. I've forgotten what I was going to say.
	j. I think you were going to give us some disadvantages.
	k. Are you saying that it raises the cost of the products?
	l. Yes, that's exactly right.
	m. Do you mean *millions* of tons?
	n. Yes, sorry. I meant to say *millions*.

D Taking part in a discussion

Set the task. Students can discuss the questions in pairs or small groups. Encourage them to try to use some of the phrases from Exercise C, if at all possible. Here are some supplementary questions you can ask (or write on the board for students to consider):

- Are looks more important than taste for customers?
- What's more important for you when you buy fruit and vegetables: looks, taste, price, freshness, etc?
- Should we buy more food:
  ○ from markets?
  ○ direct from the farmer?
  ○ from local shops?
- Should we refuse to buy food with too much packaging?

Closure

Use the discussion in Exercise D and relate back to the questions suggested for the introduction (above).

Everyday English: At the supermarket

Objectives

By the end of this lesson, students should be able to:
- use appropriate language when shopping and returning goods.

Introduction

Ask students if they shop at supermarkets; why (not)?

Ask them what happens when you shop at a supermarket, to see how much relevant vocabulary they know already. Don't push this. If they don't know the words, tell them they will learn them during the lesson.

Model answer:

- You pick up a basket or take a trolley – sometimes you have to put a coin in a slot to release the trolley.
- You take things from the shelves and put them into the basket / trolley.
- You go to a checkout and queue – usually!
- The checkout operator passes the items across the barcode reader; in some supermarkets, you can go to a self-service checkout and do the job yourself.
- You put things into a bag – which you have probably paid for nowadays.
- You show your loyalty card.
- You pay by cash or card: if card, you put the machine into the card-reader, check the amount and put in your PIN number.
- You take your receipt.

A **Activating ideas**

Set the task and go over the example, pointing out there can be more than one answer. Students discuss each phrase in pairs. Elicit ideas. If students are in the UK or another English-speaking country, ask them if they have heard these informal phrases. You could also ask students if they have heard any other informal phrases in supermarkets and shops.

Answers

1. Good morning / afternoon / evening.
2. Can I help you?
3. Would you like some assistance?
4. Could you give me the receipt?
5. Thank you.
6. That's fine. / My pleasure. / Don't mention it. / You're welcome.
7. Here you are. / This is your … / Here's your …
8. Goodbye. / Good night.

Methodology note

Although in the UK, supermarket cashiers and assistants are trained to be polite, and they generally are, the language they use is likely to be very informal. It is extremely rare these days for customers to be called *sir* or *madam*. This activity prepares students to respond to typical examples of the informal language used in supermarkets and other shops.

Another characteristic of British supermarkets, which may or may not be similar in the students' own countries, is the attempt by cashiers to engage the customer in a conversation. Common tactics that have obviously been drilled into the cashiers include asking questions or making comments such as *How's your day been so far?* and *Mm, that pasta sauce looks nice*, etc. You can spend a few minutes teaching students to deal with this interaction, if relevant, at a suitable point in the lesson. Students are encouraged to discuss the merits of this in the Closure activity below.

B **Studying the models**

1. Set the task. Students discuss possible ways to end each question in pairs. They should leave out any question beginnings they find difficult. Elicit a few ideas.

2. Now students can uncover the conversations and complete as many gaps as they can.

3. Play 🔊 **5.23**. Students compare answers in pairs. Go over any answers students had difficulty with and check understanding of phrases such as *loyalty card, cash back, refund*, etc. Elicit other ways to say some of the phrases. For example:

   Are you paying by card? – How would you like to pay?

   Do you need any bags? – Would you like a bag? Have you got a bag?

Methodology note

The conversations have been written with a large supermarket in mind that sells clothes and electrical goods as well as food items. In British shops, goods are usually refunded very easily if you have a receipt. This is true even if there is nothing wrong with the goods. There is usually, however, a time limit of 28 days. If you haven't got a receipt, or you are over the 28-day limit, most shops give a refund card. This looks like a credit card and is credited with the cost of the original goods. In many other countries, it is not possible to return goods and get a refund simply because you have changed your mind.

Transcript and Answers

🎧 5.23

Presenter:	5.23. Everyday English. At the supermarket
	Exercise B3. Listen and check your ideas.
	Conversation 1.
Voice A:	Hiya. Can you put the basket on here?
Voice B:	Sure.
Voice A:	Do you need a bag? They're 5p.
Voice B:	Er, no thanks. I can manage.
Presenter:	Conversation 2.
Voice A:	That's £14.50. Have you got a loyalty card?
Voice B:	No, I haven't.
Voice A:	Are you paying by cash or card?
Voice B:	Um, card. Shall I put it in the machine?
Voice A:	Yes, please and check the amount.
Voice B:	Um. Is it working?
Voice A:	Other way round.
Voice B:	Oh, yeah. Oh, and can I have cashback?
Voice A:	How much would you like?
Voice B:	£10, please.
Voice A:	OK. Enter your PIN number, please.
Presenter:	Conversation 3.
Voice A:	I'm sorry. Could you go to the next checkout?
Voice B:	Why? What's the problem?
Voice A:	This checkout is 'baskets only'.
Voice B:	Oh, OK. I didn't see the sign.
Presenter:	Conversation 4.
Voice A:	Hi. You alright there?
Voice B:	Well, can I return this shirt? It's in this bag.
Voice A:	Is there anything wrong with it?
Voice B:	No, it's just too small.
Voice A:	Do you want to change it for a bigger size?
Voice B:	No, thanks. I'd like a refund.
Voice A:	OK. Have you got your receipt?
Voice B:	Um, oh dear. Did I leave it in the bag?
Voice A:	Yes, here you go. Did you pay by card?
Voice B:	Yes, here you are.
Voice A:	Cheers.

C Practising the model

1. Play conversation 1 from 🎧 **5.23** again, pausing after each line for students to repeat. Students then practise in pairs. Monitor and give feedback. Repeat the procedure for the other conversations. Focus on the following suggested pronunciation areas for each conversation:

Conversation 2

Intonation: questions / being polite

Linking: *put it in*

Stressed words: *Are you paying by **cash** or **card**?*

Schwa sound in *can* in question forms

Conversation 3

Intonation: as above

Conversation 4

Intonation: as above

Linking: *d'you / leave it in*

Consonant clusters: *I'd like ...*

2. Set the task without explaining the new vocabulary. Students should be able to work out the meanings from context. Check students understand, perhaps by eliciting the first two or three lines of the conversation and writing them on the board. Students can work on the conversation individually or in pairs. Monitor and give help where necessary.

3. Students practise their conversations in pairs. Monitor and make a note of common errors. Give feedback. Ask two or three pairs to act out their conversations for the rest of the class.

Closure

Discuss some of the following points with the class as a whole-class activity or put the students into groups:

- *In what ways are British or American supermarkets similar or different to your country?*

- *What do you think about the customer service you get in British / American supermarkets?*

- *Are cashiers and assistants well trained? What staff training should they be given?*

- *Are supermarket cashiers too informal and over-familiar? Or do you enjoy chatting to the cashier at the checkout? Why do supermarkets encourage staff to engage customers in social 'chit-chat' at the checkout?*

- *Would you like a career in a supermarket? Why (not)?*

5.8 Learning new speaking skills: Referring to research

Objectives

By the end of this lesson, students should be able to:

- use a variety of ways to refer to research when speaking;

- use appropriate pauses and intonation in long spoken sentences.

Introduction

Use Exercise A.

A Reviewing vocabulary

1. Set the task. Students complete individually then compare answers in pairs. Show the correct answers using an electronic projection rather than eliciting. This will avoid students having to pronounce the phrases before they have read the Pronunciation Check.

2. Give students time to read the Pronunciation Check. Say the two example phrases for the students with the correct stress: *selective* **breeding**, **plant** *species*. Go through the pairs of words in the exercise; elicit whether they are *adjective + noun* or *noun + noun* phrases, then elicit the correct pronunciation. Play ● **5.24** of the pairs of words; students repeat each phrase.

Answers

See table below.

Transcript
● 5.24

Presenter: 5.24. Lesson 5.8. Learning new speaking skills: Referring to research

Exercise A2. Listen to the phrases above and practise.

Voice: a. selective breeding
b. uniform product
c. desirable characteristic
d. genetic code
e. edible fruit
f. sugar content
g. plant species
h. supermarket buyers

Methodology note

Students may find it quite difficult firstly to identify if a pair of words is *n + n* or *adj + n* and then to remember the correct stress. Therefore treat this activity simply as an introduction to this feature of English pronunciation. Also remember that the stress can move when the phrase is being used contrastively, e.g., *edible fruit vs inedible fruit*.

B Identifying a new skill

1. Set the task and ask students to cover the Skills Check. Students complete individually then compare answers in pairs. Do not elicit answers.

2. Give students time to read the Skills Check. Go over the notes, checking that students understand how each note relates to the example above. Now ask students to go back to their answers for B1 and make any changes if necessary. Show correct answers using an electronic projection. (Note that organizations are considered plural in American English when making the verb agree with the subject.)

Play ● **5.25** so that students can listen and repeat. Make sure students copy the pauses and use a falling intonation only at the end of the sentence.

Note that, because the sentences are quite long, a backchaining technique is used in order to assist students with the correct intonation.

Answers

a. According to the website, Farming News, ~~it says~~ uniform produce leads to a great deal of waste.

a. selective	'breeding	*adj + n*	
b. uniform	'product	*adj + n*	*uniform* is an adjective here
c. desirable	characte'ristic	*adj + n*	
d. genetic	'code	*adj + n*	*genetic* is an adjective; *genetics* is the noun and cannot be singular
e. edible	'fruit	*adj + n*	
f. 'sugar	content	*n + n*	
g. 'plant	species	*n + n*	
h. 'supermarket	buyers	*n + n*	

b. Andrews, 2011, *states* that customers are happy to buy fruit and vegetables that have skin blemishes.

c. Johnson et al., 2005, *claim* that uniform produce is easier to transport.

d. Dawson, *writing* in *The Power of the Supermarkets*, 2004, argues that the organizations have seriously damaged farming in Britain.

e. Mortinsen quotes a supermarket buyer *as saying that* customers want uniform produce.

f. Essex et al., 2009, describe ~~that~~ the difficulties of fruit farmers.

Transcript

🌐 5.25

Presenter:	**5.25. Skills Check. Listen and practise the pauses and the intonation pattern.**
Voice:	Duffy, 2005, argues that breeding for uniformity actually gives us inferior produce.
	Mather et. al., 2010, describe the problem in California.
	The British Society of Plant Breeders, 2006, states that selective breeding is very time-consuming.
	Joliffe, writing in *Plant Breeding*, 2006, says that it can take up to 12 years to develop a new breed.
	Duffy quotes a farmer as saying 'blemishes on melons, for example, are a sign of high sugar content.'
	According to the website, Waste 2, 2011, supermarkets claim that uniform products appeal more to their customers.

C Practising the new skill

1. Set the task and go over the example. Remind students the topic for Lesson 4.10 was about psychological factors affecting sportspeople. Students should select only one fact from each piece of information to quote, otherwise their sentences will be much too long. You could ask students to write sentences first for two or three of the pieces of research information. Then students can practise saying the sentences in pairs with correct pauses and intonation.

2. Set the task and remind students of the forms in the Skills Check. See the Methodology notes below for different ways of working. Students should spend a few minutes preparing sentences to say for the next stage of the activity. One way to do this is to make notes and then practise saying the complete sentence, perhaps by 'mumbling' the sentence to themselves. Students could also write out the complete sentence, but point out that in C3 they will not be allowed simply to read sentences aloud.

3. Monitor while students exchange information. Encourage responses to each piece of information, including asking for clarification where necessary. Ask students to decide in each pair or group if they think supermarkets have too much power. Give feedback.

Methodology notes

C1: If your students did not do Lesson 4.10, you can leave out this activity and go straight on to C2. Similarly, if you are short of time you can miss out this exercise or set it for a written homework activity.

C2 and C3: There are eight pieces of information in the resources. There are many ways the activity can be done. Students can work in pairs, or groups of four. Allocate different resources to each student (so that there is an 'information gap'). If you are short of time, you can select between two and four resources only for students to work with. You can put students together who have the same piece(s) of research in order to help each other to prepare sentences. Then regroup students for the information gap activity.

Closure
Ask the different pairs or groups to report on their thoughts about supermarkets from the discussion in Exercise C3.

5.9 Grammar for speaking: Complex sentences (2)

Objectives

By the end of this lesson, students should be able to:
- produce complex sentences with two clauses using pauses where appropriate;
- restate complex sentences in order to give variety.

Note: Complex sentences were also dealt with in Lesson 5.4.

Introduction

If students studied the complex sentences in Lesson 5.4, you can ask them to look back at this page to remind themselves about it.

Revise some of the information about selective breeding from the speaking section. This will help with understanding of the example sentences in the table.

Grammar box 22

Give students time to study the explanation and the sentences in the table. Point out that *when / if* are interchangeable in sentences like this, because they describe facts / general truths, rather than possible future events.

Play 🔊 **5.26** so that students can listen and repeat. Note that the sentences are given first time in full and then as a backchaining activity.

Ask students to give the same information, beginning with the subordinate clause. Elicit answers and drill the sentence, preferably using backchaining.

Answers

Because supermarkets buy so much produce, they can control food prices.

When / If you breed plants selectively, genetic changes occur naturally.

Although selective breeding is very effective, it has drawbacks.

Transcript
🌐 5.26

Presenter:	5.26. Lesson 5.9. Grammar for speaking: Complex sentences (2)
	Grammar box 22. Listen and repeat the examples. Copy the pauses and the intonation.
Voice:	Supermarkets can control food prices [PAUSE] because they buy so much produce. Genetic changes occur naturally [PAUSE] when you breed plants selectively. Selective breeding has drawbacks [PAUSE] although it is very effective.

A　Choosing the correct adverb

Give students time to read all the sentences, then elicit ideas. Keep reminding them that *when / if* are interchangeable.

Answers

1. *When / If* farmers notice a desirable characteristic they can breed from the seeds of the plants.

2. Genetic changes occur naturally in the plants *when / if* you breed plants selectively.

3. *When / If* you modify plants genetically the changes are done artificially in a laboratory.

4. *Because* it takes a long time selective breeding is very expensive for farmers.

5. *When / If* a plant has a disease its fruit can sometimes taste better.

6. Millions of tons of fruit and vegetables are wasted *because* they are the wrong shape.

B　Changing the order of clauses

1. Set the task. In pairs, students say the sentence (answer) to each other.

2. Play 🔊 **5.27**. Students compare their version with the audio. Give further explanation if necessary. Work through each sentence in the same way. Drill some of the sentences if you wish. Students write some or all of the sentences either in class or for homework.

Optional activity

The following variations are possible:

1. Students write the sentences, then listen and check their answers with the CD. Drill the sentences.

2. Students listen to the sentences with pens down, then make sentences orally in pairs. Students write the sentences.

Transcript and Answers
🌐 5.27

Presenter:	5.27. Exercise B2. Listen and check your answers.
Voice:	1. Farmers can breed from the seeds of the plants when they notice a desirable characteristic.
	2. If you breed plants selectively, genetic changes occur naturally in the plants.
	3. The changes are done artificially in a laboratory if you modify plants genetically.
	4. Selective breeding is very expensive for farmers because it takes a long time.
	5. Fruit can actually taste better if a plant has a disease.
	6. Because they are the wrong shape, millions of tons of fruit and vegetables are wasted.

C　Making complex sentences

1. Set the task. All the examples are taken from previous themes. Students complete

individually then compare answers in pairs. Do not elicit.

2. Play ⊚ **5.28** for students to check their ideas. Discuss any variations students had with the class and if they are acceptable or not. Play the CD again, pausing after each sentence for repetition. Drill the sentences if you wish, using backchaining. Make sure students pause in the correct places.

Transcript and Answers
⊕ 5.28

Presenter:	5.28. Exercise C2. Listen and check. Try saying the full sentences.
Voice:	a. If you buy a BOGOF product, you get a second one free. b. Film and television personalities sometimes endorse products although they probably don't use them. c. Bad reviews can kill a new movie, although some people go to see if the reviewer was right or wrong. d. When a film company puts a trailer of a new movie onto a website like YouTube, it hopes that the film will go viral. e. Athletes should listen to music during training because it decreases the perception of effort. f. The majority of asthmatics can prevent attacks if they take medication before doing exercise. g. Although Braille invented a better system of reading for the blind, he was not allowed to teach it at his own institute. h. Because Braille's system only used six dots, it is easier to read than previous methods. i. Because the Yangtze River floods most years, the Chinese government is diverting some water to other parts of the country. j. The government of Egypt has threatened to use force if any country takes water from the Nile without permission.

Closure
Say the first part of some two-word phrases from the lesson. Ask students to say the complete phrase in each case. Drill pronunciation individually or with the whole class, if necessary.

T:	Ss:
food	*food prices*
genetic	*genetic changes*
selective	*selective breeding*
desirable	*desirable characteristic*
television	*television personality*
bad	*bad review*
film	*film company*

Objectives

By the end of this lesson, students should be able to:
- research and present information about the ethical issues involved in cloning and intensive farming;
- use sub-skills from the course to take part in a seminar-type discussion.

Introduction
Revise some of the information from the previous lessons in this section which may be relevant to this one, for example:
- selective breeding;
- the power of the supermarkets;
- uniform products;
- food waste.

A Previewing vocabulary

Exploit the visuals and find out what students already know about the two topics of *cloning* and *intensive farming*. Set the task and go over the example. Play ⊚ **5.29**. Pause after each sentence and elicit the answer. Replay the sentence if students have difficulty or are not sure. Avoid detailed explanations at this point.

If students found the task difficult, show the transcript for the sentences using an electronic projection. Explain new words or give further explanation where necessary.

If students found the task fairly easy, ask them to remember and tell you some of the sentences they heard. If necessary, write two or three words as prompts on the board for each sentence.

Transcript and Answers
⊕ 5.29

Presenter:	5.29. Lesson 5.10. Applying new speaking skills: Cloning and intensive farming
	Exercise A. Listen to some sentences. Which photograph is each sentence related to?
Voice:	1. Chemicals are used to improve growth. 2. Each animal is an exact copy in genetic terms. 3. Farmers can create animals which are consistent in terms of productivity. 4. There have been several successful trials, although genetic defects mean that many animals die young.

5. The animals live in cramped conditions because it is easier to look after them.
6. Scientists grow cells from selected animals in a laboratory.
7. The living conditions mean that many animals experience stress.
8. The practice has been banned in the European Union.

B Researching information

1. Ask students to read the assignment. Elicit / teach the meaning of the words *ethics* and *ethical*. Definitions include:

   - a system of moral standards or principles;
   - rules / standards of behaviour;
   - what is right and wrong.

2. Allow students to read all the resources quickly so that they can decide which practice – cloning or intensive farming – to work on.

3. Once students have chosen their topics, put them into groups so that they work with others with the **same** practice.

   Remind students to:

   - read the notes and discuss with their group any new words or anything they don't understand;
   - practise pronunciation of words and sentences.

   Tell students how long the presentation should be and if necessary set a strict time limit, for example, three minutes. On the other hand, if your students are reticent, you might need to set a minimum time!

   Remind students of the topic of the presentation, *The ethics of farming*, and that therefore they should make sure they emphasize that aspect. Monitor and give help where necessary.

Methodology notes

1. If the resources are available, students can make PowerPoint slides or other visuals to accompany their presentations at this point. They could also research further information to add to their presentations.

2. When students are discussing, you can remind them of some useful discussion phrases (see previous Learning new speaking skills lessons).

C Presenting and discussing

Tell students which presentation sub-skills you want them to work on besides the ones mentioned in the Course Book for this activity (you can refer back to previous speaking lessons if you wish), e.g.,

- eye contact;
- speed and volume of delivery;
- sticking to a time limit;
- introduction / conclusion, etc.

Re-divide the class into groups with students for each topic. Make sure listening students take active part while each presentation is happening by following the instructions in the Course Book. Monitor and give feedback on:

- common errors;
- where students missed opportunities to use target language;
- where students used target language appropriately;
- using turn-taking (in)appropriately.

D Developing critical thinking

Give students time to read the two quotations. Check understanding. Students can discuss the question in pairs or in small groups. After a few minutes, elicit ideas.

Answers

Answers depend on students.

Closure
Use the discussion in Exercise D.

Reading: Should man be a herbivore?

5.11 Vocabulary for reading: Types of diet

Objectives

By the end of this lesson, students should be able to:

- demonstrate understanding of vocabulary for the section;
- use new vocabulary to understand a text about the three main types of animal diet.

Introduction

Use Exercise A. Alternatively, write some questions about food and diet on the board for students to discuss in pairs, for example:

- *Do you eat a balanced diet?*
- *How much meat or fish do you eat each day?*
- *What about vegetables, dairy, fats and carbohydrates?*
- *Do you like vegetarian food?*
- *Is there any food you never eat? Why?*

A Activating knowledge

Give students a few minutes to study the photos, then elicit the connection between the four of them. Ask students to give examples of other food chains, particularly from their own countries.

Answers

The four photos show a food chain: plant – herbivore – carnivore – carnivore.

B Understanding sentence development

Exploit the text title, *Animals and diet*. Remind students that the word *diet* has more than one meaning:

- controlling what you eat for health or weight loss;
- the food that a person or animal usually consumes.

Obviously in this context *diet* is used with the second meaning.

Revise/check the meanings of the words *domesticate* and *ethical* (from previous sections in this theme) either before you set the task or after students have completed it.

Set the task. Students work in pairs or small groups to order the sentences. When most of the students have finished, show the completed texts using an electronic projection so that students can check their answers. Ask comprehension questions to further check understanding (or provide them on a handout or electronic projection):

1. What are the three animal diets? (herbivore, omnivore, carnivore)
2. Which animal type is at the bottom of the food chain? (herbivores)
3. Why was meat-eating rare in Neolithic times? (because animals were hard to catch and kill)
4. Why did meat-eating increase in about 7000 BCE? (because people began to domesticate animals)
5. Why do some people become vegetarians? (for ethical, health or environmental reasons)
6. What are the health dangers in meat and fish? (high percentages of saturated fat and hazardous chemicals)

Methodology note

Ideally do this activity as a jigsaw reading (See Introduction, page 21). The topic of vegetarianism, and the theory that eating meat will become unsustainable in the future, is continued in much more detail in the two main texts in this section.

Answers

See next page.

C Understanding new vocabulary

Try the following variation rather than asking all the students to do all the pairs of words.

Step 1: Divide the class into pairs. Ask half the pairs ('red' group) to work on numbers 1–5. Ask the other half ('blue' group) to work on 6–10.

Step 2: When students have finished working on their allocated words, re-divide the class into pairs with one 'red' student and one 'blue' one. Students take turns to explain the meanings of their words from Step 1.

Animals and diet

|2| and cows, which only eat plants are called <u>herbivores</u>. Animals, like lions

|3| and killer whales, which only eat meat are <u>carnivores</u>. Herbivores are at

|6| cases, carnivores then eat these animals. The third kind of animal includes humans,

|7| most bears and some birds. They are omnivores, eating both animals and plants.

|5| plant like the fruit or berries, and convert them into energy. In many

|4| the bottom of <u>food chains</u>. They eat plants, such as grass, or parts of a

|1| There are three main kinds of animal in terms of <u>diet</u>. Animals, like sheep

|7| as cows and sheep, and <u>livestock rearing</u> for food became common.

|5| been quite rare at this time because animals were hard to catch and kill.

|3| <u>gatherers</u>. In other words, they <u>followed</u> a way of life which involved

|6| However, around 7000 BCE, people began to domesticate animals, such

|4| hunting animals and gathering fruit and berries. <u>Meat-eating</u> may have

|1| There is some evidence that humans have been omnivorous since <u>Neolithic</u>

|2| or Stone Age times (*c*9500 BCE). It is believed that early humans were <u>hunter-</u>

|3| animals for food. Nowadays, some people support vegetarianism for

|2| eat meat for <u>ethical</u> reasons. They believe that humans should not kill

|5| eating anymore. Others point to the health dangers of meat, including

|4| <u>environmental</u> reasons, believing that the planet cannot support meat-

|7| <u>hazardous</u> chemicals in fish, especially those which are farmed.

|6| the high percentages of <u>saturated fat</u> in red meat and the levels of

|1| Throughout history, some humans have become <u>vegetarians</u>, refusing to

Monitor carefully and make a note of any words students are having difficulty with. Give feedback on these words at the end of the activity.

Answers

Closure

Show the first two or three letters of words from the lesson on an electronic projection or use flashcards. Students predict the rest of the word. Examples:

he … rbivore   *be* … rry   *ha* … zardous

et … hical   *en* … danger / … vironmental

1. herbivore	carnivore	one eats plants, the other eats animals
2. fruit	berry	one is a large plant product, the other is small
3. food	diet	one is something you can eat, the other is what you normally eat
4. animals	livestock	livestock are animals that are reared for food
5. grow	rear	you can *grow* plants but you *rear* livestock
6. ethical	legal	the first is related to a person or cultural idea of right or wrong, the second is related to the law
7. endangered	extinct	the first means an animal may cease to exist, the second means it has happened
8. hunter	gatherer	a hunter follows and tries to kill animals; a gatherer collects fruits, berries and nuts
9. vegetarian	vegetarianism	the first relates to a person, the second to a way of life
10. hazardous	poisonous	the first means it could hurt you, the second it could kill you

Objectives

By the end of this lesson, students should
be able to:

- use context and table headings in order
  to understand a text about the reasons
  for a vegetarian diet;
- record sources in a table;
- critically evaluate information in
  the text.

Note: Students will look at the text in more detail in
Lessons 5.18 and 5.19 so they only need a general
understanding of the text by the end of this lesson.

Introduction

Revise some of the new vocabulary from Lesson
5.11, especially:

hunt   ethic / ethical   diet   vegetarian   livestock

A Activating ideas

Give students a minute or two to study the
assignment. Check the meaning of *partial*. Ask
students if they agree that some people view
vegetarians as *cranks*. Ask students to discuss
the question *What's your view of
vegetarianism?* in pairs. Elicit ideas.

Methodology note

If discussion about vegetarians arose naturally
during the Vocabulary for reading lesson
(5.11), you might instead wish to ask one or
two students to summarize some of the
points raised.

Answers

Answers depend on students.

B Understanding the text

1. Ask students to read through the
   information in the 'people' column. Ask
   students if they can predict any reasons for
   vegetarianism and/or suggest approximate
   dates where possible. Then set the task for
   individual completion. Make sure students

know where to find the references. If
necessary, remind students to read the
heading and the topic sentences first.
Monitor and give help where necessary but
try to avoid explaining too many new words
and phrases; students should be able to
complete the task without this.

Students compare answers in pairs. Go through
the correct answers, preferably using an
electronic projection to show the completed
table and the text. Make sure students
understand that, at times, the author himself is
the authority for the information, so they
should put *Ellison, 2011* in the final column for
those points. Focus students' attention on the
projection and ask what it is saying – 90 per
cent of energy is lost at each level, so it is
better for humans to eat the grain, vegetables
and fruit directly, rather than feeding it to cows
and sheep, etc.

2. Ask students to discuss the question in pairs,
   then elicit ideas. Encourage students to
   support their ideas with evidence from the
   text as far as possible.

Answers

1. See table on the next page.
2. Answers depend on students.

Optional activity

There is a photocopiable resource on page 274.
This vocabulary + definitions exercise can be set
for completion in class or for homework.
Photocopy the handout.

If done in class, you could once again (see 5.11,
Exercise C) try the following variation rather
than asking all the students to work on all the
definitions.

Step 1: Divide the class into pairs. Ask half the
pairs ('red' group) to work on numbers 1–6. Ask
the other half (blue group) to work on 7–12.

Step 2: When students have finished working
on their allocated definitions, re-divide the class
into pairs with one 'red' student and one 'blue'
one. Students take turns to give the correct
word for each definition from Step 1.

Monitor carefully and make a note of any
words students are having difficulty with.
Give feedback on these words at the end of
the activity.

people	period	reasons	source
a. early men	Stone Age	because not able to catch many animals	Piperno & Dillehay, 2008; Humphries, 1994
b. Pythagoras	c. 6th C BCE	animals should not be killed for food or clothing	Vegetarian Society, 2011
c. Buddhists	c. 6th C BCE	religious faith – non-violence and respect for all life forms	Vegetarian Society, 2011
d. poor people in the Middle Ages	c. 5th to 15th C CE	meat was expensive	author of article = Ellison, 2011
e. Leonardo da Vinci	Renaissance	ethical grounds	Vegetarian Society, 2011
f. people in World War II	not given directly but 1945 cited	not available or expensive	Vegetarian Society, 2011
g. people in recent times	1990s	meat scares; treatment of animals is cruel	Vegetarian Society, 2011 CIWF, 2011
h. people today	2011	range of reasons including not efficient	Ellison, 2011

Answers

1. an eater of both meat and plant products	omnivore
2. famous	renowned
3. from the Stone Age	Neolithic
4. group of people coming together for worship	congregation
5. limited supply, controlled by the government or another authority	ration
6. lived at the same time	contemporaries
7. people who do not accept main ideas of their religion	heretics
8. related to teeth	dental
9. say something is good or correct	advocate
10. small faith groups	sects
11. sudden increase in cases of a disease	outbreaks
12. took from different places and brought home	gathered

C Developing critical thinking

Students discuss the two questions in pairs or small groups. Encourage students to be open-minded rather than simply giving biased opinions. You might like to point out that one reason for vegetarianism is not given in the text – some people simply do not like the taste of meat.

After a few minutes, elicit ideas. Some students may make the point that it may not be necessary to become total vegetarians, but simply to reduce meat consumption.

Tell students that in the next text in this section they will look at more reasons for reducing meat consumption in the future.

Closure

Use the discussion in Exercise C. Summarize what students have learnt in this lesson:

Vegetarianism is not just a cranky idea, it is a way of feeding the world population in the future.

5.13 Learning new reading skills: Relationships between sentences

Objectives

By the end of this lesson, students should be able to:
• show understanding of marked and unmarked sentence relationships.

Introduction

Focus on the illustration. Ask students what it shows and how it was used – people could only get a particular amount/number of meat, eggs, etc., even if they could afford to pay for more.

A Reviewing vocabulary

Set the task. Students complete the collocations individually then compare answers in pairs. Elicit answers. Elicit examples of further words that could be used with some of the verbs, for example:

gather	*berries / ideas / information*
hunt (for)	*animals / birds / a killer / a criminal / your keys*
treat	*people / an injury*

Answers

Note that *hunt a person* is a possible collocation but unusual.

1. hunt	7	a person
2. gather	6	a way of life
3. provide	*1*	animals
4. practise	8	life forms
5. cite	3	evidence
6. follow	2	fruit
7. influence	5	research
8. respect	4	vegetarianism

B Identifying a new skill

1. Students discuss the question in pairs. Elicit ideas. Students may have little or no idea about the answers, in which case tell them not to worry and move on to Exercise B2 – reading the Skills Check. However, students should be able to tell you that words such as *however, for example, although*, etc., show relationships.

2. Give students time to read the Skills Check. Check understanding, in particular of the second explanation and example. Elicit key features of the second sentence in the example which show it is related to the first, as follows:

   they – replaces *Early men* in the first sentence

   hunted and *gathered* – repeats words from the first sentence (although in different forms, the basic word is the same)

Answers

1. and 2.

We can show relationships with words and phrases such as *for example, because, so / therefore, in addition*. Sometimes relationships are not clearly marked.

C Practising the new skill

1. Check students understand the task. Students read the pairs of sentences individually, then discuss the answers in pairs. Elicit answers, preferably by showing the pairs of sentences using an electronic projection.

2. and 3. Set the task and go over the example. Explain that not all the sentences listed appear exactly in that form in the text. They may need to paraphrase.

   Students discuss the remaining answers in pairs. Elicit answers. Use an electronic projection to show the answers below as this gives the actual second sentence in each case.

Answers

1.

Early men are usually described as hunter-gatherers.	reason	They hunted small animals and gathered fruit and nuts from trees and bushes.
However, there is evidence to indicate early human diets were vegetarian.	example	The dental remains of an ancient civilization in Peru are typical.
During the same period in history, several religions in Asia, including Hinduism, Brahmanism and Buddhism, were teaching their followers not to eat meat.	reason	Non-violence and respect for all life forms is what these faiths teach.
During the Middle Ages, from the 5th to the 15th century CE, meat was very expensive.	result	Only the rich could afford to eat it.

However, by the time of the Renaissance, there were some famous supporters of animal welfare.	example	The artist Leonardo da Vinci is known to have refused to eat meat.
Gradually, vegetarianism grew in popularity, especially as members of the Christian church began to advocate it.	example	For example, Reverend William Cowherd created a vegetarian congregation in Manchester in 1809.
The Second World War contributed greatly to the spread of vegetarianism.	reason	In many countries, meat was not available, on ration, or extremely expensive for the duration of the conflict.
The 'meat scares' of the 1990s … made many people concerned about where meat came from.	result	A significant number of people stopped eating meat.

2. and 3.

a. There are many sites of historical interest in Tunisia.	e.g.	Just north of Tunis City are the ruins of Carthage.
b. Cyprus has three languages.	exp	German, French and Italian.
c. In 1862, the teenage Edison saved a little boy from being hit by a train.	exp	He was selling newspapers at his local railway station when a boy fell onto the tracks.
d. Edison's invention of the electrical vote recorder was not successful.	reason	Nobody wanted to buy it.
e. Edison decided to make things which people wanted.	result	He made a device for the New York Stock Exchange, selling it to them in 1870.
f. While she was crossing the Atlantic, Hedwig met an important Hollywood producer.	result	He offered her a movie contract in Hollywood, also giving her a new name, Hedy Lamarr (from La Mar, 'the sea').

g. In the middle of the Second World War, Hedy Lamarr had an idea.	exp	'Is it possible,' she thought, 'to change the control signal constantly, so that the enemy cannot intercept the signal?'
h. Humans are experts at understanding fictional narrative even though it is written in code.	reason	We have encountered the code thousands of times since we first heard fairy tales.
i. The main characters always begin in a stable situation, married happily, successful at work or enjoying an idyllic childhood, then something happens.	result	The equilibrium is disrupted.
j. In the UK, the Forsters Education Act was the first step towards state education in Britain.	exp	It stated that all parts of the country should provide schools (UK Parliament, 2011).
k. There are other subjects that may be valuable during free time or in retirement.	e.g.	One of these is dealing with money.

Closure

Ask students to look back at another text from the course and find examples of pairs of sentences. Students explain the relationship and how they know the pairs are related.

5.14 Grammar for reading: Interrogative clauses: *who*, *which*

Objectives

By the end of this lesson, students should be able to:

- identify hidden questions in interrogative clauses;
- use hidden questions to predict information in a text.

Introduction

Ask quick-fire questions about the text in 5.12, allowing students to find the answers by reading.

Example questions:

Who did the research into a Neolithic tribe?	Jared Diamond
When did Pythagoras live?	sixth century BCE
Which religions advocated vegetarianism?	Hinduism, Brahmanism and Buddhism
When did Leonardo da Vinci live?	during the Renaissance
What were the meat scares about?	CJD, Listeria, Salmonella

Grammar box 23

Give students time to read all the information in the table. Ask one or two questions to check understanding.

A Working out the 'hidden question'

Set the task and go over the example. Students should write each question individually then compare answers in pairs. Elicit the correct questions.

Answers

See after Exercise B.

B Looking for the answer to a hidden question

Students try to find answers to their questions in the text in Lesson 5.12. After a few minutes, elicit answers.

Answers

Grammar box 24

Give students time to read the information in the table. Check understanding.

C Recognizing interrogative clauses

Set the task. Students discuss in pairs. Elicit answers. Ask students to give the 'hidden' question for interrogative clauses, and the noun / noun phrase that is referred to in the relative clauses (see answers below).

Answers

1. There is an increasing number of people in many countries *who* do not eat meat. *a*

2. The practice of vegetarianism *which* is advocated in many eastern religions is widespread in Asia. *b*

3. Vegans are very strict vegetarians *who* do not use any animal products, including wool and honey. *a*

4. It is hard to know *which* country has the highest percentage of vegetarians. *a*

5. Most countries in the world have a compulsory education system *which* is paid for by the state. *b*

6. Although many people believe that the Wright Brothers made the first powered flight, historians argue about *who* was really first. *a*

Closure

Ask students *What do we know? What don't we know?* Give some examples and ask them to give more.

Examples:

We know when dinosaurs lived on Earth.

We don't know why they died out – although there are some strong theories.

	hidden question	in text?
1. ... it is not clear which tribes began the practice of hunting.	*Which tribes began the practice of hunting?*	*not answered in the text*
2. They showed him (Diamond) what they got from a day's hunting.	What did they get from a day's hunting?	two baby birds, a few frogs and a lot of mushrooms
3. This kind of research gives some evidence of how long ago vegetarianism started.	How long ago did vegetarianism start?	Stone Age times
4. ... Compassion in World Farming started to make people aware of how some meat is produced.	How is some meat produced?	not answered directly but presumably in bad conditions with suffering to animals
5. There are a number of reasons why people have become vegetarians throughout history.	Why have people become vegetarians throughout history?	reasons given in each para of the text
6. Given these reasons, it is perhaps surprising how few people are vegetarians in the West today.	How *many* (not few) people are vegetarians in the West?	3 per cent of UK and US

Objectives

By the end of this lesson, students should be able to:

• use new reading sub-skills, grammar and vocabulary in order to understand resources about agriculture;

• read for an established purpose, rejecting texts which are not related to their need;

• work out counter-arguments to a strong viewpoint – note that this skill is continued in the writing section of this theme and is fundamental to academic life.

Introduction

Use Exercise A.

A   Previewing vocabulary

Remind students that some words go together and others don't. It's called collocation. There is not always a reason why one word is collocated and a synonymous word isn't. Set for individual work and pairwork checking.

Answers

	a	b
1. livestock	*rearing*	growing
2. arable	food	*farming*
3. endangered	organism	*species*
4. greenhouse gas	*emission*	production
5. recommended daily	*intake*	food
6. intensive	agriculture	*farming*
7. hazardous	*chemical*	element
8. saturated	protein	*fat*

B   Understanding a text

1. Make sure students understand the question, and check the meanings of *sustainable* and *unsustainable*. Remind students about the points raised in the text in Lesson 5.12 about vegetarianism and if necessary give them time to reread it. Students discuss the question in pairs. Elicit one or two ideas. This activity can be referred to again during or at the end of the lesson, as the students' ideas will be confirmed or rejected by information in the texts.

2. Divide the class into four groups. Allocate one of the four factors, *economic, environmental, ethical* and *health,* to each group. The first task of each group is to identify which texts are relevant to them. Allow plenty of time for this task. Then students should make a note of the points for their factor. Monitor and give help where necessary. Note that there are far more environmental factors than others. You may wish to give this factor to a more able group.

3. Re-divide the class into groups of four, with one student for each factor. Students should explain the information they researched in the previous stage in their own words. Ask students if they are able to answer the assignment question. Elicit ideas. If students are still struggling with some of the concepts, leave this question until after Exercise C.

Answers

Answers depend on students.

C   Using key skills

1. Remind students about the work they did on hidden questions and sentence relationships (Lessons 5.13 and 5.14). This activity practises those skills and will help with understanding the texts more deeply. Set the task. Students complete individually then compare answers in pairs. Elicit answers.

2. Set the task. Check understanding of the headings in the table. Ask students to tell you where the first piece of information – 12 times the amount of water use compared with food crops – comes from. Students complete individually then compare answers in pairs. Elicit correct answers, preferably using an electronic projection. Ask for reactions to the figures. In particular, if you had any students who earlier in the lesson were reluctant to believe that meat-eating is unsustainable, ask them if they are now convinced.

Answers

1.

a. Animals are often treated badly in intensive farming.	T – cramped conditions; small birth crates; animals can't turn round, forage for food; crowded sheds; stress
b. Humans must eat meat to get the protein they need.	F – protein in vegetables, e.g., 17% in wheat
c. A vegetarian diet is healthier than one involving meat-eating.	T – low in fat esp. saturated, high in complex carbs + vitamins and minerals
d. Bottom-trawling is a method of fishing.	T – it is destructive to the seabed
e. Crop-rearing does not involve cutting down trees.	F – preparing land for any agricultural enterprise involves deforestation
f. Wild salmon are low in their food chain.	T – they are given as an example of a species low down in the food chain
g. Dolphins are not normally caught for food.	T – they are given as examples of unwanted species caught in the nets
h. Fish-eating has not led to any environmental damage to oceans.	F – ocean food chains are threatened as a result of fish-eating = over-fishing
i. Kangaroos do not produce greenhouse gas emissions.	T – given as example of animal which doesn't produce emission

2.

water use	12 x food crops
land use	2.5 x food crops
pesticide contents	14 x food crops
calories per hectare	10% of food crops
greenhouse gases	18% of world total
effect on topsoil	85% of loss

D Developing critical thinking

Ask students to discuss the questions in pairs or small groups. Elicit ideas.

Answers

1. This is the only strong evidence in support of the livestock industry. Note that it contains separate points in favour:

   Thousands of communities around the world depend on livestock rearing. In the UK alone, 315,000 people work in the industry, producing 11 million tons of leather and 2 million tons of food, in addition to meat (Holmes, 2010). Manure from livestock contributes 15 per cent of fertilizing nitrogen. Without that, organic farming would disappear. Grazing land that supports animals often does not support arable farming (ibid.).

2. Answers depend on students but they could mention:

   • cultural traditions around meat-eating, e.g., Thanksgiving
   • nutrition – is it really true that we can get everything we need from a vegetarian diet?
   • taste
   • speed of creating meat-based meals
   • high levels of energy in meat

Closure

Ask some high-speed questions which require scanning, e.g., *What does each of the following numbers refer to?*

13.5%	emissions from world transport system
17%	protein in wheat
4 million	acres of topsoil lost to erosion every year
315,000	number of people working in the livestock industry in the UK
11 million	tons of leather produced in the UK each year
15%	percentage of fertilizing nitrogen from livestock manure

Knowledge quiz: Reading texts

Objectives

By the end of this lesson, students will have:
- reviewed core knowledge from Themes 1 to 5;
- recycled the vocabulary from Themes 1 to 5;
- practised the skill of reading for specific information.

Introduction

Tell students they are going to do a knowledge and vocabulary quiz on all the themes of the book. If you like, while you are waiting for everyone in the class to arrive, students can spend a few minutes looking back over the themes.

Methodology note

See notes in the Introduction for further ideas on how to do the quiz (page 16). As usual the focus should be more on content than using correct grammar but on this occasion, you should not have to give the correct answer to any of the questions. Eventually, someone in the class should be able to locate the information from the relevant reading text.

Exercise 1

Divide the class into groups of three or four. Ask students to prepare a page for their answers. Students discuss the questions and make notes of their ideas. They are, of course, unlikely to be able to remember many of the answers, but should be able to understand the vocabulary in the questions. Set a time limit of, say, ten minutes. Monitor but do not confirm or correct.

Exercise 2

Keep the class in groups but work through #1 with the whole class as an example, showing them that they must find 1.12 and then skim and scan for the required information.

Students try to find the information in the relevant texts. Set a strict time limit of 20 minutes, for example. Remind students of time regularly. Students can divide up the task or all try to find the answer in each text.

Finally, elicit answers, preferably using an electronic projection. Give points if you wish and declare a winning group.

Answers

See table below.

Closure

Tell students to learn the information and say you will test them again in a couple of days.

1. Which countries border Tunisia? (1.12)	Libya and Algeria
2. Which civilization first made Tunisia an important area? (1.12)	the Romans
3. Where is Cyprus located? (1.15)	in the Eastern Mediterranean
4. When was Cyprus divided into Greek and Turkish areas? (1.15)	1974
5. How many tourists visit Cyprus every year? (1.15)	more than 2 million
6. When was Edison born? (2.12)	1845
7. What was the first device that Edison patented? (2.12)	an electrical vote recorder
8. What was Edison's favourite invention? (2.12)	the phonograph – sound-recorder
9. How did Hedwig Kiesler become Hedy Lamarr? (2.15)	she was given her name by a Hollywood producer because they were on a boat at the time
10. Who did Hedwig Kiesler collaborate with to produce her invention? (2.15)	George Antheil
11. What did Lévi-Strauss believe about all narrative fiction? (3.12)	it has binary opposition
12. Who stated that narratives conventionally follow a structure of three stages? (3.12)	Todorov
13. What are the characters in narrative fiction, according to Propp? (3.12)	hero, villain, princess – perhaps donor, helper, false hero
14. What is the basic plot of a rags-to-riches story? (3.15)	a rise from humble beginnings to wealth or power

15. What is the most common force in a Tragedy, according to Booker? (3.15)	hubris – too much ambition or greed
16. When were state schools first established in Britain? (4.12)	1870
17. What were Plato's three classes of people? (4.12)	gold – the leaders, silver – the auxiliaries, copper – the farmers and craftsmen
18. How long, according to the BBC, does the average adult in Britain spend at work? (4.15)	41 hours
19. What is the current (2010) life expectancy in the developed world? (4.15)	85
20. Who believes that the state should teach children to be happy throughout their lives? (4.15)	Martin Seligman
21. What were vegetarians called in Europe until 1847? (5.12)	pythagoreans
22. Which faiths advocate vegetarianism? (5.12)	Hinduism, Brahmanism, Buddhism
23. How many people in the United States are vegetarian, according to a 2009 study? (5.12)	around three per cent
24. How much of the world's land surface is used for livestock rearing? (5.15)	30%
25. What nutrient is 11 per cent of potatoes? (5.15)	protein

1. an eater of both meat and plant products	
2. famous	
3. from the Stone Age	
4. group of people coming together for worship	
5. limited supply, controlled by the government or another authority	
6. lived at the same time	
7. people who do not accept main ideas of their religion	
8. related to teeth	
9. say something is good or correct	
10. small faith groups	
11. sudden increase in cases of a disease	
12. took from different places and brought home	

Writing: GM: The future or the end?

5.16 Vocabulary for writing: The principles of GM

Objectives

By the end of this lesson, students should be able to:

- demonstrate understanding of, and be able to spell, target vocabulary for the section;
- demonstrate understanding of basic principles of genetic modification of plant cells.

Introduction

Some words in this lesson have several different meanings. Write this list on the board and ask students to discuss different ways each word could be used:

- *cell*
- *characteristic*
- *identify*
- *resistance*
- *plan*
- *nucleus*

A Activating knowledge

Set the task. Reassure students they do not need in-depth biological knowledge in order to do the activity. Students should study the diagram and read the complete text of the first paragraph before starting to fill in the missing words.

Students complete individually then compare answers in pairs. Elicit answers. Some words here may be the same or almost the same in the students' own language, e.g., *chromosome* and *gene*. Of course, the pronunciation may be different so check students recognize the word(s) as the same. The word *nucleus* is often similar to the word *kernel* in Scandinavian or Germanic languages.

Methodology note

If students did the speaking section of this theme, especially Lesson 5.6 about using genetics in farming, you may wish to revise some of the vocabulary and content.

Answers

Inside every plant, there are millions of *cells*. Each cell has a *nucleus*, which contains *chromosomes* which, in turn, are made up of *DNA*. The DNA in a particular plant can be divided into about 20,000 sections. Each section is called a *gene*. Each gene carries the information for a particular *characteristic*.

B Building sentences

Check students understand the task and go over the example. Students complete individually as a written exercise. Monitor and make a note of common errors. Then students compare answers in pairs. Show the correct sentences using an electronic projection so that students can compare with their own sentences. Give further explanations and feedback on common errors you noted while monitoring. Check understanding of new vocabulary. Ask students to find the new vocabulary in the word list.

Methodology note

If you think the sentences may be too difficult for your students, try the following approach. With students' pens down, show the model text using an electronic projection. Highlight the new vocabulary and any grammar points you wish to make. Ask a few questions to check understanding, then remove the model text. Students write the sentences.

Answers

Model answers:

1. GM stands for 'genetic modification' or 'genetically modified'.
2. It is a form of biotechnology.
3. Biotechnologists are now able to modify the genes of a plant to produce a new variety or even a new species.
4. Firstly, biotech scientists identify the gene for a particular characteristic.
5. For example, an existing plant may be resistant to a particular pest or may produce a bigger yield.
6. Secondly, the gene for pest resistance or higher yield is removed from the plant.

7. Thirdly, the gene is inserted into a cell belonging to a different plant.

8. The genetics of the plant are modified.

9. The new variety now has the characteristic.

10. Finally, seeds are gathered from the modified plant and farmers are supplied with the new variety.

C Using new vocabulary

Check students understand the task. You can limit the activity to words from the lesson or students can use the complete list. The pairs students choose can be based on meaning, pronunciation, spelling, grammar, etc., as long as students can provide an acceptable rationale for the connection. Once students have the basic idea, they can usually suggest a wide range of pairs and connections.

You can set the task for individual or pairwork completion. After a few minutes, ask students to read out their pairs and give an explanation of the connection.

Answers

Answers depend on students, but here are some more examples:

nutrient – nutrition = different forms of same word

harm – harmful = different forms of same word

outsell – outweigh = both begin with *out~*, meaning 'do more than'

pest – resistant = collocation

seed – gene = both have long e sound (/iː/)

potentially – because of = adverbs

mutate – mutation = different forms of same word

migrate – migration = different forms of same word

despite – because of = opposites

discriminate – mutate = ending in *~ate*

many words with *~ion* ending

Closure

Dictate ten words from the lesson.

5.17 Real-time writing: The road to feeding the world?

Objectives

By the end of this lesson, students should be able to:

• know more about the advantages of feeding people with food from GM crops;

• demonstrate understanding of the organization of an Argument essay;

• use research notes to complete an essay.

Note: In this lesson students will research notes for and write about the argument *for* GM food. In the second essay, in Lesson 5.20, students will write the arguments *against* GM food.

Introduction

Write *The green movement* on the board. Ask students what it is. (People who agree with the idea that we should protect the environment by recycling, use natural processes rather than artificial, reduce our carbon footprint and perhaps not interfere with nature.)

A Activating ideas

Give students a minute or two to read the quote from Dr Ray Bressan. Check understanding of the following words or phrases:

to have your heart in the right place

low-grade

alarmist

conventional

negative impact

Students discuss the questions in pairs. Elicit answers. The quotation is quite difficult to understand but can be summarized something like this: *The green movement and scientists should be on the same side. They both agree that less land should be used for agriculture.*

Answers

1. They presumably do not agree with GM crops.

2. He seems to approve – he says 'our aim ...'

3. Perhaps because he is a professor but possibly because he works for a biotech company which, presumably, makes GM products.

B Preparing to write

1. This activity helps students to research information needed for their essay. Revise/teach the meaning of key words such as *sustainable, yield, resistant*, etc. Set the task. Tell students it does not matter if they cannot answer some of the questions but they should try to guess, if possible. After a few minutes' discussion, briefly elicit some of the students' ideas but do not confirm.

2. Make sure students know where to find the research sources. After students have checked their answers, ask them if they guessed correctly in Exercise B1. Ask students if any answers surprised them. Ask more questions to further check understanding, for example:

   a. Why are GM crops a *logical extension* of selective breeding? (because they involve changing the DNA of a plant, which is what selective breeding does)

   b. Why do some people say GM crops are *safe*? (because there is no evidence that they are harmful – but absence of evidence is not evidence of absence!)

   c. Which piece of evidence about *cost* is the most important? (probably the final quote – the rest is limited and almost anecdotal)

   d. Which do you think is the most important issue relating to GM crops? (answer depends on students)

3. Ask students to look at the spidergram. Check understanding of the notes and diagrams. Elicit answers to the question. Ask students if they can remember any points from the research sources for each topic in the spidergram.

Answers

1. Answers depend on students.
2. Answers depend on students.
3. There will be at least eight paragraphs (one for each topic) plus an introduction and a conclusion.

C Recognizing the essay type

Set the two questions and give students a few moments to discuss. Then feed back.

Answers

1. This is an Argument essay. It is not a For and against essay because you are only asked to consider the benefits.

2. The hidden thesis is that 'GM crops are beneficial'.

D Reviewing, quoting and citing

Point out to students that this is a revision activity. (If you wish you can refer students back to Lesson 3.18 before you set this task. Students also learnt about quoting verbs in speech in Lesson 5.8.)

Set the task. Students complete individually then compare answers in pairs. Elicit answers, keeping in mind that other answers may be possible. Remind students that the important thing is to vary the quoting verbs used.

Answers

Suggested answers: see next page.

E Noticing the discourse structure

Students discuss the questions in pairs. Elicit answers. Tell students to organize their own writing in the same way when they complete the essay in the next phase of the lesson. Refer them to the topic sentences and make sure they notice how the writer varies what is in effect a list – *firstly this, secondly this*, etc.

Answers

1. One paragraph for each point, beginning with a topic sentence.

2. Quotes and research information.

3. With one paragraph for each of the remaining points.

F Completing the essay

As usual the writing task can be set in class or for homework. Set the remainder of the essay as follows. Elicit the topics of the three model paragraphs then elicit the five remaining topics to be written:

Completed paragraphs:

Para 1 – farmers understand basic idea

Para 2 – safety

Para 3 – price

Discuss the benefits of genetically modified foods.

The first point in favour of GM foods is that farmers understand the basic idea. They are a logical extension of selective breeding. For thousands of years, farmers have been selectively breeding plants, which changes the genetics of the plants. *According to* American Public Media, 'Genetic engineering is just the latest form of biotechnology – the most precise method yet' (American Public Media, 2011).

A second argument for producing GM crops relates to safety. Several authors *support* the idea that GM foods are safe. A BBC journalist *claims* that 'there is no evidence that modified crops cause illness in humans'. Another journalist *states* 'GM crops are no more harmful to the environment than conventional plant varieties' (Black, 2004). Finally, scientific studies *have found* evidence to support their safety. For example, a University of Queensland PhD study *concluded* that GM crops are worth growing despite the risks. It *points* out that the benefits of GM food outweigh the dangers, *finding* 'no compelling evidence of harm to humans from GM plants' (Science Alert, 2008). A GM food producing company, ArgEvo, *maintains* that GM foods are actually safer than non-GM foods because of additional testing (BBC, 2009b; BBC, 2006).

Thirdly, there is the question of cost. It *seems* that GM crops can be cheaper than non-genetically modified foods (BBC, 2006). A Chinese professor *says* that people have been eating GM foods in China since 2000, because of their relative cheapness (Juan, 2010). Krebs (2000) *supports* this view, *saying* that 'GM tomato paste, which is slightly cheaper than non-GM paste, is outselling its conventional equivalent in J. Sainsbury plc' (Krebs, 2000). Some people *go* further, maintaining that GM foods are the future of cheap food. The *Times* *quotes* a scientist as *saying* that resistance to GM foods may mean the end of cheap food (Henderson, 2007). 'If we turn our backs on the technology which scientific learning can offer, then the end of cheap food can come to pass' (ibid.).

Incomplete paragraphs:

Para 4 – speed / yield

Para 5 – nutrition

Para 6 – disease and pest resistance

Para 7 – keep longer

Para 8 – sustainability

Elicit a topic sentence for each paragraph and write them on the board. Remind students to write an introduction and a conclusion.

Because this is such a long writing task, you could divide it up as follows:

- Divide the class into groups of five.
- Each student writes one of the remaining five paragraphs.
- Students help each other by exchanging drafts and editing.
- Finally, the five paragraphs can be put together to form one complete essay for each group.

Monitor during the writing phases and give help where necessary. Make a note of common errors.

Give feedback.

Closure

Use your feedback on the writing activities done in class.

Answers

See pages 279–280.

Model essay:

In this essay, I look at the benefits of genetically modified, or GM, foods. I consider a range of points, including the understanding of farmers, safety, cost and speed of production. I discuss yield, nutrition, resistance to pests and disease and shelf life. I also look at the ability of GM foods to increase the sustainability of farming.

The first point in favour of GM foods is that farmers understand the basic idea. They are a logical extension of selective breeding. For thousands of years, farmers have been selectively breeding plants, which changes the genetics of the plants. According to American Public Media, 'Genetic engineering is just the latest form of biotechnology – the most precise method yet' (American Public Media, 2011).

A second argument for producing GM crops relates to safety. Several authors support the idea that GM foods are safe. A BBC journalist claims that there is 'no evidence that modified crops cause illness in humans'. Another journalist argues that GM crops are no more harmful to the environment than conventional plant varieties (Black, 2004). Finally, scientific studies have found evidence to support their safety. For example, a University of Queensland PhD study concluded that GM crops are worth growing despite the risks. It points out that the benefits of GM food outweigh the dangers, finding 'no compelling evidence of harm to humans from GM plants' (Science Alert, 2008). A GM food producing company, ArgEvo, maintains that GM foods are actually safer than non-GM foods because of additional testing (BBC, 2009b; BBC, 2006).

Thirdly, there is the question of cost. It seems that GM crops can be cheaper than non-genetically modified foods (BBC, 2006). A Chinese professor says that people have been eating GM foods in China since 2000, because of their relative cheapness (Juan, 2010). Krebs (2000) supports this view, saying that GM tomato paste, which is slightly cheaper than non-GM paste, is outselling its conventional equivalent in J. Sainsbury plc (Krebs, 2000). Some people go further, maintaining that GM foods are the future of cheap food. The *Times* quotes a scientist as saying that resistance to GM foods may mean the end of cheap food (Henderson, 2007). 'If we turn our backs on the technology which scientific learning can offer, then the end of cheap food can come to pass' (ibid.).

Fourthly, GM foods can be grown more quickly and can produce a higher yield than normal crops, which means that food will be more readily available to people (BBC, 2006). The Alliance for Better Foods argues that 'Agricultural biotechnology has tremendous potential as a tool for producing more and better foods on existing farmland' (Alliance for Better Foods, 2011). This is especially important because there is a 'need to double food supply by 2025 due to population increases, changes in diets and natural disasters' (BBC, 2009b).

A fifth benefit is that GM foods can have nutrients added to them to make them even healthier than normal crops (BBC, 1999; BBC, 2006). The Alliance for Better Foods explains that 'Biotech researchers ... are field-testing rice enhanced with beta-carotene ... which is important because rice is a primary diet staple in the developing world' (Alliance for Better Foods, 2011). It could even be possible to produce crops that contain vaccines against human infectious diseases (Human Genome Project, 2008).

Sixthly, GM crops can be made to be pest and disease resistant (*Guardian*, 2003), meaning that fewer chemicals have to be used on them and more crops survive. This is especially important for developing countries that need big crop yields. This is also good for the environment as these types of GM crops need less fuel and water and less labour time spent on them (Alliance for Better Foods, 2011). Scientists can also make crops that are resistant to weedkillers (*Guardian*, 2003), which means that farmers can spray the chemicals on the field and kill all the unwanted plants without fear of damaging the food crops. Furthermore, companies are developing weedkillers that are biodegradable and so do not stay in the soil (BBC, 2009b). ArgEvo claims that 'in those countries that have adopted these new crops, farmers and growers are reporting a reduction in the amount of pesticide being used' (BBC, 2009b). Another current development in this area is plants that poison any pests themselves (*Guardian*, 2003).

A further advantage of GM crops is that food could be made to have a longer shelf-life (Alliance for Better Foods, 2011). This is again particularly useful for farmers in developing countries as currently, 'as much as 40 per cent of harvested fruit can be wasted because it ripens too quickly' (Devlin, 2010). Scientists have so far succeeded in making a tomato that stayed firm for a month and a half (Devlin, 2010). In addition, scientists are also currently trying to make crops that are hardier and therefore better able to withstand 'heat, drought, soil toxicity, salinity and flooding' (Alliance for Better Foods, 2011). This means that farmers will be able to have more reliable crop yields, which is particularly important for those in poorer countries.

Finally, biotechnology may be able to increase the sustainability of farming (Alliance for Better Foods, 2011). The Alliance for Better Foods states that 'certain biotech varieties of cotton and soybeans require less tilling, preserving precious topsoil and helping to reduce sediment run-off into rivers and streams' (Alliance for Better Foods, 2011).

In this essay, I have considered several advantages of GM foods. Despite opposition to the development of genetically modified crops, it seems that there are very strong arguments in favour. It may even be that sustainable farming is only possible in the future if we accept genetic modification.

References:

Alliance for Better Foods (2011) Promise of Biotechnology, *The Alliance for Better Foods*, retrieved on 16.08.2011 from http://www.betterfoods.org/Promise/Promise.htm

BBC (2006) Quick Guide: GM Food, *BBC News*, retrieved on 16.08.2011 from http://news.bbc.co.uk/1/hi/sci/tech/5098468.stm

BBC (2009) Special Report: Food Under the Microscope, *BBC News*, retrieved on 17.08.2011 from http://news.bbc.co.uk/1/hi/special_report/1999/02/99/food_under_the_microscope/280396.stm

BBC (2009b) GM Food: Head to Head, *BBC News*, retrieved on 17.08.2011 from http://news.bbc.co.uk/1/hi/special_report/1999/02/99/food_under_the_microscope/278490.stm

Black, R. (2004) Study Finds Benefits in GM Crops, *BBC News*, retrieved on 16.08.2011 from http://news.bbc.co.uk/1/hi/sci/tech/4046427.stm

Devlin, K. (2010) Scientists Create GM Tomatoes 'Which Stay Fresh for a Month Longer than Usual', *The Telegraph*, retrieved on 18.08.2011 from http://www.telegraph.co.uk/science/7128622/Scientists-create-GM-tomatoes-which-stay-fresh-for-a-month-longer-than-usual.html

Guardian (2003) GM Crops, *The Guardian*, retrieved on 16.08.2011 from http://www.guardian.co.uk/science/2003/jun/03/gm.greenpolitics

Henderson, M. (2007) GM Resistance is 'Threatening Cheap Food', *The Times*, retrieved on 17.08.2011 from http://www.timesonline.co.uk/tol/news/science/article3019037.ece

Human Genome Project (2008) Genetically Modified Foods and Organisms, *Human Genome Project Information*, retrieved on 16.08.2011 from http://www.ornl.gov/sci/techresources/Human_Genome/elsi/gmfood.shtml

Juan, S. (2010) Shelves Stacked with GM Foods, *China Daily*, retrieved on 17.08.2011 from http://www.chinadaily.com.cn/china/2010-02/12/content_9465789.htm

Krebs, J. R. (2000) GM Foods in the UK between 1996 and 1999: Comments on 'Genetically modified crops: risks and promise' by Gordon Conway, *Conservation Ecology, 4*, retrieved on 17.08.2011 from http://www.ecologyandsociety.org/vol4/iss1/art11/

Science Alert (2008) GM Benefits Outweigh Risk, *Science Alert*, retrieved on 16.08.2011 from http://www.sciencealert.com.au/news/20082501-16821-2.html

5.18 Learning new writing skills: Using lexical cohesion

Objectives

By the end of this lesson, students should be able to:
- use lexical cohesion in a written paragraph;
- restate sentences in a variety of ways.

Introduction

Dictate the verb or adjective form of some words from Lesson 5.17 and ask for the noun in each case.

understand	(understanding)
cost	(cost)
fast	(speed)
safe	(safety)
sustainable	(sustainability)
nutritious	(nutrition)
resistant	(resistance)
able	(ability)

A Reviewing grammar

Set the task. Students should edit the sentences (in preference, for the sake of time, to rewriting the complete sentences). Students complete individually then compare answers in pairs. Show correct sentences using an electronic projection. Students correct their own work. Go over any answers students had difficulty with.

Answers

1. In this essay, I look at the advantages *of* GM foods.
2. I consider the ability of GM foods *to increase* the sustainability of farming.
3. The first point in favour of GM foods *is (that)* they are a logical extension of selective breeding.
4. For thousands of years, farmers *have been* selectively breeding plants.
5. A second argument for producing GM foods *relates* to safety.
6. Scientific studies *have found* evidence to support the safety of GM crops.
7. Thirdly, there is the question of *cost*.

B Identifying a new skill

1. Give students time to read the two paragraphs. Ask one or two questions to check understanding (although students have seen this information before).
2. Now ask students to study the Skills Check. Ask students:

   Which noun is repeated in paragraph 1? *(crops)*

   Which verb is repeated in paragraph 2? *(add)*

   Set the task. Students complete individually then compare answers in pairs. Show the model paragraphs using an electronic projection. Students compare model answers with their own. Discuss any variations students may have had with the model answer and if they are acceptable or not.

Answers

GM crops can be grown more quickly than non-GM. They can produce a higher yield than conventional plants. Biotechnology can produce more and better grain, fruit and vegetables. This is important because there is a need to increase food supply as world population rises.

Biotechnologists can add nutrients to GM foods to make them even healthier than normal crops. Biotech researchers have produced rice with additional beta-carotene. It may even be possible to insert vaccines into crops. If scientists can do this, GM foods could protect humans from infectious diseases.

C Practising the new skill

Set the task and go over the example. Point out that this is another way of avoiding repetition and varying the way students write sentences. Students complete individually then compare answers in pairs. Elicit answers.

Answers

1. It costs a lot of money.	It is very expensive.	The cost is very high.
2. They are cheap.	They are not expensive.	They do not cost much.
3. They last longer.	They are more long-lasting.	They do not go bad so quickly.
4. Some scientists take a different view.	Some scientists have a different opinion.	Some scientists see things differently.
5. There are risks in the experiment.	The experiment is risky.	The experiment could be dangerous.
6. They are not harmful.	They do not cause harm.	There is no danger from them.
7. It seems that they are safe.	Apparently, they are safe.	They appear to be safe.
8. There are many tests on them.	They are tested a great deal.	Many tests are conducted on them.
9. Firstly, I consider price.	Price is the first issue to consider.	The first point relates to price.
10. The results were difficult to interpret.	It was hard to understand the results.	Interpretation of the results was difficult.

Closure

Give the noun forms of words from this lesson and ask students to tell you the adjective in each case. Do this high speed, orally, on this occasion.

harm	(harmful)
difference	(different)
danger	(dangerous)
safety	(safe)
importance	(important)
infection	(infectious)

Now give nouns with no specific adjective – ask for related adjective:

cost	(cheap *or* expensive)
speed	(fast *or* slow)
risk	(dangerous *or* safe)

5.19 Grammar for writing: *although / because vs despite / because of*

Objectives

By the end of this lesson, students should be able to:

- form sentences with *although / because* + clause;
- form sentences with *despite / because of* + noun phrase.

Introduction

Remind students of complex sentences in Lessons 5.4 and 5.9 (and also 2.14, 2.19, 3.14, 3.19, if you wish). Point out that today you are going to look at a different kind of complex sentence, which uses noun phrases instead of full clauses.

Grammar box 25

Give students time to study the notes and the information in the table. Elicit that *despite* and *because of* are followed by noun phrases.

Ask students to rewrite the sentences in the table beginning with the subordinate clause. Remind them to use a comma after the subordinate clause.

Answers

Although there are risks, GM crops may be worth growing.

Despite the risks, GM crops may be worth growing.

Because *they are tested more, GM foods are said to be safer than non-GM foods.

Because of additional testing, GM foods are said to be safer than non-GM foods.

*The subject could be moved forward when the subordinate clause is put first.

A Changing sentences into noun phrases

Set the task and go over the example. Students complete individually then compare answers in pairs. Show correct answers using an electronic projection so that students can self-check. Go over any answers students found difficult.

Ask students to close their books. Work on the reverse activity – producing full sentences from noun phrases. Ask students to look at the noun phrases only, then elicit the full sentences:

T: *the risks*
Ss: *There are risks.*
T: *the additional testing*
Ss: *They are tested more.*

Remind students once again that full clauses are needed after *although* and *because*.

Answers

1. There are risks.	the risks
2. They are tested more.	the additional testing
3. It doesn't cost very much.	the low cost
4. It is very fast.	the high speed
5. It takes a long time.	the amount of time involved
6. It is very difficult.	the great difficulty
7. It is very profitable.	the high profit
8. The company was sold.	the sale of the company

B ### Choosing the correct adverb

Set the task and go over the example. Tell students that the words after each space will help them to decide which word is missing (i.e., noun phrase or full sentence). Students complete individually then compare answers in pairs. Elicit answers and go over any problem areas.

Answers

1. Reality TV is popular with TV companies *because* it is cheap to make.
2. *Although* population ageing started later in developing countries, it is now happening faster.
3. Sales of fountain pens continued to decline *despite* the significant price reduction.
4. Sales of fountain pens increased later *because* the manufacturers rebranded their product.
5. *Because of* its location in Western Europe, the UK does not suffer from tropical diseases.
6. *Although* Switzerland is land-locked, it is still extremely successful economically.
7. Most parts of Italy have easy access to seaports *because* it is a peninsula.
8. *Because* of the thickness of the new ink in Biro's invention, it did not flow properly.

C ### Using clauses and phrases after subordinating adverbs

Set the task and go over the examples. Elicit ideas for the remaining sentences (2–6). Then students to complete individually. Monitor. Ask a few students to read out one of their sentences.

Answers

Answers depend on students but here are some possibilities:

1. Organic food is gaining in popularity in Britain …
   - *although it is more expensive than conventional food.*
   - *despite costing more than conventional food.*
   - *because many people are becoming worried about intensive farming methods.*
   - *because of growing concern about intensive farming methods.*

2. Many biotechnologists support GM foods ...
- *although they recognize that there may be risks.*
- *despite the potential risks.*
- *because they can provide better and cheaper food crops.*
- *because of their benefits.*

3. Audiences like reality TV ...
- *although it can be cruel.*
- *despite its cruelty.*
- *because it is a form of escapism.*
- *because of the real people it shows.*

4. Population ageing is a worldwide problem ...
- *although elderly people can be very useful for a society.*
- *despite the benefits which elderly people offer.*
- *because it is happening in every part of the world.*
- *because of the social and economic changes which it will produce.*

5. Some countries are successful economically ...
- *although they do not meet the Sachs and Gallup criteria.*
- *despite not meeting the Sachs and Gallup criteria.*
- *because they have had stable government for many years.*
- *because of their mineral resources.*

Closure

Say some sentences or noun phrases from this lesson and ask students to put *although* or *despite* in front and then repeat it, e.g.,

it is cruel	although it is cruel
its cruelty	despite its cruelty

5.20 Applying new writing skills: The road to disaster?

Objectives

By the end of this lesson, students should be able to:
- organize notes from own research into the dangers of GM foods;
- write an essay with reference to research sources and quotes;
- use target vocabulary, language and discourse structure from the section in order to produce an Argument essay about the dangers of GM foods.

Note: Students will have to spend some time researching independently before this essay can be written. Therefore you may have to spread this lesson over two or three lessons, or set the research tasks before the lesson itself. The research can be divided up between the class, so each student researches a different aspect of GM crops. Then the students can share and exchange research information in groups.

Introduction

Revise Essay 1 – the benefits of GM crops. Elicit the areas, building up a spidergram on the board with one or two points about each area.

A Reviewing vocabulary

Point out that you are going to look at the other side of GM crops in this lesson; here, the focus is on opposites. Set the task. Students complete individually then compare answers in pairs. Elicit answers; make sure students check their spelling carefully. Tell students they should be able to use these words in their essay later in the lesson.

Answers

1.	GM foods	*conventional foods*
2.	natural	artificial / synthetic
3.	benefit	disadvantage / danger(s)
4.	harmful	safe
5.	precise	inaccurate
6.	drawbacks	advantages
7.	support (an idea)	reject
8.	much more	much less
9.	add	remove
10.	long-lasting	short-lived

B Reviewing vocabulary

1. Focus on the assignment box. Check students understand some of the words and phrases in the quotation, e.g., *The realm of ... resistant, benefit*. Students discuss the question in pairs. Elicit ideas, pointing out that the answer is not really clear.

2. Set the task, which will help students to understand the questions in the assignment box. Students complete individually then compare answers in pairs. As always, check spelling.

3. Students discuss ideas for possible answers to the questions. At this stage, students may have no knowledge at all – that's fine; the activity should arouse interest in the topics and indicate to students the scope of the essay.

4. Remind students that this is an Argument essay, with a thesis. But what is the thesis in this case? Students should be able to see this easily.

5. Set the task then elicit answers. Tell students this introduction will help to guide their research and organize their essay.

Answers

1. In fact, it is not clear what he thinks. He seems to just be weighing up the arguments for and against.

2.

a. not on purpose	accidentally
b. tell the difference between	discriminate
c. go from one place to another	migrate
d. change in a bad way	mutate
e. possibly	potentially
f. give away	relinquish
g. owned by	the property of

3. Answers depend on students.

4. There are dangers involved in developing GM crops.

5. Discuss the *dangers* of genetically modified foods.

   In this essay, I look at the dangers of genetically modified or *GM crops*. I consider a range of points, including mutation and accidental modification of *genes*, and escape of genes to other *species*. I also discuss harm to birds and *insects*, and the difficulty of accurate identification of GM products in *supermarkets*. Finally, I look at the control of seed *production* and ownership of new *species*.

C The TOWER of Writing

Go through the five points, most of which students will be familiar with by now. (See previous writing sections of the course.) Emphasize the following:

- how to do the research – what to type into the search engine, etc.; make a note of websites and pages as well as sources;
- the number of sections / paragraphs for the essay (there are seven questions in the assignment task, so there should be seven paragraphs + an introduction and a conclusion).

Monitor and give feedback on all writing stages done in class.

Closure

Use your feedback for the writing activities.

Portfolio: Influences on the environment

Objectives

By the end of this lesson, students will:
- have researched a variety of sources in order to complete tasks;
- have worked independently to take part in a discussion about the environment;
- have produced and given a presentation, and taken notes of other presentations;
- have produced an essay or a poster about the environment;
- have used vocabulary, grammar, sub-skills and knowledge from the theme in integrated skills activities.

Note: On this occasion, the Portfolio brings together topics from Themes 1 to 5. However, if your students have not studied one or more of the themes or sections of themes, it will not be necessary to explain as students can discover key points during the research phase. Research, note-taking and other preparation may have to be set as assignments. The presentation and the writing can then be given at a later date in class.

Introduction

Start with students' books closed. Write *The environment* on the board and ask students to construct a spidergram of influences on the environment. Give a couple of examples to get them going, if necessary. After a few minutes, ask students to open their books and compare.

A Activating ideas

Set for small groups. Feed back, building up a table on the board. Words can appear in several columns if students can make a convincing argument.

Answers

Possible classification:

land use:	deforestation, soil erosion
farming:	growth hormone, pesticide, yield, crop rotation
livestock:	emissions, manure, stress
water use:	desalination, aquifer, reservoir
biotechnology:	DNA, cells, cloning, genetics, characteristic, modify
media:	education, research, documentary, audience
climate change:	pollution, emissions
supermarkets:	food miles, uniformity, taste, waste
diet:	vegetarianism, carnivore, saturated fat

B Taking part in a discussion

Divide the class into pairs. Ask them to discuss the questions and note down dangers and benefits for all of the areas or for those they have studied during the course. Now re-divide the class into bigger groups and tell students to take their notes with them. Students should tell each other the points they came up with earlier in pairs. Remind students about some of the language of discussions.

Students should compare ideas and add to them. Monitor.

Finally, elicit a few ideas from the whole class and give feedback on their performance in the discussion.

Answers

Answers depend on students; how deep students are able to go depends on which themes and sections the students have done.

C Gathering and recording information

Set for individual work or pairwork. Remind students about the importance of recording sources and the way of stating research during a presentation.

Answers

Answers depend on students.

D Preparing a presentation

Remind students about giving a presentation. Get students to practise by themselves while you go round and monitor and assist.

E Listening to a presentation

Remind students about tasks *while* listening and *after* listening to a presentation.

F Writing

Offer the choice and then set Exercise F1 for individual work and Exercise F2 for small groups. Students complete in their own time.

Closure

Give feedback on activities completed in class.

A

a good case	4.11
abandon (v)	4.11
abolish (v)	4.11
absence (n)	1.1
abstract (adj) [= opp. of concrete]	4.11
accelerate (v)	4.16
accept (v)	3.1
access (n)	1.16
accident (n)	2.6
account for (v)	1.16
additional (adj)	5.16
adopt (v) [= take up]	2.6
adventure (n)	3.11
advocate (v)	5.11
affect (v)	1.1
against (prep)	1.1
ageing (adj)	4.16
aggression (n)	3.1, 4.6
aggressive (adj)	3.1, 4.6
agribusiness (n)	5.6
agriculturalist (n)	5.1
ahead of its time	2.11
alien (n)	3.11
allocate (v)	2.1
alphabet (n)	2.6
analogue (adj)	2.1, 2.16
analysis (n)	2.16
analyze (v)	2.16
animation (n)	3.11
announce (v)	1.6
antagonist (n)	3.11
anxiety (n)	4.6
anxious (adj)	4.6
appeal (v)	5.6
aquifer (n)	1.6
archaeological (adj)	1.11
archaeology (n)	1.11
argument (n) [= thesis]	3.1
artery (n)	4.1
artificial (adj)	5.1
artificially (adv)	5.6
asthma (n)	4.6
asthmatic (adj)	4.6
attack (n) [= physical illness]	4.6
audience (n)	3.16
audience (n) [= target market]	3.6
authoritative (adj)	4.6
authorities	3.1
authority (n) [= expert in a field]	3.16
availability (n)	1.1
available (adj)	1.11
average (v)	1.1

B

ban (v)	3.1
ban (n and v)	5.6
bar-code (n)	2.11
battery farming	5.6
be the basis of	2.11
because of	1.16
because of (adv)	5.16
beehive diagram	4.16
beneficial (adj)	2.1
benefit (n and v)	2.1, 4.16
berry (n)	5.1, 5.11
billboard (n)	3.6
binary (adj)	2.6
biotech (n)	5.16
biotechnology (n)	5.16
blind (adj and v)	2.6
blindness (n)	2.6
blood stream	4.1
BOGOF (n)	3.6
bone (n)	4.1
Braille	2.6
brand (n) [= named product]	3.1
brand (v)	2.16
breathe (v)	4.6
breed (v)	5.6
breeding (n)	5.1
breeding (n)	5.6
bribe (n and v)	3.6
bright (adj) [= clever]	2.11
bring on [= cause to start]	4.6
browser (n)	2.1
buddy (n)	3.6
bulb (n)	2.11

C

cable (n)	2.1
calculate (v)	3.1
campaign	4.11
cancel (v)	2.16
cancellation (n)	2.16
carbon emissions	1.11
carnivore (n)	5.11
carnivorous (adj)	5.11
cartridge (n)	2.16
catchy (adj)	3.6

CD (n)	2.16
cell (n)	4.1
cellar (n)	2.11
cereal (n)	5.1
CGI	3.6
channel (n)	1.6
character (n)	3.11
chemical (n)	5.6
child-bearing age	4.16
childminder (n)	3.1
circulation (n)	4.1
circulatory (adj)	4.1
cite (v) [= quote]	3.16
citizen (n)	4.11
citizenship (n)	4.11
civil war	1.16
class (n) [= social division]	4.11
clearly (adv)	3.1
cloning (n)	5.6
code (n)	2.1, 2.6, 3.11
cognitive (adj)	4.6
collapse (v)	1.11
come into its own	2.11
come to pass	5.16
come up with	2.11
commercial use	2.11
commit (v)	3.1
compelling (adj) [= very strong]	5.16
compete (v)	2.16
competition (n)	2.16
competition (n)	3.6
complete (adj)	5.11
complex (adj)	2.1
compress (v)	2.16
compression (n)	2.16, 4.1
comprise (v)	1.11, 1.16
concrete (adj) [= opp. of abstract]	4.11
condition (n)	4.6
conflict (n)	3.11
conform (v)	3.1, 3.11, 5.6
congregation (n)	5.11
consensus (n)	1.6
consequence (n)	2.6
consider (v) [= regard as]	1.16
constant (adj)	2.11
constraining	3.11
contemporary (n)	5.11
contestant (n)	3.16

contract (n)	2.16
contribute (v)	1.16, 4.16
contributory (adj)	1.16
control (v) [~ a disease]	4.6
controllable (adj)	4.6
convention (n)	3.11
convention (n) [= rule]	3.16
conventional (adj)	5.16
conversion (n)	2.16
convert (v)	2.16
copper (n)	1.1
copyright (n)	3.11
correct (v)	2.16
correction (n)	2.16
counter-argument (n)	3.1
courier (n)	2.1
creative (adj)	3.11
criterion (n) [pl. = criteria]	1.16
critic (n)	3.11, 3.16
crop (n)	1.6, 5.1
cruel (adj)	5.11
cruise (n and v)	1.11
cultivation (n)	1.1
curriculum (n) [pl. = curricula]	4.11
customer base	2.1

D

dam (n and v)	1.6
damage (n and v)	2.6
damage (v)	1.11
deal with [= cope]	2.6
decide against	4.16
decline (n and v)	4.16
decode (v)	3.11
deliver (v)	1.6, 2.1
delivery (n)	2.1
demand (n)	1.11
demonstrate (v)	2.16
demonstration (n)	2.16
density (n)	1.1
dental (adj)	5.11
deny (v)	3.1
dependency (n)	3.1
dependency ratio	4.16
dependent (adj)	3.1, 4.16
depressed (adj)	4.6
depression (n)	4.6
deprive (v)	4.6
desalination (n)	1.1, 1.6
design (n and v)	2.16

desirable (adj)	5.6	
despite (adv)	5.16	
destroy (v)	1.6	
developed (adj) [~ countries]	4.16	
device (n)	2.1	
diaphragm (n)	4.1	
diet (n) [= normal food]	5.11	
digestion (n)	4.1	
digestive (adj)	4.1	
digital (adj)	2.1, 2.16	
digress (v)	5.1	
digression (n)	5.1	
direct (adj)	1.11	
disability (n)	2.11	
discriminate (v)	5.16	
disease	1.16	
disgusting (adj)	3.6	
distinguish (v) [= mark the difference]	3.11	
divert (v)	1.6	
diving (n)	1.11	
documentary (n)	3.16	
domesticate (v)	5.11	
domesticated (adj)	5.1	
donor (n)	3.11	
dot (n)	2.6	
downstream (n)	1.6	
drama (n)	3.11	
dramatic (adj)	3.16	
draw (v) [= take out]	1.6	
drawback (n)	2.1	
drought (n)	1.6	
dry (v)	2.16	
dry up (v)	1.6	
dumb (adj)	2.6	
dumb down	3.1	

E economic indicator 1.16

edible (adj)	5.1, 5.6	
educationalist (n)	4.11	
educator (n)	4.11	
elderly	4.16	
eliminate (v)	3.1	
encounter (v)	3.11	
endangered species	5.11	
endorse (v)	3.6	
endorsement (n)	3.6	
entrepreneur (n)	4.11	
environmental (adj)	5.11	
episode (n) [= part of a series]	3.6	

episodic (adj)	3.16	
equilibrium (n)	3.11	
equivalent (n)	5.16	
escapism (n)	3.16	
establish (v) [= make clear]	3.11	
etailer (n)	2.1	
ethical (adj)	5.11	
evil	3.11	
exaggerate (v)	3.6	
exceed (v)	1.11	
exception (n)	1.16	
exchange (n)	4.1	
exertion (n)	4.6	
exist (v)	1.16	
existing (adj)	2.16	
experience (v)	3.1	
experiment (v)	2.11	
experiment with	2.16	
expire (v)	2.11	
extension (n) [= next step]	5.16	
extract (v)	1.6	
extraction (n)	1.6	
extremely	1.16	
eye-catching (adj)	3.6	
eyesight (n)	2.6	

F fairy tale 3.1

famine (n)	5.1	
fantasy	3.11	
fatal (adj)	4.6	
fatigue (n)	4.6	
feature (v)	3.11	
feed (v) [= supply]	1.6	
feedback (n)	4.6	
feel strongly about	2.11	
fertile (adj)	5.1	
fertility (n)	4.16	
fertilizer (n)	5.1	
fiction (n)	3.11	
fictional	3.11	
fictional (adj)	3.1	
film (v)	3.16	
finger (n)	2.6	
flat (adj)	2.6	
flexible (adj)	4.11	
flood (n and v)	1.6	
flow (v)	1.6, 2.16	
follow a way of life	5.11	
follower (n) [of religion]	1.11	

invasion (n)	1.16	
iron ore	1.1	
irrigate (v)	1.6	
irrigation (n)	1.6	
J jingle (n)	3.6	
joint (n)	4.1	
joke (n)	3.6	
journal (n)	3.11	
K kill (v)	5.11	
L labour force	4.11, 4.16	
lack (n)	1.1	
lack of sleep	4.6	
largely (adv)	1.16	
laser (n)	2.16	
leak (v)	1.6	
leather (n)	2.6	
leisure (n)	4.11	
life expectancy	4.16	
lifelong (adj)	4.11	
limit (v)	1.6	
link (n and v)	4.16	
lip (n)	2.6	
literacy (n)	1.1, 4.11	
live action	3.6	
livestock rearing	5.11	
living organism	5.6	
longevity (n)	4.11, 4.16	
look like	2.11	
lose your sight / hearing / voice	2.6	
loss-leader	3.6	
lung (n)	2.6	
luxury (n)	2.16	
M mainly (adv)	1.16	
maintain (v) [= keep in good condition]	1.11	
maintain (v) [= say is true]	5.16	
make a fresh start	2.11	
manufacture (v)	2.16	
manufacturer (n)	2.16	
manure (n)	5.1	
manuscript (n)	2.16	
marina (v)	1.11	
market (n) [= general place to sell goods]	1.16	
market (v)	2.1	
marketing strategy	2.16	
mechanization (n)	5.1	
mechanize (v)	5.1	
media (n pl)	3.1	

mediate (v)	3.1	
medical innovation	4.16	
medication (n)	4.6	
medium (n)	3.1	
medium (n) [= way of sending message]	2.1	
meet (v) [= equals]	1.16	
member	1.16	
membership (n)	1.16	
mental (adj)	4.6	
message (n) [= meaning]	3.1	
messenger (n)	2.1	
migrate (v)	5.16	
migration (n)	5.16	
mineral (n)	1.1	
model (v) [= copy]	3.1	
modification (n)	5.16	
modify (v)	5.6, 5.16	
monster (n)	3.11	
motion picture	2.11	
mouth (n)	2.6	
MP3 (n)	2.16	
muscle (n)	4.1	
muscular (adj)	4.1	
mutate (v)	5.16	
mutation (n)	5.16	
mute (adj)	2.6	
N narrative (n)	3.6, 3.11	
natural gas	1.1	
natural resource	1.1	
navigable (adj)	1.16	
navigate (v)	2.1	
Neolithic	5.11	
nerve (n)	4.1	
nervous (adj)	4.1	
network (n)	2.1	
neurosis (n)	4.6	
neurotic (adj)	4.6	
nightlife (n)	1.11	
nitrogen (N) (n)	5.1	
nose (n)	2.6	
numeracy (n)	4.11	
nutrient (n)	4.1, 5.1, 5.16	
nutrition (n)	5.16	
O observe (v)	2.11	
obsessively (adv)	4.6	
obstacle (n)	3.11	
obviously (adv)	3.1	
offend (v)	1.11	

omnivore (n)	5.11	
omnivorous (adj)	5.11	
on location	3.16	
one-off	3.6	
organ (n)	4.1	
organic (adj)	5.1	
original (adj) [= new]	2.11	
outbreak (n)	5.11	
output (n)	5.6	
outsell (v)	5.16	
outweigh (v)	5.16	

P

packaging (n)	5.6
partial (adj)	5.11
partly (adv)	1.16
passionate (adj)	4.6
patent (n)	2.11, 2.16
per capita	1.16
perceive (v)	4.6
perception (n)	4.6
performance [= outcome]	1.16
personal education	4.11
personality (n) [= star]	3.6
personnel (n)	2.1
perspiration (n)	2.11
pest (n)	5.1, 5.6, 5.16
pesticide (n)	5.1, 5.11
phosphorus (P) (n)	5.1
physical (adj)	4.6
physiology (n)	4.1
physiotherapy (n)	4.1
pipe (n and v)	1.6
place (v)	1.16
planting (v)	5.1
plot (n)	3.11
plough (n and v)	5.1
plough (v)	5.6
population (n)	1.1
population ageing	4.16
populous (adj)	1.6
positive thinking	4.11
post (v) [= put in mail box]	2.1
postal system	2.1
postpone (v)	4.16
potassium (K) (n)	5.1
potentially (adv)	5.16
practical (adj) [= able to work]	2.16
precise (adj)	5.16
pregnancy (n)	4.16

prequel (n)	3.6
presence (n)	1.1
preserve (v)	5.1
principle (n)	2.1
privatize (v)	1.6
produce (n and v)	5.6
producer (n)	3.16
proofreader (n)	2.16
proportion (n)	4.16
proposal (n)	4.11
proposed (adj)	1.6
proposition (n)	3.1
prosperity (n)	4.16
protagonist (n)	3.11
protection (n)	5.1
provider (n)	4.16
provision (n)	4.11
proximity (n)	1.11
psychological (adj)	4.6
psychological need	3.16
public (n)	3.16
punchline (n)	3.6
put pressure on (v)	4.16
put X ahead of Y	2.11

Q

quotation (n)	3.16
quote (n and v)	5.6

R

radical (n)	4.11
raise the question	4.11
raised (adj) [= above the surface]	2.6
range (n) [= extent]	1.1
range (v)	1.16
ration (n)	5.11
reach a conclusion	1.16
react (v)	2.16
readiness (n)	4.6
reality TV	3.16
rear (v)	5.1
reasonable (adj) [= quite good]	1.11
reasoning (n)	2.11
rebrand (v)	2.16
rebuild (v)	2.11
receiver (n) [= object]	2.11
recognize [= see the value of]	2.11
recommended daily intake	5.11
reconciliation (n)	3.11
recover (v) [e.g., sales]	2.16
recycle (v)	5.6
reef (n)	1.11

reference (n)	3.11	sedentary (n)	4.11
refill (v)	1.6, 2.16	seed (n)	5.16
reflect (v) [= be related to]	4.11	seemingly (adv)	4.16
reflect (v) [= show]	1.1	selective breeding	5.6, 5.16
register (v)	2.11	self-starter (n)	4.11
related (adj) [= connected]	3.16	sense of self-worth	4.6
relative (adj) [= compared to something else]	5.16	sensitive (adj)	4.6
relay station	2.1	sequel (n)	3.6
release (v and n) [= a film]	3.6	serial (n) [= story in parts]	3.16
relinquish (v)	5.16	serve (v) [= help]	1.11
remains (n)	1.11	setting (n)	3.16
renovate (v)	1.11	shared (adj)	1.11
renowned (adj)	5.11	shelf-life (n)	5.16
republic (n)	1.11	shortage (adj)	1.1
reservoir (n)	1.6	shortage (n)	1.6
resistance (n)	5.6	shrink (v)	1.6
resistant (adj)	5.16	shrinkage (n)	1.6
respiration (n)	4.1	sight (n)	2.6
respiratory (adj)	4.1, 4.6	sign language	2.6
restore (v)	1.11	signal (n)	2.1
result (n)	2.6	significantly (adv)	4.16
retailer (n)	2.1	similarity (n)	1.1, 3.16
retire (v)	4.11	skeleton (n)	4.1
retirement (n)	4.11	skull (n)	4.1
review (v and n) [= of a film, book]	3.6	slogan (n)	3.6
revolutionize (v)	5.1	smudge (v)	2.16
rise / rose / risen (v)	4.16	social education	4.11
risk (n)	5.16	social security benefit	4.16
romance (n)	3.11	socialize (v)	3.1
ruins (n)	1.11	source (n)	1.6
run out of (v)	1.6	speaker (n) [= object]	2.11
rural (adj)	1.1	species (n)	5.6
		spinal (adj)	4.1
safari (n)	1.11	spine (n)	4.1
saturated fat	5.11	split (n)	1.1
save (v) [= stop death]	2.11	spouse (n)	4.16
scan (v)	2.16	sprain (n)	4.1
scanner (n)	2.11	spread (v)	3.6
scarce (adj)	2.1	stability (n)	4.16
Schadenfreude	3.16	stable (adj) [= fixed]	1.16, 3.11
schema (n)	3.11	stage (n)	3.11
script (n)	3.16	stand-alone (adj)	2.1
scripted (adj)	3.16	standard (n) [= norm]	2.6
seaport (n)	1.16	standard of living	1.1
seasonal (adj)	1.11	starvation (n)	5.1
sect (n)	5.11	state	4.11
secure (adj)	2.1	state (n) [= government]	4.11
security (n)	2.1	stock (adj) [= unchanging]	3.11
sedative (n)	3.1		

S

store (n) [= shop]	5.6	
store (v)	1.6	
strain (n)	4.1	
stranger (n)	3.1	
stream (n)	1.6	
strict (adj) [= very clear]	3.11	
struggle (n)	3.11	
sub-area (n)	1.1	
suffer (v) [= feel pain / stress]	5.6	
suffer (v) [~ from]	1.6, 1.11, 1.16, 2.16	
sulphur (S) (n)	5.1	
supervise (v)	3.1	
supervised (adj)	3.1	
supplement (v)	1.11	
supply (v)	1.6	
support (n and v)	4.16	
supposition (n)	4.11	
survival (n)	3.16	
sustainability (n)	5.16	
sustainable (adj)	5.11	
swelling (n)	4.1	
symbol (n)	2.1, 2.6	
symptom (n)	4.6	
synopsis (n)	3.11	
synthesis (n)	2.6	
synthesizer (n)	2.6	

T

tag line (n)	3.6
take into account	4.11
tame (adj)	5.1
technology (n)	2.1
teeth (n pl)	2.6
telegraph (n)	2.1
temperate (adj)	1.1
tension (n)	4.6
the EU	1.16
the extent of	3.16
the interior (n) [= of a country]	1.16
the issue of	3.16
the relationship between	3.16
the similarities between	3.16
the WHO	1.16
the World Bank	1.16
thriller (n)	3.11
throw away	5.6
thumb (n)	2.6
tissue (n)	4.1
tone down	3.1

tongue (n)	2.6
topsoil (n)	5.11
tractor (n)	5.1
trailer (n)	3.6
treatment (n) [i.e., water]	1.11
trend (n)	4.16
tropical (adj)	1.16
tube (n)	2.16
turn your back on	5.16
TV schedule	3.16

U

uncertainty (adj)	3.6
underground (adj)	1.1, 1.6
uniform (adj)	5.6
uniformity (n)	5.6
unit of production	5.6
unknown (adj)	3.6
unsupervised (adj)	3.1
unvarying (adj)	3.1
upmarket (adj)	1.11
upstream (n)	1.6
urban (adj)	1.1
urbanization (n)	4.16
useless (adj)	2.1

V

vaccine (n)	5.16
value for money	3.6
variation (n)	4.16
vast (adj)	1.11
vegetarian (n and adj)	5.11
vegetarianism (n)	5.11
vein (n)	4.1
victim (n)	3.11
viewer (n)	3.16
viewing (n)	3.16
villain (n)	3.11, 3.16
violence (n)	3.1
violent (adj)	3.1
viral (adj)	3.6
vocal chords	2.6
volume (n) [= journal]	3.11
volume (n) [= quantity]	3.16
vote (v)	3.16
voyeurism (n)	3.16
vulnerable (adj)	3.1

W

waste (n and v)	5.6
waste (n)	5.1
well (n)	1.6
wheat (n)	5.1

widely *(adv)*   1.11
wild *(adj)*   5.1
with regard to   1.1
working class(es)   4.11
worldwide *(adj)*   2.6
worth *(n)*   2.11
wrap *(v)*   2.11

Y   yield *(n)*   5.1, 5.16